WILLIAM PENN

A Biography

The Frontispiece is the "Armor Portrait," thought to have been painted during William Penn's brief military service in Ireland as a young man. The location of the original painting is unknown. This photograph is of an eighteenth-century copy owned by the Historical Society of Pennsylvania. This portrait is the only probable likeness of Penn in existence.

Historical Society of Pennsylvania

WILLIAM PENN

CATHERINE OWENS PEARE

WILLIAM PENN

A Biography

1957

J. B. LIPPINCOTT COMPANY
PHILADELPHIA AND NEW YORK

Second Impression

Printed in the United States of America

Library of Congress Catalog Card Number 56-10810

Contents

Acknowledgments

By far the most important single resource in telling the story of William Penn has been the splendid manuscript collection owned by the Historical Society of Pennsylvania. I am deeply indebted to the Society for placing its materials at my disposal and for the patient and sympathetic help of its staff members over a long period of time. Second in importance is the collection in The Library, Friends House, London. There, too, I am equally indebted for the full use of Friends' records and manuscripts and the help of the librarians.

For special assistance in research I want to express my appreciation to Dr. Nelly J. M. Kerling, of London, who worked at the Public Record Office and at the Bodleian Library for me; to Miss Hildegunde Nuth of Mülheim-Ruhr, who searched the municipal records and archives of a long list of German towns and cities; to Dr. Jacob ter Meulen, retired Director of the Peace Palace Library at The Hague; and Friends of Dorking, Reading and Bristol. I also wish to thank the librarians at Harvard University, Yale University, University of Pennsylvania, American Philosophical Society Library, the Newberry Library in Chicago, Grand Army Plaza Branch of the Brooklyn Public Library, the Fifth Avenue Library in New York, Union Theological Seminary, New York Historical Society, Swarthmore College, Haverford College, Friends' Arch Street Centre in Philadelphia, National Library of Ireland in Dublin, the Library of Trinity College in Dublin, Friends Meeting House Library in Dublin, Woodbrooke College in Birmingham, the British Museum and Lincoln's Inn Library in London, Christ Church Library at Oxford and the Municipal Library at Saumur.

And there are those whose hospitality made it possible for me to visit many scenes of Penn's life, in Northern Ireland and Ireland, Swarthmoor Hall in Ulverston, Chigwell School in Essex, King John's Farm in Chorleywood, Old Jordans Hostel, County Kent, the Worminghurst house, the Blue Idol Meeting House and Pennsbury.

I am also grateful to the following for permission to use material from the works indicated below:

Barnes & Noble, Inc.: *Narratives of Early Maryland*, 1910, and *Journal of Jasper Danckaerts*, 1913.
E. P. Dutton & Co., Inc.: *Lovely is the Lee* by Robert Gibbings, 1945.
The Clarendon Press, Oxford: *The Early Stuarts* by Godfrey Davies, 1952.
The Library of the Society of Friends, London: *Extracts from State Papers Relating to Friends 1654 to 1672*, edited by Norman Penney, 1913; *Journal of Friends Historical Society*, volumes 7 and 9; *The Journal of George Fox*, edited by John L. Nickalls, 1952.
Friends Historical Association, Swarthmore: *My Irish Journal* by William Penn, 1952; *Bulletin of Friends Historical Association*, volume 21.
Harvard University Press, Cambridge: *The Bhagavad Gita* translated by Franklin Edgerton, 1946.
Mrs. William I. Hull, Swarthmore: *Willem Sewel of Amsterdam* by William I. Hull, 1933.
John Murray Publishers, London: *Quaker and Courtier* by Mrs. Colquhoun Grant, 1907.

C.O.P.

Master! let us breathe and refresh a little; and sling a man overboard to stop the leakes. . . .
——A *Sea Grammar,* Captain John Smith, Sometime Governor of Virginia

1. Gentleman Commoner

EXHILARATED BY new hopes and mounting opportunities, Captain William Penn walked the *Fellowship*'s deck and breathed deeply of the late autumn air. It was eight o'clock in the morning with the wind to the northwest, and the *Fellowship,* which had been ordered out of the royal docks of Deptford two weeks before, was finally under way down the Thames. He'd been in luck; for, seafaring man though he was, he hadn't wanted to leave his bride just then; and the delay had given him the opportunity to make one last visit home before putting to sea.

There had been plenty of oars available to take the excited, twenty-three-year-old sea captain back across the Thames to London; and so to his home on Tower Hill. The house was most adequate, "consisting of one hall and parlor and kitchen with a divided cellar . . . and above stairs in the first story two fair chambers and in the second story two more chambers and two garrets over the same with a yard before." It stood on the east side of Tower Hill in the Parish of All Hallows Barking-by-the-Tower, within the protection of the wall. There his wife lay in childbirth. He had arrived in time to know that his first child was a boy who could be his namesake, and his sailing was delayed long enough so that he could carry the infant to the font of All Hallows, Barking, in nearby Tower Street, and have him baptized in the Anglican faith. The baby, which was born October 14, 1644, and baptized October 23, was strong, marked for survival in an age when the law of survival of the fittest operated almost rampant.

Captain Penn had been married June 6, 1643, in the Church of St. Martin's, Ludgate, to the widow Margaret Vanderschuren, but Captain Penn's was a seaman's kind of devotion, and

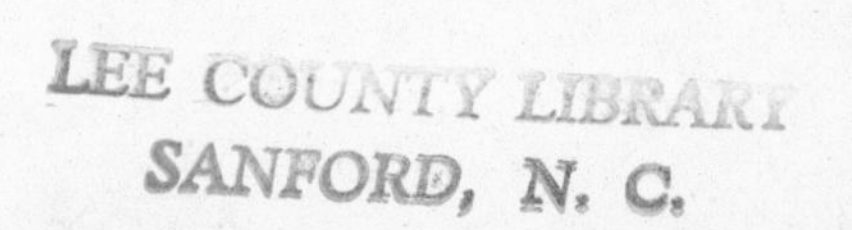

the sea had more command of his time than she. The pattern of long absences and hasty farewells had already been established, and he was setting sail once more. His sturdy legs followed the motion of the *Fellowship*'s roll, and his experienced eyes watched her sails fill and billow to his bidding as she left the Thames behind her and dipped her bow into the open sea. This was his first important command. The appointment had come to him young, but years of going to sea with his father, Giles Penn, had fitted him for it. He knew that the men under his command liked him and that he had influence with the men above. His salary as a captain was adequate for his family, it would be paid with reasonable regularity since he was now in the Parliament's employ rather than the King's, and it would improve as he continued to rise in rank. He regretted the increasingly bitter conflict between King and Parliament, but a man had to lay a good groundwork for his son's future, and he had to provide as much security for his family as possible.

William Penn was an Englishman, in the profoundest sense of the word; he was part of England's metamorphosis out of the racial amalgam of Angle-Jute-Saxon-Dane-Norman, part of her history and growth, subject of her good kings and bad, as involved as everyone else in her long, painful struggle for civil rights. Although positive genealogical record traces the direct line back only to Captain Penn's great-grandfather, William Penn of Minety, County of Gloucester, and Penn's Lodge, County of Wilts, there was a multitude of Penns in England before then—Penns, Pennes, Pens and Penes. A De la Penne came with William the Conqueror and received a land grant in Buckinghamshire for his contribution to the Conquest. Records of the Prerogative Court of Canterbury show a John Penne as early as 1383. A David Penn received a grant of land from Edward VI in 1553.

Like most amalgamated patriots, Captain Penn took a nostalgic pride in that other land from which his immediate ancestors reputedly had come—Wales. "Penn being Welsh for a *head*, as Penmanmoire in Wales, and Penrith in Cumberland, and Penn in Buckinghamshire, the highest land in England," was his son's explanation nearly four decades later; and tradition has it that the younger Penn, en route to America, said to a fellow passenger aboard the *Welcome*, "I am a Welshman myself." That remark from a man whose father may have been only partly Welsh and whose mother was either Dutch or Irish!

Margaret Vanderschuren Penn had been Margaret Jasper, daughter of John Jasper, a merchant living in Ireland. Jasper has been called Dutch, but there is no real evidence to support it; and nothing is known of his wife, who could well have been Irish. Margaret Jasper had first married a Dutch merchant, Nicasius Vanderschuren, and had been living in the Dutch-English colony of Kilrush on the River Shannon; she was already a widow when Catholic Ireland, under a specific indulgence from Pope Urban VIII, began to wage war on her Protestant residents. In 1641 the armed uprisings spread to County Clare, and the Protestants of Kilrush and other nearby settlements had to flee for their lives; the widow Vanderschuren and her father and a host of neighbors and relatives took refuge in London. Her marriage to William Penn kept her in the London environs for the rest of her life.

Her husband could indeed put to sea with racing hopes and high confidence. He was leaving at home a fine son whose soul had been given its proper divine direction, and he was moving out into times of great military activity on land and sea, when promotions came along rapidly. Cromwell had already triumphed at Marston Moor, and the winter before Parliament had wrested control of the navy from the King, appointing the Earl of Warwick as Lord High Admiral and Captain William Batten as Vice Admiral. The ship under Penn's feet had been captured at Milford Haven, where she lay at her moorings, part of the King's fleet, and added triumphantly to Parliament's Irish squadron—under *his* command. The *Fellowship*—300 tons, 110 men, and 28 guns—was now one of nine ships in the Irish fleet.

The Irish Sea was no idle patrol where a man could be forgotten, because Catholic Ireland was still waging war; and no sooner had Penn deposited some precious passengers including my Lord Broghill at Kinsale in Ireland—with a "God be praised for this safe arrival!"—than the real patrol began. When they "spied sail" they "gave chase," and it was a fortunate prey who could explain itself when overhauled. On the second of June, Captain Penn went aboard his Admiral's ship to be told that he had been given a larger ship, the *Happy Entrance*, weighing over five hundred tons and carrying thirty-eight guns. Penn was ready to return to combat a still more hopeful and optimistic man, but not until a vessel from Plymouth brought the news that the King had suffered a disastrous defeat at Naseby, and not until Penn had supped with the Admiral who gave him a letter from Margaret Penn. His first born was now nearly nine months old.

The balance of the year 1645 saw Penn helping to raise the siege of Youghall, castle fortress and town guarding the harbor of the River Blackwater; after that he sailed from Dingle to the Vintry on the west coast of Ireland and with the help of his seamen burned "all the villages and houses about that bay." When he sailed up the River Shannon to Bonratty, he was visiting the country from which his wife had had to flee, and he must have burned Irish cabins with considerable relish for his assignment. At last in the middle of August, "I received orders . . . to repair to England, and so for London."

And so home for a heartening visit with his wife and two-year-old son and a disheartening glimpse of politics on land, to see for himself the rising tide of Puritanism, the rising power of the army, and the rapid darkening of England's darkest hour. He wanted what other men in the navy wanted, a reunion between King and Parliament, with a new balance of power struck between them; but the civil war had ended with the surrender of Oxford, the King's headquarters, and with the flight of the King to Scotland. While the Scots held the King prisoner, Parliament sent him the terms under which he might be permitted to resume his throne.

Penn was a man of exceptional ability, and his popularity was mounting in maritime circles. The Earl of Warwick, the Earl of Pembroke and Captain William Batten were his personal friends. Cromwell had created his New Model army, but he needed the navy, too, and he was quick to notice gifted officers. By an act of both Houses of Parliament, Penn was made Rear Admiral of the Irish Seas.

Yet, another spring saw Penn under arrest "declared to be a rebel and traitor to the Parliament and Kingdom of England." The exact reason for his arrest isn't known, but Penn was friendly with such men as Lord Inchiquin and Lord Broghill of Ireland whose loyalty to Parliament was very much open to question. Cromwell was probably just as sensitive to Penn's underlying loyalty to his King as he was to Penn's seafaring ability, but Penn was franker about his seamanship. His apprehension was short lived, and in a few weeks he was back at his command. Vice Admiral Batten, no doubt a degree more forthright than Penn, did not fare so well; he had been relieved of his post.

Penn's recall and brief arrest gave him another opportunity to come home to London—a London alive with intrigue, excitement, quick tempers, ragged nerves; a London that had just been through a military occupation, impoverished by interrupted supply lines and disrupted lives, where soldiers dismissed with part or no pay prowled the streets, hungry and resentful, where Cavaliers taxed into poverty to pay for four years of civil war huddled into reduced quarters, and where merchants whose trade had been disturbed by the naval warfare schemed their own recovery. It was a walled, raucous, crowded town, where peddlers screeched their wares and tavern brawls were fought to fatal conclusions, where the streets were narrow and labyrinthian, cluttered with filth tossed from protruding second story windows, a town of lusty apprentices, sooty chimney sweeps, galloping horsemen, and ladies whisking by in carriages. London was peopled with saints and sinners, where everyone rabidly claimed God for his side, a town which an unhappy young religious seeker named George Fox had already visited and had seen "under great misery and trouble, where all was dark and under the chain of darkness."

When Rear Admiral Penn stepped into his home he found a personal darkness of his own: a frightened wife who had lived through the military commotions without her husband and who had nursed her son through smallpox. There was a grim comfort in the fact that once it had struck the smallpox could not threaten the boy a second time, but its fever had burned every remnant of hair from his head, and soon he would have to be fitted for a wig. His father did not resign himself to threats of other contagions like the plague arising from the garbage-strewn streets and flea-ridden houses, because, thanks to his advancements and profits made from captured prize ships, he could now afford a place in the country. He took his wife and son to a house in Wanstead near the village of Chigwell in Essex County. The village was conveniently close to London, only about ten miles northeast of the city by the Ongar Road, and William Batten, who had retired to an estate in nearby Walthamstow, would be his neighbor.

There was real emotional security as well as ruddy health in a big country house with its plentiful domestic staff, its own grain and sheep in the fields, wild game on the premises, set in the peace of the forested countryside. As Penn moved in and out of the scene, the boy and his mother could remain in constant, comfortable surroundings, and while her husband was away, Margaret Penn could oversee the boy's education.

Young William Penn was probably coached at home in his ABC's before entering school, since the grammar schools preferred not to teach those first steps in learning or waste staff time with a small child and his hornbook. According to Aubrey in his *Brief Lives* William Penn began his formal education at Chigwell School about four miles from Wanstead. There is no proof of his attendance beyond this statement of Aubrey's, but there is no record to contradict Aubrey, and tradition would have it so. An acquaintanceship existed between Aubrey and Penn in adult life. Whenever young Penn entered Chigwell, there was waiting for him a classical education, a rigorous curriculum of Greek, Latin, English grammar, spelling, catechism, daily prayers, Sunday church attendance, training in manners and morals. There was an extra charge for lessons in the skill of writing a good Roman hand with quill, ink and paper; but from the gentlemanly art of composing and delivering orations with standardized and rehearsed gestures there was no escape.

Two Chigwell schools had been founded in 1629 by Samuel Harsnett, Archibishop of York, one to teach reading, writing, ciphering and casting of accounts; the other to teach the Latin and Greek tongues. Since Penn was a classical scholar, we can assume that he attended the latter. The building which once housed the two schools is still there, now much enlarged to accommodate a greater student body. It was a rectangular, red brick structure, two stories high, with a gloomy, oaken-beamed interior, to which small casement windows gave insufficient light. Whether the boys lived at the school is not known, but we do know that they studied under the supervision of carefully chosen schoolmasters. The Latin schoolmaster, who was also the headmaster, was required to be a man "not under seven-and-twenty years of age, a man skilful in the Greek and Latin tongues, a good poet, of a sound religion, neither Papist nor Puritan"; and he was to be a strict taskmaster, too, holding his students from six in the morning until eleven and from one in the afternoon until six in the summer months and from seven in the morning until five in the winter. He could give them only three short holidays, about six days over Easter and Pentecost and about two weeks over Christmas. He had to restrain them from ribaldry, swearing, wrangling, fighting—at least, in so far as he was able—and from carrying any dagger or weapon, except their meat knives, since fingers still predated forks in William Penn's England. If the boys became too unmanageable, he could lay the rod on them up to three stripes, but he must never strike them about the head or cheek with his fist or hand. Edward Cotton was Latin master during Penn's time.

The elder Penn had acted the wise parent in moving to Wanstead and planting his son amidst the orthodox influences of Chigwell, because Puritanism was growing stronger. He proved himself an even wiser politician. Just a few weeks after he had been restored to his command, probably even before the boy started school, eleven ships seceded from the fleet, announcing their loyalty to the King and proceeding to Holland under William Batten's command to join the Prince of Wales. Penn's ship was not among them. Penn must surely have been in sympathy with the gesture, and Batten undoubtedly gave him an opportunity to join the bolt. But he obviously considered it a shortsighted, premature action. As England plunged into the second phase of her civil war, the King had the Scots on his side and a good quarter of the navy, but Cromwell had his New Model army and the other three-fourths of the navy. It was not hard for well-informed men to predict the trend developing in England, but many even of the well informed did not predict that most tragic of incidents—the trial and execution of the King.

Charles I had been more than a monarch to the Penns. They had known their King personally. Giles Penn had brought home from one of his voyages a cast of Tetuán hawks which he presented to His Majesty for falconry expeditions; and Charles I in turn had given Giles Penn letters of protection to carry on his more perilous journeys, later appointing him His Majesty's Consul at Sallee (Salé) in the Moorish kingdom of Morocco. Giles Penn's son experienced a deep personal grief at his King's death. Giles Penn's grandson was only four years old and would never see his monarch. To Royalists like the Penns the Crown, eternally symbolizing the dignity of England, had been violated. If Charles's reign had been unwise and tyrannical, punctuated by royal treachery at times, if Charles had been too much influenced by his French Catholic Queen, these problems could be solved by time; for no king rules forever. Cromwell had boasted to Algernon Sydney that they would cut off the King's head with the Crown upon it, but when the King's bleeding, severed head was raised high for the crowds to feast their eyes upon, deep resolutions were born to expiate the foul deed even if it were counted treason.

John Milton, gifted penman of the Puritan movement, viewed the death of Charles quite differently—with a kind of bitter satisfaction. An extreme advocate of republican government, a free conscience and even a free press, he had been pouring his great skills into tolerationist pamphlets for many years. For him the mad multitude had been worshiping an idol; for him the "Athenian walls from ruin bare" had been saved; Cromwell would become his "chief of men . . . guided by faith and matchless fortitude"; and he would become Cromwell's Latin Secretary. Milton saw England moving in a new and inspired direction toward liberty of conscience and greater dignity for the individual. Cromwell was saving Milton's England from anarchy and with his sword and open Bible policy would lay the groundwork for much of England's civil and religious freedoms.

Cromwell was riding the peak of a flood tide of what is loosely called Puritanism, a movement that had had its beginnings in the days of Elizabeth I. It was the magnificent daughter of Henry VIII who had organized and unified the Church of England, and no sooner had she done so than she found herself dealing with disaffections among the clergy. The disaffections spread to the lay membership until by Cromwell's time "cobblers and weavers, feltmongers and tailors, and even butchers presumed to interpret God's word." And it was quite true. Milton was a scrivener's son, George Fox the son of a weaver, and John Bunyan of a tinker.

The word "Puritan" describes almost the whole of intellectual unrest and spiritual seeking in seventeenth-century England, and more particularly the protest against ecclesiastical coercion. Puritanism was a diverse movement within itself, from the moderates who wanted merely to revise the liturgical practices within the Church of England to the most radical, Milton and Cromwell among them, who wanted the national church abolished altogether and individuals allowed to create whatever types of congregation they wished. They were all brought together militarily and politically under Cromwell, as he proceeded to set up a kind of moralistic military dictatorship. He did not do it gently. He landed in Ireland with his Puritan army the summer after the King's death and in less than a year, by outright ruthless slaughter and pillage and selling of Irish Catholics into slavery in the West Indies, he won a terrible kind of submission. The next year he marched on Scotland. He defeated Charles II's attempt to invade England, and he waged war against the Netherlands and Spain. When the last remnants of the Long Parliament's Rump refused to leave or accept any new members of whom they did not approve, he descended upon them with his musketeers and drove them from the building. He brought the arts in England almost to a standstill with his iron censorship.

The young cannot be successfully protected from the ideas of their own times. The Commonwealth lasted for eleven years, throughout most of William Penn's boyhood and teens; and while its impact upon his thinking did not show any serious effect until he reached college, the leaven of liberalism must have been at work in his soul almost from the beginning. All he understood in his earliest years was that his father continued to rise in rank and importance under the Commonwealth and achieved the proportions of a national hero with his successes at sea. When he was only six, his father was a vice admiral in command of England's third fleet with orders to proceed to the Mediterranean where the chances for prizes and triumphs were great. This was the first time an English fleet had ventured as far as Malta since the days of the Crusades. Cadíz, Málaga Road, Majorca, Sardinia, Corsica, Tunis Bay, Cape Bona, Pantelleria Island, Trapani and Malta—ships captured, booty seized and sold, sea lanes cleared for English commerce. The boy growing up in the woods and fields of Essex was seven when his father came triumphantly home from the Mediterranean expedition. Full thirteen months had passed, and there was now a second child in the house, a six- or seven-months-old daughter, named Margaret for her mother. He was old enough to thrill at the stir created by a returning hero, old enough to feel the impact of this volatile, rigorous, out-of-doors personality suddenly striding through the household or galloping down Ongar Road in his wide-topped boots, snug breeches, doublet, gauntlets, a great plume in his hat tossing in the breeze—just thirty-one, still handsome. His father! His hero! His standard! An almost remote, not-quite-real, romantic figure who descended upon his family for short exciting visits and then disappeared again.

The pattern of living for the Penn family did not change appreciably during the next four years. Vice Admiral Penn continued to bring home reports of triumphs at sea. In 1652 he joined Colonel Robert Blake in The Downs and was off once more, this time to the shores of Holland to help wage England's war against the too prosperous Dutch, to defeat Holland in her own medium—the sea—to blockade her shores, cut off her commercial life lines and starve her into submission. Commanding one of the three great squadrons Penn came home from that war "noble and renowned" with a long list of sunken men-of-war, prisoners, prizes, wounded and dead to his credit. Cromwell had little choice but to "recognize" a national hero and bestow upon him the commission of General at Sea, a rank that had heretofore always gone to an army field officer.

Penn took advantage of his top position of favor while he had it and petitioned the Lord Protector and his Council for restitution for injuries sustained to the Irish estates he had acquired from his wife, and they responded almost immediately and ordered that "lands in Ireland yet undisposed of be set forth to him and his heirs, of three hundred pounds per annum value . . . in consideration of the great losses sustained by General Penn and his wife by the rebellion in Ireland and as a remuneration of his good and faithful services performed to the Commonwealth . . . in such a place where there is a castle or convenient house for habitation upon them, and near to some town or garrison, for the security and encouragement of such as he shall engage to plant and manure the same. . . ." It was a gesture that the Commonwealth made to scores, because it served a twofold purpose: to reward the faithful without disturbing the aching national treasury and to implement the colonization of Catholic Ireland with English Protestants. Thousands of acres, nearly three-fourths of Ireland, were forfeited by the Catholic rebels as a penalty for their anti-English attitude, and parceled out to new settlers. Penn's grant was at Macroom, about twenty miles west of Cork, land belonging for hundreds of years to the MacCarthy clan, one of whom was Viscount Muskerry. The title later became Earl of Clancarty.

And there was another reward for General Penn, something that he could show an adoring son, a gold chain worth a hundred pounds, presented to him by Cromwell. Young William Penn could hope for no greater hour than the one in which this magnificent man came home in a happy commotion and sat with his lusty companions at the long family board to which were brought great joints of mutton, sizzling hot, and great tankards of English beer, listening while his father, vanity warmed with the beverage, recounted the three-day battle of Portland Isle in which the Dutch fleet was finally driven from the English Channel. In a land where the law of primogeniture guaranteed him his father's shoes, he could linger at the table with the men and fancy the day when his voice would boom in deep tones and his stomach would hold as much food. A profoundly excited boy returned to his boys' world and his Latin books, to the rigid routine of prayers and lectures, while his father went off to Portsmouth to oversee the equipping of his fleet for an expedition to the West Indies.

Cromwell was picking his quarrel with Spain, that other threat to English supremacy, shortly after the war with Holland was concluded, and he was casting a greedy eye on Spanish possessions in the New World. General Penn sailed out of Spithead on December 25, 1654, bound for the West Indies, while agents established his land titles in Ireland.

Times under the Puritan regime were pious times, pious and repressed, when even seafaring men like Penn were careful to be frankly godfearing in speaking and writing, partly because they were at heart godfearing but partly because it was politic. Religious and political destiny were one and the same; men were either believing or they were doubting and seeking; and their religious consciences (or the lack thereof) determined their personal success and failure. God was an established political fact in the seventeenth century, and a sensitive, half-grown boy, fed a rigorous diet of religion in school, could expect religious pangs when his physical growing pangs set in. Sometime during his last few months at Chigwell, at the end of his tenth year or early in his eleventh, when exciting and destiny-changing events crowded one after another upon his family life, General Penn's son underwent his first religious experience of which there is any record. In a moment of solitude, perhaps in an attitude of prayer, he felt a sudden inward peace, an enlightening of himself and a brightening of the room around him. It was his discovery of God, a thing which must always be personal. Through all the forms, catechisms, memorized prayers and required readings had penetrated a light, a knowing, a direct communication with the divine which would never be lost.

On the verge of his eleventh birthday, young Penn was called abruptly home from Chigwell, gathered up with his baby sister, and taken hastily to London to stay in rooms on Tower Hill. His father had returned from the sea again, only this time not to the house in Wanstead, covered with glory, but to London in custody where he was remanded to the Tower. The news of his father's arrest, his hero's fall, was the boy's first taste of misfortune, his first real experience with the insecurities of his times. Up to then his life had moved from event to event on an ascending plane of good fortune and increasing affluence. His father had always come home more important than he went away; changes in rank had always been upward. But the Tower! A sojourning place for those who expected to be relieved of their heads! Sir Thomas More, Sir Walter Raleigh, Sir Thomas Wyat, Lady Jane Grey, the Earl of Strafford and many more had tarried there.

As for the real cause of Penn's second arrest there is doubt again. No fragment of love had ever been lost or mislaid between Cromwell and Penn, but each had recognized the other's potency in the scheme of England's destiny. Penn had set out upon the West Indian command under sealed orders. With Penn was army General Robert Venables who had under his command more than seven thousand troops. Penn's task, he found, was to transport the troops to Hispaniola, which Venables was to capture. But, somehow, gross miscalculations had been made about the climate and the people of Hispaniola. Venables' troops suffered horribly from the heat and the lack of drinking water, and the Negroes did not desert to the English side in droves. The English army finished up in rout and disorder, and at last re-embarked. It would not have been wise to return to London with only that dismal failure to report; so they set sail for Jamaica and did a masterly job of capturing the island, "sacking their towns and returning with very rich booty." Some scholars feel that it was only the failure at Hispaniola that caused the irate Cromwell to toss both Penn and Venables into the Tower; others that the mission to Hispaniola may deliberately have been muffed, and some even that Penn and Venables may have offered the fleet and army to Charles II in exile. I think Penn was too able a commander, too deeply entrenched in the traditions of the navy, deliberately to misguide an armed engagement. As for his devotion to, or possible communications with, Charles II, events of the next few years confirm Penn's devotion to the Stuart cause. Penn was most certainly a monarchist at heart, and whether he offered the fleet to Charles at this point would have depended entirely on whether he thought it would be an effective gesture. In any event, whatever Cromwell may have suspected, he wasn't able to make his suspicions stick; and after five weeks in the Tower, punctuated with questionings before the Council of State, Penn was released upon receipt of his full and abject apology.

After this second arrest Penn did not go back to sea. For a while he and his family stayed in Wanstead, but by the middle of the summer he thought it wise to leave the English scene altogether. He took his wife and children to his recently acquired lands in Ireland, to the castle and manor of Macroom. On August 12, 1656, Captain R. Hodges of the *Basing* transported "Lord Broghill, with his lady and family, as also General Penn, with his lady and family" across St. George's Channel. Penn's party consisted of himself and his lady, his son of almost twelve, his four-year-old daughter, and a tutor for the boy. His third child, Richard, was born about this time.

Ireland wore the Cromwell stamp of poverty, destitution, famine and dislocated lives; but an English gentleman knew nothing if not how to run a country estate, especially when there was plenty of peasant labor available; and Penn went to work on his acreage, planting, cultivating, acquiring additional acres, persuading other Protestants to come over from England and settle near him. There was food enough for those who could afford it: wild fowl, fruit, oats, grains, beef, mutton. English beer was scarce, but the Irish had a drink called usquebaugh (whisky) that proved to be excellent, and foreign wines could be purchased in a city like Dublin. The castle of Macroom, a big, square, three-storied structure of gray stone, stood in a wide area enclosed by a protective wall, and the village huddled just outside the wall. In time of military attack the villagers took refuge inside the castle walls. General Penn handled his Irish lands well, and before very long they were described as "the castle, town and manor of Macromp, being a garrison wherein was constantly and conveniently quartered a foot company and troop of horse; with many thousands of acres of land contiguous; and the castle, town and manor of Killcreagh, with several lands thereunto belonging. . . ."

The adolescent William was venturing into the unknown country of mountains and forests and bogs, mists and mysticism, sullen and vengeful Celtic Catholics, coming, with the conquering colonists, to learn much, quite by accident, of the techniques of developing and colonizing a foreign land. His life patterns had suddenly exploded and he had been uprooted from public school to private tutor, from England to an un-English soil. His seafaring father had become a land dweller, a much more constant companion who taught him to manage an estate, delegate work graciously to those of lower caste, acquire skill in the use of his sword so that he could defend himself in a quarrel or against highwaymen when he traveled abroad, help him to acquire the manner, mien and finesse of a courtier so that when the exile ended—and exiles seldom last forever—he would be ready to assume his role in the courts and salons of London.

For the second half of the year 1656 that the Penns spent in Ireland, Granville Penn (the senior Penn's biographer) says he finds no record; but there is a record for 1657—a Quaker record known as the Harvey Manuscript, believed to have been delivered by William Penn, the younger, some thirty years later to Thomas Harvey. It contains the story of William Penn's first contact with the extremist sect and much more of his ultimate convincement.

The Quaker movement had begun only around 1647 in England and had not touched Ireland at all until 1654 when William Edmundson with his family and a handful of others settled the first Quaker meeting there. An itinerant Quaker preacher named Thomas Loe came to Cork from England in 1657, and the news of his presence reached the elder William Penn, who did a curious thing: he suggested that they be like "ye noble Bereans" and hear the Quaker before judging him. Whereupon he invited Thomas Loe to hold a meeting in his home. The apostolic zeal of the early Quaker ministers knew no fatigue, no discomfort, no distance; and Thomas Loe came eagerly and joyfully to the large household at Macroom, gathering family and domestic staff around him, speaking with an eloquence and conviction that must have rivaled George Fox's. Young Penn, going on thirteen, watched Loe's glowing, candid face, tried to understand his unfamiliar line of reasoning, his exciting heresy, felt himself caught up in the emotional appeal. The boy looked around him. "A Black of his father's could not contain himself from weeping aloud and he looking on his father saw the tears running down his cheeks."

Thomas Loe traveled on and the glow of his visit to Macroom faded, but it never fully disappeared. The doctrine of the Inner Light, that quickening of a man's soul by direct mystical communication with God; the right of the individual to wait upon the Lord alone or with a group unaided by any kind of priest; the simplicity of plain, honest living devoid of plumes and laces and deception; the pacifism; the dignified humility, had their impact upon the impressionable young mind that had already tasted a precious moment of divine communion.

Father and son had always been close, and the four years they spent in Ireland brought them even closer together. The maturing boy, sharing his father's exile, could also share every scrap of political news that reached him from ships that came and went at Irish ports. The elder Penn's most valuable contacts were in the navy, and so they were not at all out of touch with the affairs of state. While General Penn idled away his days on land, Blake destroyed the Spanish fleet, England was granted the first written Constitution in her history, and Cromwell lived through the peak of his power. The choicest piece of news to reach the Royalists at home or in exile was the Protector's death. John Evelyn dipped his Cavalier's quill into his ink and wrote gleefully under date of October 22, 1658, "Saw ye superb funerall of ye Protector. He was carried from Somerset House in a velvet bed of state drawn by six horses, houss'd with ye same; the pall held by his new Lords; Oliver lying in effigie in royal robes, and crown'd with a crown, sceptre, and globe, like a king . . . but it was the joyfullest funerall I ever saw, for there were none that cried but dogs, which the soldiers hooted away with a barbarous noise, drinking and taking tobacco in the streetes as they went."

George Fox saw only idolotry in the worship of an elaborately bedecked corpse, and Milton feared a return to tyrants and a loss of his beloved liberty of conscience.

Young Penn was fourteen, caught up in the excitement that infected his home—his family happy and exuberant at the change in the political picture. How much longer could a Commonwealth last that had had so much invested in a single personality? There might be a returning to England soon—a returning to the heart of national affairs, to influence and affluence. Once back in England he would be able to resume his formal education.

And there *was* a returning—in less than two years. The Protector's successor lasted only eight months, and he was succeeded by the confusion of rivalries and dissensions naturally following in the wake of a one-man rule. Rumors about the return of Charles II expanded into open talk, and Monck marched on London to cries of "A Free Parliament!" The people of England were tired of army rule and civil strife, tired of too much piety, tired of uncertainty. They wanted to return to the patterns that had been tried in the past and had worked. They wanted peace. There was indeed an election, creating the Convention Parliament, and as a result General Penn left Macroom in March to take his seat in the new House of Commons as a representative from Weymouth. "Sir," the letter from the Mayor and Corporation of Weymouth said, "The freeholders of this town have chosen your honor and the Lord-General Montagu burgesses for the borough of Weymouth, for the ensuing Parliament. It was very much to our satisfaction, that the election passed with so much cheerfulness and unanimity. . . ." Penn was still loved by thousands of his countrymen, still appreciated as one of the heroes who had helped establish England as a sea power; with the turn of the tide he was swept back into his London circles, and his family was swept back with him, to take up a new residence on Tower Hill just to the north of the London Navy Office Gardens.

William was old enough to understand what was best for England, to share in his father's deepest confidences, to know exactly why there were so many crosscurrents, quick carriage dashes to hastily called meetings, low-voiced conversations at inns, letters exchanged with His Majesty's Court in exile, toasts and pledges in the finest French or Spanish wine—and at last his father's departure the first week in April to go aboard the *Naseby*. The entire fleet of thirty-one ships under the command of General Montagu weighed anchor and stood out to sea bound for Scheveningen in Holland—to bring home their King.

General Penn had no command on this voyage; he went as a member of Parliament and a passenger aboard Montagu's ship; and whatever secret role Penn played in the service of his King was fully appreciated, because when Charles came aboard the *Naseby* one of his first acts was to lay the flat of his sword on the back of the kneeling figure of his devoted subject, William Penn, and pronounce him a knight. En route home the *Naseby* was renamed the

Royal Charles, and its most precious passenger went ashore at Dover to the cheers of waiting throngs. Charles's entry into London followed soon after, described by John Evelyn as "a triumph of about 20,000 horses and foots, brandishing their swords and shouting with inexpressible joy; the wayes strew'd with flowers, the bells ringing, the streetes hung with tapistry, fountaines running with wine; the Maior, Aldermen and all the Companies in their liveries, chaines of gold, and banners. . . ." Sir William Penn must have had his elder son at his side on this auspicious occasion, because he intended to bring the promising young man to the royal attention at the earliest possible moment.

A month after the King's London triumph the navy's top administration was completed with the Duke of York as Lord High Admiral, Sir George Carteret as Treasurer, Sir Robert Slingsby as Comptroller, Sir William Batten as Surveyor, Lord Berkeley, Sir William Penn and Peter Pett, Esquire, as Commissioners. Young Samuel Pepys, who had gone to Holland in time to join the royal party on its return voyage and had wept conspicuously when he listened to Charles's own account of his sufferings in exile, had wangled his wily way into the new political picture as Clerk. Pepys at the time of his appointment was only twenty-seven and, as his caustic pen records, he often suffered from the contempt and impatience of the older and more experienced men with whom he had to work. The complete confidence that existed between the Duke of York and Sir William Penn who occasionally neglected to tell Pepys what their plans for the fleet were, and the abiding friendship of long years' standing between the two Sir Williams were thorns that cut deeply into Pepys' soft and tender flesh.

The world of opportunity was opening up to Sir William Penn's son just as adult life was beginning. His father could now give him everything: contacts with the most influential men in the realm, a well-furnished home, the finest apparel, the best education in one of England's most ancient seats of learning—Oxford University. Sir William had come home to London in March of 1660; October 26 of the same year saw William enrolled at Christ Church as a gentleman commoner and matriculated as a knight's son.

Give me the liberty to know, to utter, to argue freely according to conscience, above all liberties.

—John Milton, *Areopagitica*

2. A Youth of Excellent Genius

LOOKING BACK over the decades the Great Colonizer may have wished that he had been sent to the Cambridge of Francis Bacon, George Herbert, Henry More and John Milton; but when William Penn was sixteen Royalist Oxford was the logical choice for him. Oxford was the academic home of Archbishop Laud, Richard Hooker and his *Ecclesiastical Polity*, and Edward Hyde, the Earl of Clarendon. Oxford University had avowed her loyalty to England's kings through the centuries, had been the financial darling of many of them; and she had been a host to royal families and their parliaments. Richard III had visited Oxford to woo the friendship of her scholars; so had Henry VIII and Elizabeth I, who felt moved to bestow upon the university the words, "God bless thee and increase thy sons in number, holiness and virtue." Charles I had paid Oxford a lavish visit in 1636, and the undergraduates had entertained him in Christ Church Hall. Charles I had returned to Oxford with his Queen and Parliament and made it his headquarters during the civil wars. Oxford dug into her university chest to lend him money; allowed her buildings to be used for storage of arms, garrisoning of troops, granaries and warehouses. Musketeers and halberdiers drilled on her grounds, and her students took up arms for the King's cause. During the siege her scholastic functions came almost to a standstill, until the King, who had entered Oxford so brilliantly, sneaked out disguised as a servant. Then Oxford felt the rough edge of Puritanism with burned books, smashed images, looted valuables, confiscated plate. And when the news of Charles I's execution reached Dean Samuel Fell of Christ Church, the devoted old Royalist died of a broken heart.

William Penn arrived at Christ Church just as the whole university was entering another traumatic experience—the Restoration;

and his enrollment was part of a significant continuity. Charles II had entered London on May 29, 1660; on July 27 John Fell, son of Samuel, was made Canon of Christ Church; in October Penn matriculated; and on November 30 John Fell became Dean. Fell, with a zeal for his task that was whetted by his father's death, busied himself with cleaning up the infectious taint of Puritanism and re-establishing the orthodoxy of the Church of England. He gave ardent attention to purifying the thinking of his young charges; and students who did not wish to conform by attending chapel regularly, by wearing the surplice, and by observing all rituals, were punished or expelled.

"I do not like thee, Dr. Fell," one of his students is supposed to have said of him; but John Fell went on doing his task full well, devoting his spare time to completing the buildings his father had started, repairing some of Wolsey's old buildings and adding new.

Fell was undoubtedly a capable and brilliant dean, but the deepest rooted academic traditions of Oxford had developed through many centuries and were much farther beneath the surface than Laud or the Puritans or Anglican Fell could reach. Oxford had begun only a little after Abelard's time; she had begun in the age when knowledge-thirsty scholars were converging upon Paris and Bologna. Oxford had begun when England, like the Continent, was shaking off the shadowy early years of the Middle Ages and gathering together the intellectual heritage treasured for her by such men as the Venerable Bede and Alcuin. She took her first impetus from the scholarly Henry I and emerged as a group of schools under Henry II. Earliest Oxford reveled along with the rest of her times in the Socrates-Plato-Aristotle discipleship. The Greek cornerstone was set too deeply in Oxford's history for an army of Lauds, Cromwells and Fells to budge.

The curriculum awaiting Penn is best reflected in a contemporary inventory (*circa* 1665) of the library available to the students of Christ Church. Its 540 handwritten pages list some two thousand volumes, more than half of which were theological—St. Andrew's sermons, the Bible in Spanish, Italian, Gallic, Hebrew, the Bishops' Bible in English, Martin Luther, Dr. Donne's sermons, Hakewell's *Apology for God's Providence, Raynaudi Theologia Naturalis.* The second largest group of books is under *Libri Artium,* both ancient and modern—Aristophanes, Aristotle, Socrates, Archimedes, Dionysius, Euclid, Homer, Petrarch, Diogenes, Seneca, along with Beaumont and Fletcher, Chaucer, John Evelyn's discourse of forest trees, Sir Walter Raleigh's *History of the World,* Will Shakespeare's plays, John Smith's geography and history of Great Britain, and Edmund Spenser's *Faërie Queene.* And there are small sections on *Libri Medici* and *Libri Juris* with Justinian's name showing plainly in the latter group. Perhaps Dean Fell ought to have examined this catalogue carefully, for such names were also sprinkled through it as Descartes, Thomas Hobbes and Hugo Grotius. Mother Oxford was continuing to nourish the inquiring mind under the very nose of Dean Fell, as she had in the past nourished John Wycliffe, John Pym, Henry Vane, John Eliot, John Hampden and John Locke; even Thomas Loe had been an Oxford man.

To me, Hugo Grotius develops as one of the most significant of contemporary influences on Penn's thinking during his college days, an influence that registered only gradually as it combined with the concepts of Thomas Loe, Moses Amyraut and the whole Quaker movement, and that ultimately flowered in Penn's *An Essay Towards the Present and Future Peace of Europe.* In *No Cross, No Crown* Penn said of Grotius: "than whom these latter ages think they have not had a man of more universal knowledge (a light, say the statesmen; a light, say the churchmen, too) witness his *Annals;* and his book, *De Jure Belli ac Pacis;* also his *Christian Religion,* and elaborate commentaries. . . ."

Grotius, the Latinized version of the Dutch de Groot, is considered the founder of modern international law. Living through the end of the sixteenth and early part of the seventeenth centuries, in an age when the waging of war was a royal prerogative and states felt no responsibility for one another's welfare except to eliminate competitors, Hugo Grotius conceived the modern idea of an international morality. Early in his ecclesiastical-legal career he had written *Mare Liberum;* in 1625 he published his immediately popular and many times reprinted *De Jure Belli ac Pacis,* this latter listed in Christ Church Library catalogue. In it Grotius raised the question as to whether war was ever justifiable; and even though he could conceive of some circumstances when a nation might be impelled to take up arms, he maintained that there was no justification for waging war indiscriminately. He was many, many generations ahead of his times, as he developed in his *De Jure* a list of unjust causes of war—the enfeebling of another power, raiding another country on the pretext of discovery, or subjugating another by force of arms. He warned princely powers not to engage in war rashly, even for a just cause.

Of the twenty-five hundred students attending Oxford, there were a hundred enrolled at Christ Church when Penn was there. They lived at the college, in the lovely quadrangle of two-story-high buildings. The great dining hall in the southeast corner stands higher than the rest, and is reached by a sweeping staircase that rises under high, fan-vaulted ceilings. The cathedral that is just outside the quadrangle on its eastern side dates back to the twelfth century. Oxford was still a walled, medieval town in design and lack of comfort, in narrow littered streets and insanitation, crowded and cramped, where rivalries between townsfolk and students and between warring student factions left few moments of quiet and peace. It burst its bounds with the rest of England when the Stuarts returned to the throne, and the twenty-five hundred young men, removed from whatever restraining influence their families may have had, contributed their vigorous share toward consuming as much beer as the town could brew and in upholding the university's tradition for riotous feasts and celebrations, roaming the streets each evening until curfew in search of mischief and singing lusty songs.

Coming from a comfortable, protected home environment, accustomed to a relatively quiet rural atmosphere, Penn referred to university life as "hellish darkness and debauchery." But while the changes both physical and emotional to Oxford must have been severe, he appears to have made a reasonably good adjustment that first year. He could have met the academic requirements easily since he had competent preparation; he couldn't help but succeed socially since his father was a personal friend of the now ruling family; and he had the financial resources that he needed. A young man turned loose among other young men in a town resigned long since to the temperaments of young men would need time to explore his adult levels. He would need to test his own poise in new situations marked "manly" by university tradition, to pit his wits against minds sharper than that of a hired tutor. After years of isolation in the frontier-like conditions in Ireland, he would need time to adjust to the rich intellectual diet, after the easy regimen of home to accept the rigidly timed schedules of college life. If it became too hellish, he was only a day-and-a-half carriage drive from London.

The death of the young Duke of Gloucester, brother of the King, the same autumn that Penn entered Oxford, sent quantities of students effusing into verse, and Penn turned out his mournful spot of Latin:

> *Publica te, Dux Magne, dabant jejunia genti,*
> *Sed facta est nato principe festa dies,*
> *Te moriente, licet celebraret laeta triumphos*
> *Anglia; solemnes solvitur in lachrymas.*
> *Solus ad arbitrium moderaris pectora; solus*
> *Tu dolor accedis, deliciaeque tuis.*

The public show of sorrow at the death of the Duke of Gloucester, and the public joy accumulating for the Coronation, were part of the pattern of the times. The Restoration was still a happy affair, unclouded by the Clarendon Code. The King's brother was buried in Westminster; Pepys bought himself a pair of short black stockings to wear over his silk ones; the Oxford men plunged back into their debaucheries and their studies. All seemed well with the world.

Young Penn came home during the spring of his first year at Oxford to attend the Coronation with his father. He found that his father and his capital city had both changed in the course of the winter. The elder Penn had always been a genial, easy-to-know fellow, in spite of his quick temper; and as soon as it became politically safe he relaxed into the man full of "merry discourse" that Pepys knew, "sociable, able and cunning." In fact, it was Sir William who taught Pepys to take "two good draughts of sack" in the morning to cure the head aching from last night's celebration. Sir William reveled with everyone else in the chance to lay aside the plain clothes and drab colors of the Commonwealth and dress more gayly. Restoration styles were borrowed from Louis XIV's Court—

furs, laces, embroidery, slashed sleeves, doublets, fine silk stockings shoes with heightening heels, magnificent wigs. The ladies turned to exaggerated coiffures, long tight bodices, and heavily gathered skirts and elaborate underskirts. And London, righteous too long, had flung open her pleasure haunts to the revelers With gaudy dress went lewd talk and drives in gilded carriages to bawdy plays, for as rapidly as the once forbidden theatres opened so rapidly were they furnished with ribald material by Dryden and his ilk. And the gardens—Spring Gardens, Mulberry Gardens—developed into elegant retreats with groves of trees, flower gardens sheltered nooks, games and refreshments, and became hotbeds of political intrigue for the cultured and highly favored.

The shockable young man, who had found Oxford a place of "hellish darkness," joined his family at their new and better London residence and became part of his father's circle of friends and acquaintances, foremost among them the Battens and the Pepyses, sat with them at the family board while they talked of intimate government affairs. He donned the elaborate clothes waiting for him so that he could witness the Coronation parade and repaired with his father; Sir William Batten, his wife and three children, and Samuel and Mrs. Pepys to the home of a Mr. Young, a flag-maker, in Cornhill. Mr. Young's windows gave them an excellent view of the procession. More than one contemporary writer found his skillful pen a little inept to decribe the elegance of that cavalcade. "It is impossible to relate the glory of this day," said Pepys. "So glorious was the show with gold and silver, that we were not able to look at it, our eyes at last being so much overcome." The "magnificent traine on horseback, as rich as embrodery, velvet, cloth of gold and silver, and jewells, could make them and their pransing horses," as John Evelyn decribed it, covered the length and breadth of London from the Tower to Whitehall, through streets strewn with flowers, under specially built triumphal arches, past houses hung with rich tapestry, windows and balconies full of beautiful ladies. "Fountains ran wine, bells rang," and joyful voices acclaimed him as His Majesty passed on his way to Whitehall. But by far the most important incident in the procession for the Penns was the fact that when the King and the Duke of York passed Mr. Young's house they looked up and frankly and warmly recognized the group. A father at that moment would have put his arm around his son's shoulders to make certain that His Majesty would know exactly which was he—that boy whose name came into their conversations at the slightest cause. And the young man—to be noticed by his King and the King's brother—it could not have helped but thrill him.

After dinner with Mr. Young, at which they were very merry indeed, they could go home—father and son—to talk and talk before the younger's return to Oxford. First, about the future, both their futures, bathed in the sunshine of the royal favor. What a magnificent opportunity was waiting for Penn as soon as he finished Oxford! Perhaps he, too, would be knighted some day. Then Sir William, garrulous from all the wine he had drunk, could recapitulate for his son the events of the past few months. Last November Sir William and Samuel Pepys had galloped out to Walthamstow to visit Sir William Batten at his country estate. Ah, yes! He was living in splendor now, the Admiral who had had the imagination and audacity to steal a piece of Cromwell's navy and carry it off to the King. Months ago the King had given Sir William Penn an Irish assignment with a nice piece of income attached to it: he was governor and captain of the castle and fort of Kinsale, "and of a foot company there, for the defence and safety thereof, to hold during His Majesty's pleasure; together with all fees, allowances, profits, and advantages thereto belonging." In December there had been a dinner at the Sun Tavern on Fish Street Hill, fine gentlemen, good music, excellent wine; and Lord Inchiquin had been there, and of course, Pepys. Confidentially, Pepys' attitude was hostile, although he pretended to great friendship for his own greedy gain. Lady Penn was the one who knew how to charm Pepys.

No doubt there was a theatre party for the young man home from college, and if he was too silent at seeing women play women's roles and display their legs on a stage, an indulgent father would have laughed good-naturedly, clapped him on the back and bade him be a man.

The William Penn who returned to Oxford, like a man walking away from a brilliant light, was dazzled by the splendor of the

Coronation and his own close association with it, and glowed with his father's hopes and enthusiasms. He could hope some day to play as intimate a role in England's destiny as his father, and he could add to his father's talents the benefit of an Oxford background. His terms at Oxford ran around the calendar, punctuated by four short vacations, and he returned in time to begin his post-Easter sessions. Not until his second year did the alter-influences of Puritanism take on sufficient strength to create a serious conflict in his thinking.

When William Penn was in his second year at Oxford, England was in her second year of Restoration, a very different year from her first. The first had been a kind of honeymoon between people and tradition, but the second saw the beginnings of persecution of the Puritan sects, the re-establishing of the Anglican Church as the only church of the land. The Corporation Act, the first of four laws known collectively as the Clarendon Code (modeled on the code used against the Church of England by Cromwell) was passed by a cruel, young, shortsighted Cavalier Parliament that was to sit from May, 1661, for eighteen years. The Corporation Act excluded from municipal office anyone who would not participate in the sacraments as prescribed by the Church of England, and since municipal officeholders usually controlled parliamentary elections its intent is apparent.

A man matures many years in one during his first academic year away from home. Under the stimulation of new friends, a new kind of teaching and new areas of subject matter and ideas, his whole mind comes alive and seeks more that is new. He is most susceptible then to intellectual adventure. Penn, older and stabler and better oriented in his second year, felt his perspective widening and his capacity for inquiry leading him to wonder about John Fell's rigid regulations, about Charles II's order that the surplice be worn by students, about the handful of fellow students who refused to attend chapel service, and were, instead, holding worship meetings of their own, and attending lectures by a Dr. John Owen. Dr. Owen had been the Dean of Christ Church, dismissed by the Restoration and replaced ultimately by Fell. Owen was a vigorous and brilliant man, a widely known Puritan preacher, a gifted penman who had contributed his share of theological pamphlets to the Puritan revolution. Lads who had been in Oxford longer than Penn remembered their Dean; they were the students who still clung to their Puritan traditions and training, were less obscene in their language, less cruel, less vain, more serious; so, when they followed their Dean to his "retirement," Penn followed them.

Penn's few isolated religious experiences—the brief moment at Chigwell, the visit of Thomas Loe to Macroom, association with the serious-minded non-conformist students, Dr. Owen's lectures—were beginning to form a pattern. Within himself, somehow, was coming to life a new kind of individual integrity. He was both led and driven: led by his non-conformist associations, and driven by the scenes in London and Oxford. The cruel, quick-tempered crowds of Royalist Oxford men, "black tribes of scholars," took their cues from the top, rushed along blindly with the times, administered duckings, beatings and obscene barbarities upon the persons of such Puritan minorities as the Quakers who came to Oxford town with their purist message. Penn was a young man turning radical when a man is most apt to turn radical—in college—at an historical moment when piety and decency were radical.

Penn may even have heard Thomas Loe speak in Oxford during his first year there. It would have been possible, but there is no certainty about it. It would not have been possible during his second year, because Loe was in Oxford jail. Loe had been in the jail of Oxford town for preaching Quakerism even before Penn entered the university; but Loe had gone to Ireland when he was released, not returning to Oxford until November or December, 1660. He was arrested again, with a group of Quakers suspected of being connected with the Fifth Monarchy uprising, during the middle of January of Penn's first college year, and held in jail until long after Penn himself had been dismissed from Christ Church. There would be time for Loe, after the leaven had worked a little longer, after Penn had removed from his own shoulders the revolting robes of prefabricated thinking, after he had listened frequently enough to John Owen and then to a greater French divine.

The sincere ardor of the Oxford men who refused to wear the

surplice and conspicuously absented themselves from chapel was as English as Oxford town herself, and Penn's joining company with them in their valiant plea for freedom of conscience came out of his own racial and cultural heritage. At first Christ Church levied an ineffective fine on Penn for his non-conformity, but Penn's own writings suggest that there was much more to be faced than a cash fine in taking up with a minority that was resisting the trend of the times. In telling his own story of his convincement he refers to his "persecution at Oxford . . . and how the Lord sustained" him, and there was plenty of opportunity for persecution from both students and faculty with official approval for any disciplinary devices that their minds could invent. But there was a restraining factor, too; Penn *was* the son of Sir William who *was* a close personal friend of the Duke of York who *was* the brother of the King. Christ Church endured the seventeen-year-old recalcitrant as long as its patience would allow, but by March of 1662 its patience ran out and Penn was expelled and sent home.

Home to an embarrassed and quick-tempered father, who had not been unaware of the developing problem. The boy had been in London in January and Sir William had had a talk with him then. Sir William had even consulted Samuel Pepys about removing him from Oxford and sending him to Cambridge. Pepys had recommended Magdalene. In February he had called at Pepys' home again and talked about his son. Penn was cautious about telling the gossiping Pepys the real nature of the problem even after the boy came home, because Pepys wrote in his *Diary* on the sixteenth of March, 1662: "Walking in the garden with Sir W. Penn: his son William is at home, not well. But all things, I fear, do not go well with them—they look discontentedly, but I know not what ails them."

William was "not well" because by his own words his father administered "bitter usage," "whipping, beating and turning out of doors," a panacea of the times, a naval commander's tactics, a hothead's clumsy approach to a problem that was subtler than he could comprehend. The turning out of doors was a rash, melodramatic act that was quickly reconsidered at the intervention of Lady Penn. Where could the boy go? How could he live without financial support? How could his family possibly protect him from further infection if he were turned loose upon the world and beyond their jurisdiction? How could she get along without him when her husband was away? The boy returned to the house and withdrew into his room and into himself, to reflect, to consider, to pray, to wonder how his life would turn out if he and his father could not agree—and they could not. In that kind of intolerable situation he could not turn to his father for advice or comfort without stirring up an emotional scene; he could not turn to his mother because she was not a scholar. There was someone to whom he could turn, Dr. John Owen, and he began to correspond with the Puritan preacher. When Sir William came upon a letter that Dr. Owen had written to his son, he was so upset and beside himself with worry that he was even willing to take Pepys into his confidence and risk the fact that Pepys would probably tattle in high places.

"Sir W. Penn much troubled upon letters come last night. Showed me one of Dr. Owen's to his son, whereby it appears his son is much perverted in his opinion by him; which I now perceive is one thing that hath put Sir William so long off the hookes," Pepys put down not a little happily.

Troubled young Penn was still at home in the heart of raucous, riotous London in May when the House of Commons passed the prison-packing Quaker Act: "An Act for preventing mischiefs and dangers that may arise by certain persons called Quakers, and others refusing to take lawful oaths." An uprising of a small, violent religious group called Fifth Monarchists who became mistakenly identified with the Quakers was responsible; the Quaker Act made it an offense for five or more of them to assemble "under pretense of worship"; fines, imprisonment, banishment and slavery being the succession of punishments. The same month the second law of the four-pronged Clarendon Code was enacted; that was the Act of Uniformity which forced some two thousand clergymen out of their posts by requiring them to follow exactly the established Prayer Book and other details of liturgy. He was still at home in June when Sir Harry Vane, bold advocate of the sovereign power of Parliament, was brought to Tower Hill to lose his head under the executioner's axe. But Penn was not home much longer than that, because his father was making swift and positive plans for his well-being.

There were many in Whitehall who loved and valued Sir William and wanted to help him save his son from ruin, and the plan that resulted was to send William Penn to France for that stint on the Continent so essential to a gentleman's education. France was a country where a man could acquire fine manners, subtle ways, a genteel air; and its Court could certainly divert a young man's thoughts from his soul. Both father and son prepared to leave London the first week of July, Sir William to Ireland to look after his holdings, particularly his recently acquired Kinsale fort, and William to France with "some persons of quality."

Before departing they dined with Pepys on the fifth of July. "Had Sir W. Penn, who I hate with all my heart . . . and his son, William, to my house to dinner. . . . I having some venison given me a day or two ago. . . ."

Robert Spencer, four years older than Penn, was one of the persons of quality on the continental tour party. (Travelers usually set out in groups because of the dangers involved.) Spencer was of a lighter substance than Penn, well inured to his high-born life, not afflicted by inner conflicts with his own soul, in no danger of becoming a spiritual seeker, yet this was the beginning of a friendship that lasted for the rest of Penn's life. Spencer eventually became the Earl of Sunderland, a powerful name in English history, a valuable name in Pennsylvania's history.

Spencer, Penn and the others made Paris their goal, and here is a portion of Penn's life about which almost nothing is known. The record of his stay in Paris is blank. Penn's Paris belonged to the same era as Penn's London; it was boisterous, haunted by night-prowling robbers, immodest, heavy-drinking and unsanitary. Its architecture was different, its houses "built rather by philosophers than architects" according to another English traveler's observation, "being seven or eight stories high. . . . Instead of wainscot and boarded floors the rooms are hung with tapestry and paved with bricks." The hotels were nobler than that, with dignified courts and porte-cochères, and inlaid floors polished to neck-breaking slipperiness. Louis XIV was, like his predecessors, expanding the old

Louvre, and in the Tuileries gardens ladies and gentlemen strolled about like peacocks in elaborate finery that had taken them all morning to don. As the inevitable complement to exaggerated wealth and idleness there was that symptom of extreme poverty, the hoards of beggars in the streets who made it impossible for one to open one's purse without drawing a crowd. There were the cabarets with almost endless wine lists and ordinaries serving curious food items. The delicate French did not serve their meat in great joints, but sliced it thin, "scarce thicker than a sixpenny steak."

Besse, to whom a contemporary biography is attributed, tells us that Penn attended the French Court, and the Court at that time was held at Fontainebleau since Versailles was not yet completed. There, nearly forty miles from Paris, buried in the forest where Louis XIV hunted stag, the Bourbons were at the height of their glory. Contrary to the fate of the Kings of England who had been losing ground to their Parliament, the French monarchs had achieved absolute power at home, and, after the Thirty Years' War, they had overcome the chief threat to their supremacy abroad, the Hapsburgs, both Austrian and Spanish. Under the guiding genius of Cardinal Richelieu and after him Cardinal Mazarin, France moved into political eminence with expanding domestic frontiers, increased power at sea and colonies in the New World. Her late-starting Renaissance in art, music and literature outstripped the Italian by the seventeenth century, and flowered with the rest of French elegance under Louis XIV. Corneille had his theatre. A young man named Jean Racine showed great promise. Molière was living on a pension from Louis XIV and performing his plays for the King. He had not yet written his *Le Bourgeois Gentilhomme*, but *L'École des Maris* and *L'École des Femmes* had already seen the light of day.

William Penn arrived in Paris in the summer of 1662. Richelieu had been dead for twenty years, Mazarin for one. Penn was not quite eighteen; Louis XIV was twenty-four. Penn stepped into the dazzle of jewels, satins, exquisite and complex manners, and he could not help but be affected. This was his first real foreign experience, and he would unconsciously have taken on the new delicacies of living, thrilled to hear his own voice turn the subtly twanging consonants and musical cadences of a new tongue.

One precious episode of Penn's French visit comes down to us in his own words.

"I was once myself in France . . . set upon about eleven at night, as I was walking to my lodging, by a person that way-laid me, with his naked sword in his hand, who demanded satisfaction of me for taking no notice of him, at a time when he civilly saluted me with his hat; tho' the truth was, I saw him not when he did it. I will suppose he had killed me, for he made several passes at me, or I in my defence had killed him, when I disarmed him (as the Earl of Crawford's servant saw, that was by). I ask any man of understanding or conscience, if the whole ceremony were worth the life of a man, considering the dignity of the nature, and the importance of the life of man, both with respect to God his creator, himself, and the benefit of civil society?"

Penn had been legally entitled to slay his attacker, but he spared the man's life instead, because in a moment of complete clarity he saw the superfluousness of man-made rank and complex custom. "Envy, quarrels and mischiefs have happened among private persons, upon conceit that they have not been respected to their degree or quality among men, with hat, knee, or title." It was his first experience in non-violence. Even amongst all the French finery and influence he still belonged to Thomas Loe; he was still a non-conformist; he could not accept the idea that the doffing of a hat was worth a man's life.

Harboring half-buried, almost forgotten challenges to his inherited patterns, William Penn moved into the aura of Moses Amyraut. He left Paris and its Roman Catholic circles—and his traveling companions, too, apparently—and went southward to the Protestant atmosphere of Saumur on the Loire, not far from that capital of Protestantism, Nantes. Saumur stretches along the left bank of the brown, sometimes shallow river that winds its way westward through the château country, its own château high on a hill overlooking the town and the meadowy countryside. Saumur is a very ancient town, called Salmurium by the Romans, plundered by the Normans in the tenth century, and visited by Joan of Arc on her way to Poitiers in 1429. The château, the sixteenth-century hôtel de ville, the home of

Duplessis-Mornay and many more of its present buildings were there before Penn's time.

The Huguenot, Philippe Duplessis-Mornay, one of the outstanding Protestant leaders of France in the sixteenth century, had placed the stamp of his personality upon Saumur. He was head of her government for many years and was responsible for Saumur's prominent role in the French Reformation. Among other accomplishments, Mornay founded two schools; one was an *académie d'équitation,* now L'Ecole de Cavalerie; the other was L'Académie Protestante de Saumur that William Penn attended in 1663 and 1664, a school that flourished from about 1591 until the Revocation of the Edict of Nantes.

The gentle, liberal, spiritually endowed Moïse (Moses) Amyraut was principal or headmaster when Penn arrived at 6 Rue St. Jean, some time at the end of 1662 or beginning of 1663. The school term ran for eleven months from the middle of October to the following September, and Penn may have attempted to reach there at the beginning of the term. Amyraut was one of the greatest and most courageous theologians of his time. His voice and pen spoke eloquently on behalf of religious liberty and toleration until he became a popular national figure. Richelieu respected him, and when Richelieu took away from French Protestants their right to participate in political affairs it was Amyraut who was chosen by his Synod to present a protest to the King. After Richelieu, Mazarin listened to Amyraut's advice. William Penn went to Moses Amyraut, sat in his classes for at least a year, even lodged at his home rather than at the inns and hostels used by the poorer students, absorbed from him at school and at home his extraordinary views on Christian morality.

Amyraut's *La Morale Chrétienne,* six volumes of fine classical French, establishes him as the most creative theologian of seventeenth-century France. Amyraut was both product and mentor of the French Reformation, and as he watched the spiritual vitality drain out of the movement and saw it settled down to rigid Calvinistic dogma and empty form, he rose to call it back to its true appointment. He rejected predestinationist thinking. The divine will, he declared, did not select favored souls; rather it yearned to save every soul. To Amyraut personal liberty was the *sine qua non* of integrity, and Christ was its agent. He saw the human soul as a free, self-determining entity; and he conceived of a spontaneous morality flowering out of the human conscience. Moral man, said Amyraut, did not develop out of externally applied, abstract principles, but his fundamental starting point was his own psychology. The self-determined, voluntary acts of a man were the only ones that had real value, and his acts were motivated either by love or aversion, his noblest by love of good and aversion to evil. Man had to judge and weigh and compare each new situation as he went along, and his own intelligence was his court of blame and praise. Amyraut spoke of a "supreme good," *le souverain bien,* as the goal toward which man's actions tended. But man could not achieve it alone; he needed the power and experience of redemption to move toward an ever closer communion with God. Therein lay supreme human happiness. The Christian religion did not give man a soul or any other faculties; it illuminated the soul with which he was already endowed. But piety was not enough, Amyraut went on to say; charity was also needed; for man's responsibility to his brother was part of his ultimate morality.

The thinking of Amyraut was the theological atmosphere of Saumur, and Penn may have been there as long as a year and a half. Classes were available to him in theology, philosophy, Hebrew, Greek, rhetoric, eloquence, mathematics; but the great emphasis was on philosophy and theology. He had arrived carrying within himself a growing accumulation of religious experiences; he remained to have those experiences verified and amplified by a doctrine of morality based upon free will, a free will guided by that of God in every man.

Why William Penn left Saumur in the spring or summer of 1664 we do not know. Amyraut died early that year, and the two events may be related. A war with Holland was imminent (the New Netherlands were seized that summer), and that may have been another determining factor.

During his stay on the Continent Penn is thought to have met Algernon Sydney, Robert Spencer's uncle, and it is perfectly possible. The most likely place would have been at the home of the Quaker merchant, Benjamin Furly, in Rotterdam. Furly's hospitable home was an intellectual center on the Continent, and we know that Sydney was in Rotterdam in 1664. Penn may have stopped at Rotterdam on his way to catch the Channel boat from Brielle to Harwich.

Sydney was an Englishman serving out a sad and dangerous exile. He was a republican who, like many more, had wanted reform, a disciplining of the Stuarts, rather than the extreme measures that resulted. There was no doubt in his mind about the legality of beheading the King, provided the King's deeds warranted it, and provided the King's trial was just. But the trial of Charles I had been so fraught with tension, haste and hatred that many had announced their opposition to the proceedings, among them Sydney, who warned that such an extreme measure would cause the people to rise up against the very Commonwealth they were trying to create. It was then that Cromwell had said to Sydney, "I tell you we will cut off his head with the Crown upon it!" And Sydney had replied, "You may take your own course; I cannot stop you; but I will keep myself clean from having any hand in this business." Sydney was abroad on a diplomatic mission when he heard that the Convention Parliament had voted to restore Charles II to the throne and that regicides were being rounded up. He decided to remain abroad, constantly on the alert for Royalist assassins, in spite of the fact that he had not been a party to the execution of Charles II's father. Vane's subsequent execution confirmed the wisdom of his decision.

William Penn's father had been a member of the Convention Parliament, and he was a Royalist in high favor. Did young Penn request the audience with Sydney? Or did Sydney ask to see him? Sydney wanted to go home. Did he hope the young man could intercede for him? Answers unknown. Whatever Sydney's confidences may have been, Penn never revealed them; and political exiles were seldom so incautious as to leave written records lying around.

William Penn arrived back in London in August, 1664, a changed personality on the surface—"a most modish person, grown a fine gentleman," said Mrs. Pepys, to which her husband added, "but a great deal, if not too much, of the vanity of the French garb, and affected manner of speech and gait"—a changed personality beneath the surface, possessed of a maturing sense of values, an accumulating set of standards by which to measure new experiences. But it was the surface man that Sir William saw. There is no verified record of William Penn's appearance, although we know by inference that he was tall and athletic in build, and if the armor portrait be a true likeness he was certainly handsome with wide, candid eyes, a sensitive mouth and firm chin. The figure he cut when he returned from France, two years older, was bound to please his father. His intellectual prowess was satisfying, too; his French was excellent, his Latin finely polished, his logic clean-cut, his capacity for discourse and quick-witted answer all that a proud parent could possibly expect.

> They that feel nothing of charity are at best not above half of kin to the human race.
>
> ——William Penn, *Reflections and Maxims*

3. The Plague Year

WILLIAM PENN, returning from France to England, stepped from youth into manhood, transformed from the learning boy to the administering adult, responsible as the older son for the welfare of his mother, his thirteen-year-old sister and his nine-year-old brother, should his father be called away to sea duty. He found his father in a rush of national affairs and the responsibilities of his naval office, and he discovered himself being drawn deeper into the network of his father's influence, brought to the closer scrutiny of the King and the Duke of York, told about events that had occurred in his absence. Charles II had just a few weeks before his return bestowed upon the Duke of York all territory in the New World along the Atlantic coast from the St. Lawrence River to Delaware Bay. Parliament had passed the third act of the Clarendon Code, the Conventicle Act, which forbade the gathering for worship except under the auspices of the Anglican Church under pain of imprisonment and deportation. But Sir William Penn was not too busy to make plans for a final touch to his son's education. It still seemed inevitable to both father and son that William Penn would move into government circles; for this some legal training seemed necessary, and Lincoln's Inn was the law school they chose.

Lincoln's Inn was one of four Inns of Court in London where young men, usually the sons of gentlemen, persons of wealth and "quality," went for their legal training. Lincoln's Inn, thought to have become a seat of legal training as far back as the fourteenth century, fronted on Chancery Lane, to the extreme west of London and well beyond the limits of the city wall. The quadrangle of buildings that were there in Penn's time was entered through a pointed Tudor arch between two, four-story, square brick gate houses. At the south side of the quandrangle were chambers, and at the north side stood the chapel with its hand-hewn oak pews, thought to have been designed by Inigo Jones. On the opposite side of the court stood the Old Hall, built at the end of the fifteenth century, with its buttresses and tall, stained-glass windows. The Old Hall, nearly seventy-five feet long, was the center of life at the school. To it came the young men to dine at long tables, to give masques and plays, to hold mootings and celebrations. Its side walls were oak paneled, its tile floor protected by a layer of rushes, and in the center of the floor a fire burned and sent its smoke up more than thirty feet to escape through the vents at the joining of the side walls and ceiling. Beyond the quadrangle lay the famous gardens of Lincoln's Inn where Ben Jonson had once walked under the stately elms. The garden had just been enlarged and improved when Penn entered Lincoln's Inn, and its wall facing Lincoln's Inn Fields to the west had been made higher, for the fields were a distasteful sight, rubbish strewn, attractive to beggars and vagabonds.

The exact date of William Penn's admission to Lincoln's Inn is recorded in the school's ancient *Black Books*: February 7, 1665—William Penn, son and heir apparent of Sir William Penn, of City of London, Knight. The school terms during 1665 were: Hilary from January 23 to February 13, Easter from April 12 to May 8, Trinity from May 26 to June 14 and Michaelmas from October 23 to November 28. Students were required to be in residence at the inn during these periods of study.

Study at the Inns of Court during the Restoration offered curious and various values. The readings and mootings must have taught the young men considerable law, but the old readings in law began to include readings on Dryden, Beaumont and Fletcher; and the mootings, mock trials intended to instruct, became more mocking and less instructive, and subject to interruption if they interfered with a social function. A swarm of young men suffering from too much wealth and too high caste carried the day with their arrogant and undisciplined vigors.

William Penn's attendance at Lincoln's Inn was short lived and further shortened by two major interruptions. War had been declared a second time against Holland, and the new and greater British fleet went into action. There were three squadrons, the first, thirty-eight ships, with the Duke of York as Lord Admiral and Sir William Penn as Great Captain Commander aboard the *Royal Charles*. Sir William removed his son from Lincoln's Inn almost immediately after his enrollment, and took him aboard the *Royal Charles* for a short while. This gave Penn an opportunity to feel the pulse of his father's kind of life, to experience the exhilaration of sailing in a great fleet toward sea warfare, and to recapture some of his childish adoration as he watched the older man in his best medium, in command of a whole squadron carrying more than eight thousand men. He could observe the frank confidence and respect that Sir William received from those under his command. He was aboard for two or three weeks, until his father sent him home as a personal messenger to the King—a brilliant first step in introducing the two. Penn wrote to his father from Harwich on April 23, 1665:

HONORED FATHER:

We could not arrive here sooner than this day, above twelve of the clock, by reason of the continued cross winds, and, as I thought, foul weather. I pray God, after all the foul weather and dangers you are exposed to, and shall be, that you come home as secure. And I bless God, my heart does not in any way fail, but firmly believe that if God has called you out to battle, He will cover your head in that smoky day. And, as I never knew what a father was till I had wisdom enough to prize him, so I can safely say, that now, of all times, your concerns are most dear to me. It's hard, meantime, to lose both a father and a friend, etc. W. P.

A serious letter, a concerned letter, a sober and righteous letter, penned as soon as he had reached the port. He proceeded from there to London and Whitehall, arriving at dawn before the King was up, but when the King heard that there was an express message from the Duke of York's ship, he donned his gown and slippers and received the messenger.

"Oh, is't you?" the King remarked with surprise. "How is Sir William?"

William Penn wrote a second, very boyish letter to his father, giving every little detail of how the King had behaved in that brief encounter.

Navy Office, 6th May, 1665

. . . He asked how you did at three several times. He was glad to hear your message about Ka [probably a code symbol]. After interrogating me above half an hour, he bid me go about your business and mine too. . . . I delivered all the letters given me. My mother was to see Lady Lawson, and she was here. I pray God be with you, and be your armor in the day of controversy! May that power be your salvation, for his name's sake! And so will he wish and pray, that is, with all true veneration, honored father.

Your obedient son and servant,

WILLIAM PENN

He paid his respects to Pepys, too, and gave him an account of the sailing of the fleet.

And so back to Lincoln's Inn and its artificialities, while his father fought a war at sea, and his mother and sister and brother minded their diplomacy at home. Ten-year-old Dicke Penn had long since chosen to be Mrs. Pepys' valentine, and Peg and her mother managed well together. Pepys called at Lady Batten's one day and found all three women together. They must have thought Pepys needed jollying up, for they seized him and flung him down on the bed and then pounced on top of him. They knew how the plump, vain Pepys loved feminine attention. "Very merry we were," said he. Another time he confessed to his *Diary* that he found it difficult to withstand an invitation from the Penn ladies, and in spite of his resolution "to follow business close this afternoon, did stay talking, and playing the fool almost all the afternoon." The Penn ladies could not have known that Pepys' *Diary* observed that "Mrs. Penn grows mighty homely and looks old," or that he had been gossiping with a neighbor of theirs, a Mrs. Turner who claimed to have known the Penns "when." When the Penns lived on Tower Hill, before their rise, he had been a "pityful fellow" and his wife had been "one of the sourest, dirty women, that ever she saw; that for many years together they ate more meals at her house than at their own . . . that she brought my Lady who was then a dirty slattern, with her stockings hanging about her heels, so that afterwards the people of the whole Hill did say that Mrs. Turner had made Mrs.

Penn a gentlewoman. . . ." But Pepys-Turner gossip must be heavily discounted for envy.

Margaret Penn's older boy was making observations of his own, observations that increased his distraction and deepened his withdrawal from the unavoidable frivolities of his father's household. As he traveled back and forth between his home and Lincoln's Inn he was seeing the direct results of the Clarendon Code, dissenters in stocks being pelted with missiles by mocking crowds, raids upon worshiping meetings, mass arrests; hearing reports of brutal tortures. He could not have escaped the fact that the religious persecutions fell most heavily upon the Quakers, who refused to meet in secret, nor could he have helped but realize that the religious persecutions were being visited upon the Puritan sects with anything but spiritual intent.

It was late spring when he returned to his classes in Lincoln's Inn, but the previous winter the terrible factor that would cause the second interruption in his law studies had been gathering in readiness for the warm weather—the plague. There were always a few cases in the most squalid areas, so when a case occurred in December in St. Giles in the Fields, comfortably outside the wall, it did not cause too much concern. The winter was exceptionally cold with heavy snow and ice on the Thames, and that held most infections in check. But a seafaring nation whose ports communicated with most of the ports of the world was paying a bitter price for her profits as the ships that carried merchandise also carried rats who carried infected fleas. The rats swarmed over the docks and through the cellars and foul underground ways of English cities bringing their deadly parasites with them, and fraternized with the native rats, exchanging flea for flea. When the frost lifted in March, the number of plague cases that occurred in the slums clustering outside the wall of the city increased. Inevitably, as the slum dwellers came into the city to beg, peddle wares, or work at their appointed tasks, the plague came in with them, and by June London knew it had an epidemic.

Lincoln's Inn at first locked most of its gates and under guard admitted "none but persons of quality," but by the middle of June most of its wealthy students had fled with their families to the countryside. The poor could not flee; it was they who stayed and died. They could only stand by the wayside, resigned, and watch wide-eyed, as the cavalcade of nobles in their coaches, household goods piled in wagons, removed themselves from danger, with no notion of any responsibility to the rest of humanity. The King and his Court moved to Hampton Court and then to Salisbury, and the Parliament met at Oxford. The Penns, so far as we know, remained in London.

The heat, humidity and rainfall of July and August gave the epidemic a terrible impetus; death rates shot up; commerce within the city came to a standstill; the streets were filled with mournful cries—of the painfully stricken, the grief stricken, the shouts of the man walking beside his horse and two-wheeled cart, "Bring out your dead! Bring out your dead!" Families with plague cases were boarded up into their houses for forty days without sufficient resources. Door upon door bore the great placard with its red cross and the plea, "Lord have mercy upon us!" The spotted death swept through the city killing so many so rapidly that there weren't enough burying grounds; great pits had to be dug wherever there was waste ground and bodies brought in great wagon loads. The madness of pain and fever, mass hysteria, ruled London life that summer. Regulations, preventives, treatments, all designed by the medically ignorant, promoted the progress of the disease oftener than they slowed it. There were no real nurses—only the hags and crones so desperately poor that they would take care of plague victims for a fee and a chance to rob the corpse. The Great Plague claimed an estimated seventy thousand Londoners before it receded.

Living in the midst of such tragedy and desolation, seeing the self-hearted flee and the magnificent-hearted come out to help the stricken, burdened by an indefinable sorrow, sensing that the increasing riddle of himself was somehow identified with the incredible suffering and sorrow all around him—this was William Penn. He had been brushed long ago by the delicate fringe of a humanitarian doctrine, and he had only a few months before left the classrooms of Moses Amyraut who had said that piety is not enough, that man's responsibility to his brother is part of his ultimate morality. He saw the Quakers, their courage quickened by human need, go about administering what relief they could in the face of arrests and persecutions that were carried on right through the plague period. Quakers took food to the well who were boarded up in their houses, they helped gather the dead, they went into the chambers of the sick to give ministry and physical aid. Even though great quantities of them died of the plague or were arrested, they went on about their errands of mercy. George Whitehead, prominent Friends' minister, knowing that he could find himself in prison any moment, always carried his nightcap in his pocket. What a deep revulsion young Penn must have experienced from the standards of Whitehall, the foolish gaiety and ornate dress of the times. The influence the French Court had had upon him must have faded almost to the vanishing point, as he began to sense the pulse of the broad base of godfearers beneath the frothy surface of the Restoration, the broad base of persistent respectability that had never ceased to exist.

The plague had a revitalizing effect on all the Puritan sects, and the non-conformists began to meet more openly. "The Great Plague," said Walter George Bell, "established English Non-conformity," and that is an exaggerated statement, since non-conformity is the original divine breath of individuality in the soul of man. But Bell does have a point. The recurrence of non-conformity during that summer and fall was so widespread that it attracted the attention of Parliament and the result was the Five-Mile Act in October, 1665, requiring a further oath of allegiance to Church and State and forbidding any non-conformist preacher to come within five miles of any corporate town. Thus the Clarendon Code was completed.

Sir William had been home in June, triumphant as usual, from the victorious battle of Lowestoft in which the English navy had routed the Dutch. He made another triumphant return in September with a host of prizes—four men-of-war, three East Indiamen and seven other merchant ships. This proved to be Sir William's last sea command, for his health had begun to fail, and he was suffering severely from the gout. But being confined to a chair with his gouty foot up on a cushion meant that he could give more attention and thought to his son; William had reached his majority in October; he was twenty-one years old.

O let us be valiant in God's cause on earth, who have but a short time and a few days to live.
——William Penn, *A Letter of Love to the Young Convinced*

4. The Young Convinced

Sir William was aging according to the life span of his times, and at forty-four his best energies had been spent. The more strenuous responsibilities for his affairs, particularly his estates, must be handed on to his heir. Apparently the two men decided that estates were more important than law, because William Penn discontinued his studies at Lincoln's Inn and went to Ireland. Many complications that needed on-the-spot supervision had arisen concerning their Irish holdings. Upon Charles II's accession to the throne, Irish Royalists began to file claims for return of their lands confiscated by Cromwell, and in many instances restitution was granted. Penn's lands at Macroom were among those returned to their original owner. Penn, always eager to please his King, had accepted in exchange extensive lands around Cork Harbor and another tract below Kinsale. Legal transfer of titles, amicable establishment of the new claim with the local tenants and residents, were all to be handled by his son.

Sir William must have hoped, too, that the Viceregal Court in Dublin, a small scale replica of the Court in London, would prove a constructive diversion for the young man whose countenance was growing more sober every day.

Penn left London in January, 1666, and appears to have sailed across St. George's Channel to Kinsale, the fort and castle to which his father held the governorship and captaincy. From there he went up the coast as far as the village of Shanagarry near Ballycotton Bay, halfway between Cork and Youghal. Shanagarry Castle, set close to its village and within a short walk of the sea, now belonged to his father. It was built of the native gray stone, and the wall around its grounds skirted the bog where extensive drainage ditches were needed. Penn made the castle of Shanagarry his residence whenever the problems of the more than seven thousand acres required his presence.

But much of his time during those first few months in Ireland was spent in Dublin with James Butler, Duke of Ormonde and Lord Lieutenant of Ireland, and Ormonde's eldest son, the Earl of Ossory; and he was completely absorbed by his companions and responsibilities. His days were filled with preparing his father's claim to be heard before the land commissioners and in settling affairs with tenants. Suddenly received as a landed gentleman in his own right, expanding under the flattery of moving freely in an adult world, he responded with an heroic flourish when a sudden need arose for his services.

The garrison of Carrickfergus mutinied, and Penn, skilled in handling both musket and sword, served under the Earl of Arran in restoring order to the gray stone fortress that guarded the long, deep harbor now known as Belfast Lough. It was his one brief record of military service. He handled himself so conspicuously well and revealed himself to be such excellent officer material that many enthusiastic letters were dispatched to London about his exploits. The Duke of Ormonde advised Sir William that he would like to make his son captain of the foot company at Kinsale, "and desire you to send a resignation to that purpose."

William Penn was still in the grip of the excitement of military victory when he wrote his own account to his father and indicated how pleased he would be to accept the military command at Kinsale:

Honorable Sir:

When I was at Carrickfergus with my Lord of Arran, Sir George Lane, in my Lord Dunagle's house, called me aside, and told me the character my Lord Arran had pleased to give his father, obliged him to write you a letter on my behalf; which was, to surrender your government and fort. . . . Sir, I humbly conceive it may be necessary you take notice of my lord's kindness in a letter by the very first . . . I beseech your answer to this, as also, if you please, an acknowledgment to my Lord Lieutenant's and Lord Arran's great and daily kindness. . . .

I am, sir, your most obedient son,

Dublin, 4th July, 1666 W. P.

Sir William had no intention of allowing his son to take the bit in his teeth and run away with the carriage.

July 17th, 1666

SON WILLIAM:

". . . I can say nothing but advise to sobriety. . . . As to the tender made by his grace my Lord Lieutenant, concerning the fort of Kinsale, I wish your youthful desires mayn't outrun your discretion. His grace may, for a time, dispense with my absence; yours he will not, for so he told me. God bless, direct, and protect you.

Your very affectionate father,

W. P.

Sir William planned to "fix in Ireland" himself in his old age; William had to content himself with managing the estates and accepting a post as victualer of the ships of Kinsale. His father wrote him a long letter of instruction about the new post, and added the suggestion: "When you have done this, which I think will take up no long time, and do find that you can settle your business so as no damage may befall us there in your absence, I think you were best make a step over to me . . . to consult upon the whole. . . . Contrive your passage so as to make it most safe. . . ." In a few weeks, just as his father had predicted, Penn had things running smoothly enough at Kinsale to be able to make a visit home.

Penn returned to a charred and ruined London over which the Great Fire had swept, raging for four days and four nights, reducing a large portion of the city to rubble and debris. It had begun in a baker's shop on Pudding Lane near the London Bridge, and the first flames had not attracted much attention in a wood-structured city where fires were so frequent. But a long period of abnormal drought had preceded the fire, and a high wind blowing in from the east accompanied it. The flames traveled down to the water front where inflammable merchandise, hay, coal and timber, lay stacked; then along the Thames as its licking flames and flying hot sparks found their way inland—up street and byway, from house to house relentlessly, past feeble fire-fighting efforts. It gutted a great semi-circle of London within the wall and then swept through the western gates to the liberties. Again the panic and hysteria of mobs fleeing from a city of tragedy, crowding the narrow streets, rushing toward the gates with their belongings in carts or on horses, or on their backs when they could find no vehicle, to live in the open fields until the fire had burned itself out. Then they could creep back and search mournfully through the ashes that remained hot for days afterward. More than thirteen thousand houses had vanished. Penn rode past acres of ruin bristling with stone pillars and solitary walls, dotted with tents and makeshift lean-tos and every kind of temporary molehole contrived out of the rubble. His own home on Tower Hill had not been damaged, because the westward traveling fire had spared the eastern end of the city.

He arrived home in ample time to attend his sister Peg's wedding to Anthony Lowther of Yorkshire the day after St. Valentine's Day. It was a private ceremony with none but the immediate families attending. A few kitchen things were borrowed from Pepys. Sir William's dowry was reported to be generous, and Peg's husband must have been a man of some means at that point, even though he did not seem to be in later years, for fifteen-year-old Peg was able to travel about in a gilt coach, wear a train held by a page when she called on the Battens, and display bracelets of diamonds and rubies.

After he had fulfilled his social obligations and held his conferences with his father, Penn returned to Ireland to take up his residence at Shanagarry Castle.

Cork had been his urban center when he lived at Macroom, and it was also the principal city for Shanagarry. Built upon a cluster of islands between the two forks of the River Lee where the river divides and then reunites before flowing into Cork Harbor, Cork was a walled city in the seventeenth century with a protecting castle and drawbridges that connected it to the marshy mainland. Many of the wide, lovely streets of modern Cork once had canals down their centers.

Penn rode up to Cork one day to purchase some clothes, and, recalling a shop he had known as a boy, one owned by a Quaker, he searched it out. The woman who kept the shop did not recognize the Cavalier customer, but she was cordial. He stood chatting with her, telling her how he had once lived at Macroom, how he had come to know about the Friends, and how his father had once invited Thomas Loe to speak to his family. He would never forget that meeting, he sighed, and he would surely walk a hundred miles to hear Thomas Loe speak again. He need not walk so far, she assured him, for there was to be a meeting in Cork tomorrow, and Thomas Loe was going to speak. He had best stay over for the meeting. Where Penn slept that night at Cork I have no idea, but knowing Friends, I know he could not have escaped their hospitality. Retiring to a plainly appointed home among plainly dressed folk, feeling a little self-conscious about his expensive fabrics and lace ruffles, his elegant wig and clanking sword, he would have felt himself captivated once more by an atmosphere of love that questioned not, judged not, and asked for itself no degree of rank.

The meeting next evening was probably in a private home. William Penn stepped inside with his companions and sat down in the silence, with not a little excitement, some sentiment, and a great deal of curiosity as he surveyed the members of the gathering. The first speaker who rose to break the silence had little or no effect upon Penn, but after that Thomas Loe stood up. Loe was older, and in the intervening years he had not spared himself.

"There is a faith that overcometh the world," Thomas Loe began, "and a faith that is overcome by the world."

Then twenty-two-year-old Penn heard a testimony that spoke deeply to his condition. Loe had found the indefinable sorrow growing within the young man, the increasing sensitivity to human need and suffering, the nebulous new direction, the strange standard of integrity, and defined it—Light, the Word, God. He had brought a blurred image into focus and showed it to Penn, and once Penn had seen it he could never forget. The image had been assembling piece by piece, the brief religious experience during his boyhood at Chigwell, the teachings of Moses Amyraut, the sufferings he had witnessed during the plague, and this day the fragilely related fragments had come together in a new and adventuresome pattern of living. The "glory of the world" that had overtaken him, and to which he had so recently given himself up, turned to ashes, and out of its ashes rose the phoenix bird of faith. That spark of God in every man had expanded to a great fire in Penn. "Being ready to faint concerning my hope of the restitution of all things, it was at this time that the Lord visited me with a certain sound and testimony of His eternal word."

Penn began to weep, and as his tears fell he felt within himself a compulsion to rise to his feet and bear witness. "How dost thou know," said his own inner voice, "but somebody may be reached by thy tears." So he stood, with no words at his command who spoke so glibly and cleverly in law class or Court circles, and let his tears be his only evidence, and when William Penn sat down he knew himself to be a Seeker.

Of course, he was noticed. Friends gathered him up and took him to one of their homes for the night, the same home in which Thomas Loe was staying, and there he had a further opportunity to converse with the minister. The young man spoke with too much haste and too much excitement, no doubt; the older with infinite patience and satisfaction. In the course of their talk Loe mentioned his need of a horse since the one he had was no longer fit for travel. Impulsively Penn offered him his own mount, a sumture horse he had brought with him from France. Loe's refusal to accept the animal was crushing, for Penn thought Loe rated him not sufficiently a Friend. He didn't understand that Loe had simply regarded the horse as too fine for himself.

William Penn began to follow the Quaker meetings. He sat with Friends in silent worship to be absorbed by their mystical powers; he listened to members rise and speak who were moved by a power which the meeting brought alive within them. He acquired a new style of companionship, traveled in a new world. The belief of the Friends in the power of the Inner Light of Christ to guide them and the right of the individual alone or with a group to communicate directly with God, the amazing messages that came out of their meetings for worship, their ability to judge lucidly and to make forthright decisions, their integrity, their capacity for self-appraisal, their absolute convincement—all these qualities fascinated the Cavalier.

He wanted more of the companionship of Friends, more of their meetings, more of their messages, more of their literature.

He already knew how badly the Quakers were harried and mistreated by the authorities, who took pleasure in disrupting their meetings and carting off whole groups of them to jail. He himself was present at a meeting on the third of September, 1667, in Cork when a soldier blundered in with the deliberate intent of creating a disturbance. To Penn, the gentleman, the intruder was a common soldier, as low if not much lower in caste than hundreds of men under his father's command. Finding himself affronted by the ruffian, Penn did what came naturally to him: he picked the man up by the collar and started with him toward the head of a flight of stairs. Friends hurried to prevail upon Penn to be gentle; retaliation was not their way. He let go his hold and allowed the soldier to depart, realizing immediately that he could have brought down upon the meeting any amount of official reprisal. He had anyway. The disgruntled soldier went straight to the magistrate with his grievance and returned with a group of officers who broke up the meeting and arrested nineteen of the Quakers. The Mayor before whom they were hailed took one look at Penn's clothes and said that since he was obviously not a Quaker he must have been arrested by mistake. Penn was therefore free to go. It was in that moment that Penn set aside his privileges of birth. He *was* a Friend, he assured the Mayor, and he insisted on being treated the same as the others. The same? Not quite; for the Oxford man and Lincoln's Inn scholar assumed the role of legal counselor to the group of prisoners and demanded to know on what charge they were held. Answer: for being present at a tumultous and riotous assembly. Further: unless he [Penn] gave bond for his good behavior he would be committed to prison. Penn wanted to know the Mayor's authority for such a sentence, since it was clear that without an act of Parliament to back such an action the Mayor would be guilty of "too much officiousness."

"A proclamation in the year 1660, and new instructions to revive that dead and antiquated order," the reply was barked back.

The Mayor was referring, of course, to the Quaker Act passed in 1662 according to the present-day calendar. But *that* law, Penn argued, had been passed against the Fifth Monarchy men. His presentation did no good; he and his eighteen companions were led away to prison.

Penn, the swashbuckling Cavalier, had a subtle sense of the dramatic that he never lost. The grand gesture was a part of his personality. Although he strove all his life from the time of his convincement to achieve the degree of modesty required by Quaker doctrine, there was always that other contrary force within him, that stimulation to be sought in an audience response. That was the manner in which he gave up his sword. Just before he stepped over the threshold of the Cork prison, he paused, unbuckled his sword and handed it with a bow to a bystander, announcing that henceforth he would walk unarmed in an armed world.

William Penn's first literary effort on behalf of Friends was his letter, written during that first imprisonment, to the Earl of Orrery, Lord President of Munster, calling attention to the unjust imprisonment of himself and his associates.

"Religion, which is at once my crime and mine innocence, makes me a prisoner to a mayor's malice, but mine own free man," he wrote, and gave a detailed account of what had occurred. "Since the King's Lord Lieutenant and yourself being fully persuaded the intention of those called Quakers by their meetings, was really the service of God, have therefore manifested a repeal by a long continuance of freedom, I hope your lordship will not now begin an unusual severity, by indulging so much malice in one, whose actions savor ill with his nearest neighbors, but that there may be a speedy releasement to all for attending their honest callings . . . and though to dissent from a national system imposed by authority renders men heretics, yet I dare believe your lordship is better read in reason and theology, than to subscribe a maxim so vulgar and untrue. . . ."

His release came almost instantly, and just as instantly I-thought-you-ought-to-know letters sprouted wings and flew to Sir William. Young Penn, meanwhile, plunged more earnestly than ever into Friends' activities. The brief moment of martyrdom had fed his ardor and made the Quakers his brothers. Now that he had tasted their life, had caught an inside glimpse of their sufferings, he could respect them more than ever. His activities were interrupted by a firm recommendation from home:

Navy Office, October 12, 1667

SON WILLIAM:

I have writ several letters to you since I received any from you. By this I again charge you and strictly command that you come to me with all possible speed. In expectation of your compliance, I remain

Your affectionate father,
W. PENN

The letter did not have the desired effect, and it was followed by another:

Navy Office, October 22, 1667

SON WILLIAM:

I hope this will find you in health. The cause of this writing is to charge you to repair to me with all possible speed, presently after your receipt of it, and not to make any stay there, or any place upon your road, until it pleases God you see me (unless for necessary rest and refreshment).

Your very affectionate father,
W. Penn

Josiah Coale, one of the many new friends Penn was making, returned to England with Penn. Josiah Coale was another man of good family who had been convinced by John Audland and John Camm when they went to Bristol in 1654 in the earliest days of the Quaker movement, and since he was also a man of means he was able to devote most of his time to the ministry and to publishing the Truth both by word of mouth and by his epistles and writings. Penn enjoyed "an intimacy with Coale above many," and found in this man in his early forties a tremendous source of strength. Coale had suffered much and had traveled great distances on behalf of Friends' doctrine; he had been attacked by an angry mob, "dragged bareheaded under the spouts in time of rain," and committed to Newgate prison in Bristol. He and twenty-seven others had written to Charles II giving the King details about the continuous persecution that Friends endured. Later he suffered imprisonment in Dorsetshire and Preston-Richard, and beatings by mobs in many towns. In 1658 he traveled with Thomas Thurston to the New World and accomplished an impossibly difficult journey on foot from Virginia to New England. The Maryland colony later banished him from its bounds. As zealous and ardent as any of the young convinced, Coale poured his positive passions into epistles to Friends in prison in London, Hartford and Kendal, to Friends in exile in Holland, Jamaica and New England; and he joined the pamphleteers in attacking the wickedness of his times. "Oh, England, England, what Lamentation shall I take up for thee," he cried in *England's Sad Estate Lamented*. "Oh, England, England, how incurable is thy wound?"

Penn and Coale stopped in Bristol, Coale's home city, on the way back to London, to visit several meetings there and woo the strength Penn would need to face his father. We know he was back in London by December, 1667, because of an item in Pepys' *Diary*:

> At night comes Mrs. Turner to see us; and there, among other talk, she tells me that Mr. William Penn, who is lately come over from Ireland, is a Quaker again, or some very melancholy thing; that he cares for no company, nor comes into any; which is a pleasant thing, after his being abroad so long, and his father such a hypocritical rogue. . . .

Sir William no longer lived in London but quite recently, probably the previous summer, had taken his wife and one remaining child out of the charred and dismal city to a great house in Wanstead, again near Sir William Batten's. This second Wanstead residence was no doubt purchased, since Sir William's widow occupied it throughout her life after his death. It is described as being a "pleasant house with a garden and wilderness." (A wilderness was a planned arrangement of trees.) The house itself had a great hall downstairs, a parlor, a dining room and kitchen. The hall was green carpeted, hung with pictures, furnished with a billiard table, two other tables and chairs. The dining room was hung with vast tapestries and filled with nearly two dozen chairs, some needlework and some turkey work, couches and tables; in the kitchen were brass kettles, ladles, warming pans, skillets and skimmers. A wide, sweeping stairway led to the second floor where there were five bedrooms, two rooms for servants and a ladies' closet. The bedrooms were replete with feather beds and bolsters, turkey work chairs, looking glasses, silk and satin quilts, heavily curtained windows and rich tapestries.

Josiah Coale drove out to the Wanstead house with William to help him through that first meeting with his father, and in front of Coale Sir William held his temper, even when the younger men spoke discourteously and their heads remained covered. But when at last father and son were alone the whole painful conflict burst forth. Why did he use *thee* and *thou*, Sir William demanded to know. 'Twas obedience to God and not intended as disrespect to him, William explained. Did he not realize how important it was to use the plural *you* when speaking to those older or of higher rank? Did that have to be explained to him after the excellent upbringing he had had? No, William retorted; the Quakers recognized no rank; they considered all men equal; therefore they had adopted the language of the commonest folk. He could use *thee* and *thou* to whomever he pleased, but he must, Sir William declared, address the King, the Duke of York and himself in the courteous plural. The younger man shook his head. He was sorry, but he must henceforth address even the King, the Duke and his father in the singular number. Sir William's temper mounted as he broached the subject of hat homage. Surely he would be willing to uncover before the King, the Duke and himself; and the incredible reply came back that drove Sir William to such a degree of rage that he dared not trust himself to pursue the argument further that night. William was sorry, but he could not comply with his father's desire. The only further instructions that his father gave him before going upstairs to bed were to arise early the next morning and be prepared to go out with him in the coach.

William Penn retired to his room, but not to sleep, because he did not know where he and his father would go—very possibly to Whitehall. When the coach drew up next morning and the two men climbed in, Sir William ordered the coachman to drive them into the park, and William Penn felt easier at once. It was simply his father's intent to have a private conversation with him that none could overhear. Non-conformity was fraught with political dangers to both of them; it could cost Sir William the King's and the Duke's favor, and it could cost William his freedom, perhaps his life.

He had been "trained up in learning and other accomplishments for a courtier—as for an ambassador or other minister," Sir William began to reason. How could he in the face of all that become a Quaker? 'Twas in "obedience to the manifestation of God in his own conscience," came the explanation, and William reminded his father that he himself had once wept to hear Thomas Loe speak. He firmly believed that his father had been convinced of Friends' doctrine then, but that the "grandeur of the world" had afterward overcome "the reaches he had received." The argument tortured on and got nowhere, until they drew up in front of a tavern and Sir William suggested that they go in for a glass of wine. They entered one of the small private rooms of the tavern, and when Sir William closed and locked the door behind him William fully expected to be caned. Instead, his father laid his hands upon the table and in a tremulous voice announced that he was going to kneel down and pray that his son would be saved from becoming a Quaker. Responding to so melodramatic a gesture with his own melodramatic disposition, William leaped toward the casement window, flung it open, and declared he would throw himself out of it before his father could pray for such a thing to come to pass.

They were both saved from the exaggerated situation they had created by a knock at the door and the entrance of a nobleman who, having seen Sir William's coach outside, came in to pass a friendly moment with him. Scarcely had he joined the Penns than he tactlessly congratulated Sir William on having so virtuous a son, a young man who eschewed the popular vices. Both father and son realized they had spent enough time alone together and that for the moment at least their quarrel could not be resolved. It was just as well that they had been interrupted. They left the tavern, paid a social call on another titled acquaintance who also complimented Sir William on having so clean-living a son, and then returned to Wanstead.

The house was big enough so that the two men could avoid each other at least part of the time, and Sir William's days were still burdened by naval affairs and the continuing war with Holland, even though he had retired from his post as Commissioner. A kind of temporary truce settled down upon the Penn family. But neither father nor son had changed, and their difference continued unsolved as William Penn sought out Friends' meetings in and about London and grew each day more deeply entrenched in their world.

"About the year 1668, being the twenty-fourth year of his age, he first came forth in the work of the ministry . . . to recommend to all that serenity and peace of conscience himself had felt: walking in the Light, to call others out of darkness. . . ." Besse tells us of Penn. He plunged into the ministry almost immediately, matching zeal for zeal, energy for energy, with an ever increasing eloquence, calling upon every ounce of training that Chigwell, Oxford and Saumur had given him. He sat in mystical silence with other Friends or rose to give his spontaneous message. He traveled about the countryside visiting meetings, evangelizing for new members, until the inevitable happened—the authorities broke up a meeting at which he was present, scooped him up with the others, and brought him before the local magistrate. The Cavalier was still conspicuously the Cavalier; and the magistrate, recognizing him, was a little afraid to send him to jail. Instead, he posted a note to his father about the "tumult" that William had been making.

Sir William was hampered by increasingly poor health, and he was up to his ears in navy department troubles as well. His enemies were launching impeachment proceedings against him. High-placed intrigue had been closing in around him, and the impeachment proceedings were well under way by the late spring of 1668. He was accused of embezzling prize goods during the war, and the long tedious case had to be heard before the House of Commons and then go on up to be heard before the House of Lords. The machinations were not clever enough to touch Penn, for the charges were dropped eventually, but he was racked with worry when he ordered his son home to Wanstead.

Young Penn obeyed the order, but before he faced his irate parent once more he stopped first at a meeting for worship and then at the home of a Friend. To be a Quaker means to live the Quaker way throughout every day in every waking and sleeping hour, to share your concerns and your life with other Quakers in a fraternity that radiates outward in every direction; and William Penn was drawn not only into the worship of the Friends but into their homes and family lives as well. As he sat down with the family a dignified and reportedly beautiful young woman entered the room and he was introduced to her—Gulielma Maria Springett, daughter of Mary Springett and stepdaughter of Isaac Penington.

Gulielma, or Guli, was twenty-four, just a few months older than William Penn. Descended from two Puritan lines of landed gentry, a convinced Friend, endowed with culture and education and blessed with a gentle, temperate disposition, she must almost immediately have become the touchstone of his ardent soul. "A match of providence's making," was his own testimony. Their first meeting consumed only a few minutes, while he paused for a word of counsel before going home to Wanstead. Her hand clasped his after the manner of Friends, and she was gone. He had seen beautifully fashioned ladies in the courts of France, England and Ireland; he had seen titled women bedecked with satins and feathers, their faces pointed up with beauty spots. Many of them must have put forth their best efforts to capture such a close associate of the Stuarts. It remained for the modest, unadorned Guli to engage his interest.

The carriage rumbled him away to Wanstead, and he crossed the threshold to an upset household, a distraught mother and an enraged father. What could father and son say to each other? All avenues of communication between them had been lost, and there was nothing left to do but accept the inevitable. Out of the depths of his embarrassment, Sir William told his son to pack his clothes and remove them and himself from the house—and further—"that he should dispose of his estates to them that pleased him better."

William Penn left—without funds—and without hesitation—to surrender himself utterly to the movement, to be welcomed by the open and loving arms of his new companions, to be cared for by them until his own funds could be restored to him, "transported with fiery zeal" at so early an opportunity to be a martyr. The Truth, the Truth! That was what the Friends sought and believed in. It was the Truth that lighted their hearts and guided their steps! Still only partially understanding this extraordinary powe that had caught him up, and endowed with some knowledge o theology, William Penn proceeded with the incredible self-confidence of the very young to write his first religious tract: *Truth Exalted*

"Jehovah, the Everlasting Power," he begins, borrowing heavily from biblical jargon, a writing fashion of the times, "that spans out the Heavens with His span, and measures the waters in the hollow of His Hand. . . . What nature, what heart, what spirit, and what ground is it in which your religions, faiths, works, words and worships stand and grow? Is it the divine, not the fallen nature? Is it the broken, not the stony heart? Is it the contrite, not the formal spirit? . . . No performances but by clean hands, and a pure heart, from whence evil doings are put away, can give acceptance with the pure God." The tract rushes on; it challenges Papist and Protestant alike to re-evaluate themselves; it demands of "ye of the Church of England, that say the Scriptures are your rule, where do they own such persecutors, false prophets, tythmongers, denyers of revelations, opposers of perfection, men-pleasers, time-servers, unprofitable teachers. . . . Whence came your forms of prayers and church government. . . ." Not from the Scriptures, surely, not as Penn reads them. He denounces idolatry, superstition, carnal ordinances and will-worship; his strength is in the "everlasting arm of strength." So "therefore, let the winds of imagination blow, the storms of persecution beat, and the sea of raging malice foam . . . we shall still confide and rejoice in that everlasting Holy God Almighty!"

Many sons have done virtuously in this day, but dear George thou excellest them all.
——William Penn, Preface to the Original Edition of George Fox's *Journal.*

5. Dear George Fox

THE IMPACT of George Fox upon William Penn was a phenomenon repeated many times throughout England, Ireland and Scotland in the middle of the seventeenth century. George Fox himself was an amazing phenomenon, a clarifying, unifying genius, destined to lift out of the Puritan movement its purest values, strip them of false and unessential impediments and weld them into a powerful and lucid faith. His magnetic, almost hypnotic, personality gathered together in one church a host of individual seekers and groups of seekers and pulled more from the undetermined and dissatisfied minorities of other denominations. George Fox was able to do it because he rediscovered in the Christian faith what the Protestant movement had lost—its inner core of mysticism.

George Fox was born in Fenny Drayton, Leicestershire, the son of a weaver, in July of 1624, less than a year before the death of James and the accession of Charles I to the throne. The Puritan movement had already reached an advanced state of maturity, and during Fox's childhood William Laud succeeded to the post of Bishop of London to combine his disciplinary measures against Puritanism with Charles I's Star Chamber in an attempt to make England a nation of one church and an absolute monarch. George Fox grew up through the days that nurtured the civil wars, the days when the deep desires for freedom of conscience were becoming a movement, when Puritans were fleeing to Holland and America, when Charles and Laud were trying to enforce a universal Prayer Book, when the English government was trying to bring Scotland and Ireland under its control, when political parties were germinating. He belonged to a religion-conscious household, "a righteous Christer" father and a "stock of the martyrs" mother. Grave and introspective beyond his years, his pious interests caused some of his relatives to suggest that he be given an education above the minimum and trained for the priesthood, but the final decision was against it, and he was apprenticed to a shoemaker. His religious vocation grew upon him anyway, and by the time he had reached his teens he was known in his own community as a devout young man of the strictest integrity. "If George says verily, there is no altering him." With the pangs of adolescence came more poignant prayers and deeper spiritual disturbances, until at nineteen Fox withdrew from his family altogether to become a religious seeker like so many more of his time, walking the highways alone, fasting, reading Scripture, listening hopefully to those who presumed to teach. There were agonizing hours of hopelessness, of struggling against the temptation to give up the search and reverse his direction, but George Fox's destiny was too powerful to let him go. He wandered all the way to London, but there he found that all was "under the chain of darkness." His family wanted him to marry; but he told them, "I am but a lad, and I must get wisdom." Others urged him to enter military service, but the very thought was abhorrent. He sought out priests, but none reached his condition. After nearly three years of wandering and seeking and withdrawal the first positive beginnings of his creed began to occur to him. "A consideration arose in me, how it was said that all Christians are believers, both Protestants and Papists." Later he realized that being educated at Oxford or Cambridge did not necessarily make a man a minister of Christ. Then why follow these men? He looked at the church buildings and concluded that "God, who made the world, did not dwell in temples made with hands." Then why did anyone need a building in which to worship? In 1647, when Fox was only twenty-three, he reached the zenith of his search: "But as I had forsaken all the priests, so I left the separate preachers also, and those called the most experienced people; for I saw there was none among them all that could speak to my condition. And when all my hopes in them and in all men were gone, so that I had nothing outwardly to help me, nor could tell what to do, then, Oh then, I heard a voice which said, 'There is one, even Christ Jesus, that can speak to thy condition,' and when I heard it my heart did leap for joy."

His strength and his vigor and his confidence grew by leaps and bounds from then on, and he began immediately to preach in his happy, ardent excitement. It was only necessary to wait in silence, he declared, the silence of the heart and mind, all earthly sounds and thoughts laid aside, maintaining an inner peace, until the mystical divine Light quickened that of God in every man. Other confused seekers drew closer to this raw-boned weaver's son in leather breeches and common attire and became filled with a new confidence. Now the priests could expect him to return and challenge them in their man-made temples; they could expect to cringe before the searching questions. They could not dare to admit that God's tabernacle was the heart of man, that in the ministry of Jesus there was liberty and freedom and in their ministry there was bondage. Fox could expect their anger and often the anger of their flocks who would set upon him and beat him or turn him over to the authorities for imprisonment.

Through town after town he traveled on his joyous way, "taken up in the love of God," his ministerial and leadership capacities expanding and flowering—to the professors at Dukinfield and Manchester to declare the Truth among them, convincing some, enraging others; to a great meeting of Baptists at Broughton in Leicestershire to feel as he opened his mouth to speak a power go out of himself and encompass them. The experience repeated itself until he knew that his career must be ministerial, perhaps even prophetic. "And I was to bring people off from all the world's religions, which are vain, that they might know the pure religion." Piece by piece he added to the doctrine that he was developing. "Moreover when the Lord sent me forth into the world, he forbade me to put off my hat to any, high or low; and I was required to 'thee' and 'thou' all men and women, without any respect to rich or poor, great or small. And as I travelled up and down, I was not to bid people 'good morrow' or 'good evening', neither might I bow or scrape with my leg to anyone; and this made the sects and professions to rage. . . . 'And I,' saith Christ, 'receive not honour of men': showing that man have an honour, which men will receive and give, but Christ will have none of it. . . . Oh, the rage and scorn, the heat and fury that arose! Oh, the blows, punchings, beatings and imprisonments that we underwent for not putting off our hats to men!" He concluded later that the oath was wrong, since it implied two levels of truth telling. "Swear not at all," the New Testament said. Gradually he saw that the original intent was lost in too often repeated rituals and that men must realize that "preaching, baptism and sacrifices would never sanctify them." And his early abhorrence for things military was clarified. "I told them I lived in the virtue of that life and power that took away the occasion of all wars."

Fox experienced his first imprisonment at Nottingham in 1649, "in a pitiful stinking place, where the wind brought all the stench of the house of office into the place." A few weeks later he was in the stocks in Mansfield. When in his travels he reached Derby in 1650 a longer and more trying incarceration was awaiting him—one year in the house of correction. In spite of his minimum education and his lack of formal training in theology, Fox strove to express himself with the written word as well as the spoken, and in Derby prison he was moved to write an eloquent lamentation for the town that was resisting his message: "Oh, Derby! as the waters run away when the flood gates are up, so doth the visitation of God's love pass away from thee, O Derby! Therefore look where thou art, and how thou art grounded; and consider, before thou art utterly forsaken. . . ." Out of his conflict with the authorities in Derby came the *Quaker* label. The Society of Friends had not yet come into being in 1650. There was still no organization and no settled name. Followers of Fox were called by such names as Professors of the Light or Children of the Light. But one of the justices of the peace who committed Fox to prison, on being warned by Fox to "tremble at the word of the Lord," laughed scornfully and called Fox and his companions Quakers. The label stuck, like a bad name to a good dog, and followed the Friends with taunts and derisions down the years—the people who quaked when the Lord visited them—until it has become accepted even by the Friends as an alternative label, at last divested of its derisive quality.

Fox's sufferings and journeyings would have killed a lesser man, would indeed have killed a very strong lesser man. Through the four seasons of the year he traveled from town to town, speaking in the market places, invading the "steeple houses" to address congregations already assembled, sleeping in the fields when no shelter was available or the innkeeper was afraid to have him on the premises. His inner resources burned so brightly that he seemed indestructible. If he was set upon by mobs armed with staves, he would extend his hand and bid them strike it, accepting their beatings as a privilege, never striking back. At Tickhill, "when I began to speak, they fell upon me, and the clerk up with his Bible as I was speaking and hit me in the face that my face gushed out with blood . . . and then they cried, 'Take him out of the church,' and they punched me and thrust me out and beat me more with books, fists and sticks, and threw me over a hedge into a close and there beat me and then threw me over again." He emerged from beatings and from the stinking holes of prisons, where all had predicted he would surely die, and went on—through Buckinghamshire, Northamptonshire, Leicestershire, Nottinghamshire and Yorkshire, all the way eastward to Hull and Patrington. In 1652 he reached the Lake Country. Near Sedbergh a great fair was in progress, and Fox reaped an abundance of followers from among the young people. At Firbank he found that Francis Howgill and John Audland had been preaching to a large meeting. Fox did not invade the chapel; he sat instead on a rock near the top of Firbank Fell (known today as Fox's Pulpit) and waited for the divine message to fill his heart. To wait upon God anywhere but inside a temple was a curious thing to do; a crowd gathered round him, "above a thousand people," and in the afternoon Fox rose to his feet and preached to them, gathering them and their preachers into his flock. Among the newly garnered souls were Howgill and Audland, and they, two years later, with John Camm and Edward Burrough, journeyed down to Bristol with the Quaker message. There they caused a great stir, convincing large numbers, drawing upon themselves mob violence and persecution; but in the process they convinced Josiah Coale who became the precious intimate of William Penn.

Fox's influence spread so rapidly that his followers as early as 1654 were coming together into an organization. The first settled meeting in the city of London was at Aldersgate Street; soon there was another in Tower Street; convening in private homes until they became too large and a public hall had to be hired. That was the Bull and Mouth in Martin's le Grand, near Aldersgate.

England was under Cromwell's firm hand in 1654, and Cromwell had said, "Own your call, for it is of God." Yet, everyone's call was of God—the Royalists and Catholics who had been excluded, the Puritans who were in power, the Quakers who were being harried by mobs and imprisoned by local constables, George Fox in particular who was apprehended by troops as he approached a meeting place in Whetstone. Protectors of the Protector were anxious for his safety, and when they heard rumors of a plot against the Protector's life they rounded up every style of rabble-rouser, Fox among them. Fox was a verbose man, and anyone who apprehended him could expect a long discourse. The unfortunate colonel of the troops who had him in custody absorbed as much as he could of Foxian conversation and then begged the young non-comformist to go home and preach no more. Fox would not. In despair the colonel handed him over to Captain Drury of Cromwell's lifeguard with instructions to take him to the Lord Protector. Surely Cromwell's own verbosity would match Fox's. And so George Fox was brought to Whitehall and into the presence of Oliver Cromwell.

Cromwell possessed the elements of greatness, and he could recognize it in others; and further, he was not likely to be too uncordial to a religious leader who had derived his impetus from the Puritan movement. Fox has been called by at least one historian "the greatest religious leader the Puritan revolution produced." His reputation had preceded him to Cromwell's presence, and so had two of his own letters offering comfort and spiritual direction. "Be still and in the counsel of God stand, and that will give thee wisdom," Fox had advised Cromwell in his first letter. In the second he had assured Cromwell of his non-violent disposition, "I, who am of the world called George Fox, do deny . . . the carrying or drawing of any carnal sword against any, or against thee, Oliver Cromwell, or any man." Cromwell's own life was one of profound theological content; his Bible was as fingermarked and worn as Fox's. They talked a long time, "And I spake much to him of Truth," Fox tells us. The conversation lasted so long that curious people began to crowd in. Fox felt it time to withdraw, and Cromwell, tears in his eyes, seized Fox by the hand and said, "Come again to my house; for if thou and I were but an hour in a day together we should be nearer one to the other." He wished Fox no ill, he declared, and told his soldiers that Fox was at liberty. Then he invited Fox to remain and dine, but Fox declined.

"Now I see," said Cromwell, "there is a people risen, and come up, that I cannot win either with gifts, honors, offices or places; but all other sects and people I can."

Fox's influence with Cromwell went a long way in alleviating the sufferings of the Friends under the Protectorate. Persecutions did not cease, because the temper of any crowd that gathered in seventeenth-century England was quick and cruel. Emotions were ragged from all the violent death pangs of medievalism, the civil wars, foreign wars, the sudden changes in personal fortunes, the tireless headsman's axe. A minister could expect to be set upon with staves, thrown into a house of correction by local authorities, or otherwise spontaneously mistreated for his zealous testimony.

When the Quakers carried their gospel to Ireland, they found additional sufferings waiting for them there, not nearly so much at the hands of the Catholics as at the hands of their fellow Protestants. William Edmundson and his family opened the way, settling the first meeting in or near Lurgan. Edward Burrough and Francis Howgill went to Dublin, and so did many more, enduring beatings, loss of goods, imprisonment, banishment, but persistently riding up and down the land, preaching from the very backs of their horses, wherever a crowd was willing to gather and listen, ignoring the accepted sacredness of church buildings, refusing to pay tithes to support "hireling" clergy, refusing to take oaths.

Still others felt compelled to cross the ocean to the New World with their message of Truth, and there in the Puritan strongholds some of their most atrocious persecutions were awaiting them. Salem lopped off ears, whipped, bored holes in tongues, imprisoned, levied fines. Boston's anger was almost psychopathic with its corded whips and starvation of prisoners. One Quaker was encased in irons and whipped; when he refused to submit he was taken out and beaten until the flesh of his back and arms became jelly. Others were stripped to the waist, lashed to a cart's tail, and whipped out of town. Boston in 1658 passed an act against the "pernicious sect," making it possible to arrest them without warrant, imprison them without bail until tried, and, if found guilty, banish them upon pain of death. Something about the awful disturbing quality of truth so enraged men, so threatened the settled dignity of their lives, so upset their thinking, that they did not dare to allow it.

Cromwell had done nothing to ease the sufferings of Friends in America, but the newly reinstated Charles II issued an order to the New England governments that accomplished the release of Friends from the local prisons. He may well have done it to spite the Puritans, since ultimately persecution of all dissenters to the Church of England reached insanely glorious levels during his reign.

The Quaker movement was just slightly younger than William Penn. Fox had begun his ministry in 1647, and Penn had been born three years earlier. So rapidly did the authenticity of the Quaker doctrine take hold that by the time of the restoration of the monarchy there were some forty thousand Friends. Not England, Ireland and Massachusetts combined had jails enough to accommodate them all, although there were certainly times when all three appeared to think they had. The earliest years of the Restoration were, of course, years of reaction and vengeance. John Bunyan was arrested in November, 1660, and committed to Bedford jail to begin his twelve years of imprisonment—and there indeed suppression was its own undoing, for it gave Bunyan the solitude and withdrawal in which to write his *Christian Behavior* and *Grace Abounding* and to conceive and begin his *Pilgrim's Progress,* books that had far wider influence than Bunyan could ever have had as a busy non-conformist pastor in a local community. In rapid succession the Puritan sects tasted each law of the Clarendon Code, and the Quakers were pounded and hounded the most grievously of all. There was no prophet among the Cavaliers to rise up and say, "You are solidifying the Puritan movement by your persecutions; you are nurturing in it the seedlings of the Whig Party." The Quaker movement flourished under chastisement, and its flocks increased. Penn flourished with the rest, and very soon produced a second tract,

The Guide Mistaken and Temporizing Rebuked, or, A Brief Reply to Jonathan Clapham's Book, Entitled, A *Guide to the True Religion.* It was a longer, much better organized and more objective piece than his first, and, as its title implies, argumentative in content.

The passionate, impatient author of *Truth Exalted* and *The Guide Mistaken,* cut off from family and resources, found himself on a higher level of exaltation in his new freedom from worldly concern. Being dismissed from home meant the opportunity to spend all of his time with his new companions; being cut off from his inheritance meant being freed of its responsibilites. His father had recovered from his gout and apparently from his political embarrassments, too, because by the end of June, 1668, he was back in the social whirl, dining at Whitehall, taking the air with Pepys in Hyde Park or appearing in a theatre box with his ladies. Two worlds—and young Penn left with a free choice between them.

Penn's exceptional position of being both Cavalier and Quaker made him a liaison between the two, and there were many times during the years that followed when his associations and friendships at Court counted heavily in the cause of religious liberty. As Fox had been the chief appellant to high places under the Commonwealth, so Penn became the chief appellant for mercy and justice under the restored Stuarts. His first effort in this new role was to arrange an interview for himself, Josiah Coale, Thomas Loe and George Whitehead with the Duke of Buckingham, to discuss the appalling "stocks, whips, gaols, dungeons, praemunires, fines, sequestrations, and banishments, for their peaceable dissent in matters relative to faith and worship." George Villiers, second Duke of Buckingham, was one of the most favored and powerful men in Charles's Court; but it wasn't hard for the son of a personal friend of the King to arrange an audience with him. It proved impossible, though, to persuade him to risk his favored position on behalf of a righteous minority. It may be that Buckingham was not fully prepared for the young man who still carried himself with the high-chinned dignity and nonchalance of a Cavalier, whose wrist still turned delicately in the French manner, whose hand still reached unconsciously for a sword hilt that wasn't there, yet who had shed his unnecessary feathers and ruffles and who failed to bare his head before one of higher rank. Undoubtedly the rudeness of the four visitors, who used the too familiar *thee* and *thou*, rubbed Buckingham's fur the wrong way; but their loving tone of voice must have counted for something, because he did admit that he favored liberty of conscience. And their appearance must have moved him, too, for they showed clearly the effects of their suffering. Coale had just been released from Reading's house of correction; Loe had recently returned from his ministry and sufferings in Ireland. Coale and Loe were both sick men, aged before their time. Whitehead had recently been in Marshalsea Prison in Southwark. But Buckingham was not moved sufficiently to give any help, and the mission proved fruitless.

That was only an opening attempt, "the first time I went to Court after I had embraced the communion I am of," Penn tells us.

George Whitehead and William Penn were associates from the time of that first return to Penn's old world. Whitehead then thirty-two was from Westmoreland. He had been convinced at seventeen, and within a year had heard George Fox speak at a meeting at Sunny Bank near Kendal. He was taken up immediately into the main-stream of the Quaker movement, a sufferer with the rest, a powerful minister who eventually succeeded Fox as leader.

"The second time I went [to Court] was the same summer, and upon the same errand, in company of G. Whitehead and Josiah Coale."

The second visit was to Sir Henry Berwick, Secretary of State. These were *Protestants* for whom he spoke, Penn persisted to Sir Henry. Their very suffering in a Protestant country "must necessarily bring the very Protestant religion under scandal abroad." They were Protestants "in all those points wherein the very Church of England might claim that title." They sought a strict and holy life, and that was why he, Penn, saw fit to bring their sufferings to the attention of those in authority.

And again—"our business had no better success than before."

For Penn the excursions to Whitehall were a plan fixed in his mind and early failures could not alter his intent.

Thomas Loe did not accompany him on the second trip and would never go with him again, because Loe succumbed to failing health that same autumn. He had been taken seriously ill after the interview with Buckingham, and Penn, Whitehead and Coale had carried him to the home of Ann Cullen. That evening he was taken by coach to the home of another Friend, Ann Greenhills; but her house was too noisy and after a week of illness and high fever they moved him once more to a quieter spot, the home of Edward Man, "where we had all hopes of his speedy recovery, inasmuch as the retirement of the chamber in which he lay occasioned great rest; but having an infirm inside and an extraordinary fever, the strength of his constitution could not long support it. For about ten days together he daily decreased, and some days before he left us we expected his departure," so Penn wrote to Isaac Penington. Four days before Loe's death Penn himself was taken ill, but when during the first week of October he was told that Loe was failing he got up from his own bed and went to Loe. Loe had been his first teacher; had lighted the candle within his soul; was still his guide and mentor; Loe was dying. The emotionally susceptible Penn found his teacher of the "faith that overcomes the world" at peace and "in a sweet readiness to be gone," speaking final words of comfort and advice to those gathered around him. Loe extended a weakened hand to the Friends beside him—Penn, Whitehead, and others—and said, "Bear thy Cross, stand faithful for God, and bear thy testimony in thy day and generation, and God will give thee an eternal Crown of Glory that shall not be taken from thee. There is no other way. . . . My heart is full, what shall I say? . . . Friends, keep your testimony for God, live with Him and He will live with you." Loe felt himself grow weaker. "I am near leaving you, I think; but am as well in my spirit as I can desire." His companions were caught up by Loe's strong mystical powers as he burst into songs of praise, dying at last in a kind of spiritual revelry.

"Whom my soul loved, whilst alive, and honors now dead," Penn wrote to a Friend, "and yet have pure fellowship with that which lives forever. This day we lay the body in the ground, as having done its Master's work, and well. . . ."

A precious scrap of Penn's autobiography that has survived tells us his next experience was with a Presbyterian minister in Spitalfields named Thomas Vincent. Vincent was in the high good graces of the Bishop of London, and that may explain why he enjoyed amazing freedom from official reprisal of the Anglican government. It seems that two members of Vincent's congregation wandered into a Friends' meeting one day and remained long enough to be convinced. Vincent burst into a fury of abuse against the Quakers, described by Besse as "fiery zeal, a thing fertile of ill language." The Quakers held most erroneous and damnable doctrines! He had as lief his flock should go to a bawdy house, Vincent declared, as to frequent the Quakers' meetings. "If ever you go again, I will give you up, and God will give you up," he cried at his two fallen souls, "that you may believe a lie, and be damned!" William Penn, in particular, he called a Jesuit—the most damaging label with which a man in Protestant England's public life could be impugned.

Ill language travels fast, and Vincent's "raised choler" reached the ears of Penn and Whitehead. As they saw it, two newly convinced Friends were being denied liberty of conscience; "all which," wrote Penn, "we could not for the Truth's sake let pass in silence." Quakers tried whenever possible to answer every challenge, every theological attack, every denial of their liberty, with their own best eloquence. Penn and Whitehead assumed spontaneous responsibility for Vincent, demanding an opportunity to meet him in public debate. Vincent was reluctant. They wrote him a letter dated thirty-first of 8th month (October according to the old calendar), 1668. Judging themselves injured as well by being refused a competent time to justify themselves as well as by the unchristian and untrue character put upon them, their letter stated, they did request a meeting to be "some day the next week about the tenth hour in the morning at your own meeting, where and when we shall not fail with a few sober Friends to meet you. . . ."

Vincent accepted the challenge, scheduling the meeting for two in the afternoon, or so he told the Friends, and carefully calling his congregation together at one so that he could rail at them before the Quakers arrived. Penn and Whitehead and a small delegation of Friends found a laughing, hissing, shoving audience waiting for them, ready to pelt them with such words as "impudent villain" and "blasphemer." The older, more experienced Whitehead did most of the talking for the Quakers, beginning immediately to explain their doctrine, but Vincent would not allow him to continue. *He*, before his own flock, would examine the intruders with questions. Did his congregation agree, he cried gleefully. Shouts of derisive agreement! Well, then, did the Quakers "own one Godhead subsisting in three distinct and separate persons?" As stated by Vincent, Penn and Whitehead retorted, the doctrine had no basis in Scripture. Vincent resorted to the verbal trickery of the syllogism: There are three that bear record in Heaven, the Father, the Word and the Holy Ghost, and these three are one. These are either three manifestations, three operations, three substances, or three somethings else beside subsistences. But they are not three manifestations, three operations, three substances, nor three anything else beside subsistences. Ergo, three subsistences. Vincent's terms were nowhere in the Scripture, Whitehead insisted. Why such complex verbiage, the visitors wanted to know. God spoke to man in plain language. But the complex verbiage persisted back and forth hour after hour while the audience grew more and more unruly, with laughing, shouting, ridiculing. At last Vincent quieted them by declaring it was time to pray. At the end of the prayer he adjourned the meeting and left his pulpit, left his visitors without having given them adequate opportunity to present their case, left them to the mercy of the congregation.

William Penn, George Whitehead and their companions attempted to address the group without benefit of a chairman, but rough hands hauled them down from the platform. Other hands extinguished the candles that had been lighted at nightfall. With the unshakable persistence for which Friends have been noted (and not always appreciated) down the centuries, they stood in the dark and continued to speak to as many as wished to remain and listen. To their profound gratification many did remain, and Vincent was obliged to return and promise them another meeting. A second attempt a few days later to invade Vincent's Presbyterian stronghold yielded little, and as far as Whitehead was concerned the matter was closed. For him it had been only one incident among many in his strenuous, fast-moving career, and he does not even mention it in his journal which is quite detailed and one of the finest of such Quaker records. He had dutifully added the case of Thomas Vincent to his already crowded schedule and then hastened on to other items. But to William Penn, eight years younger, with only a year in the movement against Whitehead's fifteen, it was a *cause célèbre.* He could not dismiss the unresolved arguments from his mind. Every hair of every head, every feather of every sparrow, every misunderstanding of Quaker doctrine, every false accusation—was the responsibility of one disciple or another. If the Presbyterians of Spitalfields, and no doubt many more, would not heed a Quaker voice, perhaps they would heed a Quaker tract. It was thus that William Penn came to write *The Sandy Foundation Shaken.*

After setting down in a Preface an account of the rude treatment they had received at Spitalfields, the author ("A builder on that foundation which cannot be moved") asks, "Would Socrates, Cato or Seneca, whom they call heathens, have treated us with such unseemly carriage?" Then he plunges into his three main topics: the Trinity, the impossibility of God's pardoning sinners without full atonement and the justification of impure persons by an imputative righteousness. Of the three the most important and most dangerous politically was his denial of the existence of the Trinity.

"For there is one God," Penn declares, "and they must necessarily conclude their kind of Trinity a fiction. . . . If there be three distinct and separate persons, then three distinct and separate substances, because every person is inseparable from its own substance; and as there is no person that's not a substance in common acceptation among men, so do the Scriptures plentifully agree herein: And since the Father is God, the Son is God, and the Spirit is God, then unless the Father, Son and Spirit are three distinct nothings, they must be three distinct substances, and consequently three distinct Gods. . . . If each person be God, and that God subsists in three persons, then in each person are three persons or Gods, and from them three, they will increase to nine and so ad infinitum. . . ." There is a Shavian quality in Penn's tongue-in-cheek treatment of the Trinity; yet the quality was no doubt unconscious because Penn was in deadly earnest. His pulse must have raced as he wrote his heresy, for he knew full well that he was flirting with official wrath. His devotion was to a God who was all things and in whom all men could unite, to a God "whom to know is life eternal, not to be divided, but ONE pure entire and eternal being."

He goes on to his second point—God's infinite capacity for mercy and forgiveness, a God who is not interested in visiting His wrath on anyone. That Christ suffered he admits freely; it is the purpose of that suffering which Penn is eager to interpret. Christ suffered for His beliefs. He was the perfect example of holy resignation to the divine will.

The third point—imputed righteousness or vicariously acquired virtues—Penn refutes categorically. Sin came not by imputation from Adam, and so neither can righteousness be imputed to anyone. God will not justify the wicked, and every man must prove his own work and make and take his own consequences in the divine scheme of things.

Events moved with lightning speed the moment Penn's *Sandy Foundation Shaken* saw the light of day. The writing, publishing, circulating, resulting furor, arrest and imprisonment of the author all took place within the space of less than a month. Early in November Penn and Whitehead had been debating with Vincent; on December 12, 1668, a warrant was issued to Sir John Robinson by Lord Arlington, Principal Secretary of State, to receive Penn and "keep him close prisoner till further order."

"I was committed the beginning of December, and was not discharged till the fall of the leaf following; wanting about fourteen days of nine months," Penn's autobiography tells us.

The most offensive heresy in the tract was his refutation of the Trinity, but the technicality upon which he was arrested was his failure to obtain a publishing license from the Bishop of London, required under the censorship law against which John Milton had launched his *Areopagitica*.

As for the tract itself, hasty and hostile readings injected into it heresies that were not there, one being the accusation that in it Penn denied the divinity of Christ. Pepys thought the tract "so well writ" that young Penn could not have been its author, and observed further that "it was not fit for everybody to read." A surprisingly large number of people did read it, though, particularly in high places. It rapidly came to be referred to as Penn's book against the Trinity, and John Evelyn observed dryly that "Sir William Penn's son had published a blasphemous book against the deity of our blessed Lord."

The authorities first picked up Penn's printer, John Derby, and clapped him into the Gatehouse Prison. No excuse for Derby; any London printer knew the censorship statute. When Penn heard of Derby's arrest, he immediately presented himself to Lord Arlington, who issued the December 12 warrant.

The whole proceeding against William Penn was, in its own peculiar way, legal. He was arrested because he had violated a law, and the "court" which exerted jurisdiction in this instance was the King's Privy Council. The Privy Council, according to Blackstone, had the King's will for its sole constituent. Under Charles II it was composed of approximately thirty men, half of whom were principal officers of state and the other half were ten lords and five commoners selected by the personal whim and wish of the King. The Privy Council could not punish an offender, but it could "inquire" into offenses against the government and commit offenders to "safe custody" while the inquiry was being pursued. Arlington, as Secretary of State, was a member of the Council; after he had placed Penn in custody he proceeded to obtain *ex post facto* approval of the Council, and the Council issued another warrant to the Lieutenant of the Tower, signed by the Duke of Ormonde, the Lord Chamberlain (Earl of Manchester), the Earl of Sandwich, the Earl of Carbery, Lord Ashley, Lord Berkeley and Sir John Trevor, a Secretary of State, directing that Penn be kept a close prisoner until the King's pleasure should be further signified.

Penn's Tower experience was rigorous. He was quartered in a tiny room under the roof, inadequately heated in winter and baked by the heat of the summer sun. His hair that had grown back only sparsely after his infantile bout with smallpox fell away. He was obliged to eat prison fare, and was permitted almost no communication with the outside world and no recreation. Not even a barber was allowed to come near him, although on December 24 his personal servant, Francis Cooke, was issued a permit to visit him. Only twenty-four, Penn was cut off from friends and family and even books, with no hope of release in sight. Yet, it was not so terrible as some of the prisons in which Fox had been kept. This he knew.

Dear George Fox could stand it, and he was willing to do the same. His was the exquisite privilege of surrendering up his life to the bidding of the Light within his heart.

The Bishop of London soon conveyed to Penn by way of Cooke an accurate knowledge of his destiny: Penn could "recant in Comon Garden at an appointed time, before the Fair of all the city or else be a prisoner during his life."

Cooke brought back his reply: "Thou mayst tell my father, whom I know will ask thee, these words, that my prison shall be my grave before I will budge a jot, for I owe my conscience to no mortal man. I have no need to fear. God will make amends for all. They are mistaken in me. I value not their threats nor resolutions, for they shall know I can weary out their malice and peevishness and in me shall they all behold a resolution above fear, conscience above cruelty and a baffle put on all their designs by the spirit of patience. . . ."

What an unfortunate embarrassment for Sir William Penn, who had so recently been impeached and who had passed the peak of his influence at Whitehall. He still attended navy board meetings, though his responsibilities had been reduced, and he was still close to the Duke of York; but even calling into play all his remaining influence, he had difficulty helping this estranged son of his who flaunted his heretical ideas in the King's face. Probably for Sir William's sake, the King on January 4 sent Dr. Edward Stillingfleete, Bishop of Worcester and the King's Chaplain, to the Tower to treat with Penn. Stillingfleete was young and abounding in enthusiasm; he could appeal to the prisoner if anyone could. But Penn told Stillingfleete, who told the King, that the Tower was the worst argument in the world to convince him.

At the end of January Derby's wife, Joane, went tremulously in person to a session of the King's Privy Council to petition for her husband's release, but they didn't let the printer go until the following May.

And during those first winter weeks in the Tower Penn received a testing piece of news—the death of Josiah Coale. Surely then he felt the subtle and gross frustrations of prison, knowing he ought to have been at Coale's bedside in the home of Thomas and Ann

Curtis in Reading when his friend died. Coale had been a counselor to Penn almost from the time of Penn's convincement. Either while he was still in the Tower or very shortly after his release, Penn wrote a testimony on Coale's life and works that was included in Coale's collected tracts and epistles. "Though I knew him not from the beginning, yet I knew him in that which hath neither beginning of days nor end of life. . . . In the eternal Light I knew him and had often and sweet fellowship with him therein to my great refreshment, even in the gloomy and dark day of my early and deep exercises. . . . My soul is often heavy and bowed down in the sense of the loss of these valiants, at this time of the day. . . ."

Edward Burrough had died in Old Bailey six years before at the age of twenty-eight; Francis Howgill had died in Appleby jail, succumbing after five years of imprisonment; Thomas Loe was gone. How long could the Friends' movement stand the persistent purging of its leadership?

As William Penn made the gradual emotional adjustment to prison life, the seclusion and the reduced physical pace; as he began to miss the spiritual nourishment he had been receiving from his associates—Whitehead, Loe, Coale, many more—he was forced to draw upon and subsist upon his own inner resources. Prison did for him what it did for John Bunyan, although at a much earlier level of his development. It forced him to pause and take stock, to examine his own faith, to tap depths within himself that might have gone unused. The onrushing river of Penn's magnificent mind met a dam and accumulated into a deep lake, and while its waters were forcibly stilled their impurities settled out, leaving his thoughts and direction crystal clear.

In a subtle sense, Penn always had the key to the Tower door in his pocket; that key was the opportunity to recant and go free. So have all other moral prisoners. Perhaps that is what makes their imprisonment so fruitful, so productive, so creative. Out of Penn's first withdrawal from the violent persecutions of the Quaker movement and the hurly-burly of London life came two essays and many letters.

The first essay, *No Cross, No Crown,* is not to be confused with the one we know today which was written twelve years later. Penn used the title twice. The later version was written by a man who had matured many more than twelve years; the Tower version by a rapidly maturing novitiate. The Tower essay is only 111 pages, including an entire page devoted to its title and intent. The tract begins in a constrained and stilted style, but as he writes his style relaxes, becomes more fluent, and a strain of poetic eloquence creeps in. First comes a covering letter: "To my Ancient Friends F.S. E.B. H.S. J.C. I.N. A.L. M.L. T.C.," who were quite obviously not Quakers and who needed to have the true intent of the Society of Friends explained to them. In the Preface Penn implores his audience to read with a serious and impartial mind. In Chapter I he gives sixteen reasons against hat honor and titular respects, in Chapter II twelve reasons against using *you* to a single person, in Chapter III thirteen reasons against the vanity of apparel. After each chapter he quotes a wide variety of authorities whose writings testify to his views—Luther, Calvin, Erasmus, Gregory, Jerome, Plato, Socrates, Aristotle, Augustine, Polybius, Cicero, Solomon, Ignatius, Charles V of Spain, Sir Philip Sydney, Grotius, Dr. Donne, Lord Bacon—sixty-eight in all; and the text of each chapter is interlarded with nearly four hundred scriptural quotations and verifications with exact citations noted in the margin. So far as we know he was able to call upon all these scholarly resources from memory!

Penn produced another document about this time, *A Relation and Description of the Nature and Fruits of the Two Kingdoms of Darkness and Light* . . . a letter to his father, which I feel he must have written while still in the Tower, because its contents imply that he had not yet been fully reconciled to the older man. In it Penn deeply yearns to make his father understand his utter inability to recant:

DEAR FATHER:
Fearing that words may create wrath, and that reasons or citations, though most true in themselves, may lose much of their native force and usual success when by a child alleged unto his parent, it seems good unto the Lord who first put it into my heart that I should only offer unto thee a few words out of His own written will, as discovering the most inward qualifications as soon as external garb and appearance of those two spirits that act or lend the sons

and daughters of man, either to prove the God of this world or the God of Heavens.

The rest of the pages are divided lengthwise into two columns of arguments, the lefthand column is headed: "The Spirit and Practice of This World," and the right: "The Spirit and Doctrine of Christ." Both columns are filled with detailed biblical quotations, the left chiefly from the Old Testament, the right chiefly from the New.

Sir William, hoping against hope that the Stuarts would be moved to mercy, must have found some encouragement in his son's loving desire for reconciliation. He may even have shown the letter to one or another of the royal family. Penn's autobiography states that his father was admitted to the Tower to see him "as my relation." The love which both Charles and James felt for the Penns was no fragile or fleeting thing. It led Sewel to speculate that the King may have been keeping Penn in the Tower to protect him. Other scholars suggest that the King may even have been holding him there at the request of Sir William. But the latter idea is refuted by the fact that Sir William presented a petition to the Privy Council on March 31, 1669, in behalf of his son and was not able to obtain his release. The Council moved, however, to direct the Bishop of London to examine the heretical views expressed in *The Sandy Foundation Shaken;* and further, the Council instructed Sir John Robinson, Lieutenant of the Tower, that Penn was to be allowed with "a keeper and sufficient guard" to go to the Bishop's consistory. Officialdom moved slowly, and Penn continued in his little attic room into the heat of the summer until at last an action of his own produced some results. On July 1 he wrote a long letter to Lord Arlington.

"I know none to whom this paper may so properly be directed as thyself. For as thou art Principal Secretary of State, the person to whom I surrendered myself, by whose warrant I was committed, and who was pleased to come to this place to take my examination about a note that was by some suspected to have dropt from me the day of my surrender. . . ."

The reference is to a "paper full of rant and treason against his Majesty" that Penn was supposed to have dropped on the day of his arrest in Lord Arlington's room. Treason, of course, could have been fatal to Penn had not Lord Arlington made a thorough investigation of the paper and found that it had not come from Penn. If Arlington was capable of being so spontaneously objective once, Penn was surely justified in expecting the same of him twice.

Penn builds his case carefully. "Strange, that men esteemed Christians should seem so indefatigable in writing, preaching, and discoursing down the reputation of an innocent man, by the most foul aspersions, black characters, and exasperating imputations. . . ." The Penn affair had really mushroomed into a babbling scandal in a few months. "What if I differ from some religious apprehensions? Am I therefore incompatible with the being of human societies? Shall it not be remembered with what success kingdoms and commonwealths have lived under the balance of diverse parties? . . . My hopes are, I shall not longer continue a prisoner, merely to assure the world I am not innocent of what in very truth I am not guilty, nor yet that matters of lighter moment be sought to prolong my restraint, because as yet there is no law to deprive an inoffensive Englishman of so great and eminent a right as liberty. . . . I beseech thee to intreat the King on my account, not to believe every man to be his enemy, that cannot shape his conscience by the narrow forms and prescripts of men's inventions. . . . Since my adversaries have overshot the mark, that the accusation is fictious, and many of them have publicly retracted their first opinions of the matter, after so strict an imprisonment, without any legal cause, or just procedure, contrary to the privileges of every Englishman, as well as the meekness, forbearance, and compassion inseparable from true Christianity; I think it's time, and I desire I may be ordered a release to follow my ordinary employments; but if it should yet be scrupled, or denied upon the least dissatisfaction unremoved, I intreat the favor of access to the King, where I shall freely and justly answer to all such interrogatories as may concern my present case; or if that will not be allowed, that it would please thee to give me a full hearing to all such objections as may be thought to carry any weight; that so if I must remain a prisoner, it may be known for what; and in the meantime that such liberty may be granted me, as is customary for other prisoners to enjoy, after the first or second month of their imprisonment, the season especially considered. . . ."

Actually it was not Lord Arlington, but Dr. Stillingfleete who contributed most to Penn's ultimate release. Eternal laurels to Dr. Stillingfleete! He called again at the Tower and spent long, pleasant hours discoursing with William Penn, reaching the conclusion that the prisoner was not denying the divinity of Christ either in or out of *Sandy Foundation.* He made a suggestion: Why did not Penn write another tract explaining his exact views? Why not an apologia for *Sandy Foundation?* If the King and Council would not see Penn, perhaps they would read a tract.

Penn agreed and set to work on his second Tower essay, *Innocency with Her Open Face. Presented by Way of Apology for the Book Entitled, The Sandy Foundation Shaken.* In *Innocency* he writes carefully and in detail; his recent disputation, he must point out, was with some Presbyterians. (Let the Anglican Church make note.) Penn realizes that his imprisonment is due to the fact that in refuting the Trinity he has been also thought to deny the divinity of Christ. Nothing could be further from the truth. "I conclude Christ to be God; for if none can save, or be styled properly a Savior but God, and yet that Christ is said to save, and properly called a Savior, it must needs follow, that Christ the Savior is God. . . . I sincerely own, and unfeignedly believe . . . in one holy, just, merciful, almighty and eternal God, who is the Father of all things." He reiterates in this second paper that nowhere does the Scripture say that Christ suffered an eternal death and infinite vengeance. Penn's God as expressed in Christ is a God, not of Old Testament vengeance and anger, but one of remission and forgiveness, a God of love and gentleness and boundless understanding.

Dr. Stillingfleete had already expressed his interpretation to the King and Privy Council of his conversations with Penn, and *Innocency* was the last necessary weight needed to tip the scales in Penn's favor. At a meeting of the Privy Council on July 28, 1669, the King being present, His Majesty signified his approval of both the report and the tract. He therefore sent an order to the Lieutenant of the Tower to liberate the prisoner and deliver him to the custody of Sir William Penn.

> Day after day I climb the hills. Heather and heath, heath and heather, cotton-grass, loosestrife, and myrtle. Lichens on the rocks, exquisite minute chalices dusted with silver, and miniature ivory antlers crested with crimson, springing through the stellate moss. Stars of the butterwort and clusters of London pride in the crannies. Dark pools whose lights shine blue. Bogs deep with sphagnum moss, peat-forming pockets in the groins of the hills. With each step upward a wider horizon.
>
> ——Robert Gibbings, *Lovely Is the Lee*

6. Among the Irish Friends

Sir William, no longer on the navy board, had retired altogether to his house in Wanstead, and there, infirm in health, he awaited the return of his son. The notoriety that had arisen around the author of *Sandy Foundation* combined with the older man's reduced earning power no doubt contributed heavily to the decision which Sir William had made. Penn was to go to Ireland once more to look over Sir William's lands and improve his rent collections, at the same time withdrawing temporarily from the overheated political situation in London. The reconciliation, while not complete, must at least have been realized to the point where they could converse and plan together. But the reconciliation was not so complete that Penn cared to dally any length of time in Wanstead, and on September 15, about three weeks after his release, he left London and started out for Bristol.

Away from the heavy atmosphere so strained by distasteful responsibilities and misunderstandings and back into the mainstream of Quaker life once more! His status in the Society of Friends had changed conspicuously. Two controversial tracts, a doctrinal rumpus and Tower hospitality had catapulted him into a role of leadership, and he found himself already a weighty spokesman of the cause. Friends flocked around him, ready to give him support, the newly convinced eager to hear his messages in meetings for worship, other leaders drawing him into their fraternity. The stimulating effect that his personality had upon Friends was noticeable even to himself, whether or not he realized that it was of his own doing, for in his *Irish Journal* he observed at this point that "meetings grew afresh." He himself was starved for the meetings after so many months of isolation, and his hunger was contagious.

For reasons not hard to fathom Penn did not follow the flight of the crow due west to Bristol. He turned northwest toward the Chiltern Hills, passing through Watford, behaving like a man with a fixed and important destination in mind, until he reached Amersham and the home of the Peningtons—the home of Gulielma Springett.

Buckinghamshire, "Beechy Bucks," is beautiful countryside with its dales and wooded hills, its roads winding through a wealth of tall, gray beech trees. Even today it has the quiet atmosphere of a natural retreat; there is still peace and healing seclusion in its rural air; and a traveler along one of its country roads may look up and find himself sheltered from the sky by a high vaulted ceiling of beech leaves, and see on either side the shorter holly trees adding their lustrous darker green. Amersham, just east of the Chilterns, is in a valley; in the center of the original village through which the old coach road winds stands the ancient red brick market building and within sight of the market is Bury Farm, home of the Peningtons.

The Peningtons had moved to Bury Farm a little more than two years before when their beautiful manor house, The Grange, at nearby Chalfont St. Peter was confiscated by the Crown.

The Peningtons had been ardent Puritans for many years; Isaac Penington's father had been one of the justices at the trial of Charles I; and under the Commonwealth the family played a prominent role in national affairs. Mary Penington had been Mary Proude and the wife of Sir William Springett, a Commonwealth hero who had died on the battlefield for Cromwell in the first year of their marriage, before the birth of Gulielma. Guli was ten when her mother married Isaac Penington in 1654 and twenty-two when the Grange, local capital of Quakerism, refuge for the distressed and center for meetings, was finally seized.

Mary and Isaac Penington had been caught up in the Quaker movement in the same year as their marriage. They suffered a lion's share of imprisonment and loss of goods including the Grange, because of their conspicuous leadership. Isaac Penington had just been released from Aylesbury jail. It was to Isaac Penington that Penn had written his long account of Thomas Loe's death.

The warm and ample family circle—all of Isaac Penington's children by both marriages and Mary's daughter Gulielma by her first marriage—welcomed the movement's newest hero. William Penn sat at family board with the Peningtons—and Guli; he joined in holy fellowship with the Peningtons, their neighbors—and Guli; he was able to find some opportunity to talk alone with Guli. There was so little time! He had to go on to Bristol and to Ireland; it was his father's bidding, and he was under a kind of parole in the custody of his father. But he could at least stay one night with a clear conscience, although the next day there was no excuse for loitering. So Penn mounted his horse, starting southward to find the westbound road to Bristol. When he had covered about fifteen miles and had reached the town of Maidenhead, he made an amazing discovery. He was "missing of" his servant and he needs must return all the way to Isaac Penington's. That day was consumed and night travel was unsafe. One day's delay logically and easily led to a second and third. Well, there was a meeting in Penn Street that Guilelma and William attended together, and another at Russell's the next day; and Penn was awaiting the arrival of a man from Aylesbury whom he had decided to employ, and that held him to the fifth day.

Thus it was during this happy sojourn at Amersham that Penn took Philip Ford into his bosom, engaging him to manage his personal affairs at a salary of forty pounds a year. Ford was a Quaker merchant of good repute, but in spite of a marked talent for business had not been too successful; so the invitation to become Penn's personal steward was no doubt a welcome one. When Ford finally arrived at Amersham, prepared to go to Ireland, some of the Penington family mounted up to ride part of the way with the two men and with fourteen-year-old John Penington who was also going to Ireland with Penn. Guli Springett and Thomas Ellwood accompanied Penn a little beyond Maidenhead, and Isaac and Mary Penington rode with him as far as Reading. The parting at Maidenhead was the last Penn saw of Guli for many months, but the roots of courtship had been well established in those five days.

Thomas Ellwood had been an intimate member of the Penington family circle for many years, but I cannot accept the centuries-old gossip that he was Guli's suitor displaced by Penn. His own journal refutes it. He was a Latin tutor to the Penington children, and he was Guli's companion, protector, adviser and friend, sometimes escorting her on journeys around the countryside. But he could not suddenly have been displaced in her affections by Penn, because he had been courting Mary Ellis since late in the previous year, and he was married to Mary on October 28, 1669, right after Penn's departure. Since he and Mary were married in meeting, they would have had to declare their intent to wed at two previous monthly meetings. Thus, they would have had to declare their intent at least by the time of Penn's first visit to Amersham in order to accomplish their wedding by the end of October.

Ellwood was a child of the English civil wars, whisked from Crowell in Oxfordshire to London at the age of two for safety's sake when hostilities between King and Parliament broke out. His family remained in London until Oxford surrendered, and it was during their sojourn in the city that his parents made the acquaintance of the young widow of Sir William Springett. Espousal of Parliament's cause united the adults; the interests and pastimes of childhood united Thomas and Guli. Thomas Ellwood became her "early and particular playfellow" and was "admitted to ride with her in her little coach, drawn by her footman about Lincoln's-Inn-Fields." The Ellwoods returned to Oxfordshire when Thomas was still a small child, and he did not see Guli again until they were adults. His next years were consumed by a stormy growing up.

Thomas Ellwood was nineteen when the former Lady Springett, now married to Isaac Penington, moved to the Grange, only fifteen miles from Crowell. He called on them almost immediately, and —true enough—when he caught a glimpse of the twenty-four-year-old Guli he was startled. Other contemporaries of Guli were equally startled by her beauty, and have left records telling us so. He created an opportunity to speak to her as soon as he dared, and found her in the garden where she was walking with her maid and gathering flowers. She must have made a captivating picture, strolling along the narrow path of the formal garden, her arms full of blooms. What startled the brash Ellwood even more was her serious mien. She was cordial and courteous, but so grave that he could only stammer an apology for having intruded into her private walk and stumble away, his thoughts and emotions in disorder.

He knew nothing of Quakerism, almost nothing of the Quakers, and the real effect of his first meeting with the adult Guli was the reawakening of his scholar's mind as well as his soul. His early schooling had been lost temporarily in careless and gay living, and now he suddenly wanted to recover it: visiting with the Peningtons led him to seek out Quaker meetings. It was Edward Burrough and later Samuel Thornton who finally spoke to Thomas Ellwood's condition, and the message that he heard was "like the clinching of a nail; confirming, and fastening in my mind, those good principles which had sunk into me at the former. . . . Now was my former life ripped up. . . ." The human soul can absorb only one intense experience at a time, and this was the time of Thomas Ellwood's convincement.

Within three years Ellwood had risen to the rank of martyr, cast into the castle in High Street, Oxford, at the same time as Thomas Loe. When the Restoration forced the blind Milton into hiding, and he wanted a young man to read to him in exchange for learned instruction, the Peningtons and others succeeded in obtaining the post for Ellwood. Martyrdom claimed Ellwood again when he had been reading for Milton only a few months; and after being released from his second imprisonment, instead of returning to Milton, he joined the Penington household as an instructor to the children. During the time of the Great Plague, Ellwood found Milton his "pretty box" in Chalfont St. Giles. Ellwood had been a member of the Penington household six years when Penn appeared on the scene and did not leave it until his own marriage.

Ellwood and Guli were harried for a while by ugly gossip that went beyond suspicion of courtship, but Mary and Isaac Penington trusted Ellwood completely and turned a deaf ear toward those who came behind Ellwood's back to whisper their "ill surmises" about him.

Gulielma Springett, Thomas Ellwood tells us, was a woman of good family, beauty and good fortune, and was crowded with suitors whom he describes as "good and bad, rich and poor, friend and foe." But with all these candidates Guli "carried herself with so much evenness of temper, such courteous freedom, guarded with the strictest modesty, that as it gave encouragement or ground of hopes to none." Guli's dignity treated all alike "until he at length came, for whom she was reserved." When William Penn arrived, all doubt and speculation could cease; for Guli was as candid in her acceptance of his intentions as he was in his courtship of her. Thus, he found an excuse to turn his horse back and spend three additional days with her, and she at last rode with him to Maidenhead, to say goodby. William Penn went on to his Irish exile, and Thomas Ellwood escorted Guli back to Amersham.

Penn reached Bristol in two days and there he remained for a full month before sailing to Ireland. His diary tells us that on the day he arrived in Bristol he visited George Fox, Margaret Fell and other Friends. He was probably already acquainted with George Fox. They could have met in London as early as the first year of Penn's ministry, and Penn's dispute with Vincent had no doubt attracted Fox's attention. The acquaintance flowered into friendship when Penn endorsed the intent of George Fox and Margaret Fell to wed.

Fox was forty-five and Margaret Fell a widow ten years older, Founder on the one hand and "Mother" on the other of the Quaker movement. Margaret and Thomas Fell, living in their manor house, Swarthmoor Hall, in Ulverston, in the Lake Country, had received a visit from Fox very early in his ministry. Margaret Fell accepted Quakerism, and although her husband never actually became a Friend, he allowed meetings in Swarthmoor Hall and as a circuit judge was able to help Friends considerably with his personal influence. Swarthmoor Hall, now a shrine, became a vital center of Quakerism, particularly after Judge Fell's death and Margaret's ultimate marriage to George Fox.

But because Margaret Fell and George Fox had worked closely together for so long before their marriage, unkind and ungenerous talk cast a shadow over the Bristol Men's Monthly Meeting at which their intent to wed was to be considered, and the testimony of many weighty Friends was called for so that all might be clear in their minds about the virtue and wisdom of the planned union. Penn, who had been accumulating some profound thoughts on marriage en route from Amersham to Bristol, attended that meeting and felt moved along with many others to speak in favor of the marriage. He did not, however, remain long enough to witness the wedding, but left on October 23, four days too soon. On the twenty-fourth he was beyond Cornwall seven leagues and on the twenty-fifth his ship lay in the Cove of Cork over night. He landed next day and within a matter of hours he was back in the center of the Irish Quaker movement.

"Dined at Thomas Mitchell's. Visited the prisoners. . . ."

He needed only one glimpse of Cork prison conditions to feel his concerned excitement mount—children in stocks, eighty Friends in one small enclosure with no food or drink except what could be pushed in through a hole, servants in the stocks who had run the risk of bringing food, bedding or tools of trade to the prisoners. The shocking thought occurred to him that these abuses were English to English, Protestant to Protestant.

When a Quaker is seized by a concern, it will not let him go, because his concern he recognizes as arising from the Light within himself, the bidding of the divine voice, and Penn was bidden to aid the Quaker prisoners in Ireland. Private affairs could wait in the face of this crying need, he concluded, and hurried to the Mayor's quarters.

". . . to no purpose."

Back he hurried to the suffering Friends, obtained admission to the prison, dined with the prisoners, held a meeting for worship with them. A couple of letters would have to take care of his father's affairs in Cork for the time being—"wrote to both baronies to prepare them"—because he had to go up to Dublin and take the case of the imprisoned Friends to government men there.

His third day in Ireland found him en route from Cork to Dublin with Philip Dymond and William Morris, both outstanding Quaker leaders.

"Dined at Kilworth, supped at Clogheen at a Friend's Inn." Next day, "Came to John Fennell's; dined at Cashel at The Cow.

Passed through Holy Cross . . . and by Clas . . . lay at Thurles the ancient Manor House of the Duke of Ormonde." The following night the travelers stopped at Rosenallis and stayed with William Edmundson. Penn was gathering strength, advice and information, and none better qualified to give Penn his direction than the seasoned pioneer Edmundson who had been working on the spot for fifteen years. Edmundson knew Irish prisons from the inside; he knew every meeting, its origin and internal problems; he knew Ireland. From Rosenallis Penn and his companions went on through Mountmellick, Kildare and Naas, reaching Dublin on November 2.

Dublin was about as Penn had left it three years before—a walled medieval town with its protecting castle on top of a hill on the south side of the River Liffey. Even the Stuart Court could not make it more of a city than it was. Its population was around nine thousand; many of its houses were crude, one-story cabins, and only a few residents lived in the Elizabethan type building of three or four stories; its narrow streets were a labyrinth. But it was advanced enough to have its own Black Dog and Newgate, imitating the evil conditions of the London dungeons, and it did incarcerate independent consciences there. Dublin's Newgate was the prison proper where the keeper charged extortion rates for minimum sustenance and cast into the felons' rooms those who could not pay, stripping and beating them, leaving them on the bare floor to die of starvation and exposure. The Black Dog was a subsidiary prison-inn, where lodging could be purchased in crowded dormitory rooms or closet-sized single rooms.

Penn stayed at the home of John Gay in George's Lane, hurrying into conference with Quaker leaders immediately. The second semi-annual National Meeting of Friends was held two days after his arrival at his lodgings, and there at further conferences a paper was prepared concerning imprisoned Irish Friends. William Penn and William Morris then waited upon the Mayor of Dublin armed with the report of the National Meeting.

The pompous Mayor, Lewis Desmynières, in spite of his Huguenot background, received his visitors with a curled upper lip and a disposition ready to ignite at the first word. They came gently and lovingly, the Quakers, and set forth in modest tones the injustice of imprisoning Friends for worshiping according to their consciences. Desmynières exploded in their faces calling them rogues, rascals, whelps. They ought to be lashed out of the town and sent to Barbados! As for their paper, he snatched it up and flung it to the ground with contempt. The Quaker visitors restrained themselves as became their non-violent convictions and withdrew.

Penn, as in the case of Vincent, could not let the matter remain unfinished. When he reached his lodgings, he took his quill and inkhorn once more and addressed his own personal letter to the Mayor:

"It is the duty of a magistrate to hear and redress the oppressed, not revile them," he reminded Desmynières. . . . "Let me tell thee that if we were as contentious as thou has shown thyself injurious, this treatment would find a resurrection in thy great disprofit. . . ."

The Mayor of Dublin was far from being top man in Ireland, and once his rank had been recognized by the courtesy of a call Penn was free to go to others. He plied back and forth between conferences with Friends and conferences with government officials. Time and again he went to the Castle to talk to this officer or that. He would receive a "slight account" from one; another would be "very civil but nothing done." Finally, Penn wrote to the Earl of Drogheda. Drogheda was Henry Moore of the old landed gentry of Ireland; Charles I had made him Governor of Meath and Louth and later of Drogheda; at the time of the Restoration he was raised to an earldom by Charles II. The name of Penn carried considerable weight with someone who had been loyal to the Stuart cause so long, and two days after his letter Penn was granted an interview.

"He treated me with all civility. Promised his utmost. Invited me to dine with him at my pleasure."

That was the first real encouragement, and in another two days Penn was back, still civilly received, and met not only Lord Drogheda ut the Earls of Arran and Roscommon and others. Arran was the on of the Duke of Ormonde, Sir William's friend, and Roscommon was of the Dillon family of Kilkenny West.

Hope began to run high. Penn and the Friends decided to petition the Council for a release of the prisoners, and they composed an address to the Lord Lieutenant of Ireland. None but the son of Sir

William Penn, friend of Ormonde, Arran, Drogheda, Roscommon, Orrery, Broghill—and the Duke of York, was qualified to carry that petition to the Council and present it; none better than he could ask and hope to receive a sympathetic hearing. Yet, when Penn attended that Council meeting the address which he himself had turned in in the morning was not read. The reversal of attitude was surprising. These men in high places had promised him their utmost! The Earl of Drogheda had himself been present. Penn returned to the Council on a later day to find that it did not meet because of the Lord Lieutenant's illness.

There was still another way, another approach; while he was at the Council chambers he talked to three of the Privy Councillors individually about the Friends in prison. Persistently, painstakingly, he began to wear down one man after another in the government, at the Castle, at his lodgings, at social functions. A Lieutenant Colonel Young came to him one morning and another afternoon a Lieutenant Colonel Walker dined with him. Penn knew that the Council would take no official action, so he continued his private calls upon one officeholder after another. Somehow, Penn's talent for high-level diplomacy, his capacity for convincing argumentation, filtered through a multitude of devious channels, until, on November 29, he entered in his *Journal*: "Friends were released in this city with great love and civility from the judges."

With a deep sense of satisfaction, Penn set out for Cork the next day, to return to the Friends still imprisoned there.

Penn was a center of interest while he was in Ireland, to Friends and non-Friends. There were the Quakers who gathered round him —the Gays, M. Canning, Morris, Dymond, John Burnyeat, George Gregson, Samuel Claridge, Elizabeth Gardner, Anthony Sharp, Robert Turner, Burrough. And there were those like the Catholic priest Roules who was drawn to him again and again to dispute the water baptism or vindictive justice. Every available minute of Penn's time was taken up with Friends, Friends' problems, distributing Friends' books which he had brought with him for that purpose, writing in his journal, writing doctrinal letters, tracts, news letters home to George Fox, the Peningtons, Whitehead, his father, Guli. Personal matters had to be fitted in somehow: "I caused my hair to be cut off and put into a wig because of baldness since my imprisonment."

An errand for Guli eased the burden of exile. She owned some land in Ireland, thought to be a little over forty-three acres on the Barony of Deece in County Meath, that had been so neglected it had fallen away to about a third of its former value.

His father's affairs had to be given their fair share of attention, and on the way back to Cork, through Rathcoole, Carlow, Kilkenny, Callan, Clonmel, he stopped to pay a visit to Captain Boles in the vale of Shanagarry, living on a farm "which he holds of my father," and found it well improved. Boles returned to Cork with Penn and the two men went on down to Sir William's fort at Kinsale. There Penn visited the fort, "gave the soldiers two cobbs or plate pieces," then paid William Crispin a visit. Crispin was related to Penn by marriage and eleven years later became one of the first three commissioners for settling the colony of Pennsylvania. From Kinsale Penn returned to his father's lands in eastern County Cork. All the while he tended to estate problems he was haunted by the memory of Friends in prison. He dispatched Ford to Cork with letters to Sheriffs Field and Harvey and to Friends John Gossage and Samuel Thornton, and while he awaited Ford's return he rode about conferring with his father's tenants, adjusting whatever questions awaited him regarding the lands. When Ford returned from Cork, Penn set him to the task of surveying and acting as liaison between Shanagarry and Cork, so that he could keep in close touch with Friends there. Philip Ford was becoming more and more important to him as assistant, secretary, emissary, courier-reporter and correspondent.

Penn executed a new lease for a Francis Smith at £42 per annum, settled with Sergeant Rouls at four shillings six pence per acre. Apparently many of the tenanted parcels of land had disputable borders, because Penn refers to several instances where he had to take time to "admeasure" the land with the help of Ford or John Gossage. In other instances the amount of annual rental was in dispute. Day after day he worked his way through a volume of administrative detail that must have irked him then but would stand him in good stead when he began to administer his great colonial experiment.

Land problems held him at Shanagarry until the end of January, 1670, when at last he was able to move up to Cork and make it the center of his activities in Ireland until the end of May. There he stepped into a new role—that of traveling Friends' minister—a role he was to play again and again. Traveling ministers provided a kind of connective tissue for the Society, keeping faith alive. The Friends in Ireland were colonists, living often in out-of-the-way and even primitive places, working desperately hard to survive, not always able to travel to a center for worship. In other places where a meeting was available it was sometimes small, lacking in ministerial strength.

Penn set out from Cork to Clogheen on his first ministerial mission, taking Philip Ford, John Penington and George Gamble with him. He pushed north to Cashel, in time for First Day meeting, then back over another route to Kilworth, "had a meeting there," and to Tallow where the meeting was "disturbed by a busy constable." Penn spoke personally to the Tallow intruder and his eloquence and sincerity seem to have won out, for the man departed and the meeting resumed its prayers. He went from Tallow to Youghal. "We had a blessed meeting. . . . Supped at the Inn." From Youghal he returned to Shanagarry, where John Penington had to be left behind because he was "ill of a stoppage in his throat." Penn went on to Cork with George Gamble, to stay at Gamble's home. "I shaved my head, dined there, did something about my book."

Among Penn's collected works is a tract called *A Seasonable Caveat Against Popery*, which may be the "book" to which Penn refers frequently in his *Irish Journal*. Perhaps the profoundly Catholic atmosphere of Ireland, conversations with such men as Priest Roules and another who walked with him along the strand of Ballycotton Bay one day in theological argument, compelled him to write the *Seasonable Caveat*. It is quite likely, for in it he refutes the Trinity once more, as well as the praying to saints and angels, the accumulation of merits, participation in the Holy Eucharist, sacrifice at the altar, prayer in Latin, prayer for the dead, and the necessity of a priest as an intercessor between God and man.

During the latter part of his stay in Ireland he was also working on *The Great Case of Liberty of Conscience*, but this piece was not finished until he returned to London. Its covering letter is dated from Newgate Prison.

A noble document of his Irish sojourn is *A Letter of Love to the Young Convinced.* He is himself one of the young convinced, and the letter, inspired by journeying among the Friends in their meet ings, their homes, their prison cells, springs straight from his hear "In you the hope of glory," he declares. "Let us not be discomforte under all our sharp and heavy exercises, whether from within or without; for this I am fully persuaded of, that the same pure principle of Light and Truth that hath appeared to give a certain discerning of our states and conditions, and wrought a convincement upon our understandings, is able to give us that succor and support, if our minds be but seriously stayed thereon. . . ." The sufferings of the imprisoned Friends, the meetings interrupted by constables, the callousness of petty officials, the backbreaking labors of peopling a strange and hostile land—these but frustrations to tempt them from their appointed course. Penn beseeches, cautions and admonishes them "never forbear meeting and assembling of yourselves with the holy remnant amongst whom we first received our blessed convincement." The short, intense piece is dated Carberry, County Cork, February 19, 1670, shortly after he had begun his second ministerial journey southward out of Cork—to Bandon, Skibbereen and Baltimore at the very southern tip of Ireland, then back to Bandon, through Rosscarbery to Cork.

He visited Kinsale again and he and Sir William kept up a running correspondence about both tracts of Irish land. As a matter of fact, William Penn was profoundly considerate of his whole family. He corresponded with his brother Richard, then traveling in Italy; he bought gifts for them, in one instance a rough woolen outer garment or frieze for his sister, Margaret.

Returning to Cork from the south there was that haunting problem awaiting him—the Friends still in prison. "Went to the prison and saw dear Friends," says his *Journal* on March 15. It was the time of the Assizes, and Penn waited upon the circuit riding judge. "Could not speak to him in the morning." Penn hurried to Lord Shannon (a brother of the Earl of Orrery) who gathered up Sir St. John Brockerick and a Redmond Barry and went back to the judge with Penn. "Effected but little, but cleared Truth and came over the judge." Later Penn sent William Morris to the judge with a letter. But at last the judge who had appeared to understand what Penn was talking about and who "seemed civil" came into court and "dealt wickedly." He would do no more for the Friends in prison than allow them to keep their tools of trade, purchase a few comforts and have a little more space in which to be housed. "The judge went out of town and left the prisons full, and Friends were fined £195 besides fees; one Friend was beaten in the court but was not regarded by judge or jury. A wickeder mayor nor judge has not been in the city of Cork since Truth came." Penn and his companions walked solemnly to the prison to tell Friends of their half a loaf of justice.

Estate matters took Penn out of town for a few days—to Imokilly and then to Shanagarry. At the end of a week he returned to Cork to find that even the judge's smallest concession had not been honored. Friends in prison were not even allowed tools of trade with which to support themselves.

All during April and May he was harassed by leases that "were not come," by the collection of quitrents, by the difficulties of determining fair annual rentals, by stubborn tenants who would not "give way" on terms offered. He made another trip down to Rosscarbery and Baltimore and there demonstrated a firm hand with a recalcitrant tenant. He stopped at Thomas Gookin's and sent for the man named Berry. When he did not come, Penn went to him at Clonakilty. "He boiled," says Penn. "I fell out with him and so returned to Rosscarbery to settle that business." Berry was stubborn, even when Penn sent representatives to the farm to distrain his cattle. But eventually Berry surrendered, acknowledged his fault, and accepted Penn's terms. Penn magnanimously paid him six pounds twenty over and above the finished matter. Penn even made a trip up to Macroom, his father's earlier grant in Ireland. Sir William must have had either a continuing title to some land there or some uncollected accounts. Gradually the real estate problems were being ironed out. April 25: "I went to Ladysbridge. Colonel Osborne and Major Woodley came and took their leases." April 28: "I ended with Rous at £33 per annum. May 3: "The Irish inhabitants came. They had their houses and gardens as before. Two were made sergeants to keep the grass, etc." In the first week of June he was able to write in his *Journal*: "My father's business is also done."

In a small place like Cork every visit to Lord Shannon and Lord Barrymore (another member of the Boyle family and relative of Orrery, a great-nephew of Lord Shannon), every trip between Shanagarry and Cork, every dispatching of Philip Ford to Cork or to Dublin was easily noticeable. On the twelfth of May Penn went to the Cork prison and stayed overnight with the prisoners. He did the same thing again two nights later. Perhaps as a result, his lodgings in Cork must have been raided, for a quantity of his books were seized. He hurried to the Mayor about it and was treated to such epithets as "cockscomb, jackanapes, fellow, fool." So again he found himself writing to the Earl of Orrery about a mayor's malice.

The reply was immediate from Charleville: "So soon as I received your letter I showed it to my brother O'Bryan who hath promised me to do something for you; had I as much power as formerly I have had, it would be employed to serve you, and at the capacity I now am in I'll do you what kindness I can; I much wonder that the Mayor of Cork should give any gentleman be he of what religion or sect soever such ill language as you sent me word he gave you. . . . I shall come very speedily to Cork and then I'll get him to deliver you your books. . . . BROGHILL"

O'Bryan wrote the next day: "My brother Broghill showed me yesterday a letter of yours wherein you complain of the Mayor of Cork's severity. Whatever be your opinion, I shall never encourage him to be uncivil to a person of your quality, therefore I have writ the enclosed to him, and wish it may work the effect that you desire. . . . Your books, upon the enclosed, will be restored. . . ."

Penn was glad enough to have won this particular point, but the great problem—the Friends in prison—went unsolved. He and other Friends drew up an account of sufferings and sent it to Dublin with Philip Ford, who returned two days later to report that nothing had come of it. By the latter part of May Penn's patience with officialdom ran out, and he boarded a midnight post for Dublin, arriving at dawn the second day. There he met, among others, Robert Turner, who later became one of the First Adventurers in Pennsylvania. Penn wrote at once to the Lord Lieutenant of Ireland and requested an audience; for double assurance he also wrote to the Chancellor. On the first day of June he saw both men as well as the Earl of Arran, and in their company he went before the Council. This time the Council was more cordial; it heard the reports on Friends' sufferings and saw Penn again on the third, when it issued a release of Maryborough Friends. The resistance was cracking! Penn took the next diplomatic step and gave a dinner for Arran, Shannon, Kingston, Major Fairfax and many more of his befeathered and beruffled friends. None other in the Society could have made this social gesture more competently or with more grace, and none but Penn could have moved with such complete ease from that elaborate banquet to an unadorned meeting for worship next day. In fact, many of the high-caste gentry, among them the Countess of Clancarty to whom Macroom had been restored, came to that First Day Meeting for Worship. They wanted to hear Penn speak! Monday found him closeted with the Chancellor, Lord Arran and the Lord Lieutenant of Ireland, and at last with the Lord Lieutenant.

"He promised to release our Friends and did so by order of Council in the afternoon."

It was the same day on which Penn had written in his *Journal*, "My father's business is also done."

With all of the Friends out of prison and his father's work completed, William Penn could dare to consider himself. The letters exchanged with Guli Springett fed the young suitor's longing to be home, and although none of these letters survive we know from his *Journal* that there were many.

Sir William wanted him home, too. He had been indicating in his letters a strong desire to become completely reconciled with his son. At the end of April he had written: "I wish you had well done all the business there and that you were here for I find myself to decline." The snappy old sea dog had lost his snap; he was tired, ill, failing; he had learned during these last few months how capable a man his son really was despite his religious disaffections, and he wanted the young man at his side.

Some time shortly after the first of August in 1670, Penn sailed for England, leaving Philip Ford in Ireland to handle his affairs.

This forcing of men's consciences is contrary to sound reason, and the very law of nature. For man's understanding cannot be forced by all the bodily sufferings another man can inflict upon him.

—Robert Barclay, *An Apology for the . . . Principles and Doctrines of the People Called Quakers*

7. For All Thou Art Penn's Son

PENN'S HOST in Dublin, John Gay, had come to London weeks ahead of Penn and had written to him about his father's declining health. But his letter, with those of several others, had fallen into the hands of officialdom and never reached its destination. The news it had contained was waiting for Penn when he arrived in England.

John Gay had paid a visit to Wanstead and had found both Sir William and Lady Penn indisposed, the former too ill to see him and Lady Penn abed. But the servant brought word back to the caller that Lady Penn wanted very much to chat with him about her son. "Much discourse we had full of tears." She had not had one letter from her son and wondered whether her husband was keeping them from her. It wasn't like her dutiful and affectionate son not to write to her at all. John Gay gave Lady Penn a detailed report of her son's activities in Ireland, and Lady Penn wept as she listened to his strange interests. His father, she said, had intended to make William a great man but the boy would not hearken. Then she gave Gay all the family news: William's sister had just two weeks before given birth to a baby girl, and his brother, Richard, was a little wild but had been greatly entertained in Italy. As for Sir William's health, he was "very ill of a dropsy scurvey and jandies and hath a very great belly and full of water and the fisick was to get out the water if possible, but the doctor had given over and had said . . . that the fall of the leaf would put him hard to it, and that if not then the first of the winter would carry him away. He seldom walks in the garden and not at all abroad. . . ."

Penn learned, too, that Margaret Fell Fox was in prison, with child, close to the time of her delivery, and Friends were making every effort to obtain her release; that Isaac Penington had been rearrested and placed in Reading jail, "after a great deal of discourse and reviling language. . . . It is like to come to a praemunire unless God put a stop to the wicked intentions." Penn must have been glad to be back where so much was happening that concerned him, where his parents needed him, the Quakers needed him and Guli needed him.

English history had ground ruthlessly on in his absence. Charles II, at heart a Catholic, son of a French Catholic mother, longed to see England back in the Catholic fold almost as much as he longed for absolute personal power. For years he had been secretly planning, with the aid of a group of his partisan ministers, to re-establish Catholicism in England with French support, at the same time openly supporting the Triple Alliance of England, Holland and Sweden to keep the "menace" of French power in check. In the spring of 1670, when Penn was winding up his father's affairs in Ireland, Charles II concluded his secret Treaty of Dover with the French under the terms of which he was to declare his conversion to the Roman Catholic Church and England was to assist France in a war against Holland. Only the war against Holland materialized. The Anglican Parliament meanwhile renewed the Conventicle Act. The brief respite from persecution that had followed Clarendon's fall from power a little earlier vanished less than three months before Penn's return to England, and on the tide of renewed persecutions Isaac Penington was one of those who had been arrested.

The purpose of the Conventicle Act was clearly stated in its preamble: "for providing further and more speedy remedies against the growing and dangerous practices of seditious sectaries, and other disloyal persons, who, under pretence of tender consciences, have or may at their meetings contrive insurrections, as late experience hath shown." Although the burden fell heavily upon the Quakers, the real fear was Catholicism. "Any subject of this realm, of the age of sixteen years, or upward, being present at any assembly, conventicle, or meeting, under color or pretence of any exercise of religion, in other manner than according to the liturgy of the Church of England" would be subject to specified fines, sale of the offender's goods and chattels, collectable by local justices of peace who were in turn to pay it in to the quarter sessions court. The fines for anyone daring to preach at a conventicle, or for anyone daring to act as host to a conventicle, were appropriately heavier. Ultimate impoverishment under the law, as a result of scaled-up fines, could end in debtors' prison where life was often allowed to waste away.

George Fox was in London when the Conventicle Act went back into effect. A wise, well-informed and wide-visioned leader, he knew immediately what it could mean, and he determined to test it with his own person. On First Day he went to the most conspicuous Friends' meeting house in London, the one built in Gracechurch Street to replace the Bull and Mouth destroyed in the fire, "where I expected the storm was most likely to begin."

The streets were crowded with the curious and the tense, all waiting for violence to break out, many thirsty for the entertainment of a quick riot, broken heads, damaged property, eager for an excuse to join in a melee or hurl missiles. It was a raw-edged age, its moods sharpened by the crowding and slum conditions of a still only partially rebuilt city, by the utter lack of police protection, by the continuously perilous living. A London crowd in that tenth year of the monarchy was accustomed to seeing whole rows of freshly executed prisoners dangling from gibbets, or to expressing its frank juridical sentiment toward a victim in the stocks. It was an age that believed in witchcraft and gathered from far and wide to watch a burning at the stake, and it gathered on that First Day morning in May, 1670, to see what would happen to the Quakers.

Fox found guards stationed at the door of the Gracechurch Street Meeting House to prevent Friends from entering to worship. He went around to the side door on Lombard Street and found the same. But Friends were there, too, because it was time for group worship, and they never convened in secret. William Warwick was already preaching to the group gathered outside the building. When he finished, George Fox began to speak. He had not been talking long when a constable and an informer and an "officer with a file of musketeers" appeared and dragged Fox, Warwick and John Burnyeat away. Fox took the sense of the crowd milling around him as he was being taken away, and it indicated clearly a turning in the tide of public opinion. It suggested that the English people had reached a saturation point on gross injustice. "Have a care of him, he is a princely man," shouted one at the guard who held Fox. Others mocked at the great bevy of armed might come to capture a people who would neither resist nor bolt. Fox and his two companions were brought before the Lord Mayor, and the case dissolved under Fox's eloquence. The Act did not apply, said Fox, since Friends were a peaceable people and did not gather to contrive insurrections. The Lord Mayor, Sir Samuel Starling, was remarkably tolerant in his attitude toward Fox. "Mr. Fox, you are an eminent man amongst those of your profession, pray will you be instrumental to dissuade them from meeting in such great numbers?" To which Fox's reply was, "If Christ had promised to manifest His presence in the midst of such an assembly where but two or three were gathered in His name, then how much more where two or three hundred are gathered in His name." The Mayor was not a little afraid of Fox's potential leadership capacities. Fox was respected and loved far beyond the confines of the Society of Friends; he had a tremendous popular appeal, the Mayor knew, and he could, had he chosen to misappropriate his own talents, have roused whole masses of people with his homely eloquence. The Mayor was not at all confident that Fox would never do so. The three Quaker ministers were released.

Well-established legal precedent would go a long way in saving the Friends from persecution under the Act, and about a month later George Whitehead made a similar test case, going to the center of trouble, the meeting house in Gracechurch Street. There he rose in the gathering of Friends and prayed publicly. The arrest which everyone anticipated followed, but Whitehead talked his way out of custody on the grounds that he had been praying and not preaching. Three weeks later Whitehead came again to Gracechurch Street, where he found the Friends quietly assembled, listening to a priest whom the Lord Mayor had sent. Whitehead waited patiently through the reading of the common prayer and the preaching of the sermon. Then he stood up and preached a sermon of peace and love, with the inevitable result—dragged down by two soldiers and committed to Gatehouse at Bishopgate. He and others arrested with him were given a hearing before the Mayor and heavily fined—Whitehead twenty pounds.

William Penn arrived back in London three months after Fox's experience with the Conventicle Act at Gracechurch Street, and he hurried to confer with Quaker leaders. In the light of his own legal training he agreed with Fox's interpretations: the Act did not apply to the Society of Friends. But it most certainly was being applied to the Friends. Their meeting houses were policed, boarded up; their membership carted off to the jails. The purpose of the Act was to "force a general conformity to the liturgy and practice of the Church of England," wrote George Whitehead. "The agents employed for that work were generally a company of idle, loose, profligate and mercenary informers, by that law let loose to seek honest people's ruin." George Fox called it a "cruel bloody persecuting time."

William Penn was still in the early flush of religious conversion when he found his way to Gracechurch Street Meeting House, at the optimum point of youthful idealism, eager for more tests, privations and dramatic opportunities to prove himself worthy of the God whom he had only just begun to know. A healthy animal vigor carried him along—and carried others along with him who might not have been strong enough to make their way alone.

It was First Day morning once more, and Friends would be waiting upon the Lord with their usual gentle stubbornness. Penn knew he was courting arrest, and his deliberateness stirs memories of the Great Salt March to Dandi where Mahatma Gandhi publicly broke the law and forced the government to arrest him, thereby calling attention to the iniquitous salt tax. Other Indians could have done the same, but they would have made little news. Other Quaker leaders had been arrested under the Conventicle Act, and they had either talked their way out or merely paid a fine. It was Sir William's son, newly returned from Ireland where he had used his name and position in behalf of Friends, who arrived to find the meeting house door barred and guarded by soldiers, who found Friends gathered quietly in the street, who felt the compulsion to stand forth and give ministry. It was Sir William's son, addressing the worshipers, who caused the small gathering to be swelled by a multitude of the curious. It was he who would draw the throngs to his trial at Old Bailey, and who would convey to his jury the inspiration that awakened their integrity.

Speaking to that gathering at the corner of Gracechurch and Lombard, he waited patiently for the inevitable, and when the constables arrived and took hold of his elbow he went quietly—he and one other, William Mead. He had sampled prison life in the Tower, and as the Lord Mayor's men dragged him away toward the west side of London, it looked as though he would sample it again in infamous Newgate, joining in the company of debtors, murderers, clippers of coins and highwaymen. But the authorities were apparently hesitant about going so far as to place a friend of the Stuarts within the foul confines of Newgate itself, and they took him and his companion to the sign of the Black Dog in nearby Newgate Market. The tavern looked out upon the haggling of the street venders of flesh, fish and fowl, and its own atmosphere was almost as unwholesome as the jail itself. The "Dogge Tavern in Newgate" had operated its extortion upon prisoners for many years, serving fine Bordeaux and Gascony wines to those who could pay.

Penn was arrested on August 14, 1670. "Receive into your custody the body of William Penn herewith sent you, who was taken in the street called Gracious Street [Gracechurch Street] preaching seditiously and causing a great tumult of people on the royal street to be there gathered together riotously and routously, and him safely keep until he shall be legally discharged," says the document signed by the Mayor, addressed to the keeper of Newgate.

That evening Penn and Mead were taken before the Mayor who proceeded against them "according to the ancient law," and with much mockery and many rude jibes. They stood with their heads covered, and the Mayor remarked that Penn would have his hat pulled off for all he was Admiral Penn's son. Penn replied that he "desired to be in common with others, and sought no refuge from the common usage." Penn insisted upon disputing the hat issue, and did not answer quickly enough when asked his name; so the Mayor threatened the men with Bridewell where he would see them whipped himself, repeating the jibe about Penn's parentage. The Mayor didn't carry out the Bridewell threat, though, for the prisoners were back at the Black Dog, and from there the next morning Penn dispatched a letter to his father.

Second day morning, 15th of 6th Month
[August] 1670

MY DEAR FATHER:

This comes by the hand of one who can best allay the trouble it brings. As true as ever Paul said, that such as live godly in Christ Jesus shall suffer persecution, so for no other reason am I at present a sufferer. [He related his brief interview with the Mayor.] He bid his clerk write one [mittimus] for Bridewell, and there would he see me whipped himself, for all I was Penn's son, that starved the seamen. Indeed these words grieved me, as well as that it manifested his great weakness and malice to the whole company, that were about one hundred people. I told him I could very well bear his severe expressions to me concerning myself, but was sorry to hear him speak those abuses of my father, that was not present, at which the assembly seemed to murmur. In short he committed that person with me as rioters; and at present we are at the sign of the Black Dog, in Newgate Market.

And now, dear father, be not displeased nor grieved. What if this be designed of the Lord for an exercise of our patience? . . . I doubt not but I may be at liberty in a day or two, to see thee. I am very well, and have no trouble upon my spirits, besides my absence from thee, especially at this juncture, but otherwise I can say, I was never better; and what they have to charge me with is harmless. . . .

Correspondence shows that there had been a complete reconciliation between father and son upon William's return from Ireland, and it is fortunate that it was so, since the next few months were to test the depths of their mutual understanding. Their lives and their names were inseparable in the scheme of things, and whatever befell one also befell the other.

When the son of Sir William Penn was brought before the Lord Mayor, the Mayor's attitude was conspicuously harder than it had been to Fox or even Whitehead. It was as though petty officialdom had been waiting for this protected young man to make a mistake that they could catch him on. He had escaped from the Tower; he had been conspicuous in the Irish Quaker movement for a whole year without being arrested, had even been able to enlist the aid of the higher-ups; he had returned to London to follow the same patterns there. They had him at last—this gentleman of quality, this fellow who enjoyed so much favor and protection, this friend of Catholic Stuarts and espouser of radical movements!

The Conventicle Act contained a clause providing for the right of appeal in writing from the "person or persons convicting, to the judgment of the justices of the peace in their next quarter sessions . . . such offender may plead and make defence, and have his trial by a jury thereupon." Penn and Mead quite obviously refused to pay their fines and demanded a trial by jury in the court of quarter sessions, which met at Old Bailey, conveniently close to Newgate. They were brought to trial on the first of September, only two weeks after their arrest, escorted out of the Black Dog and around the corner to the courthouse.

William Penn, gentleman, and William Mead, linen draper—what strange companions!—united across caste barriers by a ray of light. Penn had come from the Cavaliers; Mead, some sixteen years older, had been a lusty Roundhead, serving in Cromwell's model army. Mead was also a learned man with a fair knowledge of the law, a minor leader in the Quaker movement, who later married one of Margaret Fell's daughters.

The two men were led into the courtroom and bade to stand before the bench on which Sir Samuel Starling presided in company with the Recorder, five aldermen and three sheriffs; and there began four days of what Besse terms "monstrous and illegal proceedings." To the cries of "*Oyez, Oyez,*" the twelve London citizens who had been impaneled as jurors were called—Thomas Veer, Edward Bushel, John Hammond, Charles Milson, Gregory Walklet, John Brightman, Wil. Plumstead, Henry Henley, James Damask, Henry Michel, Wil. Lever, John Baily—men whose individual and collective courage would advance legal history. The court required them at the outset to bind themselves by an oath that would cling to their memories throughout the reading of the indictment and the trial:

"You shall well and truly try, and true deliverance make betwixt our Sovereign Lord the King, and the prisoners at the bar, according to your evidence: So help you God."

Penn had assured his father that what they had to charge him with was harmless; but as he and Mead listened to the reading of the indictment the whole case took on a grimly harmful complexion.

"That William Penn, gentleman, and William Mead, late of London, Linen-Draper, with divers other persons, to the jurors unknown, to the number of three hundred, the 14th day of August, in the 22nd year of the King, about eleven o'clock in the forenoon the same day, with force and arms, etc. . . . in the street called Gracechurch Street, unlawfully and tumultously did assemble and congregate themselves together, to the disturbance of the peace of the said Lord the King. And the aforesaid William Penn and William Mead, together with other persons, to the jurors aforesaid unknown, then and there so assembled and congregated together; the aforesaid William Penn by agreement between him and William Mead before made, and by abetment of the aforesaid William Mead, then and there in the open street, did take upon himself to preach and speak, and then, and there, did preach and speak . . . by reason whereof a great concourse and tumult of people in the street aforesaid, then and there, a long time did remain and continue, in contempt of the said Lord the King, and of his law; to the great disturbance of his peace, to the great terror and disturbance of many of his liege people and subjects, to the ill example of all others in the like case offenders, and against the peace of the said Lord the King, his Crown and dignity."

The whole weight of the Conventicle Act was being thrown at Penn and Mead, and the court was going to strain every effort to find the two defendants guilty of sedition and insurrection. But there was the jury. It would have been difficult to impanel twelve Londoners no one of whom knew anything about the peaceable intent of Friends, and who would not have seen through the sham of such words as "with force and arms," "tumultously," "great terror," and "by agreement before made." But seventeenth-century juries were inclined to do as they were told, to avoid vindictive consequences, particularly in so touchy and tender a case.

"What say you William Penn, and William Mead, are you guilty, as you stand indicted, in manner and form as aforesaid, or not guilty?"

To which Penn responded, "It is impossible that we should be able to remember the indictment verbatim, and therefore we desire a copy of it, as is customary on the like occasions."

The Recorder was on solid ground; he knew he had strong backing; and he snapped, "You must first plead to the indictment, before you can have a copy of it."

"I am unacquainted with the formality of the law," said Penn with tongue in cheek, "and therefore before I shall answer directly, I request two things of the court. First, that no advantage may be taken against me, nor I deprived of any benefit, which I might otherwise have received. Secondly, that you will promise me a fair hearing, and liberty of making my defense."

"No advantage shall be taken against you; you shall have liberty; you shall be heard."

"Then I plead not guilty in manner and form."

William Mead followed suit.

That consumed the morning session, and they were required to wait all during the afternoon session while other prisoners were tried. Court then adjourned until the day after next. On September 3 the "monstrous proceedings" got under way, and when Penn and Mead were brought before the Lord Mayor the first device used against them was the one by which a Quaker could always be trapped—the hat service. Somewhere along the line both men had lost their hats, either in the scuffle of being arrested or the confusion of their living quarters.

"Sirrah, who bid you put off their hats?" demanded the Lord Mayor. "Put on their hats again."

An officer placed hats upon their heads and led them forward to the bar.

"Do you know where you are?" the Recorder demanded.

Penn replied that he did, that he knew it to be a court, he supposed the King's court.

"Do you know there is respect due to the court?"

"Yes."

"Why do you not pay it then?"

"I do so."

"Why do you not put off your hat then?"

"Because I do not believe that to be any respect."

"Well, the court sets forty marks apiece upon your heads, as a fine, for your contempt of the court."

"I desire," said Penn, "it may be observed, that we came into the court with our hats off and if they have been put on since, it was by order from the bench; and therefore not we, but the bench, should be fined."

The jury was sworn in once more, the indictment was read a second time, and the court began to call witnesses. James Cook testified that he had been sent from the Exchange to disperse a meeting in Gracious Street and that he had seen Mr. Penn speaking to the people. He admitted, though, that he could not hear what Penn was saying because of the noise. Richard Read testified that he, too, had seen Penn preaching but couldn't hear what he said for the noise.

"Jury, take notice, he swears now a clean contrary thing to what he swore before the Mayor, when we were committed. For now he swears he saw me in Gracious Street, and yet swore before the Mayor, when I was committed, that he did not see me there."

A third witness had *seen* Penn but had not heard his words, and had not seen Mead there at all.

"What say you, Mr. Mead," asked the Recorder, "were you there?"

"It is a maxim in your own law," Mead replied, "that no man is bound to accuse himself."

The riotous attitude of the spectators, drawn by the extraordinary news value of the case, began to reach nuisance proportions. They liked a court wrangle as much as they liked a cockfight, and the verbal duelings in Old Bailey this morning were really worth an admission fee.

"I desire we may come more close to the point," said Penn, "and that silence be commanded in the court."

"*Oyez!* All manner of persons keep silence upon pain of imprisonment. Silence in the court."

Then Penn stated his case: "We confess ourselves to be so far from recanting, or declining to vindicate the assembling of ourselves, to preach, pray, or worship the eternal, holy, just God, that we declare to all the world, that we do believe it to be our indispensable duty, to meet incessantly upon so good an account; nor shall all the powers upon earth be able to divert us from reverencing and adoring our God, who made us."

"You are not here for worshiping God," put in one of the sheriffs, "but for breaking the law. You do yourselves a great deal of wrong in going on in that discourse."

Penn affirmed he had broken no law, and desired to know by what law he was being prosecuted.

"Upon the common law."

"Where is the common law?"

"You must not think that I am able to run up so many years, and over so many adjudged cases, which we call common law, to answer your curiosity," said the Recorder contemptuously.

"This answer I am sure is very short of my question; for if it be common, it should not be so hard to produce."

"Sir," demanded the Recorder, "will you plead to your indictment?"

Penn replied, "Shall I plead to an indictment that hath no foundation in law? If it contain that law you say I have broken, why should you decline to produce that law, since it will be impossible for the jury to determine, or agree to bring in their verdict, who have not the law produced, by which they should measure the truth of this indictment, and the guilt, or contrary, of my fact."

"You are a sawcy fellow; speak to the indictment."

"I say, it is my place to speak to matter of law; I am arraigned a prisoner; my liberty, which is next to life itself, is now concerned; you are many mouths and ears against me, and if I must not be allowed to make the best of my case, it is hard; I say again, unless you show me, and the people, the law you ground your indictment upon, I shall take it for granted, your proceedings are merely arbitrary."

Penn was required once more to plead to the indictment, and again he refused, maintaining that the question before the court was not his guilt but the legality of the indictment.

"Certainly," he told the court, "if the common law be so hard to be understood, it's far from being very common; but if the Lord

Coke in his *Institutes* be of any consideration, he tells us that common law is common right; and that common right is the Great Charter Privileges."

The court labeled him troublesome. He persisted, pointing out that he had asked but one question so far—the question of the common law under which he was being accused. He could ask questions until tomorrow morning, he was assured, and be none the wiser.

"I must plainly tell you," declared Penn, "that if you will deny me the oyer [hearing] of that law, which you suggest I have broken, you do at once deny me an acknowledged right, and evidence to the whole world your resolution to sacrifice the privileges of Englishmen to your sinister and arbitrary designs."

That was stating it too clearly.

"Take him away!" shouted the Recorder.

"Take him away!" echoed the Mayor. "Take him away! Turn him into the bale-dock."

Rude hands seized him and dragged him to the cylindrical enclosure in a corner of the courtroom.

"I am not to be silent in a case wherein I am so much concerned; and not only myself, but many ten thousand families besides," were his last words before they popped him into the tiny cupboard.

Mead remained, and he spoke in the same vein as his fellow, repeating Penn's request for an oyer of the law. The recorder had given that as much answer as he was a mind to. Mead turned and faced the jury.

"You men of the jury, who are my judges, if the Recorder will not tell you what makes a riot, a rout, or an unlawful assembly, Coke, he that once they called Lord Coke, tells us what makes a riot, a rout, and an unlawful assembly. A riot is when three, or more, are met together to beat a man, or to enter forcibly into another man's land, to cut down his grass, his wood, or break down his pales."

The Recorder interrupted, removing his own hat with a mock gesture of deference to Mead, thanking the speaker profusely for explaining the law.

"Thou mayst put on thy hat," said Mead dryly. "I have never a fee for thee now."

"He talks at random," sneered another sheriff.

Mead replied in Latin.

"You deserve to have your tongue cut out," declared the Mayor, who may not have been a sufficient enough scholar to understand. The Recorder added another threat.

"Thou didst promise me," said Mead, "I should have fair liberty to be heard. Why may I not have the privilege of an Englishman?"

The Recorder retorted that he looked upon Mead as an enemy of the laws of England, and with that Mead, too, was dragged away to the bale-dock. The Recorder then proceeded to charge the jury.

"You have heard what the indictment is; it is for preaching to the people, and drawing a tumultous company after them; and Mr. Penn was speaking. If they should not be disturbed, you see they will go on; there are three or four witnesses that have proved this, that he did preach there, that Mr. Mead did allow of it; after this, you have heard by substantial witnesses what is said against them. Now we are upon the matter of fact, which you are to keep and to observe, as what hath been fully sworn, *at your peril*."

Penn poked his nose between the bars of the bale-dock and shouted:

"I appeal to the jury, who are my judges, and this great assembly, whether the proceedings of the court are not most arbitrary, and void of all law, in offering to give the jury their charge in the absence of the prisoners. . . ."

"Why ye are present," observed the Recorder sarcastically. "You do hear. Do you not?"

Penn's tempestuous soul, that so often sweated under the Christian harness of self-restraint, burst its bounds, and in a rage he clambered to the top of the paling and shouted over it:

"No thanks to the court, that command me into the bale-dock; and you of the jury take notice, that I have not been heard, neither can you legally depart the court, before I have been fully heard, having at least ten or twelve material points to offer, in order to invalidate their indictment."

"Pull that fellow down! Pull him down!" the Recorder commanded.

Mead took a turn at shouting, "Are these according to the rights and privileges of Englishmen that we should not be heard, but turned into the bale-dock for making our defense, and the jury to have their charge given them in our absence? I say, these are barbarous and unjust proceedings."

"Take them away into the hole!" said the Recorder, and they were taken away and locked in a "stinking hole" to await the verdict of the jury.

After an hour and a half the jury stood eight to four with no hope of a decision, and the court sent for them. Edward Bushel, one of the recalcitrant four, drew a special rebuke from the Recorder,

"Sir, you are the cause of this disturbance, and manifestly show yourself an abettor of faction; I shall set a mark upon you, sir."

"Mr. Bushel," one of the aldermen added, "I have known you near this fourteen years; you have thrust yourself upon this jury, because you think there is some service for you; I tell you, you deserve to be indicted more than any man that hath been brought to the bar this day."

Strictly speaking the alderman was right. Bushel had caught an infection from the young man on trial, and he was every bit as guilty as Penn of treasuring his free conscience.

After more threats from the court the jury was sent back to its retirement and eventually all twelve filed into their box to give a decision. With a flurry and flourish court reassembled and prisoners were brought out to hear the verdict. The foreman rose in place.

"Look upon the prisoners at the bar. How say you? Is William Penn guilty of the matter whereof he stands indicted in manner and form, or not guilty?"

"Guilty of speaking in Gracious Street," said the foreman.

The pompous faces on that bench must have flushed up scarlet to hear their own instructions flaunted in their faces. They were after Penn's hide!

"Was it not an unlawful assembly?" demanded the Mayor. "You mean he was speaking to a tumult of people there?"

"My lord," replied the foreman, "this was all I had in commission."

Vilifying language was hurled at the men in the jury box; tempers rose; the jurymen stood their ground. They were told they would not be released until they had given a verdict! They *had* given a verdict, they retorted. When they were ordered to go and consider their verdict once more, the jury demanded pen, ink and paper, and the court recessed for half an hour, to reassemble and glower at one another grimly.

"Here is our verdict," said the foreman, handing a piece of paper to the Clerk of the Peace, which stated:

"We the jurors, hereafter named, do find William Penn to be guilty of speaking or preaching to an assembly, met together in Gracious Street, the fourteenth of August last, 1670, and that William Mead is not guilty of the said indictment."

"What?" cried the Mayor. "Will you be led by such a silly fellow as Bushel, an impudent canting fellow?"

"Gentlemen," echoed the Recorder, "you shall not be dismissed, till we have a verdict that the court will accept; and you shall be locked up, without meat, drink, fire and tobacco. You shall not think thus to abuse the court. We will have a verdict by the help of God, or you shall starve for it."

It was no longer Penn who was on trial, but the jury system itself; and Penn became its champion.

"My jury, who are my judges, ought not to be thus menaced; their verdict should be free, and not compelled; the bench ought to wait upon them, but not forestall them. I do desire that justice may be done me, and that the arbitrary resolves of the bench may not be made the measure of my jury's verdict."

"Stop that prating fellow's mouth," said the Recorder, "or put him out of the court."

The Mayor tried to reason with the jury once more about the evidence, and Penn refuted his arguments. But there had to be an end of the unfortunate session; no more could be accomplished by remaining in the courtroom. The jury was returned to its chambers, placed under lock and key, and the prisoners to their jail. Before Penn left the courtroom, he gave one more opinion.

"The agreement of twelve men is a verdict in law, and such a one being given by the jury, I require the Clerk of the Peace to record it, as he will answer it at his peril. And if the jury bring in another verdict contrary to this, I affirm they are perjured men in law. You are Englishmen," he told the twelve, "mind your privilege. Give not away your right."

The jury was detained all night, without "so much as a chamber pot"; and when court reconvened at seven the next morning the foreman again announced the verdict: "William Penn is guilty of speaking in Gracious Street."

"To an unlawful assembly!" the Mayor barked at the twelve.

"No, my lord," spoke up Bushel, "we give no other verdict than what we gave last night. . . . I have done according to my conscience."

"That conscience of yours would cut my throat," was the Mayor's reply, suggesting that he feared the results for his own sake.

Penn tried to separate Mead's destiny from his own, since Mead had been fully acquitted by the jury, but the court would not allow it; they were indicted for a conspiracy, he was told, and it could not be a verdict unless they were both convicted.

"If *not guilty* be no verdict, then you make of the jury and Magna Charta a mere nose of wax," said Penn.

"How! Is *not guilty* no verdict?" demanded Mead.

Of course, there was no satisfactory answer to that question. There was only more wrangling back and forth, more threats directed at the jury.

"It is intolerable that my jury should be thus menaced," said Penn. "Is this according to the fundamental law? Are not they my proper judges by the Great Charter of England? What hope is there of ever having justice done, when juries are threatened, and their verdicts rejected? I am concerned to speak, and grieve to see such arbitrary proceedings. . . ."

"Stop his mouth," shouted the Mayor. "Bring fetters, and stake him to the ground."

"Do your pleasure," said Penn grandiosely. "I matter not your fetters."

Penn had already had his impact upon the twelve jurors; he had already awakened their Englishmen's hearts within them, and the English heart has an enduring civic sense, nurtured gradually through hundreds of generations. Englishmen had wrested Magna Charta from King John in 1215 more than four hundred and fifty years before Penn's trial and thus laid the cornerstone of English liberties, of English law, of English dignity. "To no man will we sell or deny, or delay, right or justice," the Great Charter stated, but the total structure of justice and liberty was still in the building in Penn's lifetime, and he was one of its builders. Slowly the toilsome metamorphosis was taking place; Magna Charta survived annulments, ruthless monarchs, corruption; and all the while the great body of common and constitutional law was being fashioned out of medieval custom, fitted piece by piece to the structure going up around Magna Charta. Juries developed from the ancient remanding of local witnesses to the impaneling of impartial judges of the evidence; courts of justice evolved from royal and ecclesiastical audiences; a Parliament emerged from the sixth- and seventh-century moots or meetings of villagers. Star Chambers and Cabals occurred from time to time to hamper progress, but the building went on. Parliament drew up a Petition of Right for the signature of Charles I; the writ of Habeas Corpus was strengthened and improved under Charles II; the Bill of Rights was accomplished at the accession of William and Mary. Miraculous personalities had already appeared—John Ball, Francis Bacon, Edward Coke—to hasten and refine the building. "You are Englishmen, mind your privilege," Penn had told his jurymen. "Give not away your right."

Again the twelve were detained all night without physical comfort, and at seven next morning they came into court, asking to have their written verdict returned to them.

"That paper was no verdict," said the court, "and there shall be no advantage taken against you by it."

The jury had obviously changed its verdict, and with high hope the clerk asked, "What say you? Is William Penn guilty or not guilty?"

Foreman: "Not guilty."

The court deeply regretted that the twelve jurors had thought to follow their own judgments in the face of the good and wholesome advice given them. Penn demanded his liberty since he had been freed by the jury.

"Oh, no," said the Mayor. "You are in for your fines."

Fines for what? For contempt of court, was the reply. As he was being dragged away to Newgate, Penn cautioned the men on the bench that they were violating the fourteenth and twenty-ninth chapters of the Great Charter of England.

A fine of forty marks a piece was laid upon the twelve jurymen, and when they refused to pay they, too, were carted off to Newgate, there to remain until they paid their fines. Eight of the twelve soon capitulated, paid their fines, and went free; but the other four, Edward Bushel, John Hammond, Charles Milson and John Baily, resolved to become a test case, and they remained in prison. The "phenatique jurymen," Sir Samuel Starling called them. With Bushel in their vanguard they remained in Newgate, retaining counsel to argue their cause. After two months they were able to move the Court of Common Pleas for a writ of Habeas Corpus and were brought before the Common Bench. That court transferred them to the Fleet, while their attorneys argued on. At last Common Pleas granted bail and the four were at liberty, but their case hung fire for about a year. The case became a "business of great consequence to His Majesty's Government"; it was argued many times before the justices, until at last the justices rendered a unanimous verdict: that the Penn jury had been illegally fined and imprisoned. In their opinion *a jury could not be punished for its verdict.* Lord Chief Justice Sir John Vaughan wrote the opinion:

"I conclude, therefore, that this return, charging the prisoners to have acquitted Penn and Mead against full and manifest evidence first, and next without saying that they did know and believe that evidence to be full and manifest against the indicted persons, is no cause of fine or imprisonment. And by the way I must here note, that the verdict of a jury and evidence of a witness, are very different things in the truth and falsehood of them. A witness swears but to what he hath heard or seen, generally or more largely to what hath fallen under his senses: but a juryman swears to what he can infer and conclude from the testimony of such witnesses, by the act and force of his understanding, to be the fact inquired after; which differs nothing in the reason, though much in the punishment, from what a judge out of various cases considered by him infers to be the law in the question before him. . . . A man cannot see by another's eye, nor hear by another's ear; no more can a man conclude or infer the thing to be resolved by another's understanding or reasoning. . . . It is absurd, a jury should be fined by the judge for going against their evidence, when he who fineth knoweth not what it is. . . ."

Only three years earlier a case tried before Lord Chief Justice Keeling, in which the justice had imposed restraints upon the jury, had been appealed to the House of Commons. The House had resolved that "the precedents and practice of fining or imprisoning jurors for verdicts is illegal." With Penn's further vindication of the free jury system another important stone had been added to the centuries-long process of building civil liberties.

When William Penn passed under the iron-spiked gate of Newgate Prison, he had no idea whether he would ever see Wanstead or his father again. Newgate could be his last resting place; it had never lengthened anyone's life. The lurid and revolting conditions inside had undergone a partial cleansing four years earlier when the fire damaged a portion of it, but the old vices were still there. Crowding and filth and jail fever, hysteria, hopelessness, insanity, drunkenness and prostitution, still stalked the corridors.

"Dear Father," Penn wrote from Newgate at the conclusion of the trial. "Because I cannot come, I write. These are to let thee know that this morning about seven we were remanded to the sessions. The jury, after two nights and two days being locked up, came down and offered their former verdict, but that being refused as not so positive, they explained themselves in answering, not guilty, upon which the bench were amazed, and the whole court so satisfied, that they made a kind of hymn, but that the Mayor, Recorder, etc. might add to their malice, they fined us to the number of about twelve of us, for not pulling off our hats, and kept us prisoners for the money. An injurious trifle which will blow over, or we shall bring it to the common pleas, because it was against law, and not by a jury sessed. . . ." He described in detail the treatment the jury had received and concluded with a hopeful note: "Their verdict is accepted for us [acquittal], because they did not dare deny it. . . . I am, dear Father, thy obedient son, Willian Penn."

His father was bound to worry, and worry would aggravate his illness; so on the second day in Newgate Penn wrote again.

DEAR FATHER:

I desire thee not to be troubled at my present confinement; I could scarce suffer on a better account, nor by a worse hand, and the will of God be done. It is more grievous and uneasy to me that thou shouldst be so heavily exercised, God Almighty knows, than any living worldly concernment. . . . I intreat thee not to purchase my liberty. . . .

Sir William knew he was dying, and he wanted his son with him in his last hours; and so, under pressure of his own illness, he paid the fines for his son and for Mead, and the two men were released from Newgate. The four jurymen remained to their permanent glory.

William Penn came home to a wasted, bedridden man, a man within whom an amazing tolerance had been awakened.

"Son William, I am weary of the world; I would not live over my days again, if I could command them with a wish; for the snares of life are greater than the fears of death. This troubles me, that I have offended a gracious God, that has followed me to this day. O have a care of sin! that is the sting both of life and death."

Was the father teaching the son? Or had the son ultimately taught the father?

"Let nothing in this world tempt you to wrong your conscience; I charge you, do nothing against your conscience; so will you keep peace at home, which will be a feast to you in a day of trouble. Whatever you design to do, lay it justly, and time it seasonably; for that gives security and dispatch. Lastly, be not troubled at disappointments; for if they may be recovered, do it; if they can't, trouble is vain."

William Penn had returned home on the ninth of September, and his father sank rapidly during the week that followed; but the dying man was able to do one more thing for his son, make one more real effort to protect him. Sir William wrote to the King. Both the King and the Duke of York sent their profound solicitude and their promise to continue their favor to Sir William's son.

Growing at last delirious, Sir William began to succumb to the pressures that secret high politics had exerted upon him for so many years. "Woe to thee, O England!" he cried out at one time.

"God will judge thee, O England!" None knew better than he how "dissolute and profane" men in high places could be and what terrible consequences to mankind their profanity could have. Recovering his clarity at the very end he spoke once more to the man attending him, "Son William, if you and your friends keep to your plain way of preaching, and keep to your plain way of living, you will make an end of the priests to the end of the world. Bury me by my mother. Live all in love. Shun all manner of evil. And I pray God to bless you all; and He will bless you."

Sir William died on September 16, 1670, and in accord with his wishes his body was carried back to the port city of Bristol and laid in the churchyard of St. Mary Redcliffe.

His last will and testament was dated only the previous January, suggesting that he had been a long time forgetting the threat he had made to his son to "dispose of his estates to them that pleased him better." He could not, however, under the prevailing law of primogeniture, have left his lands to any but his elder son, but Sir William had accumulated considerable cash and chattels. An inventory values his chattels at more than £732, his plate alone at £240. To his wife Margaret he left three hundred pounds sterling and all his jewels and the use and occupancy during her life of his plate, household stuff, coaches and horses. Lady Penn continued to live in the Wanstead house for the rest of her life, apparently at her son's consent. To his son Richard went four thousand pounds sterling, a diamond ring and all his swords, guns and pistols. His elder son would not have wanted the weapons of war. To his daughter, Margaret, went one hundred pounds sterling. There were smaller bequests to other relatives: among them his nephews James Bradshaw and William Markham; William Penn, son of Sir William's brother George; and grandchildren. To William Penn went all the rest and residue together with a very sentimental gift—the gold chain and medal that had once been bestowed upon him by Cromwell. William Penn was sole executor, and Sir William Coventry was to act as mediator in the event of any difference among the heirs.

Sir William was no more. The line had passed on, and his heir, who had stepped into the responsibilities of estate and station, was no longer the "son of Sir William"; he was William Penn.

No freeman shall be taken or imprisoned, or disseised, or outlawed, or banished, or anyways destroyed; nor will we pass upon him, or commit him to prison, unless by the legal judgment of his peers, or by the law of the land.——*Magna Charta*

8. Newgate After All

PENN LEFT his mother and Wanstead for a while, left the scene of poignant memories—canings, quarrels, misunderstandings, estrangements, reconciliations—and rode in the direction in which he was drawn, to Buckinghamshire and Amersham and Guli Springett. Besse tells us he took up his residence for a while in the village of Penn, only about five miles from Amersham, and it is perfectly possible, since a family of Penns lived there who William Penn claimed were his relatives, although there is no genealogical record to prove it. Penn went to Buckinghamshire seeking peace after the strains of trial and imprisonment and family grief, peace in the gentle affection of the Springetts and Peningtons, healing and replenishment in the quiet, rural countryside. During this respite he either wrote or completed *A Seasonable Caveat Against Popery*; its covering letter is datelined Penn, Buckinghamshire, January 23, 1671.

His healthy energies bounded back, and in a very short time he began to cast about him in Quaker affairs in Bucks. A Baptist preacher named Ives, in his pulpit in near-by High Wycombe, was thundering abuses against the Friends. The universality of the divine Light was false, declared Ives, and drew Penn to him like a magnet. Ives must be answered just as Vincent and others had been answered, at whatever cost, and Penn requested an opportunity to debate him publicly. The debate was agreed upon, to be held at West Wycombe, and Ives sent his brother Jeremy Ives to act as proxy. Thomas Ellwood went with Penn to West Wycombe, but he was dubious about the wisdom of it all: "I have rarely found the advantage equivalent to the trouble and danger arising from those contests."

A religious debate always drew a crowd, if for no other reason than that it was a cheap form of entertainment. Jeremy Ives, according to debating courtesies of the times, was to speak first, and he arrived with a "stock of syllogisms ready framed for his purpose." After a lengthy discourse he played a trick on his opponent; he left the platform immediately at the end of his talk, thinking to break up and disperse the meeting. But Penn's own reputation was well tinged with notoriety by that time, and in the eyes of many non-Quakers he was a genuine martyr for liberty of conscience; so the vast majority of the audience remained to hear him. In fact, the audience was so attentive to Penn, and he spoke so well and so convincingly, that Ives came back in an "angry railing manner." He was too late. William Penn had won the day, and Thomas Ellwood could lay aside his misgivings and report to Isaac Penington: "Truth hath prevailed, the enemies did fly; we are in safety; praise to God on high."

Penn began to travel about the countryside in a wider sphere, and November found him at Oxford investigating the sufferings of Friends there. The Conventicle Act was still operating in full strength, and the university was encouraging the scholars in their old sport of Quaker-baiting. Penn the Oxonian was thoroughly familiar with their raucous activities and their adolescent cruelties. He addressed a letter to the Vice Chancellor:

> Shall the multiplied oppressions which thou continuest to heap upon innocent English people, for their peaceable religious meetings, pass unregarded by the Eternal God? Dost thou think to escape his fierce wrath and dreadful vengeance, for thy ungodly and illegal persecution of his poor children; I tell thee, No. Better were it for thee, thou hadst never been born. Poor mushroom, wilt thou war against the Lord, and lift up thyself in battle against the Almighty? . . .

I find no record of a reply received from the Vice Chancellor, nor of any immediate results from Penn's letter; but it must have done Penn's soul some good to call his subject a mushroom.

The disgruntled authorities who had lost their quarry at Old Bailey were watching Penn, waiting for him to make another mistake. And he very soon did. He was in London on the fifth of February, and under their very noses he attended a meeting in Wheeler Street near Spitalfields. Spies and informers must have been at every hand, for after he had sat down in the meeting for worship a sergeant and some soldiers came and "planted themselves in the door," not interfering with the meeting itself nor with anyone else who spoke. They simply stood and waited. Word would have traveled through the meeting with lightning speed that there were soldiers present; in a matter of seconds Penn knew they were there even though he may have been sitting with his back to the door. Again, the minister, the leader, the tester of laws, the man who was "above the fear of man," arose, climbed upon the platform, turned a love-laden face to the assembled worshipers and began to preach. They must not be dismayed at the rattling of weapons of war, he told them, nor must they consider giving up their meetings to worship the Lord. Yes, he knew of their bitter trials from all powers, but God would continue to strengthen and protect them. They must endure in patience the wrath of men and resort to no visible means of relief or defense, and they must shun all plots and conspiracies.

The intruders allowed him to speak for about half an hour, and then the soldiers clattered forward, pulled Penn from the platform, and led him out into the street where a constable and his assistants were waiting. Penn was taken to the Tower and allowed to cool his heels there for three hours until Sir John Robinson, the Lieutenant of the Tower, could arrive to question him. On the way to the Tower the soldiers who escorted Penn were friendly and courteous and even apologetic at the meanness of their calling. It was grossly unfair that innocent assemblies should be disturbed, they grumbled. When the Lieutenant of the Tower and his associates—Sir Samuel Starling, Sir John Sheldon, Lieutenant-Colonel Josiah Ricroft among them—arrived, it was apparent that they had "taken their cups as well as their council together." They dispatched an officer and a file of musketeers to escort the pacific Quaker into their presence, and gave orders that in the name of prudence no unnecessary witnesses be admitted to the hearing. Besse describes them as men "afraid of their work however well they wished it."

Once again William Penn had to stand before the Lord Mayor while the Tower Lieutenant put him through a long, tedious, repetitious questioning, beginning with the insistence that they did not know him and that he must state his name. When they moved to swear in witnesses, Penn stopped them and admitted freely that he had been speaking to an assembly of people at Wheeler Street. The witnesses were sworn in anyway.

"Mr. Penn," said Robinson, "you know the law better than I can tell you, and you know that these things are contrary to the law."

"If thou believest me to be better known in the law than thyself, hear me, for I know no law I have transgressed. All laws are to be considered strictly and literally, or more explanatorily and lenitively. In the first sense, the execution of many laws may be *extrema injuria,* the greatest wrong; in the latter, wisdom and moderation. I would have thee make that part thy choice. Now whereas I am probably to be tried by the law, Act against Conventicles, I conceive it doth not reach me."

Then Robinson could lick his chops and inform the prisoner that he was not being tried under the Conventicle Act this time, but under the Oxford Act of Six Months. Robinson was referring to the Oxford Five Mile Act which forbade non-conforming clergymen to come within five miles of any city or town where they had ever preached in any conventicle or had ever been a parson, vicar or lecturer. The penalty for violating the Act was six months in prison without bail or mainprise.

"That of all laws can't concern me," declared Penn, "for first, I was never in Orders, neither episcopally nor classically, and one of them is intended by the preamble of the Act."

No, no! the court protested. The Oxford Act applied to anyone who spoke in unlawful assemblies, and that Penn certainly had done. Penn refuted the contention and pointed out again that he had never been ordained and further that the Act did not define an unlawful assembly. But other acts did! They could not borrow a piece of law here and a piece there, Penn told them.

There was more than one way to catch a Quaker, so Robinson required Penn to take an oath. Penn was to swear that it was unlawful to take up arms against the King. What need had he to take such an oath, he asked, when it was his faith not to do so? They had a case against him in his refusal to take an oath, but the dickering went on since it amused the men on the bench, and soon it deteriorated into personal insult.

"You are as bad as other men," Penn was told.

"I make this bold challenge to all men, women and children upon earth justly to accuse me, with ever having seen me drunk, heard me swear, utter a curse, or speak one obscene word (much less that I ever made it my practice). . . . Thy words shall be thy burden, and I trample thy slander as dirt under my feet," was his reply.

"Well, Mr. Penn, I have no ill will toward you; your father was my friend, and I have a great deal of kindness for you," said Robinson.

"But thou hast an ill way of expressing it. You are grown too high to consider the plea of those you call your forefathers for liberty of conscience. . . ."

The hearing had run itself into the ground, but they could not let him go; so they renewed their accusations that Friends stirred up the people to sedition, that they preached sedition, that they meddled with the government.

"We have the unhappiness to be misrepresented," sighed Penn. ". . . As for the King, I make this offer, that if any living can make it appear, directly or indirectly, from the time I have been called a Quaker . . . I have contrived or acted anything injurious to his person, or the English government, I shall submit my person to your utmost cruelties. . . ."

"Well," replied Robinson, seeming more and more like the man afraid of his work, "I must send you to Newgate for six months; and when they are expired you will come out."

"Is that all?" Penn asked in surprise. "Thou well knowest a larger imprisonment has not daunted me. . . ."

They knew that; they knew they hadn't accomplished anything; that Penn would soon be out of prison and back preaching in meetings.

Robinson requested a corporal and a file of musketeers to accompany the prisoner.

"No, no," replied William Penn. "Send thy lackey; I know the way to Newgate."

There were to be six months from the fifth of February, 1671, the date on the mittimus issued by Robinson and Ricroft, into the heat of July; six months with no sight of the Chilterns and no passing of pleasant hours with Guli Springett; six months of health-destroying foul air. Nor would this imprisonment even afford the withdrawal that the Tower had done, for Newgate was crowded with prisoners. There were some accommodations available—separate quarters, beer—for those who wished to and could pay, but when Penn was apprised of the extortionist rates he would have to pay for a modicum of privacy, he rejected the opportunity and elected instead to dwell in the loathsome common quarters. There were plenty of Quakers already there to bear him company, mingled in with every variety of felon, the poorest and the meanest who could not afford to purchase better. During the day the prisoners were permitted to walk in the hall which was on the second floor and above the gate, and there were other rooms where they could move about and work. At night, though, they were all herded into one room—a huge, circular affair with a great oaken pillar in the center that supported the chapel floor just above it. Prisoners strung their hammocks from the central pillar to the wall, in three tiers because there were so many of them, and those in the top tier had of necessity to climb up to bed first. The sick and dying lay on pallets scattered about the floor.

William Penn's animal energy, his boundless ardor, his absolute conviction, his unshakable willingness to obey in all things his "lamp of the Lord," his Light, made it possible for him to make a spontaneous adjustment to his suddenly changed situation and to make even the evil wilderness of Newgate flower into literature. He knew how long his sentence would be this time—six months—and six months would not last forever. Not a precious moment of it must be wasted.

Two days after his commitment he had completed the tract begun in Ireland, *The Great Case of Liberty of Conscience*, and written its covering letter "To the Supreme Authority of England," signing it, "From a Prisoner for Conscience-Sake, W.P."

"By liberty of conscience," says the tract, "we understand not only a mere liberty of the mind, in believing or disbelieving this or that principle or doctrine, but the exercise of ourselves in a visible way of worship." Penn sees long range dangers in persecution; it is an evil which will "overthrow the whole Christian religion," since the persecutor in destroying the freedom of others ultimately destroys all liberty including his own. "We are pleading only for such a liberty of conscience as preserves the nation in peace, trade and commerce; and would not exempt any man or party of men from not keeping those excellent laws that tend to sober, just and industrious living." Again he dips into his scholarly sources—Cato, Livy, Tacitus, Chaucer, Wycliffe, Luther, Grotius and others—and draws examples from contemporary governments—the present affairs of Germany show plainly that toleration is the preservation of their states; the same in France where the discreet toleration of Richelieu and Mazarin saved the kingdom from being ruined by the Spaniards; and look at the wealth, trade and power of Holland, which she chiefly owes to her indulgence in matters of faith and worship. "It was the saying of a person once, too great to be named now, that liberty of conscience is every man's natural right, and he who is deprived of it, is a slave in the midst of the greatest liberty."

Penn wrote continuously and voluminously in Newgate, turning out three long tracts that we know of, as well as several epistles. Through them all runs the single theme of liberty of conscience.

Truth Rescued From Imposture, or A Brief Reply to a Mere Rhapsody of Lies, Folly and Slander. Written by a Professed Enemy to Oppression, W.P., is dated Newgate, Twelfth Month [February], 1671. Thomas Rudyard, who was in Newgate at that time, wrote a long Appendix to it, and Penn himself wrote a postscript dated March, 1671. It is a reply to a tract written by "S.S." that attacked the trial of Penn and Mead, as well as the reputation of the late Sir William Penn. In it Penn has another opportunity to defend the authority of juries and the fundamental laws of England. In the absence of anything resembling objective news coverage, the only reviews of his case that were circulated were those written by himself and his associates or his enemies. So when the tract by "S.S." appeared, it was of the utmost importance that it, like every other misrepresentation of the Friends, be refuted in detail and in kind. An exact narrative of the trial had been told in *The People's Ancient and Just Liberties Asserted, in the Trial of William Penn and William Mead, at the Sessions Held at the Old Bailey in London, the First, Third, Fourth and Fifth of September, 1670, Against the Most Arbitrary Procedure of That Court.*

The third Newgate tract was *A Serious Apology for the Principles and Practices of the People Called Quakers.* Part I, dated Kingston-upon-Thames, First Day of Second Month [April] 1671, had been written by George Whitehead. William Penn wrote Part II, dated Newgate in London, the twenty-ninth of the Fourth Month [June], 1671. It was addressed particularly to the King's Lieutenant General and General Governor and Council of Ireland.

Penn also wrote a postscript to his earlier *Truth Exalted,* and a comparison of the language of the tract written in 1668 and its postscript written in 1671 shows that his tone, style and thinking had vastly matured in three short years.

There was a free flow of news in and out of Newgate, and when Friends within its confines learned that the Conventicle Act was to be stiffened with amendments they gathered together with William Penn in April to compose a letter to the "High Court of Parliament" expressing their protest.

Within the prison the turnkey and the keeper abused and exploited them as long as they could conscientiously bear it, until in May, the fourth month of Penn's incarceration, they addressed a letter to the Sheriffs of London giving details of conditions in the "common stinking jail."

At another time Penn engaged in a strenuous correspondence with a Roman Catholic writer named R. Lany.

But through all the foul, crowded conditions, the concern for Friends' sufferings inside and outside of Newgate, the hours spent in writing tracts, Penn's heart was filled with a love theme. In an old letter book there is a much corrected and scratched-over copy of a short essay on *Right Marriage As It Stands in the Light and Council of the Lord God,* and in the same letter book there are five stanzas of doggerel, *An Holy Triumph,* which begin:

Your jails and prisons we defy
By bonds we'll keep our liberty
Nor shall your racks, or torments make
Us, e're our meetings to forsake . . .

and are annotated, "Sent to dear G. M. Springett, my dear wife since, writ in Newgate, 1671."

The racking six months reached their inevitable end, and some time during the last week in July or the first week in August William Penn went free. George Fox's *Journal* records him almost immediately afterward in the company of Guli Springett.

My true love hath my heart, and I have his,
By just exchange one for another given:
I hold his dear, and mine he cannot miss,
There never was a better bargain driven.
—Sir Philip Sidney, *The Bargain*

9. The Love of My Youth

William Penn and Guli Springett and her mother, Mary Penington, accompanied George and Margaret Fox to Gravesend on the twelfth of August, traveling down the Thames in a barge. Isaac Penington was still in Reading jail, but in spite of his absence it was a happy, tender time. Margaret Fell Fox had just a few weeks before been released from Lancaster prison and had come up to London to be reunited with her husband, who himself had just recovered from a serious illness contracted on a trip through Sussex and Kent. Guli Springett and William Penn were experiencing their own shyer kind of reunion. And it was an adventuresome moment, too; for George Fox had felt called to visit America, and they and a few more had gathered to see him off.

Evangelizing Friends had gone early to the New World; the first had been two women, Mary Fisher and Ann Austin, in 1655 who landed and preached first in Barbados and then had invaded the tight-lipped Congregationalist strongholds of New England. When they reached the stony heart of Boston, where they were anticipated, they were removed from the ship, incarcerated, their books publicly burned; then they were stripped naked and examined for signs of witchcraft. After several weeks of indignity they were placed upon an outgoing vessel and sent back to Barbados. News of such an event, of course, merely sent up the signals to Quakers that Boston needed them. And Boston did! But even before the signals could be noted, eight more Friends were sailing into Boston Harbor, and a year after the visit of Mary Fisher and Ann Austin the theological attack on Boston was in full swing, martyrs suffering through fines, imprisonments, whippings, stocks. Flourishing meetings in Barbados and other Caribbean islands joined with England in supplying personnel to replace the fallen. Tolerationist Rhode Island was more cordial; there meetings were established and there persecuted Friends whipped out of Massachusetts at the cart's tail could find asylum.

Friends felt called to all of the English colonies. Penn's mentor, Josiah Coale, had traveled with Thomas Thurston on foot through raw wilderness from Virginia to New England in 1658. New York and Long Island, particularly Flushing, already had Quaker settlers when Coale and Thurston passed through. Coale and Thurston made the first recorded Friends' missionary visit to Virginia, and during their six months' stay established Quakerism permanently. They went on to Maryland where Elizabeth Harris had preceded them with the message, and added their efforts to hers. John Burnyeat went to America some seven years after Coale's first trip, and during the summer of 1665, while the plague raged in London and William Penn suspended his studies in Lincoln's Inn, worked tirelessly in Maryland and Virginia to establish the Society of Friends there and help it to acquire the dignity it needed to command officialdom's respect. The powerful "seed" sprouted all up and down the American coast. The first yearly meeting in America had been established in Newport as early as 1661. The second was organized in Maryland, the Baltimore Yearly Meeting, in 1672; and George Fox arrived in time to attend its first sessions.

There was a constant flow among Friends of conscientiously detailed epistles exchanged between individuals and between meetings. Their contents were shared and read aloud wherever Friends gathered. It is impossible to know just when William Penn first became interested in America, since the idea may have been germinating in his system long before he became aware of it on any conscious level. He had been attending Friends' meetings almost constantly since his convincement in 1667 and had had a multitude of opportunities to hear news-laden epistles from the New World. So far as we know he had not expressed any particular interest in America up to the time that he and Guli gathered at Gravesend to see George Fox off on his trip.

The ketch, *Industry,* lay about three miles below Gravesend, and Margaret Fox and a few more went down in the barge and spent the night aboard ship with Fox. William Penn and most of those who accompanied him lodged the night at Gravesend. Margaret Fox sailed with her husband as far as Deal and parted company with him there. Penn and Guli must have returned to London from Gravesend. Theirs had to be a parting too, and soon, for William Penn left that same month on a traveling minister's mission to the Continent.

Penn traveled with Thomas Rudyard who had been in Newgate with him, and he was joined by Benjamin Furly, an English Quaker merchant living in Rotterdam. Furly had made the Dutch city his permanent home at least a decade earlier, and it became a cultural mecca for such men as Leclerc, Limborch, Algernon Sydney and John Locke. Furly was a brilliant scholar and a linguist, and possessed a library of nearly four thousand volumes, largely theological. He gave Holland's religious community an aggressive leadership, and his merchant's prosperity allowed him ample facilities for entertaining guests under his roof. Furly, some nine years older than Penn, tall, his sharp features a little fierce, his eyes burning with righteous concern, presided over his ever expanding sphere of influence dressed in indifferent, often worn-out, clothing, a black velvet ribbon tied around his head to keep his hair out of his eyes. He had come originally from the English village of Colchester, but trade brought him to Holland, and there he became the Dutch translator, pamphleteer and publisher of the Quaker movement. Penn and Rudyard must have repaired immediately to Furly's house, since they could not have gone far without his services as an interpreter.

From Rotterdam the three traveled up to Amsterdam, a distance of fifty-odd miles, depending upon how many digressions they made along the way to visit some of Holland's multitudinous villages. The shockable and emotional young Penn looked about him at a Holland at the peak of her middle class prosperity, a land where vigorously applied industry, frugality, integrity sharpened by shrewdness had built lovely cities full of wealthy homes and created a merchant navy to market her wares throughout the world. In the seventeenth century Holland was just beginning her large-scale land reclamations due to the invention of the windmill with the revolving top. She had been reclaiming small amounts of land since the twelfth century, but now really vast and ambitious projects were in her future. Creaturely, creaturely! was all Penn could think of the wealth that he saw. Worldly and wanton! Well, other Englishmen in those same hours were looking with as intense distaste at Holland's prosperity, but with dissimilar motives. Charles II and Louis XIV were secretly planning to attack the Low Countries and partition them, and Holland was teetering on the brink of her third war with envious competitors when Penn, in the role of Old Testament prophet, came through the land crying her doom. On the ninth of September, 1671, in the walled city of Amsterdam, having looked upon her busy, tree-lined canals, her stately brick houses with their marble floors and tile decorations, Penn addressed an epistle to the Netherlands, which Furly translated into Dutch: "A trumpet sounded in the ears of the inhabitants of both the High and Low Dutch nation of what state, principality, quality, sex, sect and soever. . . ." As Isaiah had once cried, "Give ear unto the law of our God, ye people of Gomorrah!" so Penn's letter proclaimed an awful destiny for the Dutch: "O ye inhabitants of these countries, the spirit of the Lord is upon me, and by the same I am necessitated to proclaim the great and dreadful Day of the Lord which is already come unto many and hasteneth to come upon all nations, as a thief in the night . . . my soul laments over your condition. . . ."

But Holland was not nearly as godless as Penn's alarming language would suggest. Martin Luther had made a deep impression on Holland, and so had Calvin. A multitude of lesser religious teachers had been as well received. Ever since she had thrown off the yoke of Spanish colonialism, Holland had furnished a refuge for persecuted minorities and independently thinking individuals from other countries.

Very little is known, now, of Penn's first journey through the Netherlands and Germany, except for fragments that can be gleaned from his letters and one or two other sources. In his diary of a later journey through these countries he describes his meeting in 1671 with the physician, Dr. Johann Wilhelm Haesbert, and his wife, at Emden. Penn and Furly must have passed through the northern part of Holland and crossed the Dollart Bay from Delfzijl to Emden. Emden was completely Dutch in appearance at that time, with dikes, windmills and canals; its architecture was similar, and Dutch was the prevailing language. The city had taken the Reformation to her heart early and had become a refuge for Protestant exiles from other lands—rich, appetizing fare for sectarian evangelists.

There were no Quakers in Emden until Penn's arrival, and his meeting with the remarkable Haesbert is credited with bringing the Emden Meeting into being. Haesbert and his wife were Mennonites, already deeply religious folk and sensitive to a spiritual message. Within three months after Penn's visit they had become not only Friends but leaders of a new group of Friends who met in the Haesbert home.

The minutes of the Monthly Meeting at Friedrichstadt for 1671 state: "It has been among Friends to meet on the first day of the week, also to meet in the afternoon, hereto advised and encouraged by William Penn, who considered it to be right that Friends should meet more with each other." Friedrichstadt is about twenty-five miles southwest of the city of Schleswig, on the Eider River which flows into the North Sea. I do not know whether Penn visited Friedrichstadt before or after going to Herford, but I think he would have found a watery route more comfortable than an overland route, and that would place his visit up into the Danish peninsula between his visits to Emden and Herford. From Friedrichstadt he would then have traveled southward into Germany.

A keen concern was drawing him toward Herford. He was planning to call on a religious sect there known as the Labadists and try to draw them into the Quaker community.

Jean de Labadie enjoyed an international notoriety, partly deserved and partly exaggerated to luridness by excitable observers. He had begun his checkered career as a Jesuit, but at about the age of twenty-nine he left the order of St. Ignatius and went forth to preach. He was a gifted preacher, blessed with a spellbinding eloquence, but he was also an egotist who drew attention to himself by taking shocking departures from prescribed doctrine. By the time he was forty he had left the Church of Rome and joined the Reformation movement, but he still kicked against the traces and caused such disturbances wherever he went that his life is a series of flights from one pastorate to another: from Amiens, to Montauban, to Geneva, where accusations of immorality and licentiousness finally forced him out. By that time he had his own community of followers gathered around him, and he declared he strove only for innocence in human relations and wanted men and women to live equally together. But the gossips declared, "They practice community of property and community of women." His next parish was the Walloon Church in Middelburg in southern Holland, but even the tolerant Dutch who bent over backward to grant liberty of conscience to a multitude of sects found his doctrines shocking, and after three years he was dismissed from Middelburg. He wandered from one Dutch town to another, and his devoted flock wandered with him. When the frightening rumor began to circulate that he was still secretly a Jesuit, the Dutch who remembered the bitter war they had fought to throw off the Catholic-Spanish yoke raised an outcry against him. At that point, one of his prominent followers, Anna Maria von Schürman, wrote to her friend of many years' standing, the Palatine Princess Elizabeth, now Abbess of the Protestant Convent of Herford, and asked her to give shelter to the Labadists. The Abbess responded with a gracious invitation.

The Labadists talked of an inner light as a primary expression of the divine being in the human soul, and of other mystical concepts. Those who dwelt in De Labadie's colony renounced worldly goods and dressed simply without benefit of adornment. Such doctrine drew the Quakers to them like moths to a flame. Robert Barclay and George Keith are thought to have visited the Labadist colony in Herford the year before Penn's journey. If so, the Quakers must have pulled their cloaks tightly around themselves in horror to discover that the inner light of the Labadists sometimes made them so ecstatically happy that they burst into dancing and exuberant revelry.

Slow and toilsome and wearing, in wagon or on horseback, was the overland route that Penn, Furly and Rudyard took to Herford. During the summer in the North Sea countries, rainfall is heavy and frequent, and they were a weary and bedraggled party of missionaries when they arrived at their goal. In Penn's own words, "I and my companions had put ourselves to the trouble and expense . . . of the extraordinary journey, at least, from the common road, and subjected ourselves" to inconveniences. It was late at night when the men ended their forced march to Herford, but they did not waste a minute. As soon as they reached the inn, they dispatched a message to the Labadist colony asking at what hour they assembled next day, for—lucky mortals—they were to hear the Quaker message. The reply came back from Jean de Labadie himself, who advised the travelers of the customary hour of morning assembly and then slyly scheduled it an hour earlier. Penn and his companions, "poor, simple men, filled with zeal for God," and with love for the souls of the Labadists, rain pelting their heads, arrived on the scene as the meeting was dispersing. Penn showed distinct signs of bitterness at that slight: "I can truly say, Satan, that old serpent, hindered, yea, instead of receiving us as Angels of God." And the slight was extended, for De Labadie led the visitors in the pouring rain into an open garden instead of offering them so much as a shred of physical comfort.

De Labadie's attitude is perfectly understandable. He was then fighting for his group's existence against the whole community of Herford, and allowing an eloquent zealot like Penn to speak to them could have caused dissension within the ranks. When Penn reached Herford, the hostility of the town toward the Labadists had reached the point of hysteria. Town tradesmen would not sell food to them; unruly crowds drove them away from the public well; when they walked abroad they could expect to be hooted at and pelted with mud. Elizabeth asked the Elector of Brandenburg for troops to keep order in the town and to protect herself, since community wrath was also directed against her for harboring the colony. Stubbornly Elizabeth stood her ground while the Elector of Brandenburg deliberated over the situation. The Town Council of Herford lost patience and applied to the Stadtholder of Cleves, then to the Imperial Tribunal of Spires. The latter group ordered Elizabeth to expel the Labadists; she merely shrugged her shoulders at their instructions.

It seemed like a supreme piece of bad judgment on the part of the Abbess to grant refuge to such an ill-reputed group and risk the peace and safety of Herford, but her attitude was understandable, too. Her entire life, until she became Abbess at the age of forty-eight, had been insecure, filled with trials of political exile, haunted by a loneliness relieved only infrequently by such extraordinary intellectual friendships as that with Descartes. Elizabeth understood the refugee's anguish. Her father, Elector Palatine Frederick V (The Winter King), had lost the Bohemian Crown when she was one, and she had to live with her grandmother at Heidelburg Castle after her parents fled to Holland. She spent some of her growing years in Holland where she had the protection of the House of Orange, since William of Orange had been her great-grandfather. She was also a Stuart. Her mother had been a sister of Charles I and daughter of James I; Prince Rupert was Elizabeth's brother. Elizabeth was a brilliant woman who derived happiness from her studies and found her deepest friendships with her teachers of theology and philosophy. At the death of Charles I, it was Descartes who wrote her a long letter of comfort. Descartes' death in 1650 had robbed her of a source of strength. Elizabeth was gifted in many fields—languages, painting, engraving, wood carving, tapestries. She had not been Abbess of Herford very long when the appeal from Anna von Schürman to give asylum to the Labadists reached her. Elizabeth's studies in philosophy and theology and her loneliness had long since led her into the realms of mysticism and spiritual seeking, and when De Labadie entered her life he arrived in time to fill a deep need. His "inner light" that was "the proof of God" lighted a faith within Elizabeth and brought her spiritual seeking into focus, and no doubt rendered her blind to De Labadie's shortcomings.

It was equally understandable that William Penn, after being so grossly rejected by De Labadie, should make his next appeal to the Palatine Princess Elizabeth, and even more understandable that she should receive him graciously. This was a friend of the Stuarts come knocking at her door, and a Quaker as well. She had already met the itinerant Quakers William Caton and William Ames when they traveled through Germany nine years earlier. Penn's visit to Elizabeth resulted in a deep friendship between the two and in winning her friendship for the Quakers until her death nine years later. It did not alter her faith in the Labadists, and Penn had to leave Herford as troubled in his heart about them as when he had arrived. But before he left Herford, early in October, he addressed a long letter to the Labadists pointing out to them the errors of their ways.

Penn landed back in Harwich on October 24, 1671, as an informer gleefully and dutifully wrote to Whitehall on the twenty-sixth: "On Tuesday out of one of our packet boats from Holland arrived here Sir William Penn's eldest son, the great opinionist. He went presently and associated himself with the Quakers of this town. I can hear of no more."

In spite of a deep desire to return to Guli, Penn remained in Suffolk for at least a month. To that magnificent first generation of Friends the cause always came ahead of themselves, and had Penn felt any indecision between his desire to see Guli and his desire to serve where he was, Guli would have bidden him remain with his responsibilities in Suffolk County. In Cambridgeshire, just west of Suffolk, was the administrative county known as Isle of Ely where Friends were enduring what Penn described as "lamentable sufferings" from the "illegal and inhuman practices" of the local justice.

News flowed to him from his English Quaker world, news of its continuing impoverishment under the Conventicle Act. They were short of leadership at that point. Fox, Edmundson and Stubbs were in America; Whitehead, who had just recovered from a debilitating illness, was carrying on almost singlehanded the fight to ease the sufferings of the Friends' meeting in Southwark. Margaret Fell Fox was in the north of England. When Penn learned that Friends in London, in the absence of their wisest minds, were going to seek legal redress, to end their sufferings for refusing to swear, by cunningly finding a loophole in the law, he became alarmed. They had lost their perspective, he realized; they had not thought through their problem carefully. "My dearly beloved Friends and Brethren," he wrote from Suffolk on the fifteenth of November. . . . "I have understood by several good Friends that there are some endeavors . . . to commence a suit with the King for the delivery of our dear Friends that are sufferers upon the oaths by formal course of law. I confess I was not a little startled at it." Did they not realize that if they went through formal court procedures they would have to accept the results? The device they intended to use, he had learned, was that the required oath was worded in the name of King James, now dead, and therefore not legal. "The King never dies in their law," he warned the misguided Friends, and should Quakers win this case—and they could if the courts agreed to substitute the present King's name—they would find themselves obliged to submit to the oath. No, no! it was the swearing itself that was wrong. All oaths were grounded on falseness; to swear was to suspect one's own honesty. They dared not make so bold with God as to summon him to every controversy. And, remember! Christ Himself forbade. They must remember their "immovable foundation, the law of the spirit of life, which makes free from the laws and lawyers of sin and gives the tongue of the learned into every mouth wherewith to plead his own righteous cause, and so a good conscience becomes an able and bold advocate. . . ."

Penn returned to London shortly after writing that letter—to London and to Buckinghamshire; and on February 7, 1672, he and Gulielma Springett appeared before the Jordans Monthly Meeting to declare their intention to wed. "William Penn of Walthamstow in the County of Essex and Gulielma Maria Springett of Tiler's End Green in the County of Bucks, proposed their intention of taking each other in marriage. Whereupon it was referred to Daniel Zachary and Thomas Ellwood to inquire into the clearness of their proceedings and give an account to next meeting," states the minute. Tyler's End Green, or Tyler's Green, is a tiny hamlet joining the village of Penn, where the family of Penn lived who William Penn claimed were his relatives and where Besse says Penn went to stay after his father's death and before his Newgate imprisonment. It may have been another temporary address for Guli or her whole family. In a letter thought to be dated during Penn's imprisonment in Newgate, George Fox had written to Penn at "Tilleringreen," a forwarding address, and no more likely custodian for his mail than Guli. At Monthly Meeting of March 6 the declaration was repeated and received the approval of Friends. The Monthly Meeting convened at the home of Thomas and Mary Ellwood at Hunger Hill (Ongar Hill).

After four years of courtship the wedding was accomplished on April 4, 1672, in a little house in Chorleywood called King John's Farm, because it is thought to have been a hunting lodge built for King John. It is still there, at the end of Shepherd's Lane, just northwest of the village of Rickmansworth where the couple planned to live, and just over the Bucks County line in Hertford. It has been built upon and added to, but the original four rooms are intact—two rooms downstairs and two upstairs with a chimney up the front and back walls to provide four fireplaces. The living room where the wedding took place is low-ceilinged with heavy oak beams overhead, white plastered walls divided into panels by narrow strips of wood, and floors of wide, uneven planks.

The solemnity and beauty of a Quaker wedding is a profound experience, even to the untrained observer. Its simplicity, its dignity, its gentleness, create a devotional atmosphere in which the full significance and authenticity of the occasion can develop. The bride and groom sit side by side in the meeting as its silence deepens into worship, and after a time, when they feel that members have had sufficient opportunity to dwell upon the sacred union, the couple stand up and clasp hands, and in the simplest language take one another for man and wife, promising to be loving and faithful as long as they both shall live. That is all. No ring, no flowers, no attendants, no vows of obedience. They sit down again, and the meeting re-enters its silent meditation, until one member after another rises to give a message. The messages that follow are full of blessing, encouragement and hopefulness. At the rise of the meeting for worship, the marriage contract is spread upon a table and after the newly wed couple have signed their names as many as wish sign it as witnesses.

William's and Guli's certificate, written by Thomas Ellwood who was clerk of the Monthly Meeting, was signed by forty-six wedding guests. At the head of the list was Margaret Penn (no doubt his mother); next came his brother, Richard Penn; then Isaac and Mary Penington and three of their children. There were other prominent names among them: George Whitehead, James and Helena Claypoole, Thomas Rudyard, Thomas and Mary Ellwood, John Harvey.

Solemnity gave way to the celebration of happiness as the conversation, begun first in hushed tones, gradually gained volume and soon became punctuated with laughter. At last William and Gulielma Penn, laughing, protesting, thanking well-wishers, could escape into their new coach and drive away down Shepherd's Lane toward the village of Rickmansworth to the big, many-gabled Basing House set among lawns and gardens on the north side of the curving coach road (now High Street) where they are thought to have lived. Another building stands on the site of the old Basing House. They were not very close to Wanstead, perhaps because Lady Penn was a petulant, complaining and dependent kind of woman who sometimes suspected others of being in league against her—of the sort who lose their sons early and never really understand why.

Although Rickmansworth is close to London and close to the whole cluster of little villages about which the Penn-Penington-Springett-Ellwood story revolves, Friends and relations saw little of William and Gulielma during the first five months of their married life together. They had waited a long time for this honeymoon; they had been in love a long time; they had bided the months faithfully and devotedly through arrests, imprisonments, foreign assignments and all the incidental vicissitudes of seventeenth-century dissenters. At last these few precious weeks were theirs, and they could seek in one another the peace and safety they had needed so long. Their twenty-two year record of marital devotion suggests that Guli must have found in her bridegroom all that she had hoped for; and Penn found that the bride he at last could gather to himself was "good, wise, chaste, humble, plain, modest, industrious, constant and undaunted."

We speak what we know, and can but declare what we have felt of the work of God in our hearts.
—William Penn, *The Christian Quaker and His Divine Testimony*

10. On Truth's Account

"I AM at peace with all men," William Penn wrote to Friends in the United Netherlands in June. Until the blessed, healing respite of his honeymoon, he had not spared himself soul or body since his convincement.

But all men were not at peace with one another. Just before Penn's wedding England and France had declared war against Holland, and militaristic excitement was spreading as their fleets combined and French land troops gathered to attack Holland across the Rhine. The brilliant politician, Charles II, recognizing the value of peace on the home front when he was fighting abroad, issued a Declaration of Indulgence a few days before the declaration of war, suspending all penal laws against Protestant non-conformists and Catholic recusants. It was a popular-appeal tactic, easily achieved while Parliament was not in session, and it spelled relief and freedom to many. Informers and persecutors withdrew into the background; meetings assembled without molestation; and in May, under a special pardon issued by the King's most excellent majesty and his Council, nearly five hundred non-conformists, most of them Quakers, were released from thirty-eight prisons throughout England. Isaac Penington, already out "by permission," was on the list of those pardoned, and from Bedford jail stepped John Bunyan carrying his partially written *Pilgrim's Progress.*

There appears little record of Penn's participation in public affairs at this time; in fact, the next five years of his life are a kind of interim between his service as a young martyr and his role as a politico-religious leader in creating Quaker colonies in America. From the time of his marriage until his second trip to the Continent with Fox and Barclay in 1677 he lived a rather withdrawn life, serving the Friends' movement with his writings and in its legal and administrative problems. Except for one short trip through the southern counties of England, his activities were confined to London and his own community. Philip Ford continued to handle his financial affairs, rendering scrupulous statements, and Penn grew to trust him and depend upon him more and more.

Penn and Barclay probably first met at the London Yearly Meeting of May 1672. The Yearly Meeting was new, and its very newness may have brought Barclay down from Scotland. There is no record of Barclay's having come down before 1672, but in that year he made a town-to-town, meeting-to-meeting journey through the northern counties. A few months after the 1672 Yearly Meeting, Barclay wrote to Penn, "I have often remembered thee in a sense of God's love"; and in May of 1673 Penn and Barclay were definitely together in London, for they both attached their signatures to an epistle sent out by Friends at that time.

Barclay was a Scotsman who had been convinced at eighteen and plunged into the martyr's role almost immediately. He was four years younger than Penn, and, like Penn, had been sent by his family to a French theological school, although Barclay's training had been Catholic rather than Huguenot. He fell under the influence of the Scottish Quaker minister, George Keith, and for many years both men contributed greatly to the growth of Quakerism in the north. Barclay was a gifted penman as well as a scholar and became the great apologist for Quaker doctrine.

Not until five months after his marriage did Penn emerge from Basing House and set out on a traveling minister's journey through the counties of southern England. *My Journey on Truth's Account Through Kent, Sussex and the Skirt of Surrey* gives us the chronicle of his twenty-six days' trip beginning September 8, 1672. He first took Guli to Watford, no doubt because she was pregnant. His two traveling companions throughout the journey were "A.P.," who Dr. Cadbury suggests was Alexander Parker, and his sixteen-year-old brother-in-law John Penington. He lodged the first two nights in London at the home of "W.G." identified as William Gibson on Bull and Mouth Street, "seeing of Friends and dispatching some papers then in the press."

At last, their cloaks wrapped around them against the chill autumn air and frequent drizzle, the three turned their horses' heads in a southeasterly direction along the ancient road that connects London with Canterbury and the chalk-cliffed coast. Tinsbery was their first stop where they held a small meeting that same evening, but in Penn's own language they weren't clear in themselves and so the worship experience was unsatisfactory. Local Friends were dissatisfied, too, that the visitors spent such a short time with them. They reached Rochester the next morning, and there the results were quite different—a "large, living and open meeting," in which exalted hecklers and self-appointed theologians were laid low by the Quaker message. The circuit riders were up and away, pausing at Sittingbourne and arriving in Canterbury that same afternoon.

The first Christian missionary to set foot on English soil could not have walked through the streets of Canterbury with a more dedicated purpose. Over a millennium had passed since St. Augustine had found the ruins there of an old Roman building and had made them into a cathedral. After him had come the Norman invasion, the destruction of the old cathedral and the building of the new. Thomas à Becket's blood had stained the stones of the little transept between the cloisters and the north aisle of the choir, and the feet of thousands of pilgrims had passed through Canterbury to view his shrine, but William Penn does not indicate that he so much as glanced at the imposing Anglican edifice. He sought out the house of a Quaker shoemaker, "an honest, tender man and whose wife is of a sober, grave and exemplary deportment," and there he lodged the night and planned a meeting for the next day. A handful of Canterbury Friends came, and were comforted, but there were few others. Perhaps the cathedral cast too long a shadow after all. Penn's susceptibility to changes in mood found him frankly depressed by the scanty meeting as he, Parker and Penington sat down together afterward. They were interrupted by the arrival of a young ruffian, a "high, peremptory, knowing but pragmatical" fellow, who came to devastate the Quakers with his great fund of information and a torrent of talk, some of it highly abusive; and they reasoned with him gently and watched him go, wondering whether they had done him any good. That night the boy crept back, the leaven having had time to work in his soul, to make his humble apologies and promise to attend First Day meeting on the morrow. The gathering up of at least one mortal was gratifying; the Quakers realized that they must accept their due as it was meted out to them.

But next day, when the hour of their meeting arrived, they found to their amazement that a huge, enthusiastic crowd was gathering, people "base and noble, rich and poor, young and old, learned and unlearned, men, women and children." Penn had been too impatient with Canterbury; he had not given Canterbury time to learn that there were Quaker ministers in town; and naïvely he had reckoned without the drawing power of his own recent notoriety as a martyr. A new fear arose in the minds of the ministers—that so large and motley a crowd could not be held to worship. They were mistaken. A glorious power rose in Penn and his companions, and they felt themselves reaching that great group and felt the response come back from almost everyone, "and the grass withered in our presence." Happy men were they indeed when they swung up into their saddles and at last rode away from Canterbury, "in triumph over all, and Truth was set upon the head of the great city."

Some of the Canterbury Friends, as happy as they over the results, rode with them to Sandwich, and there in the pouring rain they repeated their triumph with another big meeting. They rested that night with a ship's master and then went on to Nonington in time for the Monthly Meeting, reaching Deal late at night and lodging with a glover. The next day produced another "very convincing, open, powerful, and exceeding tender meeting, to the bringing all under our spirits." The story was the same at Dover with a further harvest of convincements. Luke Howard, who had joined the travelers in Canterbury, was a resident of Dover and Penn's host there.

From Dover Penn and an accumulation of traveling companions that included Luke Howard followed the coastline past Margaret's Bay, leaving behind the ancient Norman castle perched high on the massive chalk cliffs. Soon they came out upon a hill looking down at Folkestone, huddled on the flat land close to the shore. Success and enthusiasm greeted them again. Penn left next morning in order to reach Swingfield in time for the Monthly Meeting, and Alexander Parker stayed behind to be with Folkestone Friends for their First Day Meeting. Lydd was Penn's next immediate goal. It was far out on a promontory of flat, desolate land, flanked by the Romney Marshes and soggy grazing meadows.

The value of the journey began to seem like the spreading ripples on a pool as it attracted one large meeting after another and the travelers' ministerial powers reached new high levels and gave more powerful messages. Penn was leaving refreshment and encouragement behind him all along the way, for down in these parts of England the Friends had suffered a great deal. They needed the tonic of his visit as well as the re-enforcement of increased membership.

The next stopping point in his journey Penn calls Wey; Dr. Cadbury thinks this may be Wye. In any event, it must have been virgin territory, for Penn was obliged to book a room at the local inn. He didn't use it, though. He gave the folk there such a religious experience in which "God's dreadful power trampled false coverings under foot, and the plain, simple Truth was set over all" that some of the newly convinced carried him home with them and entertained him with "exceeding openheartedness." Word went out to the surrounding countryside, and next day there were many in the meeting who had traveled great distances to hear Penn's words. Some had come from Ashford, and that was the next town on his itinerary. In a second Wye meeting "the glorious power was so strong, opening, piercing and tendering that Truth became of good savor, and all seemed to confess and rejoice." And the rejoicing flew ahead of him along the road to Ashford, where the crowds fought and struggled and trampled one another to get close enough to hear his searching eloquence. The house in Ashford chosen to accommodate the meeting was crammed throughout the parlor, kitchen and entry, "in so violent a manner that people were forced to go out for breath," and more gathered in the garden. Penn was fearful lest the true spirit of the occasion be lost in such rowdy conditions, but his fears were groundless, and that meeting melted together in a spiritual unity that gave incontrovertible testimony to the living Light. It was the zenith of Penn's southern journey.

Next morning Ashfordian Friends asked Penn if he would hold another meeting with them privately, but their caution was of little avail, for non-Friends found out about it and pressed eagerly in.

Penn left the dark green muted hills of the North Downs behind him and rode down toward Tenterden, where he was rejoined by Alexander Parker. Luke Howard had turned back at Ashford. Penn was headed for the coast again, reaching Lewes "through much wet" by the twenty-eighth of September, and Rottingdean not far from Brighton the following day, stopping at the home of Nicholas Beard. Next morning he moved on through "Kingston Bowsey" and Blechington to Storrington. The following night he spent at Horsham. Gulielma Springett Penn owned considerable property in Sussex, and his purpose in routing his journey this way may have been twofold. This lovely section of England so densely wooded with elm and oak, lying between the North and South Downs, would eventually become their home. He does not mention giving time to a meeting in Horsham that October 2, and October 3 found him passing through Charlwood on his way to Reigate in Surrey. After an early morning meeting, Penn was back in the saddle, riding toward London. Parker left him about five miles out of Reigate to depart to his own home in Enfield. Penn took a road that veered to the left through Kingston. Kingston saw him only for one hour; the needle was too close to the magnet now to resist. "Cross the country to my dear wife and got home before the seventh hour in the evening."

Penn the evangelist strode into the house to report his spiritual victories, just as his father had once come striding into the house at Wanstead to recount his victories at sea.

Upon his return he began immediately to produce the prodigious volume of copy that was to highlight the next few years, chiefly letters and tracts. In November, 1672, a long letter went to Dr. Haesbert in Emden and another to De Labadie in Herford.

During the respite from persecution under the Declaration of Indulgence the multitude of Puritan sects were indulging themselves in an orgy of free expression, and many that resented the Quakers were taking this opportunity to make virulent attacks upon them. Friends made it a policy to reply to every attack in kind; letter with letter, speech with speech, tract with tract, book with book. Penn assumed responsibility for a great deal of this work.

Two men named John Reeve and Lodowick Muggleton appeared

on the public scene that year, claiming to have had wonderful revelations from Heaven, to being, in fact, the true last witnesses mentioned in Revelation. Reeve considered himself a new Moses and Muggleton a second Aaron. They were the sensational kind of "witnesses" who will always draw some followers, and they did succeed in making enough of a stir to upset William Penn and a few more Quaker leaders. On December 15, 1672, Penn wrote to Muggleton briefly and to the point, calling him to task for his "ungodly and blasphemous practices," and enclosed a copy of the "discourse" he had written to expose the blasphemy. This is the tract, *The New Witnesses Proved Old Heretics.*

A nameless author wrote a tract called *The Spirit of the Quakers Tried,* and Penn wrote in reply *The Spirit of Truth Vindicated.* The anonymous attacker had taken great pains to make George Fox out to be an imposter and the Quakers to be heretics, and Penn produced an essay of over fifty thousand words that is a forerunner of the great *No Cross, No Crown* to appear a decade later. He develops the Friends' concept of Light, and responds to the oft-repeated accusation that Friends denied Christ. In the style of the times, the tract is cluttered with quotation and repetition, but the Truth Penn wishes to vindicate is there, and the tract contains passages that stand out like gems. Friends are honest-hearted men, he says, and that "which reduces man . . . to an honest heart and a life good and laudable . . . must be the Grace of God." As for notions that God is shaped like a man and that Heaven is a visible place to be lived in, such thinking belongs to the "vain anthropomorphites of old." God is the spirit indwelling in man, the invisible pillar of cloud or fire that guides him. Quakers are they who "perform their worship to God in the motion of the Eternal Spirit. . . . And be it known to all the world, that as our religion stands not in the doctrines, meanings, preachings, or notions of men's devising or deducting from the Scriptures themselves, but in the living, quickening power of the Eternal God."

During December, 1672, and January, 1673, Penn locked verbal horns with a John Morse of Watford. Morse had attacked both Penn and the Friends, particularly Penn's *Spirit of Truth* tract. Penn at last gathered together the letters he had written Morse and published them with an explanatory Preface under the title, *Plain-Dealing with a Traducing Anabaptist.*

A *Winding Sheet for Controversy Ended* was Penn's reply to a paper by a Henry Hedworth called, *Controversy Ended.*

But the quasi-prophets and divine messengers of doubtful vintage, who seemed to be popping up like mushrooms on every side, could not upset Penn too badly in those days; for while they tried to invade his world with their semantics, a joyful army of chattering housewives and women relations invaded Basing House to help Guli bear her first child. Gulielma Maria Penn, born January 23, 1673, must have been very frail indeed, considering her short life, and she must have required the utmost in vigilant care. She survived only seven and a half weeks and was laid to rest in the graveyard at Jordans.

Death struck a second time that spring, claiming William Penn's eighteen-year-old brother, Richard. The lad who had once been Mrs. Pepys' valentine and later appears to have gone to sea under Captain Sir William Poole on the *Jersey* was buried April 9 at Walthamstow.

These losses brought a sudden seasoning to the young couple, and the double sorrow deepened their already sober manner. William and Gulielma Penn remained in their state of semi-retirement, and he returned to his writing table to resume the ever mounting volume of argumentation.

The two paper disputes that consumed a lion's share of Penn's time and energy and prodded him into doing his best writing of this period were with John Faldo and Thomas Hicks. Both situations began early in 1673 and ran on well into 1674. Faldo was an independent preacher near Barnet who began to develop anxiety tensions as one after another of his flock drifted away to the Quaker congregations. As Besse puts it, Faldo, "being sensible that every sheep lost carried away wool on his back, was grievously incensed," and he at last burst forth with a tract, *Quakerism No Christianity.* Penn's reply, *Quakerism, A New Nickname for Old Christianity: Being an Answer to a Book, Entitled, Quakerism No Christianity; Subscribed by J. Faldo,* is another long and wordy tract, but it is a meticulous and painstaking presentation of the "doctrine and practice of the abused Quakers." Faldo's was a losing fight, but he stayed with it, stubbornly trying to hold his congregation, and published another book to vindicate his first. Penn retorted with a still longer reply, *The Invalidity of John Faldo's Vindication of His Book, Called, Quakerism No Christianity.* Faldo quieted down, but only for a while, and soon he sent Penn a challenging letter enclosing a further paper he had written. Penn acknowledged it immediately with a letter of his own and agreed to answer it even though, he pointed out, "these things mentioned in thy paper are now in controversy between T.H. [Thomas Hicks] and us." Faldo wrote one more paper, *A Curb to W. Penn's Confidence,* and Penn patiently replied on November 12, 1674, with a short paper, *William Penn's Return to John Faldo's Reply.* Faldo was a persistent pest and went so far as to ask Penn to debate him publicly, but he proposed a meeting time that conflicted with "dispatch of an affair about four years standing," and Penn had to decline. No doubt feeling that the affair had run on long enough and that all the good had been wrung from it, Penn did not suggest another meeting date, and neither apparently did Faldo.

Thomas Hicks was a Baptist preacher who seems to have had a classical scholar's nostalgic fondness for dialogues. He wrote a dialogue between a Christian and a Quaker in which he made the Quaker the weaker member, easily confounded by his adversary on theological points. The piece was highly effectual and did the Quakers a great deal of harm, many thinking it to be the report of a real conversation, until William Penn produced his essay, *The Christian Quaker and His Divine Testimony, Stated and Vindicated, by Scripture, Reason and Authority.* This was published in 1673, and soon republished with a Part II added by George Whitehead. Most biographers of Penn have paused to pay homage to this piece. It is by far the most competent thing Penn had written to date, and it deserves a prominent place among his works. It is less argumentative in tone than his other work of this period. It sets forth in positive, straightforward language an explanation of "the Light of Christ within, the great principle of God in man, the root and spring of divine life and knowledge in the soul; that by which salvation is effected for man, and which is the characteristic of the people called Quakers, their faith and testimony to the world." Hicks was soon off the presses with a *Continuation* of his damaging dialogue, and Penn replied with *Reason Against Railing, and Truth Against Fiction.*

Penn's *Reason Against Railing* came out after the middle of May, 1673, and late in June or early July he and Guli took a short holiday from both tract writing and recent grief and journeyed out to Bristol to welcome George Fox back from America. Fox's epistles from the New World had circulated throughout the meetings in England, and interest ran high after his absence of almost two years. Margaret Fell Fox came down from Ulverston with her son-in-law Thomas Lower and two of her daughters, Sarah and Rachel; Friends came from London and from other parts of England. Battered and worn by wilderness living and illnesses and thirty-eight days at sea, Fox landed in Bristol on June 28. He glowed with all the news and inspiration he must impart, and his flock gathered round him to be electrified once more by his homespun eloquence, his absolute confidence, his authenticity. A great fair was taking place in Bristol at that time which drew still more multitudes to which Fox could preach. "Glorious, powerful meetings we had there," says Fox's *Journal.* He had suffered, but that was not important; what mattered was that the Seed was flourishing in America in the very face of persecution. Meetings were already settled, up and down the Atlantic seaboard. He had landed first in the West Indies, visiting Barbados and Jamaica, and had then landed in Virginia, going on to Maryland to attend the first session of what is now Baltimore Yearly Meeting. Fox had covered great distances, "through bogs, rivers and creeks, and wild woods where it was said never man was known to ride," on up through New Jersey, Long Island, Rhode Island where the General Meeting lasted six days. Fox traveled winter and summer, visited with the Indians, administered to the sick, gave the movement in the New World the encouragement it needed to expand still further, then returned to England to infect others with his fervor.

William and Gulielma returned from Bristol and the refreshing meetings with George and Margaret Fox with enthusiasms restored in many ways. Gulielma in particular had been afforded the comforting conversations of an older woman who had raised many children and had recently lost an infant of her own. Gulielma could re-enter her home with new hope and a happier step, for she was expecting another child, and her husband could return to his tract and letter writing and find it considerably less tedious.

That Penn did not relish the role of tract writer is apparent both in his personality and in his writing style. There was not enough physical exertion in it for a man of Penn's up-and-into-action disposition. Further, through all his life he gave signs of a lack of patience, and a long, painstaking desk assignment must have been a nerve-racking tedium, driving him to jump up and pace the floor at frequent intervals to work off his accumulation of tensions. Penn had great writing talent, as the frequent occurrence of beautiful, even poetic, phrases in his work shows; but he did not have writing temperament, as the uneven quality of his work indicates. He did not love writing for its own sake, but rather was using another personal resource—his exceptionally fine education—on behalf of Quakerism. Robert Barclay, on the other hand, was a true writer who could produce consistently polished prose. Penn turned out a great volume of material that was most valuable and sorely needed in his own time; Barclay wrote a timeless interpretation of the faith. The force that held Penn to his desk was his devotion to Fox and to the movement. Fox was a superb administrator, who had the vision to see the value in specialized talents and not to waste them.

Penn's spiritual help radiated out from Rickmansworth to those at home and abroad. A Justice Fleming in Westmoreland received some recommendations about liberty of conscience; suffering Friends in Holland and Germany, an epistle of consolation; so did his "Little Flock and Family of God" in the United Provinces. The name of an unknown English woman, Mary Pennyman, has been immortalized because William Penn in November, 1673, wrote her a loving reply after she had taken umbrage at the contents of one of his tracts.

George Fox, meanwhile, had returned to his role of creator-adviser-minister-administrator of the Society, traveling through Gloucestershire, Wiltshire and Buckinghamshire, and at last arriving in London, where he found the greatest concentration of "lying, wicked, scandalous books" attacking the Friends. He must have breathed a quiet prayer of thanksgiving for William Penn's scholarship and willingness to devote so much energy to combating this very real danger.

After Fox had visited London meetings and Friends' schools and meetings in Essex and Middlesex, he and Margaret, his stepdaughter Rachel and son-in-law Thomas Lower paid William and Gulielma a visit at Rickmansworth. Fox wanted to confer with Penn about the troubled England he had returned to, where the Declaration of Indulgence had been nullified by an irate Parliament and where renewed persecutions were being stimulated and abetted by a Test Act. Charles II had needed funds to carry on his war against Holland, and for that he had had to reconvene Parliament. Once in session, its temper whetted by public sentiment, Parliament forced the King to withdraw the Indulgence before it would appropriate any war funds, and it further forced upon him the Test Act which automatically weeded out Catholics from public office, including the King's own brother James who resigned from the Admiralty. The Test Act required that all those who wished to hold public office in England must accept communion in the Anglican Church and swear allegiance to the King. In the case of the Quakers, who sought no public office, the loyalty oath was deliberately misapplied. Penn, Fox and all the rest knew that this rendered every member of the Society susceptible to imprisonment for the slightest offence.

From Rickmansworth George Fox and Thomas Lower and the rest of his party set out through Aylesbury, Oxfordshire and Worcestershire, until they arrived at the home of John Halford in Armscote. There, on December 17, 1673, the inevitable meeting was held. After it had dispersed and there was no longer a visible meeting, a local justice and companion arrived, took George Fox and Thomas Lower into custody and deposited them in Worcester County jail. The charge was for holding not one but many meetings "upon a pretence of exercise of religion otherwise than what is established by the laws of England." That would not keep them in jail beyond the Quarter Sessions, though; the loyalty oath was to be the real legal stumbling block set up before them.

News of Fox's arrest went out over the communication lines of the Society, and its leaders—George Whitehead, William Penn, William Mead, Ellis Hookes, Thomas Moore, and others—hurried into conference to search out every possible means of obtaining Fox's freedom. William Penn's legal training as well as his devotion to Fox brought him into the center of the case. One of his first steps was to have his mother at Wanstead write a letter to Lord Windsor, Lord Lieutenant for the county, with whom she was "well acquainted," asking that the oath be waived at the quarter sessions. Lord Windsor "promised fair" but to no avail. When Fox and Lower were brought before the quarter sessions, the justices of the peace shrugged their shoulders at the fact that they had no case, released Lower, and turned their full venom on Fox. Again, as in Penn's trial at the Old Bailey, it was *whom* they were trying, not *why*.

"You, Mr. Fox, are a famous man . . . that we may be better satisfied, will you take the Oath of Allegiance and Supremacy?"

Of course, he could take no oath, and they knew it, and so they clapped him back into jail and further secured him there with that pet device, a writ of praemunire.

The praemunire does not occur in American law. It is an ancient English term dating back to Edward I. Praemunire was an ecclesiastical crime, a kind of treason, defined by Blackstone as "the offence of introducing a foreign power into the realm, and thus creating *imperium in imperio* by paying that obedience to the papal process which properly belonged to the king alone." It was an offense committed directly against the King, since encouraging papal power diminished the authority of the Crown. The most ancient writs of praemunire literally placed the person beyond the protection of the Crown; he could be killed on sight by anyone, since he was the King's enemy. But under Elizabeth I and subsequent monarchs the writ of praemunire was refined to the point where a person against whom it had been issued could "bring no legal action for any private injury, being so far out of the law that it will not guard his civil rights. And no man, knowing him to be guilty, can with safety give him comfort, aid or relief."

It was perfectly apparent to William Penn and the others that the situation in Worcester County was too hostile to give any hope of justice. They therefore managed by the end of January, to have Fox brought down to London on a writ of Habeas Corpus to the jurisdiction of the King's Bench Bar. At the same time that they were working through legal channels, they were using whatever influence they had in high court circles.

The assignment to the royal Court of the Stuarts fell logically to William Penn. Six years had elapsed since his last visit to the world of laces and velvet and brilliant plumes, six years in which his ornate wig had become a little civil thing, his dress had become plain and his boyish features seasoned and sweetened into the deeper lines of a father who had lost one child and was worried about his next. Penn's judgment apparently was against going directly to the top, for he and William Mead first waited upon the Earl of Middlesex, who advised them to go to the Duke of York. The Duke of York, forced out of his own position in the Admiralty by the same law that was keeping Fox in prison, and bound by a deep personal love for the late Sir William Penn, would have been more than ready to grant an audience. Still Penn did not go to him directly, but toiled through the tiring hierarchies of satellites that cluster around any high-ranking figure. He was first introduced by Fleetwood Shepherd to the Duchess's secretary at the Duke's palace, which functionary merely shrugged his shoulders and showed him the great crowd of favor-seekers ahead of him and told him he could do nothing. But standing in the room was a Colonel Aston, who recognized Penn.

"Looking hard at me, thinking he should know me, asked me in the drawing-room, first my name, and then my business, and upon understanding both, he presently gave us the favor we waited for, of speaking with the Duke, who came immediately out of his closet to us," is how Penn tells it in a fragment of autobiography.

The reunion of Penn and the Duke of York was momentous.

"Perhaps that with some was the beginning of my faults at court," Penn remarked years later, after the Duke of York's devotion to his own religious beliefs had cost him his throne, and after Penn's devotion to the Duke had almost cost him his liberty.

But on that day of renewed friendship at the palace, Penn lived but to help the leader of the Quaker movement, and the interview ended to the extraordinary satisfaction of himself and his companions. The Duke had "told us that he was against all persecution for the sake of religion. That it was true he had in his younger time been warm, especially when he thought people made it a pretence to disturb government, but that he had seen and considered things better, and he was for doing to others as he would have others do unto him. . . . When he had done upon this affair, he was pleased to take a very particular notice of me, both for the relation my father had had to his service in the navy, and the care he had promised him to show in my regard upon all occasions." Penn's report to Fox was full of hope.

Fox's case was heard before King's Bench in Westminister Hall, but it was footballed back to the Worcester Sessions, to drag on shuttlecock fashion between the two courts for more than a year.

Penn was a burdened man at this point; even though as a gentleman of sufficient means he could give his full time to Friends' affairs, the volume of nerve-racking detail piled up around him and to it was added more private grief. On February 28, 1674, shortly after Fox's King's Bench trial, the Penn twins, William and Mary (or Margaret) were born—two more frail babes who would reckon their life spans in months. Their inability to survive must have been painfully apparent even to hopeful young parents, and no amount of loving care was able to carry them through. William died that same May and Mary the following February. During the summer of 1674, while Penn and Guli were hovering anxiously over the failing Mary and while Penn was straining every effort to bring about a second trial for Fox before the King's Bench, the Thomas Hicks controversy broke out afresh, developed into a public dispute between the Baptists and the Quakers, and combined with the earlier dispute with Jeremy Ives, Baptist preacher of West Wycombe.

Thomas Hicks published a third *Dialogue*, and Penn had no choice but to write a reply, *The Counterfeit Christian Detected and the Real Quaker Justified*. The Baptists were losing too many members to the Society of Friends, and they had to persist in the competitive struggle for existence. Ives returned to the battle ranks, and the Baptists held a big public meeting at their London center, the Barbican, on August 28, and had a rousing time of attacking Whitehead and Penn for not appearing. William Penn had not appeared, because he did not know of the meeting. The letter notifying him of the occasion was delivered to his London agent, Philip Ford, who replied at once that William Penn had gone "into the east of England about three weeks ago, and I know not how to give him notice thereof." George Whitehead had been in Bristol. Penn and Whitehead demanded another opportunity to debate their attackers, and the second meeting materialized in the early part of October. Eager, excitable crowds of upward of six thousand gathered to watch the theological cockfight. George Whitehead, Stephen Crisp, William Penn and George Keith represented the Quakers; Jeremy Ives, Thomas Hicks and three others spoke for the Baptists. The dispute, which in the final analysis accomplished nothing conclusive, ran on so long that the meeting had to be convened a second time. The details covered in it are peculiar to that period and quite foreign to present-day thinking. One of the most amazing questions raised by the literal-minded Baptists was: "If Christ was the Light within, where was His manhood?" Like other sects, they were eager to establish the fact that the Quakers denied Christ, and they tried to do so by distinguishing between the physical man Jesus and the indwelling spirit. "I prove ye deny the man Christ Jesus," Hicks maintained. "One of your own writers saith that Christ was never seen with carnal eyes, nor heard with carnal ears." George Keith answered, "Christ as God was never seen with carnal eyes; but as man He was seen with carnal eyes." A little later Penn contributed, "Wicked men might see Him in that bodily appearance, and yet not see Him to be the Christ of God. They saw His manhood, but not His Christ-ship." It was an age in which Christ was laid upon the debaters' table and examined bit by bit. If the first century had crucified him, the seventeenth certainly dissected him.

Ives published A *Sober Request . . . to the Quakers,* which meant that Penn had to write *Jeremy Ives's Sober Request, Proved in the Matter of It, to be False, Impertinent and Impudent.* "Very late last night," Penn began, "came Jeremy Ives's *Sober Request* . . . to my hands; so soon as I had read it, I could not but cry out, Parturiunt Montes, nascitur ridiculus Mus: What! but a sorry Mouse, the product of Jeremy's great Mountain, after so many days travail?"

"William Penn has labored hard and spent himself very much," a Friend reported to George Fox in Worcester jail.

Penn made his own report to Fox on the Baptist controversy: "It was managed with much levity and enmity, all coffee houses and such like public places are filled with the news of it. . . ."

Meanwhile Fox had been tried once more at the Worcester Quarter Sessions and indicted by a jury for not taking the oath. He was confined to the prison there under the writ of praemunire, and from his prison cell he continued to administer the affairs of the Society and to keep in touch with those who were working on his case. He wrote to William Penn on August 28, 1674:

To whom is my love and to thy wife and Friends I here trouble thee with another letter enclosed from Maryland, by which thou mayst see that an order upon word is entered in their assembly books touching Friends' yea and nay instead of an oath, and they only stay for an order for confirmation from the old Baltimore. When thou goest to speak with him [Lord Baltimore], thou may take Sam Groome with thee. He knows the condition of Maryland.

The Maryland case drew Penn's attention once again toward the New World. He called in person on both the Attorney General of the Colony of Maryland and on Lord Baltimore, father of the Proprietor who figured so prominently in Penn's life. The Maryland Friends were in danger of being driven out of the colony and, after his conference with Baltimore, Penn wrote to them, urging that they stand their ground firmly on their beliefs: "That your coming thither as to a sanctuary makes it reasonable that they should not drive you thence for mere conscience so well grounded and confirmed by scripture, reason and authorities."

Throughout all these problems Penn worked continuously on Fox's case. In two letters to the imprisoned Fox, Penn refers to "a great lord, a man of noble mind," and a "person of quality" who was interceding with the King on Fox's behalf. By inference this must be the Duke of York. "He prevailed with the King for a pardon, but that we rejected," Penn says in his first letter. "Then he prest for a more noble release. It sticks with the Lord Keeper, and we have used and do use what interest we can. The King is angry with him [the Lord Keeper], and promiseth very largely and lovingly; so that, if we have been deceived, thou seest the grounds of it. But we have sought after a writ of error these ten days past, well nigh resolving to be as sure as we can; and an Habeas Corpus is gone or will go tomorrow night." In his second letter Penn tells Fox: "A person of some quality has undertaken it as with the King who will not be known. So as to the King he desires that none may move for three or four days more, till he sees what may be done. . . . As for the errors, we have [handled] in that also, and I forbear to mention anything yet about those errors till I have taken more counsellers [minds]. I love not to give encouragements without grounds. Some have been consulted and they think that thou mayst be released upon a writ of error, at last. More per next."

A writ of error is a judicial writ showing technical flaws in the proceedings and allowing a review of the case, and all during the summer and fall Penn was endeavoring by this means to have Fox's Worcester indictment set aside.

On the twenty-fifth of November Fox wrote to Penn again: "My love to thee and thy wife and the rest of the faithful Friends. I am glad to hear of the prosperity of Truth. I received thy last letter wherein thou signify that the King has granted my release under his hand and that it sticks with the keeper; here was a Friend of Banbury with me, that said if the matter sticks with the keeper he could improve some interest by some Friends of his to remove that obstacle . . . as for the other proceedings in the court I leave it to you. It is much if the King have signed my release that the keeper should stop it. What reason doth he pretend for it, for if the King hath granted such a thing, there needs no more than a warrant to the sheriff to set me at liberty."

Margaret Fox who was herself traveling frequently between Worcester and London on her husband's behalf wrote to Penn at the same time: "If thou think that my coming up concerning this business of my husband's that sticks with the keeper, if I could be any way serviceable in it, I am willing to come up. . . . Dear William, let me know thy answer by the next post, for if I come I would do so by the first opportunity. . . ."

The petitions to the King, the writ of error, and endeavors to bring Fox back to London on a writ of Habeas Corpus were concurrent efforts. In October Margaret Fox went in person to the King, but in November the release the King had granted still stuck with the keeper. The King apparently offered Fox a pardon, but he and his advisers refused to accept it since that would have implied admission of guilt. "If thou canst effect my release without the title of a pardon, thou mayst," Fox had written to Penn in October. Penn was handling the royal contact with utmost caution. "The King knows not that thou refusest a pardon," he told Fox in December, "only that we choose rather a more clear and suitable way to thy innocency."

Fox trusted Penn's legal judgment implicitly, for at a later date he said in a letter: "Dear William, I shall not strive with thee about matters of law, or law points. . . ."

These months of trial drew Fox and Penn closer and closer together on a deeply personal level, and the letters which they exchanged were full of private news. "My wife is toward a little one," Penn reported to Fox at one point, and in December, shortly before the death of the second twin: "My wife is well and child; only teeth, she has one cut."

While the child who had cut one tooth was still alive, William's and Guli's fourth child was born, the boy Springett, January 25, 1675. This child was to achieve his majority, and so there was a lustier cry from a huskier infant to fill the big rooms and corridors of Basing House. Unlike the other three, Springett was born at Walthamstow, where Guli must have been staying while Penn was so tied to the city of London. The second twin died a month after Springett's birth and was buried beside her brother and sister in Jordans.

Again, in the midst of personal anguish, Penn worked on with Whitehead and others to procure a new writ of Habeas Corpus that would bring Fox down for another trial before the King's Bench, and they succeeded around the end of January. The trial took place during the second week in February. Thomas Corbett acted as Fox's attorney and pivoted his case upon a new argument—that a man may not be imprisoned upon a praemunire. He won his case and won Fox his freedom, and the new interpretation of the praemunire was another Quaker contribution to English jurisprudence. In Fox's own words, "many lawyers came to him [Corbett] and said he had brought to light in the nation that which never was known before concerning their not being able to imprison any man upon a praemunire, which spread over the nation and was of great service."

Penn's mind was working along other lines. Actually, as far as the immediate welfare of the Quakers was concerned, the stumbling block had been the Oath of Allegiance and Supremacy, as a closing incident of the trial had shown. After the case was won, some prominent observers in the courtroom—Fox calls them "great men, Lords and others"—urged the judge to tender the oath to Fox once more. The judge would not allow it, and Fox left the courtroom a free man. Less than four months after Fox's release William Penn produced his tract, A *Treatise of Oaths: Containing Several Weighty Reasons Why the People Called Quakers Refuse to Swear*. It was endorsed by twelve other Quaker leaders, including Alexander Parker, George Whitehead, William Mead, James Claypoole, Thomas Rudyard and Richard Richardson. It was signed by William Penn and Richard Richardson. The piece was no doubt processed through a weighty editorial conference to bear such multiple endorsement, but Penn is unquestionably the basic author; it is in his style. According to its title page it was presented "to the King and Great Council of England Assembled in Parliament."

William Penn's wide perspective told him that in attacking an isolated problem like the oath, the Friends were really treating a symptom instead of searching out the causes of all religious persecution. Such tracts as the *Treatise* were needed, since Friends' views must be reported accurately; but other groups than the Friends were suffering, and the causes of their suffering were to be found in the political conditions of the times. The rights and privileges and security of all Englishmen were England's concern, and England's greatest interest could best be served by nurturing and cherishing those rights. She could not achieve the role of a great nation otherwise. "What is most fit, easy and safe at this juncture of affairs to be done, for quieting of differences, allaying the heat of contrary interests, and making them subservient to the interest of the government, and consistent with the prosperity of the kingdom?" Penn asked the question in order that he might answer it: "An inviolable and impartial maintenance of English rights." Any government must rule either by men or by laws; and Penn sees England as a land where the law is above men. The most fundamental laws must maintain title and security of estate and liberty of person from the violence of arbitrary power, they must provide for a voting upon every law that is made whereby the ownership of property may be maintained, and they must guarantee to the people a great share in the judicatory power through the use of juries. Penn sees more. He sees a balance achieved among the several religious interests. It is impossible "to prevent, even by force, the arising of any new opinion," especially "where a kingdom is of many minds." Governors are foolish "to blow coals in their own country," for "he that hath been forced to break his peace, to gratify the humor of another, must have a great share of mercy and self-denial to forgive that injury." Penn shakes his head severely at the "partiality of sacrificing the liberty and property of all dissenters to the promotion of a single party," and it is a prescient comment, casting a long shadow into the years when William Penn will play a conspicuous role in England's first opposition party. "Peace, plenty and safety" are "the three great inducements to any country to honor the prince and love the government, as well as the best allurements to foreigners to trade with it." And he does not hesitate to prophesy that plenty will be exchanged for poverty if the intolerant persecutions continue. England must stop the ruination of herself by the destruction of thousands of families and the fostering of suspicion and hatred among neighbors. The danger extends beyond England to the whole Protestant world, he warns. He deplores the notion of absolute conformity to the Church of England; there have been dissenters since that church first came into existence. Toleration, in fact, would strengthen the church more than persecution; for "the church is less in danger when she knows the worst, than where the danger is hid." Penn calls for "a sincere promotion of general and practical religion" based upon the Ten Commandments and the Sermon on the Mount. "If men would but live up to one half of what they know in their own consciences they ought to practice, their edge would be taken off, their blood would be sweetened by mercy and truth. . . . Tis want of practice and too much prate that hath made way for all the incharity and ill living that is in the world."

Such is the sum and substance of his essay, *England's Present Interest Discover'd, with Honor to the Prince, and Safety to the People,* that followed close upon the heels of the *Treatise.* It is another plea for liberty of conscience addressed to the source best qualified to grant it, the government itself, the source that was responsible for the recurring persecutions. Penn wrote it, he explained, to clear his conscience for his country. But his soul was still torn by continuous reports from various parts of England of cruelties suffered and civil liberties infringed upon, and so he wrote for the "serious consideration of the King and both Houses of Parliament" his *Continued Cry of the Oppressed for Justice.* It named names of the sufferers and gave specific details of fines, imprisonments, destroyed property—"their very bed clothes, wearing clothes and working tools escaped not the violence or avarice of their persecutors"—county by county: Leicestershire, Nottinghamshire, Norfolk, Cambridgeshire, Oxfordshire, Somersetshire, Berkshire, Cheshire, Yorkshire.

The pressure on Penn's soul was increasing. A way had to be found to ease such suffering—a way or a *place.*

At least as early as 1660, and probably before, Quaker leaders had been turning over in their minds the possibility of a New World colony as a place of refuge for persecuted members. Josiah Coale had written a letter to George Fox from Maryland in 1661 which indicates clearly that he had been investigating a site in the Susquehanna Valley. "As concerning Friends buying a piece of land of the Susquehanna Indians," he reported, "I have spoken of it to them, and told them what thou said concerning it, but their answer was, that there is no land that is habitable or fit for situation beyond Baltimore's liberty till they come to or near the Susquehanna's fort. . . ." The habitable land along the Atlantic coast was all taken up by one claim or another, and since such land grants were political plums they would hardly be bestowed upon so politically unpopular a sect as the Quakers. But early in 1674 a way suddenly opened up. A colonial property dispute was laid in William Penn's lap for arbitration.

The land was the western portion of New Jersey. New Jersey had been in its colonial beginnings a Dutch possession, and along with the rest of New Netherland had passed to English control in 1664. The entire area of New Netherland was granted to the Duke of York who in turn bestowed the proprietorship of the portion westward of Long Island and Manhattan and bounded on the east by the sea and the Hudson River and on the west by the Delaware River—the present state of New Jersey plus Staten Island—to two royal pets, members of the King's Privy Council, Sir George Carteret and John, Lord Berkeley, Baron of Stratton. Carteret had been Lieutenant Governor of the Isle of Jersey and had earned a magnificent naval record there during the civil wars. After the restoration of the monarchy, he became a member of the Privy Council and Vice Chamberlain of the Household, and for seven years, including the second Dutch war, he was Treasurer of the Navy. Charges of mismanagement of naval affairs during the war cost him his high post; but when, a few years later, the Duke of York was forced out of his own post as Lord High Admiral of the Navy, Carteret returned to favor and was made a member of the commission that replaced the Duke. Berkeley was Lord Lieutenant of Ireland from 1670 and before that had held several other favored posts in the Stuart regime.

There had been very few settlers in New Jersey under the Dutch—a scattering of Puritans along the Raritan, an occasional Quaker family near the coast, a handful of Swedes and Dutch on the Delaware. Under the English, colonization moved forward. Berkeley and Carteret issued a set of *Concessions and Agreements* to entice new adventurers, a document which is a forerunner of others to come, offering a government under an Assembly elected by the freemen of the province, guaranteeing many private rights—freedom of opinion and religious practice, taxes levied only by the General Assembly. A settler need only swear allegiance to the King to become a freeman of the province. Quitrents were to be waived until 1670. Adventurers began to move in both from England and from other colonies. Bergen (now part of Jersey City), Monmouth, Elizabethtown and Milford (now Newark) began to develop.

From the start, Berkeley and Carteret were involved in a controversy over their right to govern the province, since the King had never formally sanctioned the conveyance of the proprietorship to them. Troubles accumulated around the question. Resistance to their proprietary authority grew among the colonists and in 1670, when quitrents first became due, developed into organized revolt. The province was temporarily recaptured by the Dutch in the war of 1672, but, even before it was restored to England, Berkeley had given up all hope of growing rich from his colonial holdings in New Jersey, and so he sold his share for one thousand pounds to John Fenwick in trust for Edward Billinge. Both men were Quakers. Billinge, an insolvent London brewer, had a host of creditors clamoring at his heels who suspected him of having paid for the grant with money that ought to have been used to pay his debts to them. The controversy waxed hot and unpleasant and developed into a feud between Fenwick and Billinge. Since Friends preferred to settle their differences among themselves without going to court, William Penn was asked to act as impartial arbitrator.

The substance of the quarrel between Fenwick and Billinge is no longer known, but it was apparently not insoluble; for Penn succeeded in persuading the two men to accept a settlement. One tenth of West New Jersey was conveyed to Fenwick and nine tenths to Billinge. But Billinge's creditors were still vocal, and Billinge himself on February 9, 1675, conveyed his share to the administrative care of three trustees—William Penn, Gawen Lawrie and Nicholas Lucas. Fox's long Worcester imprisonment ran through all of 1674, and his final trial and acquittal before the King's Bench took place in February, 1675; so the early phase of the New Jersey tangle was yet another problem for Fox's "Will Penn" to add to his host of overlapping responsibilities.

After fifteen years of searching for a place to create a colony in America, the Quakers suddenly found themselves on the threshold of an opportunity, and William Penn's legal background and his colonizing experience in Ireland laid upon him the weight of leadership. He and the other trustees moved cautiously, first reaching an agreement with Fenwick for a united plan of settlement of all of West New Jersey, and then attacking the legal difficulties. They wanted before any adventurers went out to obtain from the Crown a formal acknowledgment of their proprietorship and their right to govern the province; the recent unfortunate experience of

Berkeley and Carteret pointed the way on that. They wanted the dividing line between East and West New Jersey exactly defined so so that there could be no border disputes in the future. And they wanted to draw up a framework of government.

But Fenwick proved himself stubborn, cantankerous and quarrelsome, impatient to begin his colonizing. He was Penn's neighbor in Rickmansworth, and Penn strove to placate him, but to no avail. Ignoring the agreement he had entered into for a united plan of settlement, Fenwick went ahead with his own plans, selling portions of his tenth to colonists, and soon set sail with a group of adventurers in the *Griffin*, arriving in the lower Delaware River in June, 1675. Some discovered all too quickly that their grants lay in swampy unhabitable areas, and they left the Fenwick project and went to other colonies; but those who remained took up their claims and founded Salem, the first English settlement on the left bank of the Delaware.

The Billinge trustees continued with their cautious and sober approach; not until two years later did they send out their first ship, the *Kent*; and not until 1680 were their legal problems ironed out. The line that was finally agreed upon was to run due north from the east side of Little Egg Harbor to a point on the Delaware in forty-one degrees of north latitude. The *Concessions and Agreements* that were finally drawn were a dramatic step forward in social philosophy. The Quaker scholar Amelia Mott Gummere has said, they "gave to the spirit of liberty a wider range than had heretofore been the case in any record of Anglo-Saxon organic law." They were to be the springboard for a greater social experiment on the other side of the Delaware five years later.

"We have made concessions by ourselves, being such as Friends here and there will approve of. . . . There we lay a foundation for after ages to understand their liberty as men and Christians, that they may not be brought in bondage, but by their own consent; *for we put the power in the people*, that is to say, they to meet and choose one honest man for each proprietary, who hath subscribed to the concessions; all these men to meet as an assembly there, to make and repeal laws, to choose a governor, or commissioner, and twelve assistants to execute the laws during their pleasure; so every man is capable to choose or be chosen. No man to be arrested, condemned, imprisoned, or molested in his estate or liberty, but by twelve men of the neighborhood. No man to lie in prison for debt, but that his estate satisfy as far as it will go, and be set at liberty to work. No person to be called in question or molested for his conscience, or for worshiping according to his conscience. . . ."

Thus did the proprietors themselves describe the frame of government they had designed. After his achievement at Old Bailey, Penn could not have set his hand to a document that did not provide trial by jury, and his precious liberty of conscience received forthright treatment in the words: "That no man nor number of men upon earth hath power or authority to rule over men's consciences in religious matters. . . ." The New Jersey Indians, who were merely to be treated "with humanity" under the Berkeley-Carteret *Concessions,* were given the right to bring grievances to the commissioners, and to have an impartial trial before six Indians and six settlers whether they were the accusers or accused.

The creative essence of the *Concessions* had been centuries in distillation from the days of the writing of Magna Charta, and even before. Faithfully the heretics of every generation had fed the fires under its retort, until the precious substance began to emerge in the doctrine of such groups as the Quakers and the social documents they produced. The *Concessions* were written at a time of tremendous social and intellectual advancement in England. On the political scene there was emerging the phenomenon of a representative Parliament that exerted increasing control over the King and showed a growing sense of responsibility to the country. Politically conscious philosophers like Thomas Hobbes, who talked of a contract between governing and governed, added their stimulation. Social ethics was a growing factor in England's political thinking. The pure mathematicians and such physical scientists as Halley, Boyle, Woodward, Hooke and Isaac Newton encouraged the trend. Individualism, so dear to the Quakers and the whole Puritan movement, grew more widespread as it went beyond theological areas, and the inquiring mind found new knowledge exhilarating and new thought patterns exciting as the spirit of experimentation gained momentum—in the laboratory, in the psychology of the human mind, in the wilderness.

Several writers (though not Besse) have called William Penn the author of the *Concessions,* but while Penn, the lawyer and visionary, may have drawn the first draft, Lawrie, Lucas, and many more of the 151 signers of the document, certainly had a voice in the final form. Penn's own conscience would not have permitted so important a document to depend upon a single personal judgment. The Quaker way is to develop ideas from the inter-creative group mind.

A broadside, *The Description of West New Jersey,* was circulated among Friends, followed by an epistle from Penn, Lawrie and Lucas. The project attracted wide interest, and when the *Kent* finally sailed she carried 230 passengers most of whom were Quakers. The *Kent* made her way up the Delaware River in August, 1677, and dropped anchor near the present site of Burlington, and there the little group of peacefully intended went ashore. The first arrivals were a little startled at the great numbers of snakes and the clouds of mosquitoes; they found the land really wild and had to build hasty shelters until they could erect substantial homes. Many had brought English brick with them for the purpose. Conscientiously they paid the Indians for their land before they occupied it, in the kind of currency the Indians wanted: kettles, petticoats, guns, hose, knives, axes, combs, needles, bells, rum, tobacco, scissors. When their communities were settled they could see their children play with the Indians without alarm and nod happily when Indian children came to the Friends' schools.

The first settlers followed the prearranged plans, laid out the town of Burlington that became their capital and most important port, built their homes, meeting houses and schools. Many were skilled artisans who had brought the tools of their trades with them: weavers, tailors, shoemakers. Most were husbandmen who, once they had cleared the forest from the rich, virgin soil, produced more than enough and saw the crops of their fruit orchards and grain fields go aboard export ships at Burlington.

The social experiment in a rankless community, where the right of self-determination of every individual was sacred, where God was the final source of authority, succeeded and prospered, and it did so on the simple formula: love-industry-integrity.

> Therefore, arise, thou Son of Kunti! brace
> Thine arm for conflict, nerve thy heart to meet—
> As things alike to thee—pleasure or pain,
> Profit or ruin, victory or defeat.
>
> —*Bhagavad-Gita* II

11. *Through Holland and Germany*

THE QUAKER movement was still in its revelatory stage when the New Jersey experiment was launched; new concepts were continually being added to it as they developed out of the mystical experiences of Fox and his followers, and the experimental community was one of these. Another was a definite church organization, which George Fox considered necessary. This latter development caused an internal strife in the Society, led by John Wilkinson and John Story, beginning as a local dispute among the northern meetings and spreading until an actual split in the ranks occurred which took all of the ability of Fox, Penn and others to heal. Fox's administrative genius could steer a course that would create an organization and still maintain the initial and fundamental Quaker concept of the individual's direct personal guidance by God, but followers of Wilkinson and Story watched Fox's organizational program with a dubious eye. Tyranny was a very real thing then, and the words "tyranny" and "government" were inseparable. Those who doubted Fox's wisdom saw real danger in creating a church government that could turn behemoth. Actually, Fox was preventing the concentration of power in a single individual or handful of individuals by distributing it throughout the Society in local centers, giving the individual meetings almost complete autonomy. As Fox traveled all over England, settling meetings, encouraging the development of women's meetings, drawing them together into monthly and quarterly business meetings, the disaffection he roused developed into the Wilkinson-Story Separation, about the time of his Worcester imprisonment. Such men as Whitehead, Parker and Penn stood solidly with Fox, and so did the vast majority of the membership.

Again Fox depended more upon his "Will Penn" than upon his other leaders. In April, 1675, Penn sent a lengthy paper to the northern meetings urging unity, and so did Parker, Whitehead and Fox. The following year, when constant efforts still had not brought the split to an end, William Penn traveled the more than two hundred and thirty miles to a special four-day conference at Draw-well near Sedbergh at the home of John Blaykling, going first to Swarthmoor, to see George and Margaret Fox. In the isolated gray stucco house set high on a hill overlooking the town of Ulverston, William Penn found Fox still weak and ill from his long Worcester imprisonment, unable to go to Draw-well in person, and Penn escorted Margaret Fox, her daughter Sarah and her son-in-law Thomas Lower, to Draw-well. After the conference they could report to Fox that the rift was at least partially healed.

The expense of so much traveling and the neglect of his personal affairs soon created a financial pinch in Penn's life, and an indenture dated June 3, 1676, reveals that some of Gulielma's properties in Sussex, inherited from her late father, had to be sold "for the rayseing of moneys for the supplying of such want and necessityes as by the providence of God they are att present fallen unto by reason the said William Penn is not able at present to recover such debts as are due unto him here in England, or to procure payments or retornes to be made unto him here in England of such rent as are due unto him, the said William Penn, for his estate in the Kingdome of Ireland. . . ." The schedule of properties sold yielded three thousand pounds. That Penn owned income properties in Ireland is certain, and it can be inferred that he owned them in England as well, since the above document suggests it, and so does another of a later date in the Granville Penn Collection which refers to "the said William Penn having a considerable real estate in England and Ireland." A closely attended estate yields more than a neglected one, and down through the years the declining income on the Irish properties alone tells its own story of Penn's devotion to the Quaker movement.

Shortly after the sale of Guli's Sussex property, William Penn moved his family from Rickmansworth to Worminghurst Parish in Sussex, about fifteen miles from Brighton. It is thought that this house may have been part of Guli's inheritance from her father; at least part of the land they had just sold was very nearby, some in the neighborhood of Shoreham and some described as "lying by the seaside." The thirty-two-year-old couple and their only living child, the year-and-a-half-old Springett, and a retinue of servants took up their abode in an ample red brick manor house on top of a hill between the North and South Downs. The place commands a magnificent view of the surrounding countryside, an area known as the Weald, covered in the seventeenth century with dense forest of oak and elm; and the air is brisk and brackish because of the nearness to the sea. A shell of the house is still there. A lane winds up the hill from Thakeham Village and approaches it from the north, and on that side it is a long, rectangular, straight-fronted, two-storied structure, with a gently pitched slate roof. On the south side, where there were once wings and attached outbuildings, and even a bell tower, the land falls away abruptly into a valley that held a lake in Penn's day. The insides of the walls of the house still show stumps of the heavy beams that once supported the floors and the scars of great fireplaces, chimneys and staircases. High and isolated, the Worminghurst estate was a place of peace and vast perspective, a visionary's aery.

The arrival of the Penns in Worminghurst brought much needed leadership to the local meeting; the Monthly Meeting (Horsham) frequently met at Worminghurst, and the meeting for worship met there every other Sunday, and alternately at John Shaw's until 1691, when John Shaw's house in Thakeham was made over into a meeting house, known today as the Blue Idol Meeting House, about four and a half miles from Worminghurst. The big manor house afforded ample opportunity for the kind of openhearted hospitality that Quakers love, and very soon after the removal of the Penns to Sussex the guests began to arrive.

Penn brought a quantity of Friends home with him from London Yearly Meeting in June, 1677, his first summer in southern England: George Fox; John Burnyeat; George Keith; Guli's stepfather, Isaac

Penington; Robert Barclay who had just been released from Tolbooth Prison in Aberdeen, and others. According to the Haistwell diary, most of them were there from the twentieth of June until the middle of July, and such an assemblage of outstanding personalities drew other visitors, until the premises took on the appearance of a full-fledged conference. It drew the attention of anti-Quaker sentiment as well, and when a huge meeting for worship was scheduled for July 12, the rumor flew that informers would be present. This could mean arrest and persecution; it could mean the beginning of a whole new set of unpredictable responsibilities for the Penns. Several hundreds of Quakers responded to the challenge and attended the meeting, and Fox asked them to be cheerful and fearless, while he took a walk in Penn's gardens to meditate and gather his own resources. In a quiet mingled with some tension Fox at last joined the worshipers and spoke to them at great length. The meeting lasted several hours and adjourned peacefully; the informers had either not come, or having come, had given up their troublemaking intent in the atmosphere of worship.

Fox and Burnyeat remained at Worminghurst longer than the other visitors, because they and Penn had a special task to perform—to answer an attack made upon Fox by Roger Williams of Rhode Island. True enough, Rhode Island had given persecuted Quakers from New England an asylum; and true enough, Roger Williams believed in toleration to a degree way beyond his own times; but that did not make him any less a Baptist, nor did he relinquish his right to disagree in public debate and in print with Quaker doctrine. The number of converts Friends were winning in America, with special inroads upon other sects made by the American journeys of George Fox, Burnyeat, Edmundson and others, was grating on the patience of many religious leaders. Roger Williams had published a pamphlet called, *George Fox Digg'd Out of His Burrows,* and so Fox and Burnyeat composed their reply, *A New England Fire-Brand Quenched.*

Penn's decision to go on a second ministerial trip through Holland and Germany may well have grown out of this meeting of Quaker leadership at Worminghurst, because he set out on his journey nine days after the departure of Fox and Burnyeat. When they left, on July 13, he rode out with them for about twelve miles, then hastened back to Worminghurst to give detailed instructions to servants and prepare himself, his wardrobe and his family for his absence. This second continental trip was to mark the end of the five-year interim period of his life, and it was to be his first lengthy absence from home since his marriage. He may or may not have known before he left that his wife was just beginning another pregnancy, but parting from the devoted, loving, lovely and understanding Guli would have been difficult in any event. For both Guli and William his "service of the Gospel" had first claim on their lives, and if he felt compelled to revisit the meetings through Holland and Germany, his "little flock and family of God in Emden," the struggling group in Friedrichstadt, Benjamin Furly in Rotterdam, the Princess Elizabeth in Herford, the misguided Labadists, the chain of little Quaker meetings that had developed along the routes of traveling missionaries, there would have been no word from Gulielma to detain him.

Robert Barclay had gone to Holland and Germany just the year before, and since that time had had a continuing correspondence with the Abbess of Herford and with one of her ladies-in-waiting, the Countess of Hornes. Later when Barclay was arrested and placed in prison in Aberdeen, the Abbess used her influence with her brother, Prince Rupert, to help secure the release of Barclay and his companions, and it was finally accomplished through her cousin, the Duke of York. Barclay's visit to Worminghurst after his release tied a lot of threads together in the Penn story—Penn's friendship with Elizabeth, his recently renewed relationship with the Duke of York and the King, his growing friendship with Barclay, and their impending trip to Europe together.

On the twenty-second of July, on First Day, William Penn left Worminghurst and took the road to London, reaching the city that same night, and all the next day he employed himself "on Friends' behalf that were in sufferings." Of this journey he kept a careful record, *An Account of W. Penn's Travels in Holland and Germany*. The second night he went out to Essex to pay his mother a visit. Margaret Penn by then was sixtyish, old for those times, left largely to herself in a big country house, grateful indeed for a visit from this first-born son who had moved his wife and child so far away from her, eager for news of her grandchild, ready to discuss her financial and estate affairs with him. Next morning he set out for Colchester and lodged with John Furly, brother of Benjamin of Rotterdam. A large group of Friends was going over to the Continent. John Furly, George Watts, William Talcot and others continued on with Penn to Harwich where they were joined by George Fox, Robert Barclay, George and Elizabeth Keith, and Isabel Yeamans. The party that set sail from Harwich consisted of nine Quakers and two servants; one of the travelers was the devoted diarist to Fox, Edward Haistwell.

They went aboard the packet in the evening and set sail at three o'clock in the morning. Haistwell reports a "fair wind" and a clear, calm day—a blessing in a Channel crossing. When the boat came to within a league of the opposite shore and Brielle and cast anchor, it was night. The sensible thing to do was to wait for daylight, but Penn was so driven on by the urgency of his mission that his natural lack of patience forced him to go ashore at once. Barclay, a hotheaded Scotsman, became infected with the same idea, and he and Penn climbed into a small boat. Their impatience only cost them unnecessary inconvenience, for the city gates were shut, and there were no houses outside the walls. They had to lie in a fisherman's boat until morning. With the returning day and the opening of the gates, they found that Benjamin Furly and others had come to Brielle to meet them with a boat and take them to Rotterdam.

Fox, Penn, Barclay, Keith—four of the greatest names in the first generation of Quakerism—traveling together! Barclay's *An Apology for the . . . Principles and Doctrines of the People Called Quakers*, the great theological treatise on Friends' doctrine, had just been published in Latin in Amsterdam the previous year, and would appear in the English language in another year. George Keith, ten years older than Barclay, was also a Scotsman and had been the great apologist's spiritual mentor in the early days of his convincement. He was an outstanding and substantial Friends' minister who later settled in East New Jersey, and became the Surveyor-General there.

Benjamin Furly's house in Rotterdam was their first major stop, and there a great, eager assemblage awaited them. Furly had been translating Penn's works into Dutch and publishing them in Holland; *Truth Exalted* was among them, and his *Letter of Love to the Young Convinced* came out in Rotterdam about the time of this visit. Two meetings at Furly's house were so successful that they touched off Penn's zeal to a degree like that of his earliest martyr days. "The gospel was preached, the dead were raised, and the living comforted!" he reported. Then came a canvass of homes to visit with small meetings all over the city. Several of them "dined and supped at two great men's houses." The seed had indeed sprouted and flourished during the six years between Penn's two visits to Holland. It was even more evident in Amsterdam, where such a large general meeting awaited them, that their organizational enthusiasms flowered and they established a Yearly Meeting to serve Friends in the entire area: Palatinate, Hambrough, Lubeck, Friedrichstadt, as well as a schedule of Quarterly and Monthly Meetings.

Penn must have sensed that he was moving back into the swiftest currents of Quakerism, and that his shore duties were ending.

After a huge meeting in Amsterdam in which the Quaker leaders took on a group of Baptists, Presbyterians, Seekers, Socinians, Collegians and Brownists, and "declared the Everlasting Truth" to them, Penn, Keith, Barclay and Furly left George Fox and went on to Naarden by boat, only stopping long enough to refresh themselves and then clamber into the common post-wagon for Osnabrück in Germany. Beyond Osnabrück lay Herford. "Now give up, O give up thy all, that thou mayst inherit eternal life!" Penn was going to say to the Princess Elizabeth. He and his companions reached Osnabrück late in the evening after a day and a half of traveling; they stopped at an inn, which suggests the lack of any meeting there, left some books on Quakerism in the Dutch language for the edification of the innkeeper, and set out early next morning. Penn was very conscious of a change that had taken place within himself since his previous trip over these routes. "We passed through a very dark country to that place; yet I felt not so great a weight and suffering in my spirit as six years ago, when I went through the same places." His emotional stability had vastly increased.

Late at night on August 9, a Thursday, they reached the city of

Herford. Elizabeth and the Countess of Hornes were expecting the visitors, and the fifty-eight-year-old Abbess sent word that she would receive them the next morning at seven. Six years had wrought their changes in Herford. The fuss and fury that had arisen around the Labadist colony had died away, because De Labadie had had the good grace finally to remove his colony when he realized that the situation there was insoluble. De Labadie had been dead three years, and the Labadist colony was carrying on in the Dutch city of Leeuwarden. The Quakers presented themselves at the appointed hour, and the Princess was frankly eager for the company of these spiritual emissaries. Her continuing loneliness had driven her deeper and deeper into her mystical devotions, and the minister in Penn responded at once to the gravity and scope of his opportunity. He surrendered up his whole ability and capacity to sessions with the Princess, her associates and staff, that lasted all day with only an intervening respite for luncheon. The Princess urged the Friends to return next morning, and the intensive gatherings were repeated. During an interlude, when Barclay was engaged in a conversation with Elizabeth, the Countess of Hornes drew Penn aside and whispered to him to "get a meeting for the more inferior servants of the house who would have been bashful to have presented themselves before the Princess." Penn followed the suggestion, and with exquisite tact the Princess withdrew to make the meeting possible, only returning after it was over to bid her visitors goodby.

The Quaker party spent three full days in Herford, leaving no soul untapped, from travelers who continued to arrive by post-wagon at the inn, to titled personages in the immediate community of the Abbess. On the evening of the second day this inner circle of "quality" drew Penn into a meeting in the Princess's private chamber and pleaded with him to extend his visit. He could not do that, he explained tenderly, for he "knew not when the Lord would give me such an opportunity." It pained him to have to refuse, for he could see that he was having some success in winning the Princess's friends to an understanding of Quakerism. He remained with them until around ten, talking, answering questions, explaining.

On their last afternoon in Herford they held a big meeting for town people as well as the inner circle of the abbey. Herford could be cordial to religious messengers when it wished; in fact, it responded with such vitality in that meeting that Penn's florid prose burst forth once more: "And by His own power He made way to their consciences, and sounded His wakening trumpet in their ears. . . . Oh, the day of the Lord livingly dawned upon us, and the searching life of Jesus was in the midst of us! Oh, the word that never faileth them that wait for it, and abide in it, opened the way, and unsealed the book of life!" Nothing thrilled Penn more, nor stimulated greater literary ardor in him, than a successful worship session, and this one left him almost beyond the bounds of language.

Elizabeth hurried to Penn and clasped his hand as soon as the meeting rose. She wanted to speak to him of the experience it had given her, but suddenly she turned away, clasped her hands to her breast and in a choked voice cried, "I cannot speak to you; my heart is full!"

Penn stood silently beside her until she could recover her poise, whispering just a few soft words of comfort. At last he made a move to withdraw, and she faced him once more.

"Will ye not come hither again," she pleaded. "Pray, call here as ye return out of Germany."

"We are in the hand of the Lord," he told her regretfully, "and being His cannot dispose of ourselves."

Others crowded about him when he left the Princess's side, and not until the ninth hour did Penn and his companions return to their lodgings. Princess Elizabeth, Abbess of Herford, had one parting message:

"Let me desire you to remember me, though I live at this distance, and that you should never see me more: I thank you for this good time; and know and be assured, though my condition subjects me to divers temptations, yet my soul hath strong desires after the best things."

If only she could be brought into the fold. . . .

From Herford Barclay turned back to Amsterdam, and Penn, Keith and Furly traveled deeper into Germany toward Frankfurt. They had a long stretch ahead of them, and they plotted their course through Paderborn, "a dark Popish town, under the government of a Bishop of that religion"; through Cassel in "great foulness of weather, having only naked carts to ride in"; only arriving at Frankfurt a week later. Wherever they stopped they declared their testimony and distributed reading matter. They must have left England happily loaded down with books, and they no doubt picked up more volumes in the Dutch and German languages in Rotterdam, for they scattered them like manna throughout their journey.

It was August when they passed through Germany, the month in which the *Kent* reached the Delaware with her adventurous passengers.

Having written ahead from Cassel of their forthright intent to harvest souls in Frankfurt, they were met well outside the city by "two considerable persons," who bore the glad tidings that there would be a meeting convened that same afternoon to hear them. One of their hosts was a merchant who had the meeting at his home, and there the weary but joyful travelers were greeted by "people of considerable note, both of Calvinists and Lutherans; and we can say, they received us with gladness of heart." Such gladness of heart, in fact, that they remained another day in Frankfurt and held a further meeting, convincing many more: two nobly born women, a student, a doctor of physick. Their impact upon the community was deep and lasting. "Their hearts yearned strongly toward us." Seized by religious ecstasy one young woman declared, "It will never be well with us till persecution come, and some of us be lodged in the Stadthouse [prison]." Many who attended the Quaker meetings were members of the Pietist group, a revitalizing movement taking place within the Lutheran faith, although their most prominent leader, Dr. Philipp Jacob Spener, never came to the meetings himself; and the effect upon the Pietist circles was so lasting that six years later it brought Pastorius to America and stimulated the formation of the Frankfurt Company to attempt to settle a community of people from Frankfurt, Duisburg, Wesel and the area in Pennsylvania.

In the midst of it all Penn found time to write his long epistle, *To the Churches of Jesus Throughout the World.* It is rather a Pauline thing, begging the scattered and the oppressed not to be discouraged; reminding them that they will always be visited in prison, fed when hungry, clothed when naked, ministered unto when sick. It is filled with comforting thoughts and good news of the success of his journey, urging the struggling little churches to be true to the Word and remain closely united.

Passing through the ancient city of Worms where major religious history had been made—the Concordat of the twelfth century, the Diet of the sixteenth at which Martin Luther had valiantly argued the cause of reform—Penn, Keith and Furly reached Krisheim in the Palatinate country. William Ames, William Caton, Samuel Fisher and John Stubbs had all visited these parts as Quaker missionaries in the first decade of Quakerism. Ames had paused in Krisheim in 1657, and the meeting that was waiting for Penn's message twenty years later was of Ames's creation. In this community, too, Penn's personal impression would result in the removal of several Dutch Quaker families to Pennsylvania. The town itself was not cordial, however, and the chief officer of the town, under pressure from the Calvinists, forbade the Quakers to preach. They went ahead and held their meeting anyway without being molested, but the threat of persecution troubled them, and they endeavored to obtain an interview with the ruling Prince Palatine, Princess Elizabeth's brother, living in Mannheim. Failing in this, Penn did the next best thing. He wrote to the Prince, asking him the searching question: "What encouragement a colony of virtuous and industrious families might hope to receive from thee, in case they should transplant themselves into this country, which certainly in itself is very excellent, respecting taxes, oaths, arms, etc." It was the eternal quest for a place of refuge where liberty of conscience could flourish.

Penn, Keith and Furly floated down the Rhine once more to Mainz, and from there took another side trip in an open chariot to Frankfurt, remaining over night and returning by boat down the Main to Mainz. Ancient center of the Holy Roman Empire, home city of Gutenberg, Mainz was to Penn a "dark and superstitious place," and he was frankly glad to remain there only long enough to change boats and continue the journey down the Rhine.

The Rhine Valley through which the travelers were passing is wide and flat around Mainz with rolling hills in the distance. Below Mainz the mountains close in gradually on the river until they rise sheer and precipitous from the very edge of the water. Today those steep green sides are partly wooded, partly covered with the traceries of terraced vineyards. In Penn's day they were covered with dense forests, punctuated infrequently with the turrets of a castle or Teutonic fortress. The travelers floated past Bacharach and Coblenz to Cologne. Below Coblenz the mountains begin to give ground and allow the river to grow wider, and at Cologne the Rhine Valley is wide and green and fertile. The Quaker missionaries reached the "great Popish city" of Cologne around three in the afternoon, and there they sought out a merchant whom they knew to be a "serious seeker after God," persuading him to arrange a meeting for them. They called on the town Resident, too, and were permitted to present their testimony.

"We gave him an account of how the Lord had appeared in the land of our nativity."

And so back to their boat and on to the city of Duisburg, at the juncture of the Ruhr and Rhine rivers. The Ruhr Valley city with its neighbors Mülheim and Broich was then in the Cleve-Mark portion, a disjoined colony, of the Brandenburg-Prussia dynasty. Armed with a letter of introduction from the Cologne merchant, Penn and his friends repaired immediately to a Dr. Mastricht. They wanted access to the Countess of Falkenstein of the House of Broich (Charlotte Auguste of Dhaun-Falkenstein), they told Dr. Mastricht. She was, they had heard, referred to derisively as a "Quakeress" and she suffered severe treatment at the hands of her father because of her deep interest in religion. Dr. Mastricht agreed to write to the Countess for them, but warned them not to embarrass her with open attention. He suggested that they go immediately, since it was Sunday, when she left her father's castle and spent the entire day across the river at the home of the minister of Mülheim. Like eager knights-errant the three set out to walk the six miles to Mülheim. They skirted cautiously about the back of the Count's castle and orchard and found a young schoolteacher who agreed to carry their message across the Ruhr River to the Countess. The Ruhr is not very wide; the messenger was back within the hour to report that the Countess wanted to see them but did not know where or how. A little discouraged, they started back toward Mülheim, and as luck would have it they passed in front of the castle just as the Count of Falkenstein was emerging. Who were these strangers? Attendants brought the three travelers before him. They were Englishmen come from Holland, going no farther in these parts than his own town of Mülheim, they explained humbly. What a spectacle they must have created before the haughty, well-turned-out Count, in their extra-plain, travel-battered garments, their hats firmly on their heads, bending neither neck nor knee.

Did they realize before whom they stood? Yes. Then why did they not deport themselves after a proper manner before noblemen? Why did they not pull off their hats? It was their practice, they explained, in the presence of *their* Prince, to remain covered. Suddenly the Count understood. Quakers! He could not have known that one of the offensive fellows was a friend of the Stuarts to whom he himself was related, and Penn did not enlighten him.

"We have no need of Quakers here! Get you out of my dominions," ordered the Count. "You shall not go to my town."

And he detailed some soldiers to escort them beyond the limits of Mülheim.

That was not the last episode in an eventful day, for when Penn, Keith and Furly reached Duisburg around nine at night, the city was huddled safely within its walls and the gates were locked. There was no choice but to lie down in a field and sleep. Awaking at three and finding themselves still alive and safe, they walked about together for the next two hours, grateful in voices and hearts for the protection they had enjoyed during the night. The great town clock soon struck five, the gates swung open, and the men went to their inn.

Penn sent a comforting letter to the unhappy Countess of Falkenstein. "I had seen thee, had not thy father's strange sort of severity hindered," he told her regretfully. A second letter of sterner stuff went to her father: "Art thou a Christian? How canst thou be rude, uncivil and persecute then? Thou art to love enemies, not abuse friends, harmless strangers." Dr. Mastricht made no effort to conceal his fear when they reported their experience, and cautioned them that no matter what risks they were willing to take in behalf of the Countess they would only be aggravating her situation. Reluctantly they prepared to leave Duisburg, but before they were gone a message came from the Countess echoing the warning. "For at some he sets his dogs, upon others he puts his soldiers to beat them."

August was gone and September was upon them, and they traveled with greater speed toward the Dutch border, holding meetings as they passed in Wesel, Rees, Emmerich and Cleves. From Cleves they traveled by wagon to Nijmegen in Holland, then by wagon all night to Utrecht where their paths divided. Keith and Furly went to Rotterdam, and Penn went to Amsterdam.

Fox was on his way back from Friedrichstadt, Penn learned, and the Haistwell diary places Fox in a boat crossing from Emden to Delfzijl on the fifth of September. Soon Penn could join Fox; soon they would be able to spend excited hours together comparing experiences, reporting results, taking off the newest tally of Truth's account.

A letter from Elizabeth awaited Penn in Amsterdam. She knew the hostile attitude of the House of Falkenstein at Mülheim. "It would be of much use for my family to have them disabused," she assured Penn. The same thought had been in Penn's mind. Oh, to disabuse them of their wrong thinking! It was an item of unfinished business that would continue to disturb him, until at last he would have to go back to Mülheim before returning to England.

On the evening of September 10 he left Amsterdam by boat for Hoorn. Peter Hendricks, one of the most important Quakers in Amsterdam, accompanied him. It was a grueling trip. They left their boat at Hoorn and continued by wagon to Enkhuizen, where they took another boat across the Zuider Zee to Workum in Friesland, and then went by wagon to Harlingen. At Harlingen George Fox, Isabel Yeamans, Frances Taylor, Thomas Rudyard and Jan Claus awaited them at Hesell Jacobs' house; and the combined vitalities coming together at this point had a tremendous impact on the Quaker community. Penn reports "two blessed meetings."

The reunion with Fox, though rich, was brief for Penn, lasting only a day. That same night William Penn with Jan Claus for interpreter took a boat up a long canal to Leeuwarden. Jan Claus who had been traveling with Fox was an Amsterdam merchant and a prominent Friend there. At this phase of his journey Penn was laboring under the directive of three items of unfinished business: the Labadist colony was near Leeuwarden; the Princess Elizabeth was in Herford and would be on his route after he came down from Schleswig-Holstein; and a "Quakeress" in Mülheim needed a rescuing knight.

Tensions must have accumulated in his soul as he approached the Labadists. He had been shabbily treated on his earlier visit to them, and he had failed that other time to convey any fragment of his message to the unfortunate, misguided colony. After the death of De Labadie the group had fallen under the leadership of one Ivon, an unknown quantity to Penn. Penn and Claus reached Leeuwarden around nine in the morning and held a meeting at ten, and as soon as Penn had swallowed his midday meal he wanted to be off again. He was too close, now, to be able to rest. The village of Wieuwerd where the Labadists were housed in the Somerdyke mansion was only a few hours' wagon ride south of Leeuwarden. Like a falling missile that increases its speed through each unit of time as it approaches its objective, Penn's intensity of purpose mounted as he pushed on in the jogging wagon for three hours. As soon as the house came into sight, he was out of the wagon, hiking across an open field toward a young man who turned out to be a Labadist. Penn wanted to see Ivon, the pastor, he made clear at once, and he wanted to see Anna Maria von Schürman. To his joyful amazement his reception this time was civil. Ivon appeared without any reluctance, explaining that Anna von Schürman was old, feeble and ill. Could not Penn forego an interview with her? Penn plunged immediately into a recitation of the treatment he had received at the hands of the Labadists six years ago, and his words flowed so eloquently that he was not only permitted to see Anna von Schürman, but promised an opportunity to address the entire group the following morning.

That night was not meant to be one of sound sleep for William Penn. The urgency of so many souls, the yet unknown temper of the group, the honest doubts a minister must entertain about his own adequacy if he be a true minister, the fatigue of his forced journey, all bore down upon him at once.

"That night a great weight was upon my spirit."

And it was still upon his spirit the next morning as he and Jan Claus rode the two miles from their village lodging to the Somerdyke mansion.

But William Penn could not have hoped for a finer gesture than was made to him by the Labadists. He was admitted immediately to Anna von Schürman's chamber, and there he not only talked with the learned "ancient maid" but with one of the Somerdyke women who attended her. Later the Labadists themselves and Ivon joined him there.

What, Penn asked by way of pivoting the conversation, had induced them to separate themselves from the common way they formerly lived in? And Ivon spoke at length. They had been dissatisfied with all of the Protestant churches and the "Babylonish assemblies of the world." Anna von Schürman spoke, and so did one of the Somerdykes and several more. They had all felt a deep need of closer communion with God, and to do that they had had to lay aside the vanities and encumbrances of the world.

Penn to his own happiness and comfort sensed a deep integrity in the group. "They are a serious, plain people, and are come nearer to Friends, as in silence in meetings, women speaking, preaching by the spirit, plainness in garb and furniture," he noted later. With complete fairness, they listened as he set forth his own testimony, beginning from his own earliest religious experiences as a child, as an Oxford undergraduate, as a student of Amyraut, as a witness of human suffering in the time of the London plague, and as a spiritual child of Thomas Loe. The Labadists were deeply reached by Penn's message and by his suggestion that the work of the true ministry was not to keep people to themselves in an isolated community but to turn them to God.

When he finally took his departure it was with the certain knowledge that he had found a deep fellowship among them, and that satisfying knowledge was pointed up by the fact that two of the lesser pastors and a doctor came as far as his waiting wagon to hold one last precious fragment of conversation.

Was it not true, one of them asked, that the Truth rose first amongst a poor, illiterate and simple sort of people?

"Yes," he told them, "that was our comfort, and that we owed it not to the learning of this world."

"Then," concluded the Labadist, "let not the learning of this world be used to defend that which the Spirit of God hath brought forth; for scholars now coming among you, will be apt to mix school learning amongst your simpler and purer language, and thereby obscure the brightness of the testimony."

A disturbed area of Penn's mind was at peace as he left the now-better-understood Labadist colony behind him and pushed on to the port of Delfzijl and on the sixteenth of September took an early morning boat across the bay to Emden. He took advantage of the four hours aboard ship to write a letter of counsel to Friends in England, *To Friends Everywhere Concerning the Present Separatists and Their Spirit of Separation,* because he knew the weight of his counsel could continue in that way to heal the Wilkinson-Story rift.

In Emden Penn came upon another disturbing situation. The Friends there had been "bitterly and barbarously used." He had known of it and had been sending letters of consolation to them as well as appeals for mercy to the Senate of Emden; and yet, seeing the tragic results of persecution at first hand, gave the knife in the heart a painful twist. The meeting, some twelve families in all, was scattered and broken; Dr. Haesbert and his wife were both dead. The members had suffered fines and imprisonment, were expelled from the country many times only to return persistently each time. Dr. Haesbert had been arrested again and again and finally died in prison. Penn hunted out the house of Dr. Haesbert's mother's family, and after a conference and meeting with them went away so burdened by the terrible need of Friends in Emden that he sat down in his lodgings to compose a letter to the President of the Council of State. The task palled; the scholarship failed. Who possessed sufficient language or eloquence to meet such a need? Not he, certainly! He threw down his quill and announced to Claus, "I must go myself to plead the innocent and suffering cause of our Friends with him."

The high-ranking gentleman was frankly astonished by his visitors and heard them as much out of curiosity as interest. He was not so much their enemy as they supposed, he assured them, and said that if Penn would write a letter to the Senate, he himself would deliver it. Every human being has a redemption point! The Friends had learned that lesson over and over again. As a result of Penn's appeal the persecutions in Emden were stopped, and Friends were permitted to convene in peace.

From Emden Penn traveled overnight by water to Leer and from Leer next morning took a wagon the rest of the way to Bremen, where he and Claus were joined once more by Keith and Furly who had come directly from Amsterdam. Circumstances in Bremen were not as tragic as in Emden, but they were not easy, and the Quaker group was only just beginning to take form. The traveling ministers found public officials shy of being associated with them, but in the city there were private citizens who offered powerful potential. The travelers pushed southward from Bremen—toward a lodestone—inevitably, even though they hadn't promised that they would or could return—toward Herford and its extraordinary Abbess.

The men arrived in Herford on the morning of the twenty-second, and by two that afternoon the Princess was able to see them. Happy reunion! Their supper together Penn called "a true Supper to us, for the hidden manna was manifested and broken amongst us." Here was a minister's opportunity to be dwelt upon longer. Could they not call on her again tomorrow?

"With all my heart," said the Abbess, "but will ye not come in the morning, too?"

And so in a heavily emotionalized atmosphere, from seven in the morning until ten at night of the following day, William Penn, Jan Claus, George Keith and Benjamin Furly met with the Abbess and her household and townsfolk—a three-hour morning session, a midday break, an afternoon session, supper and an evening retreat with only the Princess and Countess. On the third day the Friends conferred with the Princess on her governmental role regarding the sufferings of Friends in England. When evening had fallen, the Princess drew the Quakers into her private chambers for a farewell meeting—"eternally magnified, richly flowing," is the descriptive language that comes down to us. "Let my soul never forget the divine sense that overwhelmed all."

And Penn was gone from Herford once more, jouncing along in a wagon bound for Wesel in the Rhine Valley. The two hundred-odd English miles overland from Herford to Wesel without lying down on a bed or sleeping otherwise than in the wagon for three days and three nights was the most taxing stretch of the entire journey. To further harass the fastidious Friends, their company was increased to twelve by some hymn-singing Lutherans. Profane talk one hour and psalms to God the next! Penn declared that his soul was "sad even unto death." A day in Wesel and he and his companions turned southward up the Rhine Valley, because they were not quite ready to return home. Here in the lower Rhine country existed challenges to their lifetime mission that could not be ignored—in Düsseldorf which they had missed on the first leg of their journey, in Cologne, in Duisburg and in Mülheim where the Quaker-inclined Countess of Falkenstein lived. They soon learned that a man named Reiner Coppers was parson of the Mülheim reformed church, and that it was he who stood in the way of their meeting the Countess. The Friends appealed once more to Dr. Mastricht and were once more told that it would be unwise to try to see Charlotte Augusta because of the Count. Penn remembered well enough the disposition of the man who had said, "We have no need of Quakers here!" And so they withdrew and set out for Wesel next day. They passed through Cleves and Nijmegen to Utrecht where they caught a night boat for Amsterdam, reappearing once more in Amsterdam on First Day morning, October 7, in time to join their beloved George Fox in meeting for worship.

Quakers had been kicking up considerable theological dust in Amsterdam and interest in them was widespread enough to draw some flattering opposition. Among the opposition was Galenus Abrahams. Abrahams is defined by Haistwell as "the greatest Baptist in all Holland," by Herman van Lil as "the father of Socinianism" (sometimes known as Old Unitarianism), and by Penn the "great father of the Socinian Menists in these parts." Any of these definitions implies an eloquent, scholarly, forceful and captivating personality, a man skilled in argument, a worthy opponent. Abrahams' challenge of Quaker principles resulted in two meetings, the first a public debate on October 9 between Abrahams and Penn, Fox and Keith; the second on October 11 was a private meeting of

Penn and Keith with Abrahams at the home of Cornelis Roeloffs. On the intervening day the travel-weary Quakers held a public meeting with Fox, Penn and Keith as the principal speakers, and to it hundreds came. Furly and Claus worked diligently throughout as interpreters. At the end some priests of other denominations made their customary challenge, and it was William Penn who arose to meet it with a splendid effect upon the gathering.

After four days of extraordinary meetings, Fox, Penn and Furly set out for The Hague, pausing over night at Leiden. During the brief pause Penn's travel fatigue dissolved when he learned that in the village of Wonderwick, an out-of-the-way place they had just passed, lived a family who showed great interest in Friends' principles; but matters called him and the others to The Hague first, and after The Hague they must go to Rotterdam. Wonderwick preyed on Penn's mind like some kind of personal bidding. Something or someone at Wonderwick needed *him,* and he knew that before he left Holland he must search out the family there. Furly and Fox planned to spend seven full days in Rotterdam, and Penn was deeply devoted to them and their mutual calling; but that which is within a man is stronger than all outside influences. Penn managed to remain in Rotterdam for three days during which time he wrote four expostulatory epistles: *A Call to Christendom, Tender Counsel and Advice, To All Those Professors of Christianity,* and A *Tender Visitation in the Love of God.* But even as he wrote his epistles "the sense of the serious retreat of the great man we heard of at Leiden was so strong upon me, that I could not see myself clear to leave the country before I had given him a visit."

Although Benjamin Furly's home was in Rotterdam, its ample hospitality may have been overtaxed at the time, for Penn was lodging with a family named Sonnemans, two of whom, B.F.A. Sonnemans and M. Sonnemans, accompanied him to Wonderwick. They reached the village late in the evening, engaged lodgings at the inn and proceeded directly to the man's house. There awaited Penn a vivid verification of the Light Within that had bid him go, in the warm reception the family gave him, in the earnestness with which they sat with him in silence, and in the need they showed to hear his testimony and tell him of their own experiences in seeking the

Truth. It was late when Penn finally rose to go; and his host had tears in his eyes as he clasped Penn's hand and said,

"My house is blessed for your sakes; and blessed be God that I ever lived to see you."

Could Penn and the Sonnemans not stay the night? No, they were sorry, but they had "pre-engagements" elsewhere. It was a "scandal to their house that they should let such good people go!" For reasons which Penn does not explain, he and the Sonnemans returned to the inn for the night; and they set out next morning to make the day-long trek back to Rotterdam.

Here in Rotterdam was the end of William Penn's second ministerial journey on the Continent. Here in Rotterdam must come the personal summing up and self-evaluation. What had he achieved? What seen? What had been the effect upon himself? His achievements were those of the movement, all intertwined with the efforts and accomplishments of the whole complement of ministers making this evangelical effort, of old hearts replenished and new hearts reached, of confounders confounded, of life lines tightened and organizational structures extended and improved. He had seen at the same time Friends persecuted and scattered, officials cold to appeals for mercy or cautious of their own reputations, and royal attitudes turned suddenly evasive when confronted with the direct question: "What encouragement would a colony of virtuous and industrious families hope to receive from thee, in case they should transplant themselves into this country?"

Penn was moving with increased momentum toward the close of this inconspicuous and relatively quiet phase of his life. Actually, he had been living through a kind of withdrawal not unlike the withdrawal that Arnold J. Toynbee describes as that followed by "creative personalities when they are taking the mystic path which is their highest spiritual level." For Penn this was a preparative, resource-gathering period, when his impulsive imagination seemed to allow him some respite, and now the grand extravagance in his nature was reawakening and gathering itself to break forth into one of the most extraordinary programs that a man could dare to attempt singlehanded.

He that acts doubtfully is damned.
——William Penn, *The Great Case of Liberty of Conscience*

12. The Seed of a Nation

Fox, Penn, Keith and others boarded a packet boat at Brielle, and the return Channel crossing was probably one of the most unfortunate that has ever happened to a group of passengers. Foul weather and raging waves kept them at sea for three days and two nights in a leaky vessel that required the use of two pumps going constantly to keep out the water, while wind, rain and hail beat down. When the devout little group at last set foot on English soil, God received full credit for their safe arrival.

When Penn awoke next morning in Harwich, he felt refreshed enough to write to Friends in Holland and Germany, and by another day he and Keith were mounted on saddle horses and headed for Colchester, leaving Fox to follow later in a coach. They lodged with John Furly, attended a great meeting next morning, and set out once more to make the two-day journey to London on horseback.

Alarming circumstances awaited Penn there. The campaign of the Cavalier Parliament to exterminate Puritan sects was still in full force and gave no indication of lessening in the near future. Relieved of the restraining influence of the King's late Act of Indulgence, local magistrates were gleefully riding their judicial responsibilities roughshod. The news of further persecutions and sufferings of Friends is undoubtedly what caused Penn to delay until November first before returning to Guli and Worminghurst. Instead, he set out on a town-to-town, meeting-to-meeting canvass to pick up the threads of information. He learned that in New England persecutions had worsened since Quakers there no longer had a patron in England, and from Scotland came similar reports. The times called for a miracle to relieve such suffering, before the souls of Friends passed the point of maximum endurance.

Penn returned to Sussex only for a brief visit, and when he ascended the winding road to the great, many-roomed house on top of the hill, he found "my dear wife, child and family all well." Guli expected her next child soon; his son, Springett, would be three in January. In a letter to Margaret Fox Penn described Springett as "a large and active child," and said of Guli, "my wife is big, and expects to lie in the first week in the first month [March]. Let her condition be remembered by thee."

Within two weeks he was back in London with George Fox, at Meeting for Sufferings, a group of the Yearly Meeting that convened every week to gather reports of suffering Quakers anywhere in the world and consider ways and means to ease their trials. From the middle of November to the middle of February Penn is recorded so often in London at Meeting for Sufferings and in Bristol that it is very likely he did not get home during those weeks at all. In London he sometimes lodged at the home of a William Hages (probably William Hedges). The first week of December, he, Fox, Mead and Alexander Parker were in Ratcliff.

Even Penn's exceptionally vigorous health protested at the constant drain of its resources, and he was forced to admit that he felt the accumulation of fatigue. "I have been lately very ill-oppressed in body and spirits, but blessed be the God of my life."

Penn wrote to those he could not reach in person—to Margaret Fox in the northwest assuring her of her husband's safe arrival from Europe, to Peter Hendricks promising him a complete account of the debate with Abrahams.

A letter came to him from the Princess Elizabeth. She had searched her soul, she told him, and had at last been compelled to write and say that she could not see her way clear to embrace the Quaker faith. Penn must have nursed that disappointment a long time.

At the beginning of January Penn was in Bucks County, at Thomas Ellwood's, helping Fox, Parker, Keith and others draw up a paper on the sufferings of Friends under the Test Act; and by the end of January he was in Bristol with George Fox to try to wind up the Wilkinson-Story dispute. Story's stubbornness held Penn in Bristol until the nineteenth of February, much longer than he could conveniently remain, and the matter still had to be held over until they could meet again in London at Ellis Hooke's chambers in October.

He could have been home in time for the birth of his next child. At any rate, no record appears of his being elsewhere from the time he left Bristol until he appeared back in London the latter part of March. Letitia Penn, destined to survive the hazards of childhood and enjoy her womanhood for many years after her father's death, was born at Worminghurst, on March 6, 1678—fifth birth, second survival.

William Penn appeared in person before a committee of the House of Commons on the twenty-second of March, to represent the Quakers in an appeal for toleration. The audience was the direct result of a petition sent in by the Friends in which they pleaded that the real problem was the loyalty oath itself, not their loyalty to King and country. Could not a clause be inserted in the law allowing them to give their word instead of their oath? Many industrious families were being ruined by excessive fines resulting from laws that were really designed against the Papists.

Friends had been eager to get their appeal before Parliament, for the complex national picture kept changing like a kaleidoscope. Charles had called Parliament into session only very recently, and there was no foreseeing how soon he would prorogue it. The convening, proroguing and dissolving of the legislative body was a royal prerogative. Charles's position was difficult and dangerous. Not only was the Parliament gaining rapidly in strength and influence but its membership had been gradually changed in quality by replacements and the King no longer had its wholehearted support. There was a strong element within it that had begun to take on the appearance of a political opposition party, and the element within the Parliament was indicative of the growing movement throughout the country. The King could not allow such a Parliament to sit in session too long; neither could he permit a new one to be elected and run the risk of strengthening the opposition. This new social phenomenon, an actual opposition group known as the Country Party that had such men as Lord Russell, Sir William Coventry and Shaftsbury conspicuous in its membership, would in time become the Whig movement, and its immediate motivation was fear of Charles's Catholicism.

Penn made two speeches before the committee of the House of Commons, in which he gave a lucid representation of what the Quakers really meant by freedom of conscience. He had himself often been mistaken for a Papist, he told the committee, but he did not wish his intent to be mistaken. Even though he proclaimed against the injustice of whipping Quakers for Papists, he was far from thinking that Papists should be whipped for their consciences. "For we must give the liberty we ask, and cannot be false to our principles, though it were to relieve ourselves, for we have good will to all men, and would have none suffer for a truly sober and conscientious dissent on any hand." The obvious integrity of the Quakers convinced the committee, and a relief clause was agreed upon and did pass the House of Commons, but before it could work its way through the House of Lords, Parliament was once more prorogued by the King.

Penn drew upon himself a virulent wave of criticism and accusation for having dared to speak a word of tolerance, not for Catholicism, but for the right of Catholics to worship according to their own consciences. So much so that those who knew and loved him were deeply concerned for his reputation, as was John Gratton of Derbyshire who wrote to Penn pleading for evidence of Penn's innocence to show his friends:

> In that binding seed of life I question not but thou art right sensible of my love in the Truth unto thee and at this time in the weighty sense of God's love it was in my heart to write unto thee to acquaint thee that here is in thy country a very malicious lie and false accusation cast upon thee and so forcibly affirmed. . . . The thing is this: they say thou art turned to be a Jesuit and doth hide thyself or art fled thy country, a thing so far from thee as east and west . . . therefore, for the staying the mouth of lies and for Truth's sake . . . I would have thee if thou see and find it with thee so to do, to write as speedily as thou can to me or William Stors of Chesterfield that we may show it to some who seem to believe it and in this belief of it seems to bemoan us for your deluded men and women. . . .

The problem persisted, and almost a year later the Meeting for

Sufferings in London recorded this minute: "Friends being sensible of the great scandal cast on William Penn and that his absence adds to the same, it's the desire of Friends that Tho. Zachary write to him this post."

I cannot explain what is meant by Penn's "hiding" or "absence" referred to in these two items, unless he was taking a much needed rest at Worminghurst and indulging in a few happy hours with Guli, his young son and brand-new daughter. He could only have been "hiding" during the summer months of 1678, since he appeared before Parliament the end of March and by the following December was prominent in Sydney's election.

The whole attack upon Penn was part of a greater fury. In that year of 1678 the rising tide of anti-Catholic hysteria was reaching its peak, for Titus Oates had just burst upon the English scene with his infamous lies, accusations and rumor-mongering. Oates had behind him a checkered career that included indictment for perjury and expulsion from a Jesuit college. Disgruntled and nursing a grudge against the Catholics, Oates arrogantly presented himself in the role of devout Anglican and pleaded for an audience with the King's Privy Council so that he could reveal a dastardly popish plot being hatched by the Jesuits to conquer England with the aid of French and Irish Catholics, murder the King, and convert every Englishman at the point of a sword. Oates's magnificent lie had enough fragmentary evidence to feed upon. The immediate heir to the throne *was* an avowed Catholic; the Irish Catholics were perfectly capable of murdering Protestants; the Stuarts had already had many dealings with the King of France, in fact, a temporary military alliance with him in the war against Holland. True, Charles II had just married his niece Mary, the Duke of York's daughter, to Protestant William of Orange, but that reassuring item was lost in the hysteria that followed in the wake of Oates's testimony and engulfed England in a reign of terror that lasted almost three years. The witch-hunting was launched, warrants issued against Jesuits, many served by Oates himself, arrests made, witnesses of doubtful vintage heard. Tragically, some damning correspondence between the Duke of York's secretary and Catholic church representatives at the French Court was uncovered, giving Oates's whole yarn the semblance of truth.

On top of that Sir Edmund Godfrey, a Protestant magistrate connected with the case, was murdered. The discovery of his body and its public display was all that was needed to raise public passions to fever pitch. England was in danger! Everyone was in danger from the infiltrating Catholics plotting to overthrow the government. Reputations crumbled, heads were lost on the gallows, in an inquisition that lasted from the fall of 1678 well into 1681.

Because they could not avail themselves of the protection of the loyalty oath, the Quakers were susceptible to the worst suspicions of the anti-Catholic witch hunt, and Penn was particularly susceptible because of his personal association with the Stuarts, his renewed visits to Court, and his statement before the committee of the lower House that not even Catholics should be whipped for their faith. At this point what appears to be a sharp contradiction in Penn's views must be examined: his devotion to the Stuarts versus his role of increasing leadership in the Whig Party. During those years of turmoil aggravated by Titus Oates, when confidence in the King and the Royalists sank to a new low, the Whig Party matured—dedicated to Protestantism, to toleration for Protestant dissenters, and to the supremacy of Parliament. The principle of toleration drew individual Quakers inevitably into the Whig ranks, although they shrank from the extremest wing that was willing to resort to violence and arms. In embracing Whigism Penn was being true to his Quaker disposition. His faith required him to follow the bidding of the guiding Light within him, the divine spark that revealed the difference between right and wrong as he went along and did not permit him to count the consequences. If the principles for which the conservative Whigs stood were right, then he must risk the esteem of the Stuarts in embracing them, even to the extent of campaigning for a Whig candidate in the general election that Charles II was soon forced to allow. On the other hand, his association with the Stuarts was founded on a deep personal love that had come down from father to son on both sides. Penn's purist type of toleration would not permit him to renounce a personal friendship because of a difference in political and religious viewpoints. Time and again over the years his was the role of true friend when he went to either Charles or James and pleaded with them to change this policy or that plan. That they so seldom heeded his warnings and advices was to their own undoing.

William Penn was taking the whole evil political picture upon himself as his personal cumulative burden, and he was increasingly viewing England as a place impossible for the pure in heart. From Worminghurst the first week in November, 1678, came a passionate message *To the Children of Light in This Generation*, an epistle of concentrated intensity.

"Many days and weeks, yea some months hath my heart been heavy, and my soul unusually sad for the sake of this nation, the land of our nativity! For I have not only long beheld with a grieved eye, the many abominations and gross impieties that reign therein, the lusts, pleasures, wantonness, drunkenness, whoredoms, oaths, blasphemies, envy, treachery and persecution of the just; but for some time I have had a deep sense that the overflowing scourge of God's wrath and indignation was just ready to break out upon the people, confusion, amazement and misery! The weight of which hath caused me to cry within myself, Who shall save us? Who shall deliver us? . . . My friends, whilst the sense of this distress, that is coming as a dreadful visitation . . . lay so heavy upon my spirit, the Lord presented before me all the truly conscientious, and well-inclined people in these nations; and more especially you, His dispised, but chosen generation, for whose sake He would yet have mercy. And, in the midst of His judgments, this I received for you from the Lord, as His Holy Will and Counsel, and it often sprung in my heart with a very fresh and strong life, TO THY TENTS, O ISRAEL!" In the rest of his epistle he exhorted Friends to be more scrupulous than ever of their principles. "We are the people above all others that must stand in the gap," he cautioned them, "and we shall yet be called, The Island Saved by the Lord."

Penn had had a vision that he was not quite ready to interpret, and visions do not just happen; they come only after many, many hours, days, weeks, of searching and seeking.

The lusts, the wantonness, the treachery, the persecution of the just, went on fanning his righteous fears for the destiny of England and Englishmen, and when on January 24, 1679, Charles was at last obliged to dissolve the Cavalier Parliament and allow a general election, Penn's meditations produced a further literary fruit, *England's Great Interest in the Choice of This New Parliament: Dedicated to All Her Freeholders and Electors.* He did not sign it with his own name but with the pseudonym, Philanglus, a word he apparently coined himself from the Greek word for love and the Latin word for English, thus declaring himself a lover of England. In this short tract he set forth permanent standards of integrity for both governed and those who govern as well as what amounts to a party platform. He called upon Englishmen to act with wisdom, caution and integrity, for all was at stake. This new Parliament they were choosing would have to discover and punish the plot (even he believed Oates at that point), to remove corrupt ministers of state who had been giving the King wrong advice, to punish corrupt members of the former Parliament, to create new laws that would curb corrupt ministers and ease the burden on Protestant dissenters. "Guide and fix your choice upon men that you have reason to believe are well-affected, able, bold, to serve the country in these respects." Then he went on to state the three fundamental rights of Englishmen:

Property:—"right and title to your own lives, liberties and estates. In this every man is a sort of little sovereign to himself."

Legislation—or the power of making laws: "No law can be made or abrogated without you," he told the electorate. "No law can be made, no money levied, nor a penny legally demanded without your own consent."

A share in the judicatory power—this was Penn's precious jury.

Penn fully planned to implement this theory of government with practical application, for he had in mind a highly esteemed neighbor of his who possessed the necessary qualifications of wisdom, integrity and boldness. That man was Algernon Sydney, whom Penn may have met on his first trip to France with Sydney's nephew, Robert Spencer. Sydney was now fifty-eight; he had returned to England from his long exile only the year before, about the time that Penn returned from his journey through Holland and Germany. Penshurst, ancient home of the Sydneys, was near Tunbridge Wells in Kent, some twenty-five miles to the east of Worminghurst. A medieval, gray-walled mansion, it stood deep in the same chain of wooded hills between the North and South Downs. Residents of the two estates had visited back and forth for many years. Penn was acquainted with Algernon's father, Philip Sydney, the Earl of Leicester, and Algernon's brother, Henry.

Algernon Sydney's political thinking ranked with the most advanced of his times, and in some respects it went beyond his times. His was the open-minded, inquiring approach to each problem as it arose. "Implicit faith belongs to fools, and truth is comprehended by examining principles," he said. And his was the kind of bold, open-faced intellectual honesty that had led others like him in times past to lay their brilliant heads on the axeman's block. Man was entitled not only to create the form of government that he preferred, but he was further entitled to abrogate it, Sydney believed; and the best governments came out of the combined judgments of many, they must never be left to the will of one man. He believed that all governmental power came from the consent of the governed and was set up in the interest not of the governors but of the governed. "Power is not an advantage, but a burden." He declared openly against the divine right of kings: "There is no natural propensity in man or beast to monarchy." His dream for England was a republic with a monarch at its head whose powers were carefully limited by laws created by an elected Parliament.

That Penn should want Algernon Sydney to stand for election when the opportunity arose was inevitable, and he along with others must have exerted considerable pressure on Sydney to persuade him to squander his fading energies in the primitive, raucous brawl of a seventeenth-century style election. But, as William Penn had already stated in his pamphlet: "There seems never to have been a time, wherein this kingdom ought to show itself more serious and diligent in the business of its own safety. To be plain with you, all is at stake!" And Sydney knew he was right. England in this confused hour, this time of testing through the electorate the Parliament's weight against the Crown, this time of wresting from rampant political infamies a genuine liberty of conscience for Englishmen, needed all of her Sydneys.

Guildford in Surrey, some thirty miles northwest of Worminghurst, was the town chosen from which Sydney would seek a seat in Parliament, as a candidate of the Country Party, which the Whig

Party was still called. The appearance of Penn and Sydney upon the scene in Guildford caused an immediate uproar from demonstrating crowds inspired by the Court Party. When the two men presented themselves to the Mayor to make formal announcement of their intent, the Mayor was thrown into a blustering quandary. An opposition candidate? It wasn't done! The electorate of this town simply came forward to shout its approval of candidates chosen by the Mayor and Corporation, and since the candidate was Mr. Delmahoy, Sydney had best go home. Sydney refused. The Mayor then told him he was not a freeman (one entitled to citizenship and franchise in the town) and therefore could not be elected. When the intruders still stood their ground, the Mayor told them he would have to consult the Corporation and that they would hear soon. Knowing perfectly well they would not, Penn and Sydney went ahead and launched their vote-raising campaign, trudging from door to door, talking, persuading, working at their canvass for three weeks. Sydney was not well known in Guildford when he started, but Penn was, and many of Penn's acquaintances there were Quakers. The canvass was rolling up an obviously substantial support for Sydney, and the Court Party realized that measures, fair or foul, would have to be taken to prevent Sydney's election.

At last Penn and Sydney called again on the Mayor to ask what day the election was to be held, and were told it would be either "Friday week or Monday fortnight." But shortly after noon on Friday the Mayor suddenly announced that the election would be at nine the next morning—Saturday and market day. Intense public interest drew a melee to the hustings, Penn in their midst, still persuading and campaigning. The whole country was stirred up with electioneering, pamphleteering, name-calling and "Visions, seditions, and railing petitions." "Let Tories guard the King, Let Whigs on halters swing," said one side. "As rascals changing rags for scarlet coats, Cudgell'd before, set up to cut Whig throats," retorted the other. The shouting, jostling crowd in Guildford could barely be quieted sufficiently by the Mayor as he propounded to Sydney the original excuse for barring him from office: Was he a freeman? No? Then in that case he could not be elected, "although he had the plurality of voices." In the milling uproar that followed many declined with dignity to register their votes; others retired from the onslaught of ridicule. To make certain of the results the Mayor allowed even almsmen and other unqualified persons to vote. Worked up to a high pitch of excitement, Penn continued to plead and persuade among the electorate, ignoring such epithets as *Jesuit*, until the Mayor ordered him removed.

It had been a grossly illegal affair, as Penn realized; and he realized, too, what it must have cost Sydney in anguish; but they were into it now and they could not withdraw midway. Home in Worminghurst, William Penn composed a careful letter to Sydney:

Dear Friend:

I hope you got all well home, as I, by God's goodness, have done. I reflected upon the way of things passed at Guildford, and that which occurs to me as reasonable is this, that so soon as the articles or exceptions are digested, we should show them to Sergeant Maynard, and get his opinion of the matter. Sir Francis Winnington and Wallope have been used on these occasions too. Thou must have counsel before the Committee; and to advise first upon the reason of an address or petition with them, in my opinion, is not imprudent but very fitting. If they say that . . . they believe all may amount to an unfair election, then I offer to wait presently upon the Duke of Buckingham, Earl of Shaftesbury, Lord Essex, Lord Halifax, Lord Hollis, Lord Gray and others, to use their utmost interest in reversing this business. This may be done in five days, and I was not willing to stay till I come, which will be with the first. Remember the non-residents on their side, as Legg and others. . . . I hope a disappointment so strange (a hundred and forty poll-men as we thought last night considered) does not move thee. Thou, as thy friends, hast a conscientious regard for England; and to be put aside by such base ways is really a suffering for righteousness. Thou hast embarked thyself with them that seek, and love, and choose the best things; and number is not weight with thee. . . . 'Tis late, I am weary, and hope to see thee quickly. Farewell.

Sydney did follow Penn's advice and petition the House of Commons to have the results of the election reversed, but it was either pigeonholed or lost in the confusion. Penn and Sydney decided to try once more, and when they learned that the first Whig Parliament had been dissolved and that a new election was to be held, some time in the autumn of 1679, they chose Bramber in Sussex, close to Worminghurst. There Penn's influence was even greater than it had been in Guildford. The Court Party retaliated with vicious humor; it nominated Sydney's brother Henry to run against him, gleefully exploiting a family difference. In spite of the tremendous appeal Sydney and Penn were able to make in their pre-election canvassing, the two Sydneys received an equivalent number of votes and the final decision devolved upon the House of Commons. The second Whig Parliament convened in October and was immediately prorogued for a year by Charles. Sydney never obtained his seat.

Immediately after the Bramber election Penn published another short tract, again signed Philanglus, *One Project for the Good of England; That Is, Our Civil Union Is Our Civil Safety. Humbly Dedicated to the Great Council The Parliament of England.* It is packed with earnest pleading for a government of laws rather than of men under which "civil interest is the foundation and end of civil government," and within the framework of which the integrity of the individual non-conformist is respected.

The evil mood of the two elections cast a shadow over his hopes for governmental integrity in either low or high places. The local picture had been corrupt in the Guildford election; the corruption had come down from the top at Bramber. It expressed itself in other ways. Penn's steward, Philip Ford, had been arrested and fined in March because of his pacifist convictions; he had failed to report for duty with his arms when summoned. In July the Meeting for Sufferings again listed Ford among those who suffered distraint of goods. And corruption wasn't confined to England. Barclay wrote Penn of the persecution of Friends in Aberdeen, and Penn himself felt compelled to write to the Prince of Orange to enlist his aid in helping a group that had been banished from Krefeld. Early in 1680 a friend of the Friends both in England and on the Continent died —Princess Elizabeth, Abbess of Herford. Her memory persisted a long time; two years later a memorial to her appeared in his most important tract, *No Cross, No Crown.*

Spring brought William and Gulielma Penn a touch of real happiness—another child—to be his father's namesake. William Penn, Jr., was born March 14, 1680, and like Springett and Letitia this lad would achieve adult life. The deep ballast in Penn's life during these years was his home. While we have only fragmentary biographical knowledge of Gulielma Penn, what we do have tells us of a quiet, unobtrusive devotion of more than twenty years' duration and a gentle competence expended almost entirely on her home. Gulielma provided the stability, the constancy and good faith needed to steady her husband against the treacheries and difficulties of the world in which he worked.

In that world he could see no real solution for the Friends, and the thread of an old idea—an American refuge—persisted in his mind, kept alive by the success of the West New Jersey project and by its legal problems that reached a solution in the summer of 1680 when the opinion was handed down that Friends had purchased the government of West New Jersey as well as the soil. The decision had pivoted upon a test case. The government of New York, which then extended all down the west side of the Delaware River to the border of Maryland, was imposing a tax on all imports and exports that came up the Delaware River. The Duke of York's agent simply assumed that he had jurisdiction of the whole river, and since West New Jersey had no other access to the sea he had little difficulty in collecting. "We have not lost English liberty by leaving England," declared the Jersey Quakers. They could not "give up the right of making laws" and resign themselves to the will of another government. "By this precedent we are assessed without law, and excluded from our English right of common assent to taxes."

West New Jersey was already a prospering community with her plenitude of venison, fowl, fish, fat bucks, orchards laden with apples, peaches, cherries, fields bursting with corn, wheat, strawberries, cranberries; but West New Jersey could not hold everyone. And there were so many—so many in England, Ireland, Scotland, Germany and Holland who needed a place to rebuild their lives! The land across the river from West New Jersey possessed the same rich soil, the same abundance, and it was scantily peopled. From the Delaware it extended westward into raw, dense and unexplored wilderness known to none but the primitive native inhabitants. On its southern flank lay Maryland, and its northern side was lost in more wilderness. Space enough for a hoard of refugees, and the land was part of the Duke of York's grant.

Land grants in America were political plums. Only when the Jersey plum had rotted did Berkeley toss it aside and allow it to fall into the hands of Quakers. The Stuart kings in the face of the rising threat of Whigism could not be expected to hand out a plum to a group of Whigs; such a gesture could cost Charles the support of his own Court Party, and it would at least arouse their wrath. Charles was too clever a politician to make such a mistake. Few Englishmen were better informed about their own times and about English politics than William Penn; few Englishmen understood their King better than he. He knew the King would have to refuse such a conspicuous favor as a land grant. In this dilemma, I believe, lies the explanation of the official reason given for the granting of Pennsylvania to William Penn. Penn had to find some face-saving approach, and the approach lay in the large sum of money the Crown owed his father for services and outright loans. In those days a gentleman gave money to his King out of a sense of responsibility and devotion, and the higher the title the more generous the giving was expected to be. It is hard to believe that, even though Sir William may have considered back salary a good debt, he would ever have expected (let alone asked for) repayment of any sums earmarked "loan." It is even harder to believe that Charles II would have worried about paying a debt. He had a host of creditors who disturbed his royal conscience not at all. William Penn asked Charles to pay a debt owed his father, thus giving the King a publishable reason for the land grant; and the self-preserving Charles could then turn to his Privy Council and sell them the attractive idea of exporting whole shiploads of the Whig faction. That Penn was aware of this latter motivation, if not at once, certainly eventually, is apparent in a letter he wrote in later years to Lord Romney in which he said, ". . . after the government at home was glad to be rid of us at so cheap a rate as a little parchment to be practiced in a desert 3,000 miles off. . . ."

To the complexity of royal motives must be added the indestructible bond between the Penns and Stuarts that bespoke a debt, unexplained to posterity, that even a Stuart would not fail to honor. The speed and precision with which red tape was cut in Whitehall is nothing short of amazing; fewer than nine months elapsed from the time of Penn's formal petition to the issuing of the Charter. Was Penn going into secret exile because the King wanted to save his life? In a letter dated "1681" which by the present calendar could have been as late as March, 1682, Penn wrote to Henry Sydney at The Hague, "I perceive . . . thou art resolved to keep out of harm's way. So shall I, too, when I am got to my new granted province in America, where the change of the voyage shall secure me from the revenge of my enemies." Perhaps Penn's monarch was again protecting him as he had when he held him in the Tower under custody as an impetuous and radical young man and then required his father to send him to Ireland. Charles dissolved Parliament permanently and crippled the Whig Party before Penn left for America, and some prominent Whig heads were destined for the block while he was away, Algernon Sydney's among them. Penn, the purist, with his consuming concern to create a refuge for others, would have been easy to save on this level. If Charles II sent William Penn to America to save him from the royal purge, he was motivated by a personal love; and six years later when William Penn remained loyal to his King during the Protestant Revolution, his motive was the same.

Only a mutilated fragment of that petition remains to tell us that Penn specifically asked for the piece of land lying west of the Delaware, north of Maryland, and extending as far north as plantable, to be in lieu of an old, old debt owed by the Stuarts to his father for loans and services of "at least eleven thousand pounds." In a letter to Robert Turner, Penn later quoted the figure at sixteen thousand pounds, and most sources agree that the amount must have run that high when interest was included. Penn's petition was presented to the King some time before the first of June, and on that day the Earl of Sunderland (Robert Spencer), by then a Secretary of State, conveyed to the Privy Council His Majesty's wish for constituting William Penn, Esq., absolute Proprietary of a tract of land in America. "The Lord Sunderland was one of the first in the business of my American country," Penn said in a letter to him three years later. On the twenty-fourth of the same month Penn was present at a meeting of the Lords Commissioners for Trade and Plantations, a committee of the Privy Council, to answer questions as to the exact extent of the land he wanted. Regarding its northern boundary, Penn assured them, he would be content with three degrees to the northward. Copies of Penn's petition were then sent to the agents of the Duke of York and of Lord Baltimore, since the chief problem would be to reconcile his boundaries with theirs. By the end of October a letter was received from Sir John Werden, Attorney General and the Duke of York's agent, to the effect that "he is very willing Mr. Penn's request may meet with success; that is, that he may have a grant of a tract of land which lies on the north of New Castle colony, part of Delaware, and on the west side of Delaware River, beginning about the latitude of 40 degrees, and extending northward and westward as far as His Majesty pleaseth, under such regulations as their lordships shall think fit."

The Maryland boundary would not be so easy to define. Penn and Werden held some lengthy private conferences over it. Werden recommended that the line be drawn twenty or thirty miles above New Castle, but Penn protested that if that happened he would have so little of the river left "as very much to prevent the hope he hath of improving the rest within his Patent."

There were three principal towns along the west bank of the lower Delaware, with Dutch and Swedish populations, New Castle (formerly New Amstel), Upland (later renamed Chester), and Whorekill (later Deal). New Castle, with its fortifications and port facilities, was the largest and most important; under the Dutch it had been the principal port of New Netherland; its trade declined sharply when the English made New York their trade center, but it still commanded the entrance to the Delaware.

Sir John Werden wrote to the Committee on Trade and Plantations on December 3, "He [Penn] is willing that twelve English miles north of New Castle be his boundary, and believes the distance will fall under the beginning of the fortieth degree of latitude . . . but I confess I do not understand why it is precisely necessary to insist on just such a number of miles, more or less, in a country of which we know so little." But if Penn had not insisted on that measurement from New Castle his southern boundary may have ended eventually north of Philadelphia, the true location of the fortieth degree.

By the middle of December, Lord Baltimore's agent was summoned before the Lords of the Committee on Trade and Plantations to present any exceptions to the contents of Mr. Penn's patent, and by the end of December the Attorney General rendered his opinion—that Mr. Penn's patent did not infringe upon Baltimore's province. Baltimore's northern limits he described as being bounded as follows: "by that part of Delaware River which lieth in the fortieth degree of latitude, and so by a direct line westward through the continent." In the Charter that was finally issued Penn's grant was described as "bounded on the east by Delaware River, from twelve miles distance northwards of New Castle town, unto the three and fortieth degree of northern latitude, if the said river doth extend so far northward, but if the said river shall not extend so far northward, then, by the said river, so far as it doth extend; and from the head of the said river, the eastern bounds are to be determined by a meridian line, to be drawn from the head of the said river, unto the said forty-third degree. The said land to extend westward five degrees in longitude, to be computed from the said eastern bounds; and the said lands to be bounded on the north by the beginning of the three and fortieth degree of northern latitude, and, *on the south, by a circle, drawn at twelve miles distance from New Castle, northward and westward, unto the beginning of the fortieth degree of northern latitude*; and then by a straight line westward to the limits of longitude above mentioned." The fact that a point twelve miles north of New Castle and the fortieth degree of northern latitude lay many miles from each other marked the beginning of more than seventy years of intermittent litigation over the Pennsylvania-Maryland boundary.

There remained only the final reading and approval of the completed Charter, and at a meeting of February 23, 1681, His Majesty having approved the draft prepared by the committee for constituting William Penn, Esq., absolute Proprietary of a tract of land in America, the Privy Council "did order that one of his Principal Secretaries of State do give directions for preparing a bill for His

Majesty's royal signature to pass the Great Seal of England, according to the said draft (which was thereunto annexed) and that His Majesty's Principal Secretary of State do receive His Majesty's pleasure, what name he will give the said Province, to the end the same may be inserted in the said bill accordingly." Five days later Charles signed the King's Bill authorizing the Charter, the bill cleared through the Privy Seal Office, the offices of the Secretary of State, and the Lord Privy Seal, and finally reached the Lord Chancellor. It was the Lord Chancellor's office which prepared the final document dated March 4, 1681.

The body of the royal Charter contains twenty-three sections. It defines the bounds of Pennsylvania in the language already recommended by the Attorney General. It gives Penn free and undisturbed use of ports, harbors, waters, soil, woods, mountains, all living things in the waters and forests, all precious minerals and gems that may be discovered. Under its terms William Penn is absolute Proprietary of the country beholden only to the King of England, holding his title in free and common soccage, that is, in consideration of a specific fee of two beaver skins "to be delivered at our castle of Windsor on the first day of January in every year," and one fifth of all gold and silver ore. (Soccage is a kind of tenancy in which the lands are held in consideration of specified services; it is contrasted with an estate held in fee simple which in its absolute form gives the land title without limitation or condition.) For these considerations the country and islands are raised to the rank of province and seigniory, thus further emphasizing Penn's role as absolute lord over his vast manor. To Penn is granted the power to make and publish laws with the assent of the freemen or their delegates, the power to establish judges and other legal officers, to pardon and abolish crimes (except treason and murder), and do whatever else is necessary for the establishment of justice, provided it is not contrary to the laws of England. England, rising rapidly into her sea-trading role, requires that the exchange of raw materials and finished goods that is bound to develop must be with England and no other country. Only after goods have lain in an English port for a year and not been taken up may they be taken to foreign ports to be sold. Penn is given the power to divide the land into towns, hundreds and counties, to create ports of entry for trading vessels, although the ports at all times must receive the King's officers, deputies and commissioners of customs. William Penn must appoint an agent residing in London who shall be available at all times to represent the colony in any of the courts. Penn is denied the power of waging war, although he may create a militia for internal defense; thus making his personal power a degree less complete than that of a palatine prince. (Lord Baltimore had this additional power, and Maryland was considered a palatinate.) To Penn is reserved the rent on the land he parcels out. As a direct result of the recent West New Jersey decision, no taxes shall be levied on the residents of Pennsylvania without the consent of the Proprietary, or Chief Governor, or Assembly, or by Act of Parliament in England. There is one concession to the Church of England—the right to send a preacher to any twenty inhabitants requesting it of the Bishop of London; but this was gratuitous, since Penn's purist toleration planned freedom of worship for all.

Once he had received assurance of his land grant from the Crown, Penn, with his boundless energy and ardent faith, his contagious capacity for inspiration, plunged into his planning. He needed brave adventurers, men with strong backs and wide vision, "men of universal spirits, that have an eye to the good of posterity," men with practical talents—husbandmen, craftsmen; and he needed anyone who needed hope. Actually, he had known long before the date of the Charter that he would receive the grant, for some of his land grants to individuals are dated earlier than the Charter. All the while the Charter was being pushed through Whitehall he worked, consulted and planned. But on March 4, when the last piece of red tape was severed, he could begin in earnest, and his letter to Robert Turner in Ireland is dated March 5. Robert Turner, a Dublin merchant, had been a Quaker almost from the beginning of the movement. He had started the meeting at Grange and was already an outstanding national leader in 1669 and 1670 when Penn went to Ireland as a young exile. Now, more than eleven years later, William Penn chose Robert Turner to be a key person in his great program:

Dear Friend:

My true love in the Lord salutes thee and dear friends that love the Lord's precious Truth in those parts. Thine I have, and for my business here, know that after many waitings, watchings, solicitings and disputes in council, this day my country was confirmed to me under the Great Seal of England, with large powers and privileges, by the name of Pennsylvania; a name the King would give it in honor of my father. I chose New Wales, being, as this, a pretty hilly country, but Penn being Welsh for a head, as Penmanmoire in Wales, and Penrith in Cumberland, and Penn in Buckinghamshire, the highest land in England, called this Pennsylvania, which is the high or head woodlands; for I proposed, when the Secretary, a Welshman, refused to have it called New Wales, Sylvania, and they added Penn to it; and though I much opposed it, and went to the King to have it struck out and altered, he said it was past, and would take it upon him; nor could twenty guineas move the under secretary to vary the name; for I feared lest it should be looked on as a vanity in me, and not as a respect in the King, as it truly was, to my father, whom he often mentions with praise. Thou mayest communicate my grant to Friends, and expect shortly my proposals.

It is a clear and just thing, and my God that has given it me through many difficulties, will, I believe, bless and make it the *seed of a nation.* I shall have a tender care to the government, that it be well laid at first. No more now, but dear love in the Truth.

Thy true friend,

Wm. Penn

For the matters of liberty and privilege, I purpose that which is extraordinary and to leave myself and successors no power of doing mischief, that the will of one man may not hinder the good of an whole country.

——Penn, Letter to Turner, Sharp and Roberts, April 12, 1681

13. *The Frame of Government*

CHARLES FURTHER verified his royal will by issuing on April 2 a declaration requiring that "all persons settled or inhabiting within the limits of the said province, do yield all due obedience to the said William Penn. . . ." On the eighth of April Penn wrote his own letter to the inhabitants of Pennsylvania to allay any fears they might have of the effect of the change upon their lives. The European population of his province was then about one thousand. "You are now fixed at the mercy of no governor that comes to make his fortune great," he assured them. "You shall be governed by laws of your own making, and live a free, and if you will, a sober and industrious people. I shall not usurp the right of any, or oppress his person. . . . In the meantime, pray submit to the commands of my deputy, so far as they are consistent with the law. . . ." The letter was to be carried to America by his newly appointed Deputy Governor, William Markham.

William Markham was a direct descendant of the founder's grandfather, Giles Penn; he was Sir William's nephew and William Penn's first cousin. Markham had been mentioned as a beneficiary in Sir William's last will and testament.

To Lord Baltimore William Penn composed another letter, offering the olive branch, and introducing William Markham: "The bearer is a gentleman and my kinsman to whom I have left the manage of my affairs as his integrity will insist upon my right, his prudence and experience will always guide him from an indecent thing. . . . I shall conclude with this request that it would please thee to give my cousin and deputy all the dispatch possible in the business of the bounds that observing our just limits in that and all other things we may begin and maintain a just and free intercourse. . . ."

Penn's commission to Markham bears the date, April 10, 1681, and it endows the trusted cousin with sweeping interim powers and responsibilities. Markham, upon arrival in America, is to form a council of nine, and as his first act as its presiding officer is to read Penn's letter and the King's declaration of April 2 to the inhabitants, accepting their acknowledgment of Penn's authority. He is then to settle boundary discussions, erect courts, set up sheriffs, justices of the peace and other officers; and he may call upon the inhabitants for assistance in keeping order and putting down riots.

Under the first heat of inspiration Penn's creative thinking flowed as fast and clear as it had in his earliest years as a convert. He was moving outward and upward, drawn on by the mushrooming vision of a world free of the debauchery of the times, "the plagues of wars," a world unburdened by a nobility, a world where even the poorest countryman could hope to provide amply for his family, and where the godliest could live in whatever godly manner they chose. In the West New Jersey *Concessions* he had placed *the power in the people* and his faith had been gratifyingly rewarded; now he would place more power in a larger and more diverse group of people with an even more implicit faith.

In order to give his full time to Pennsylvania, he resigned as a trustee of the New Jersey project in April, 1681; his writing table had never seen a greater volume of work. Two tracts came off the press, probably at once, though they bear the date, 1681, with no indication of the month or day. The shorter, *A Brief Account of the Province of Pennsylvania*, appears to be the more hastily gotten up. It contains a crude map of the province, a short paragraph to "give some public notice," an abstract of the patent, text of the King's declaration, and some scanty copy describing Pennsylvania and setting forth preliminary terms under which lands will be distributed. The second tract, *Some Account of the Province of Pennsylvania in America*, is longer and more carefully written. "The place lies 600 miles nearer the sun than England," it declares joyfully.

Two days after his commission to Markham he wrote his letter to

Robert Turner, Anthony Sharp and Roger Roberts in Ireland enclosing a descriptive booklet and hinting at the joy he felt. "This I can say, that I had an opening of joy as to these parts, in the year 1661, at Oxford, twenty years since; and as my understanding and inclinations have been much directed to observe and reprove mischiefs in governments, so it is now put into my power to settle one. For the matters of liberty and privilege, I purpose that which is extraordinary, and to leave myself and successors no power of doing mischief, that the will of one man may not hinder the good of an whole country. *But to publish these things now, and here, as matters stand, would not be wise; and I am advised to reserve that till I come there.*"

Matters stood in a very dangerous way in England, particularly for Whigs, and those who advised Penn to be cautious and a little close-mouthed about his advanced concepts of government were indeed wise. When the Parliament for which Sydney had made a second attempt was convened, its Whig forces in the lower House passed a second bill (the first in 1679 had been supported by only a portion of the Whigs) to exclude Roman Catholic James from the throne, and favoring Mary of Orange. King Charles prorogued the unruly, presumptuous lawmakers on January 10, 1681, and then, to stem the rising tide of Whigism, whose capital was London, he reconvened Parliament at Oxford in March (the month in which Penn received his Charter). When the Whigs brought forth a third Exclusion Bill against his brother, Charles swooped down with secrecy and dispatch, appearing in person, and without the glimmer of a warning dissolved England's legislative body permanently. There would be no more parliaments to threaten the remainder of his reign or James's heredity. This action by the King destroyed the strength of the Whigs for years to come, and the life of every Whig leader—Shaftsbury, the Earl of Essex, Lord Russell, Algernon Sydney—was in immediate danger. As Penn sat down to design a Whig-influenced form of government for his colony, Whig leaders were rushing into hiding.

William Penn was in a position to be discreet, because he enjoyed widespread confidence in the Society, and the First Adventurers were willing to go to America long before the frame of government was written. "I do judge William Penn as fit a man as any in Europe to plant a country," wrote James Claypoole to Samuell Clarridge. In this atmosphere of trust Penn campaigned for adventurers, worked out the exact terms under which property was to be distributed and designed a government.

(By First Adventurers and First Purchasers I mean those settlers who came to Pennsylvania from the time of the colony's founding through 1685.)

The first major governmental document to be produced was *Certain Conditions and Concessions Agreed Upon by William Penn, Proprietary and Governor of the Province of Pennsylvania, and Those Who Are the Adventurers and Purchasers in the Said Province, the 11th of July, 1681.* This was a purely provisional and preliminary piece of twenty articles, the first ten of which described how land was to be laid out in Pennsylvania, the next five making specific provisions for dealing justly with the Indians, and the last five stating that the laws of England would apply until altered, that cattle should be marked for ownership, ships properly registered and debts honored. A large plot was to be laid out for a town or city, and every purchaser would "by lot, have so much land therein as will answer to the proportion which he hath bought or taken up upon rent," ten acres for every five hundred. Purchasers of five thousand acres or more could cast their land together into a township. Every man must plant his land within three years. Trading with Indians must be carried on fairly in public market. As in the Jersey *Concessions* offenses against or by Indians were to be heard before a jury of six Indians and six settlers.

In his pamphlets Penn had already set forth the prices of the land. An adventurer could either purchase or rent. Under the terms of purchase a share consisted of five thousand acres and was called a propriety; it was purchased for one hundred pounds and after 1684 was subject to a quitrent of one shilling for each hundred acres. An adventurer could rent not more than two hundred acres at one penny an acre. Out of every one hundred thousand acres, Penn reserved ten thousand for himself.

The quitrent was "reserved for the security of the title." The concept of private property was still in an early growth period, and the quitrent system was a lingering vestage of feudal times, under which a tenant made a specific payment and rendered himself "quit and free" of any other services to his immediate overlord. Sometimes the quitrent was a mere token, a pepper corn or a red rose, or in the case of Penn to the King two beaver skins per year. Quitrents were a source of discontent in many of the colonies, as they were destined to be in Pennsylvania. After colonists had wrestled with the wilderness and tamed it, they resented the additional assessment.

To encourage the well-to-do to aid the unfortunate, Penn offered each master fifty acres at four shillings per year quitrent for each servant that he brought over, and fifty additional acres were to be given each servant when his term of service expired at a quitrent of two shillings per year, which would make him a freeholder of the country.

The journey would cost six pounds per head for masters and mistresses and five pounds for each servant, fifty shillings for each child under ten, sucking children free. Freight was forty shillings per ton, but each passenger was to be allowed one chest free. Philip Ford in Cheapside, Thomas Rudyard and Benjamin Clark in Lombard Street were his London agents for consulting potential adventurers. James Harrison, a shopkeeper in Bolton, Lancashire, was another; as was Benjamin Furly on the Continent. Robert Barclay was his liaison in Scotland. In a letter dated August 25, 1681, he instructed James Harrison to "bargain and sell any parcel of land in Pennsylvania, not below 250 acres to any one person, from time to time. . . . Lay out the best and first land to the First Adventurers. . . . As to my voyage, it is not like to be so quick as I hoped, for the people upon whose going both my resolutions and service in going depended, though they buy, and most send servants to clear and sow a piece of land against they come, not one fifth can now get rid of their concerns here till spring. When they go, I go. But my going with servants, will not settle a government, the great end of my going. . . . For my country, I eyed the Lord in the obtaining of it, and more was I drawn inward to look to Him and to owe it to His hand and power, than to any other way. I have so obtained it, and desire that I may not be unworthy of His love, but do that which may answer His kind providence, and serve His Truth and people;

that an example may be set up to the nations; there may be room there, though not here, *for such an holy experiment.*"

As Penn hoped, his settlers eventually came from France, Germany, Holland, England, Wales, Scotland, Ireland and other European areas, but the first settlers came from England, Ireland and Wales. England contributed such leadership as Markham, Rudyard, Edward Shippen, Samuel Carpenter, James Harrison; Ireland sent Robert Turner of Dublin and Thomas Holme of Waterford who became Penn's Surveyor-General and laid out the city of Philadelphia, as well as James Logan from County Armagh, one of Penn's most trusted and trustworthy officeholders. Both Thomas and David Lloyd came from Wales. They were soon followed by the migration from the lower Rhine Valley.

Robert Barclay wrote his first reactions to the scheme from Leith in August: ". . . Now I neither have any great genius for such adventures, or money to spare that way, but if thou judgest it may do thyself kindness to let me have a Proprietary without money to bring in several others, I may concur to the stocking of it." Barclay's roots were too deep in Scotland to be budged no matter what the political discomforts, and a later letter from him indicates that other granite-headed Scots wanted something more solid than Penn's passionate optimism to invest their faith and resources in. "Since my last I have been discoursing with several persons hereaway touching thy plantation, and do find that we are generally so ignorant in such matters, by reason there is none belongs to this country that neither thy printed paper, nor any account I can form of thy letters, gives that satisfaction as to the method and manner of proceeding in order to the profit which people would desire to know before they engage." The Scots eventually found East New Jersey more to their liking.

Penn traveled almost continuously in and out of London, telling the Friends about his colony. "Mine eye is to a blessed government, and a virtuous, ingenuous and industrious society." The London Meeting for Sufferings was a source of help and a kind of clearinghouse, where information came in from Friends everywhere regarding their sufferings and circumstances. To its weekly meetings Penn,

Ford, Rudyard, Claypoole, Whitehead, Stephen Crisp repaired frequently, and to it George Fox came whenever his journeys brought him to the city. One of Penn's journeys on behalf of his colony had been to the western part of England in August where suffering Friends received him with warm enthusiasm and "where the Lord prospered me beyond wonder." By August about thirty-four Friends had signed and twenty were ready to depart.

Markham had left England almost immediately after receiving his commission from Penn in April, 1681, and had reached New York the middle or latter part of June.

"There is a ship going to Pennsylvania from Bristol and William Penn is gone thither to take his leave of Friends," wrote James Claypoole on September 24. That was no doubt the *Bristol Factor*. In October the *John and Sarah* sailed from London, and the following spring the *Amity* sailed. The *Bristol Factor* arrived in Chester on December 11, 1681, though the *John and Sarah* is thought to have been the first arrival.

William Crispin, John Bezar and Nathaniel Allen became Penn's land commissioners in America, and he set forth their detailed instructions in a letter dated September 30, 1681. They were to be under the direction of William Markham and theirs was the responsibility for sounding the best channels in the river and selecting a high, dry and healthy site for the town, and laying out ten thousand acres for it. They were to see that each purchaser of five thousand acres was to have some water-front land in the town, even if his whole hundred acres could not be on the water. Penn wrote to Markham on October 18:

My sincere love salutes thee, wishing thy prosperity every way. With this comes instructions and *Concessions*, with some company. I hope thou hast made convenient provision for them. I have sent my cousin William Crispin to be thy assistant, as by commission will appear. [Crispin had married a first cousin of Penn's.] His skill, experience, industry and integrity are well known to me, and particularly in court keeping, etc. so that it is my will and pleasure that he be as chief justice to keep the seal, the courts and sessions; and he shall be accountable to me for it. The profits redounding are to his proper behoof. . . . He is a man my father had great confidence in. . . .

Unfortunately Crispin never reached the mainland of America. He is thought to have arrived at Barbados where he died. The other two commissioners probably sailed on the *John and Sarah*.

Penn had already sent one reassuring letter to "the inhabitants" of his province, but that did not satisfy him. Under date of October 18, 1681 (no doubt included in the same packet with the *Concessions* and Crispin's appointment) he wrote his well-known and much loved letter to the Indians of Pennsylvania:

My Friends:

There is one great God and power that hath made the world and all things therein, to whom you and I and all people owe their being and well-being, and to whom you and I must one day give an account, for all that we do in the world; this great God hath written His law in our hearts, by which we are taught and commanded to love and help, and do good to one another, and not to do harm and mischief one unto another. Now this great God hath been pleased to make me concerned in your parts of the world, and the King of the country where I live hath given unto me a great province therein; but I desire to enjoy it with your love and consent, that we may always live together as neighbors and friends, else what would the great God say to us, who hath made us not to devour and destroy one another, but live soberly and kindly together in the world? Now I would have you well observe, that I am very sensible of the unkindness and injustice that hath been too much exercised toward you by the people of these parts of the world, who have sought themselves, and to make great advantages by you, rather than be examples of justice and goodness unto you, which I hear, hath been matter of trouble to you, and caused great grudgings and animosities, sometimes to the shedding of blood, which hath made the great God angry. But I am not such a man, as is well known in my own country, I have great love and regard towards you, and I desire to win and gain your love and friendship by a kind, just and peaceable life, and the people I send are of the same mind, and shall in all things behave themselves accordingly; and if in any thing any shall offend you or your people, you shall have a full and speedy satisfaction for the same, by an equal number of just men on both sides, that by no means you may have just occasion of being offended against them. I shall shortly come to you myself, at what time we may more largely and freely confer and discourse of these matters; in the meantime, I have sent my commissioners to treat with you about land, and a firm league of peace; let me desire you to be kind to them and the people, and receive these presents and tokens which I have sent to you, as a testimony of my good will to you, and my resolution to live justly, peaceably and friendly with you.

I am your loving friend,

WILLIAM PENN

Penn worked prodigiously, administering and acquitting an amazing volume of detail, arranging for land grants, laying the groundwork for the Free Society of Traders, designing a new government, preparing his home and family for their own departure. He felt impatient and frustrated because it all moved so slowly—"I shall not I think go till next spring"—but actually all of this was accomplished in a year and a half from the date of the royal Charter.

"William Penn is extraordinary busy about his new country, and purchasers present daily."

On November 9, 1681, he was elected a member of the Royal Society.

Late in 1680 Sir George Carteret, Proprietor of East New Jersey, had died, and his widow on February 1, 1682, put up all his New Jersey lands for auction. Twelve Quakers, William Penn and Thomas Rudyard among them, bid in the land and purchased it for £3,400. Thus Quaker interests were extended all the way to the seacoast.

Plans for a Free Society of Traders were completed in February, 1682. This was a corporation to which Penn assigned twenty thousand acres. It was really a merchants' pool which Penn hoped would "encourage the settling of a company for trade," and it offered a further opportunity to stockholders to share in the profits of Pennsylvania commerce. Penn furnished one of its earliest representatives in America with a letter to the "Emperor of Canada," a high Indian chieftain, in the hope of opening up trade with the northern Indians. The Free Society was never a success and eventually ended in financial failure, largely because it wasn't needed. Enough experienced merchants were among the early adventurers with sufficient capital to open the life lines of trade with the mother country and with the Indians.

To fill the gap left by Crispin's death, Penn appointed Thomas Holme of Waterford, Ireland, as his Surveyor-General. Holme carried another letter from Penn to the Indians of Pennsylvania. Holme was a First Purchaser of five thousand acres and a member of the Free Society. Penn gave him "full power and authority to enter into, survey and admeasure, or cause to be entered into, surveyed and admeasured . . . all the said Province of Pennsylvania," and to Thomas Holme, therefore, fell the responsibility of selecting the site and laying out the streets of the great town.

The town was on everyone's mind, since it would encompass the most valuable land, and since Penn's vision soared to new heights in describing the kind of city he wanted. His city was not to grow up in an unplanned shamble, neither was it to suffer from the unwholesome crowding and congestion of London and Paris. Penn had seen London ridden by plague incubated within her own premises; he had seen her destroyed by fire and rebuilt largely upon the same unplanned, inconvenient lines; he had seen too many houses grow back into too little space and labyrinthian streets reappear. He had in mind something quite different—an entire, planned city—a town with straight streets running "uniform down to the water from the country bounds," and "houses built upon a line," and every house placed in the "middle of its plat, as to the breadth way of it, that so there may be ground on each side for gardens or orchards, or fields, that it may be a green country town, which will never be burned, and always be wholesome."

Penn was far from being the first town planner; the art goes back to very ancient times—to Egypt, Greece, Babylon and the Roman Empire. The Chinese were town planners and so were the Dravidians of northern India whose civilization goes back at least five thousand years. Nor did Penn invent the gridiron or chessboard pattern for streets. The streets of the Dravidian city at Mohenjo-Daro were wide and laid out at right angles to each other. The plans of ancient Piraeus and Carthage are gridiron, and original portions of towns founded by Roman occupation on the Continent and in the British Isles often show rectangular streets.

The thing nearest and dearest to Penn's heart when he was setting up Pennsylvania was the creation of a frame of government. In performing this particular task William Penn reveals his true greatness more clearly than any other time in his life, first in his sincere humility in seeking the counsel and wisdom of other learned men, and second in being able to sign away personal power.

In the archives of the Historical Society of Pennsylvania there are treasured today the originals of nineteen manuscripts, sixteen of them proposing all or some provisions for a form of government, two others dealing exclusively with liberty of conscience, the third a short memorandum; they are in almost as many handwritings, and some of them are marked over with notations in Penn's hand showing that he studied them carefully.

Algernon Sydney was one of Penn's consultants. A letter written by Penn to Sydney shows clearly enough the many conferences that took place between the two men, the many drafts written by both Penn and Sydney, and the "considerable argument" they exchanged before the final version was produced. Another important consultant was Benjamin Furly in Rotterdam who wrote a long, detailed, article-by-article critique of the drafted *Frame* that Penn sent him, and whose influence was even felt in revisions of the *Frame of Government* in later years. Penn no doubt consulted his economist friend, Sir William Petty, too, for in a letter to Penn very shortly before the latter's departure to America Petty wrote: "Old friend, my opinion is that not only Pennsylvania, but all the habitable land upon the face of the earth will (within the next 1500 years) be as fully peopled as England is now," and further cautioned Penn to have a "perfect survey" made of "every ferule within the territory and jurisdiction."

As for his renunciation of personal power, Penn did that which was extraordinary then and is still extraordinary in our own times—he so designed the government "that the will of one man may not hinder the good of an whole country." It takes a great man to achieve power, a greater man to abrogate it, and in this moment of decision, when he resisted the temptations of personal power, William Penn rose to a level achieved by only a rare few. As Proprietor of Pennsylvania Penn had received almost absolute power from his monarch; the few limitations placed upon him were specified in his royal Charter, and he was answerable only to Whitehall where a Stuart set the standards. Deliberately and with his own hand, Penn divested himself and successors of any opportunity of "doing mischief."

The *Frame of Government*, that went through so many conferences and revisions before its approval by the First Adventurers and William Penn, consisted of two parts: a document with a Preface and twenty-four sections which Penn specifically called *The Frame* signed by Penn April 20, 1682, and a body of forty laws signed by Penn on May 5, 1682. Penn blanketed them under the one long title, *The Frame of Government of the Province of Pennsylvania, in America, Together with Certain Laws Agreed Upon in England, by the Governor and Divers Freemen of the Aforesaid Province, to be Further Explained, and Continued There, by the First Provincial Council That Shall be Held, if They See Meet.*

"Government seems to me a part of religion itself, a thing sacred in its institution and end. For, if it does not directly remove the cause, it crushes the effects of evil, and is as such . . . an emanation of the same Divine Power, that is both author and object of pure religion. . . . They weakly err that think there is no other use of government than correction, which is the coarsest part of it; daily experience tells us, that the care and regulation of many other affairs . . . make up much the greatest part of government." As for a particular frame, Penn has not found a model of government anywhere that "some singular emergences have not necessarily altered; nor is it easy to frame a civil government, that shall serve all places alike." There were three common ideas of government: "monarchy, aristocracy and democracy, the rule of one, a few and many"; for his government Penn chose a distinction that belonged to all three: "any government is free to the people under it . . . where the laws rule, and the people are a party to those laws. . . .

But, lastly, when all is said, there is hardly one frame of government in the world so ill designed by its first founders, that, in good hands, would not do well enough, and story tells us, the best, in ill ones, can do nothing that is great or good; witness the Jewish and Roman states. Governments, like clocks, go from the motion men give them; and as governments are made and moved by men, so by them they are ruined too. Wherefore governments rather depend upon men, than men upon governments. Let men be good, and the government cannot be bad; if it be ill, they will cure it. But, if men be bad, let the government be never so good, and they will endeavor to warp and spoil it to their turn." This is the substance of the Preface to his *Frame of Government*, or *Charter of Liberties*.

The twenty-four articles that followed described the form of government he would have in Pennsylvania. "The government of this province shall, according to the powers of the patent, consist of the Government and freemen of the said province, in form of a Provincial Council and General Assembly, by whom all laws shall be made, officers chosen and public affairs transacted." There were to be automatic annual elections by ballot to choose members of both upper and lower houses. The Council was to consist of seventy-two persons with a revolving membership, one third to dissolve each year, and the first election was to be February 20, 1683. The Governor would preside over the Council with a triple vote. The Governor and Council would bear executive responsibilities, enforce laws, give judgment upon criminals impeached, erect courts, plan towns, found schools, plan cities, ports, roads, market places, public buildings, exert power over the treasury. The Assembly was not to exceed two hundred members (for the time being). All laws were to arise in the upper house and be approved by the lower. The General Assembly met annually on April 20, and its entire membership dissolved each year. Except for the initial group Penn did not reserve to himself the choosing of judges, treasurers, masters of the rolls, and until courts were erected, sheriffs, justices of the peace and coroners. The Council was to choose a double number of these, and out of the names submitted Penn would indicate his choice. This document contained the keystone clause, the growth factor, that had been lacking in the New Jersey *Concessions:* it could be amended by six sevenths of the freemen in Provincial Council and General Assembly and the consent of the Governor, his heirs or assigns. And Penn further bound himself with the pledge, "my heirs and assigns, have solemnly declared, granted and confirmed, and do hereby solemnly declare, grant and confirm, that neither I, my heirs, nor assigns, shall procure or do any thing or things, whereby the liberties, in this charter contained and expressed, shall be infringed or broken. . . ."

The forty laws agreed upon in England, known eventually as the Great Law, defined a freeman as any inhabitant owning one hundred acres or upward, ten acres of which were cultivated, every bondsman who had completed his service and taken up fifty acres and cultivated twenty, and every inhabitant or other resident who paid "scot and lot" (a tax laid upon persons according to their ability to pay) to the government. It guaranteed free elections. Taxes were not to be levied upon any but by law. All courts were to be open and conducted in the English language, and a man was entitled to plead his own cause. Of course, a jury trial was guaranteed, so was bail except in the case of capital offenses, and anyone wrongfully imprisoned was entitled to double damages against the informer or prosecutor. Penn introduced considerable prison reform: prisons were to be workhouses and they were to be free as to fees, food and lodging. The Quaker wedding without benefit of clergy, so often not recognized in England, was made legal: "and it shall be solemnized by taking one another as husband and wife, before credible witnesses." A public register was provided for marriages, land titles, births, burials, wills and letters of administration "to prevent frauds and vexatious suits." The oath was replaced by simple affirmation for witnesses, but this question would not be settled for many years, since laws in Pennsylvania could not contradict English law. A public officeholder had to be a Christian, but it was only necessary to "confess and acknowledge the one Almighty and eternal God," to live in the province. None were to be "molested or prejudiced for their religious persuasion, or practice, in matters of faith and worship, nor shall they be compelled, at any time, to frequent or maintain any religious worship, place or ministry whatsoever." Penn mentions only two offenses subject to capital punishment:

treason and murder. The royal Charter gave him permission to pardon and abolish crimes with the exception of these two offenses, and so he eliminated the death penalty on all others. At that time in England a long list of crimes was punishable by death; the historian Stephens lists for the literate high and petty treason, piracy, murder, arson, burglary, housebreaking, highway robbery, horse stealing, stealing from a person above the value of a shilling, rape, and abduction with intent to wed; for those who could not read, all felonies including manslaughter and every kind of theft above a shilling and all robbery. Penn held morality of supreme importance to the success of a state and several of the laws forbade corruption, fraud, bribery, extortion, slander, and a long list of offenses against God including swearing, lying, drunkenness, incest, sodomy, whoredom, duels, felony, bull- and bear-baiting, cockfights and any things "which excite the people to rudeness, cruelty, looseness and irreligion."

There was to be human dignity in Pennsylvania for everyone, and freedom of conscience and expression; every man's sovereignty over his own estate was to be respected; and the whole people was to participate in the making and enforcing of laws and in the judging of infringements against them. This, indeed, was the seed of a great nation.

William Penn was the product of his own times, and of his own educational and religious experiences. His ideas, in a continuous state of growth for more than twenty years since he had first opened the pages of Plato, Aristotle and Grotius, sat in the classrooms of Moses Amyraut, and returned to discover the integrity of Coke and absorb Puritan social concepts, reached their maturity by the time he designed the extraordinary documents setting up Pennsylvania. The mark of his classical education is more pronounced at this point than anywhere else. Plato, in *The Republic*, said: "A State arises out of the needs of mankind"; and, while Plato's communal state is not Penn's, the dialectician's ability to project his thinking into a completely new social pattern most certainly is. The strain of Aristotle is stronger. Aristotle, having found man by nature to be a political animal, set him up in a state of law and justice where he could be the "best of animals," and concluded that separate from these influences he was the worst. Again, the ideal state that Aristotle envisaged is not Penn's since it conceived society divided into class layers, but Aristotle disapproved of communal ownership. "No one, when men have all things in common, will any longer set an example of liberality or do any liberal action." Aristotle's three types of government—rule of the one, the few, or the many—occur bodily in the Preface to Penn's *Frame;* and Aristotle's classification of governmental functions—deliberative, executive and judicial—appears in modified form in Penn's *Frame.* There had been a plenitude of ideal states—on paper—before the setting up of this American experiment, and Penn must have read many of them: Sir Thomas More's *Utopia,* Bacon's *New Atlantis,* James Harrington's *Oceana.* Penn, the practical, the doer, took the best thinking that men had done and created the working synthesis.

Through all of his labors for Pennsylvania ran the thread of his personal life. Around the first of March in 1682 his mother died at Walthamstow. So sudden was the severing of the maternal tie that Penn fell ill for several days. True enough, his Quaker's life and his own family had separated him from his mother in both thought and miles, and true enough in his adult years he seldom sought out the scene of his youth and the conversation of a petulant, aging woman; but maternal bonds run deep, and there was the added factor that Penn was severing so many ties at that point—with his native land and with his wife and children.

During the year and a half of planning and negotiating for the province, his family was preparing to be without him, for he was to go to America first and they were to follow later—Guli, Springett, Tishe and Bille. Some servants would go with Penn; others would follow with Guli. Guli's mother, Mary Penington, was at Worminghurst late in the summer of Penn's departure. Very probably she had come down to Sussex to keep her daughter company during Penn's absence, since Guli was expecting another child.

The domestic establishment at Worminghurst was a small community in itself; Penn never stinted himself on household space and domestic help. The expansive ménage was governed, not unlike Pennsylvania, with "certain good and wholesome orders" which he labeled their *Christian Discipline*. They began each day by assembling to wait upon the Lord; at the eleventh hour they gathered to read either Scripture or some martyrology; the practice was repeated at the sixth hour in the evening. They were constrained from neglecting any of their public meetings, from using unsavory words, from calling one another bad names, from wrath or railing, from drunkenness, lying, backbiting, talebearing, swearing, taking the name of God in vain, flattery, slothfulness and a host of other unattractive traits. That was their religious pattern. On the secular side, everyone rose in the spring and fall months at six in the morning, in the summer months at five and in the dark English winter months at seven. Breakfast was about nine, dinner about twelve and supper about seven. Every servant after supper must come and render to his master and mistress an account of what had been done that day and receive instructions for the next. At the end of the day all gates and doors must be bolted, all fires and candles extinguished and all persons in bed by ten.

When Penn prepared to leave this assortment of mortals in Guli's charge, and servants in those days were almost as personal a responsibility as one's own children, he blessed her with a great volume of detailed instructions and advices; and he endowed his wife and children with an expression of love in a letter that has become a permanent memorial to him and to them:

My love, that neither sea, nor land, nor death itself, can extinguish or lessen toward you, most endearedly visits you with eternal embraces, and will abide with you forever; and may the God of my life watch over you and bless you, and do you good in this world and forever. Some things are upon my spirit to leave with you in your respective capacities, as I am to one a husband, and to the rest a father, if I should never see you more in this world.

My dear wife! remember thou wast the love of my youth, and much the joy of my life; the most beloved, as well as the most worthy of all my earthly comforts: and the reason of that love was more thy inward than thy outward excellencies, which yet were many. God knows, and thou knowst it, I can say it was a match of

Providence's making; and God's image in us both was the first thing, and the most amiable and engaging ornament in our eyes. . . .

This was a long epistle, to which Penn devoted many loving hours; perhaps late at night while Guli slept he sat in a sequestered corner of the house whose members had repaired to their chambers at ten, and in the quietness dwelt upon the decade of happiness through which he had passed. He felt keenly that a period of his life was drawing to a close and that this could be a last farewell. Ships that started out from England did not always arrive at their destinations; passengers who did reach the shores of America did not always survive the wilderness.

Now I am to leave thee, and that without knowing whether I shall ever see thee more in this world, take my counsel into thy bosom, and let it dwell with thee in my stead while thou livest.

He exhorted her first to the vital source out of which their two lives had flowered—to the meeting for worship. " 'Tis thy duty and place." At home he cautioned her to keep careful daily accounts of her income and remain within its compass; and in the care of the children, though he and she wanted the same results, he reviewed his wishes anyway: "I love sweetness, mixed with gravity, and cheerfulness tempered with sobriety. . . . Breed them up in a love one of another. . . . For their learning, be liberal. Spare no cost . . . but let it be useful knowledge. . . . I recommend the useful parts of mathematics, as building houses or ships, measuring, surveying, dialling, navigation, etc; but agriculture is especially in my eye; let my children be husbandmen and housewives. . . . Rather keep an ingenious person in the house to teach them than send them to schools, too many evil impressions being commonly received there. Be sure to observe their genius, and don't cross it as to learning. . . ."

And—lest he really never see them again—

When grown big have most care for them; for then there are more snares both within and without. When marriageable, see that they have worthy persons in their eye, of good life, and good fame for piety and understanding. . . . Of cities and towns of concourse beware; the world is apt to stick close to those who have lived and got wealth there; a country life and estate I like best for my children.

The second part of the letter was addressed to the children themselves. Springett was seven, Letitia four and William, Jr., two; Springett was probably the only one who could read, but its counsel would be waiting for them as they grew. He called them, too, to a pious life; instructed them to obey and honor their mother; and recommended for them honest, industrious lives, listing the virtues to be emulated and the vices to be avoided.

And as for you, who are likely to be concerned in the government of Pennsylvania and my parts of East Jersey . . . let justice have its impartial course, and the law free passage. Though to your loss, protect no man against it; for you are not above the law, but the law above you.

The letter was dated the fourth of August, 1682, and so that his children would feel that his personal interest was individual he addressed separate letters, dated August 19, to each of them:

My dear Springett:

Be good, learn to fear God, avoid evil, love thy book, be kind to thy brother and sister and God will bless thee and I will exceedingly love thee. Farewell dear child

Thy dear father,

Wm. Penn

Dear Letitia:

I dearly love thee and would have thee sober; learn thy book, and love thy brothers. I will send thee a pretty book to learn in. The Lord bless thee and make a good woman of thee. Farewell

Thy dear father,

Wm. Penn

Dear Bille:

I love thee much, therefore be sober and quiet, and learn his book. I will send him one, so the Lord bless thee. Amen.

Thy dear father,

Wm. Penn

Penn was separating himself painfully from many sources of love and strength as a letter to Stephen Crisp shows: "Stephen! We know one another, and I need not say much to thee; but this I will say, thy parting dwells with me, or rather thy love at my parting."

Sometime during the summer of 1682, not long before his departure for America, an abortive arrest episode almost canceled his trip. He and George Fox attended meeting for worship on First Day morning at Gracechurch Street Meeting House, and in the course of the worship William Penn arose and spoke. "And while he was declaring the Truth to the people," says the first edition of George Fox's *Journal*, "a constable came in with a great staff and bid him give over and come down; but William Penn held on, declaring the Truth in the power of God. After a while the constable drew back; and when William Penn had done, I stood up." Fox in turn was threatened with great staves and ordered to stop speaking. He stopped only long enough to explain that the Quakers were a peaceable people intent on worship and nothing more. Even though they were allowed to finish their meeting in peace, Fox and Penn knew the trouble was not over. The constables and some soldiers returned to the empty room after the congregation had left, and the two men, who had retired to a smaller room, sent a messenger out to tell the constables where they were. One constable, staff in hand, did seek them out. Did he have an arrest warrant? Penn and Fox wanted to know. Yes, but he obviously lacked the enthusiasm to use it. The informer, he told Fox, had bolted and run. Fox and Penn offered to go to the alderman with the constable to clear up the matter, but he declined and said he would let them know. "We . . . bid him set an hour to come to us again, or send for us, and we would come to him. So he appointed the fifth hour in the afternoon, but neither came nor sent for us, and a Friend meeting him afterward in the evening, the constable told him he thought it would come to nothing."

On August 13 Penn went to Enfield just north of London to see Fox once more before leaving.

Penn's religious capacities had been deepening and ripening for as long a period as his social concepts, and at this time of departing for America they, too, seemed to reach a peak development in the tract for which he has been most honored by posterity, *No Cross, No Crown.* Thirteen years earlier, during his Tower imprisonment, he had written a short, amateurish piece under the same title. Penn called the second an enlargement of the first, but it is not. So many changes had taken place within Penn's soul, his abilities had so increased, his scholarship so expanded and his writing skill improved; he had lived through so many experiences, some of them personal tragedies, that the two tracts are as unlike each other as if they had been written by two different men. The second *No Cross, No Crown* sets forth much of the very essence of the Quaker faith and is the finest thing he ever wrote.

In August, shortly before his departure, Penn received from the Duke of York a complete release of the province, and, to protect his rights to the Delaware River two deeds of feoffment and accompanying leases for an additional tract of land known ultimately as the three lower counties. It was approximately the present state of Delaware, but at that time defined as "all that tract of land lying within the compass or circle of twelve miles about the same, situate, lying, and being upon the River Delaware, in America, and all islands in the said River Delaware, and the said river and soil thereof, lying north of the southernmost part of the said circle of twelve miles about the town . . ." and "all that tract of land upon Delaware River and Bay, beginning twelve miles south from the town of New Castle, otherwise called Delaware, and extending south to the Whorekills, otherwise called Cape Henlopen, together with free and undisturbed use and passage into and out of all harbors, bays, waters, rivers, isles and inlets, belonging to or leading to the same. . . ." Penn took the precaution to obtain these feoffments because he knew by then that a discrepancy in the Pennsylvania-Maryland boundary had arisen. A feoffment (an obsolete feudal term, meaning a kind of gift, literally bringing the donee into the feud and requiring certain homage and fealty, actually making him a tenant) gave Penn a much more limited title to the Delaware portion of his grant than he had to the upper portion.

Penn gave Philip Ford an authority for receiving all money due him on any account during his absence in America, and Ford agreed to continue at his annual salary of forty pounds. All seemed to go well until the last few days preceding the final rush of Penn's departure, when an unpleasant incident cast a long grim shadow before itself. Shortly after August 23, when Penn came up to London prepared to depart for Deal, where his effects were already aboard a ship, Philip Ford and his wife, Bridget, who seems to have been a grasping woman with considerable influence over her husband, presented Penn with an account covering the period July 6, 1682, to August 23, a sum of £2,851/7/10. They claimed it was money they had laid out in Penn's behalf. On the brink of an extraordinary adventure, about to step into an unknown world that had a reputation for the fatal difficulties it could present to the newcomer, Penn was in a state of terrific elation. He had neither the powers of concentration at that moment, nor the time, to sit down and study the papers thrust upon him. Ford had been his trusted agent since September, 1669—thirteen years—and Penn the dealer in vast ideas had never found it easy to be meticulous about clerical details. Ford, the Quaker, solemnly affirmed the contents of the statement to be true, and Penn, the colonizer, subscribed to it and rushed off—without having read the paper or received any copy of it for himself.

According to a news item dated August 29 in the *Epitome of the Weekly News* Guli and several others accompanied William Penn as far as the Dover Road (probably to Canterbury where it turns south) and bade him a final farewell. There were some thirty sail of merchant ships in The Downs at that time, says the *London Gazette*, all outward bound, two or three destined for Pennsylvania. About a hundred Friends were sailing with Penn, many of them from his own county of Sussex, most of them English, although at least one family was from Ireland and two were from Wales.

Philip and Bridget Ford accompanied Penn all the way to Deal, and there in the final moments just before he went aboard, they confronted him with three more documents for his signature, "ready engrossed," two deeds of lease and release dated August 23 and August 24, 1682, conveying to Ford and his heirs three hundred thousand acres of land in Pennsylvania unless Penn should pay to Ford three thousand pounds within two days, and a third document which was a double indemnity bond dated August 24 guaranteeing payment of the three thousand. From the language of the formal Bill of Complaint filed by Penn in 1706, I infer that Ford assured Penn these three papers were merely more "accounts" that required his signature for approval. Once again, in the rush and confusion of the moment, Penn signed the documents without reading them and without receiving any counterparts.

William Penn joined the other adventurers aboard the *Welcome*, a ship of three hundred tons, a total length of 108 feet and three square-rigged masts, larger and safer than the *Mayflower* had been. Robert Greenaway was her captain, and he was also a First Purchaser of 1,500 acres.

As though clinging to his farewells, Penn wrote from The Downs a last epistle to Friends. It bears the date of August 30, and this title, *An Epistle Containing a Salutation to All Faithful Friends; A Reproof to the Unfaithful; and a Visitation to the Enquiring, in a Solemn Farewell to Them in the Land of My Nativity.*

"Ye are the beloved of me above all the sons and daughters of men who have received and bowed to the blessed appearance of the Lord Jesus Christ in your hearts, and that have not counted anything dear for the testimony of his cross and gospel, but have unfeignedly loved and obeyed his light within and not been afraid to confess it without. . . . To you doth my soul reach in the love that many waters cannot quench, nor time nor distance wear away. . . . O Friends, go on, ye are called to a high and heavenly calling, the trumpet hath given a certain sound, follow your captain, be valiant, fight the good fight of faith, that ye may finish your course with joy."

The *Welcome* weighed anchor and spread her sails either on the last day of August or the first of September with her burden of adventurers and exiles, most of them leaving their homeland for the first time in their lives and all of them prepared never to see her again.

Farewell, England! Farewell, sorrowful and troubled land!

To reign, 'tis necessary first to suffer.

14. "No Cross, No Crown"

THE GREAT business of man's life is to answer the end for which he lives, thus begins this important tract, and that end is, to glorify God and save his own soul. But man has brought himself to a lamentable pass by disobedience to the law of God in his heart. If, reader, thou art such an one, Penn's counsel to thee is, to retire into thyself and take a view of the condition of thy soul. For the times are Babylonic, rent with lusts, wars, idolatry and hate. Penn seeks thy salvation; that's his plot. Penn offers a leaven, a medicine whose virtue is the same as of old and cannot be exhausted. Christ's Cross, he declares, is the way to Christ's Crown. He speaks emphatically and often of the daily cross, and the God that pursues his readers is the unerring, tireless Hound of Heaven. The true worshiping of God is doing God's will. Penn's appeal possesses a primitive, apostolic fervor as he cries, O Christendom! My soul most fervently prays, that after all thy lofty profession of Christ and His meek and holy religion, thy unsuitable and un-Christlike life may not cast thee at that great assize of the world. His plea is addressed to all of Christendom to allow herself to be redeemed.

What is Christ, and where is He to be found? Penn sees Him as the great spiritual Light of the world, that enlightens everyone that comes into the world. He stands at the door and knocks. What door can this be but that of the heart of man? Wherefore, O Christendom! Believe, receive and apply Him rightly. If men truly believe and their ear is attentive to the knock, they will yield to the discoveries of the Light, and they will take up their daily cross and live in the True Testimony of the Light. They will be endowed with great power against the assaults of evil through their inward obedience to the manifestations of that blessed Light, and once the Light is allowed to operate in their hearts their lives will be directed into meekness, mercy, self-denial, suffering, temperance, justice and goodness, and away from superstition, idolatry, pride, passion, envy, malice, selfishness, drunkenness, uncleanness, lying, oppression, fraud. That is Christ's business.

What is the Cross of Christ? Where is it to be taken up? How and after what manner is it to be born? What is the great work and business of the Cross? The Cross, Penn explains, is a figurative speech, borrowed from the outward tree, or wooden cross, on which Christ submitted to the will of God, and the preaching of the Cross was called in primitive times by Paul the power of God. The Cross mystical, with which Penn is concerned, is that divine grace and power which crosseth the carnal wills of men, and gives a contradiction to their corrupt affections, and that constantly opposeth itself to the inordinate and fleshly appetite of their minds, and so may be justly termed the instrument of man's holy dying to the world, and being made conformable to the will of God. It appears and is taken up within the heart and there also is where it is borne. They that cannot bear the Cross, and they that cannot endure the Cross, must never have the Crown. To reign, 'tis necessary first to suffer. The great work and business of the Cross in man is self-denial.

Self-denial is a word of much depth in itself and of sore contradiction to the world. The great princes of the world, and conquerors, too, were lacking in it, and therein they differed from Christ. For Christ made Himself of no reputation to save mankind; but these plentifully ruined people, to augment theirs. They vanquished others, not themselves; Christ conquered self, that ever vanquished them.

Penn sees two selves in every man that the Light may require us to deny, the lawful self and the unlawful self. The lawful self is that conveniency, ease, enjoyment and plenty, which in themselves are so far from being evil, that they are the bounty and blessings of God to us: as husband, wife, child, house, land, reputation, liberty and life itself. These are God's favors, which we may enjoy with lawful pleasure, and justly improve as our honest interest. But when God requires them, at what time soever the lender calls for them, or is pleased to try our affections by our parting with them, Penn says, when they are brought in competition with Him they must not be preferred, they must be denied. This made honest fishermen quit their lawful trades and follow Him, when He called them to it.

The unlawful self is the immediate concernment of much the greater part of mankind, and it is twofold: that which relates to religious worship and that which concerns moral and civil conversation in the world. In religion it sets up invention and performance of worship, exterior pomp and superstitions. Such stately buildings, imagery, rich furnitures and garments, rare voices and music, costly lamps, wax candles and perfumes appeal to the external senses, so that religion falls from experience to tradition. Christ drew off His disciples from the glory and worship of the outward temple and instituted a more inward and spiritual worship. What house will ye build me, saith the Lord? Or what is the place of My rest? Hath not My hand made all these things? Penn wants Christians to have meeting places, but plain, devoid of pomp and ceremony, suiting the simplicity of their blessed Lord's life and doctrine. Man is God's temple, and the place of God's appearance. But as Penn disapproves of gaudy display and ceremony on the one hand, he also disapproves of the recluse life. Men cannot exempt themselves from the conversations of the world; that is a lazy, rusty, unprofitable self-denial, burdensome to others to feed their idleness. Again, the true monastery is within, and there the soul is encloistered from sin. Not that he would be thought to slight a true retirement, for he not only acknowledges but admires solitude. Mountains, gardens, seasides are requisite to the growth of piety; but solitude should be free, not constrained, a place to wait undisturbedly upon God and be strengthened. Divine pleasures are found in a free solitude. 'Tis not performing duties of religion but the rise of the performance, the fruit therefrom, that God looks at. True worship can come only from the heart.

What then, shall Christians do when they come together to pray? The soul of man, however lively in other things, is dead to God, till He breathe the spirit of life into it; therefore in worship we are not to take thought what we shall say when we come before our Heavenly Father. His spirit speaketh in us. Be our relation to Him as children, and He will help us. Thus not only the mouth, but the soul, is shut until God opens it; and then He loves to hear the language of it. What is the preparation for this? Waiting patiently, yet watchfully and intently upon God. Here it is thou must not think thy own thoughts, nor speak thy own words, but be sequestered from all the confused imaginations, that are apt to throng and press upon the mind in those holy retirements. It is not for thee to think to overcome the Almighty by the most composed matter, cast into the aptest phrase. No, no! One groan, one sigh, from a wounded soul, an heart touched with true remorse, a sincere and godly sorrow, which is the work of God's spirit, excels and prevails with God. Wherefore stand still in thy mind, wait to feel something that is divine . . . thus taking up the Cross and shutting the doors and windows of the soul against everything that would interrupt this attendance upon God . . . the power of the Almighty will break in, His spirit will work and prepare the heart, that it may offer up an acceptable sacrifice. 'Tis He that discovers and presses wants upon the soul; and when it cries, it is He alone that supplies them. Penn lists four things necessary to worshiping God aright: the sanctification of the worshiper, the consecration of the offering, what to pray for, and faith. No man knows what to pray for that prays not by the aid of God's spirit, since God knows better than we what we need. As for faith, it purifies the heart, overcomes the world, and is the victory of the saints. What is it? A holy resignation to God, and confidence in Him, testified by a religious obedience to His Holy requirings, which gives sure evidence to the soul of the things not yet seen, and a general sense and taste of the substance of those things that are hoped for.

As for the second phase of the unlawful self which relates to worldly affairs, it is a subject of pride, avarice and luxury. The care and love of all mankind are either directed to God or themselves. Those that love God above all, are ever humbling self to His commands, but those that are declined from that love to God are lovers of themselves more than God. Self-love joins pride, and pride is a most mischievous quality that doth extremely seek after knowledge, power, deference, worldly furniture and ornaments. The lust of pride after power creates wars, ruin, slavery, misery. Its need for excessive personal honor and respect requires such customs as pulling off the hat and bending the knee; it gives people gaudy titles and epithets. Friends spurn such artifices, for real honor consists not in a hat, bow or title, because all these things may be had for money. True honor belongs to God. Honor *all* men, Penn therefore advises, because they are the creation of God, and the noblest part of His creation, too; they are also thy own kind. He grants that such honor is more hidden, not so discernable by worldly men, and that Quaker plainness is odd, uncouth, and goes mightily against the grain; but so does Christianity, and that for the same reasons. Another piece of Quaker non-conformity to the world, that renders them clownish, is their use of *thou* for *you*, and that without difference or respect to persons, a thing that to some looks so rude it cannot well go down without derision or wrath. But Friends have the same original reason for this as for other customs averse to pride. Penn speaks of his own renunciation of the false standards of the world. It was extremely irksome to him to decline and expose himself, but having an assured and repeated sense of the original of these vain customs, that they rise from pride, self-love and flattery, he dared not gratify that mind in himself or others. And for this reason he earnestly advises his readers to be cautious how they reprove the Friends on this occasion, and to weigh seriously in themselves whether it be the spirit of the world or of the Father that is so angry with the Friends' honest, plain and harmless *thou* and *thee*.

Avarice, the love of money or riches, the unlawful desire of lawful things, is a pitfall upon which Penn discourses with eloquence. It is hateful to God, a form of idolatry, an enemy to government, a destroyer of families, a betrayer of friendship. Hoarding up riches is unprofitable anyway, for the rich man's talents are hid in his bags out of sight, in vaults, under boards, behind wainscots, growing but as under ground where it doth good to none. O man of God, flee these things, and follow after righteousness, faith, love, patience and meekness.

Luxury, an excessive indulgence of self in ease and pleasure, is the last great impiety, a disease both epidemical and killing. It is an enemy to mankind, because it undermines health, shortens life and encourages idleness. Penn particularly admonishes the people of his own land. He has been with them and among them, their lives and pastimes are no stranger to him, and he bewails their folly. The best recreation is to do good, and all Christian customs tend to temperance. The temperance he pleads for is not only religiously but politically good; it helps create a stabler and sounder economy and enriches a land. A godfearing people does not want more than it needs, does not incur exorbitant debts, alleviates one another's woes, visits the sick and the imprisoned, relieves the needy, preys not upon the small.

Alas! Why should men need persuasions to what their own felicity so necessarily leads them? Let it be so, O you Christians, and escape the wrath to come! Why will you die? Remember, that without a cross of suffering there can be no crown of fulfillment.

And thou Philadelphia, the virgin settlement of this Province, named before thou wert born, what love, what care, what service and what travail has there been to bring thee forth and preserve thee from such as would abuse and defile thee. Oh! that thou mayst be kept from the evil that would overwhelm thee; that faithful to the God of thy mercies in the life of righteousness thou mayst be preserved to the end. My soul prays to God for thee, that thou mayst stand in thy day of trial, that thy children may be blessed of the Lord, and thy people saved by His power. My love to thee has been great, and the remembrance of thee affects my heart and mine eye! The God of eternal strength keep and preserve thee to His glory and thy peace.

—From Penn's letter to Thomas Lloyd and others, August, 1684, from on board the ketch *Endeavour*

15. *A Peaceable People*

In a letter to the Lords of Trade and Plantations William Penn referred to the date of his arrival in America as October 24, 1682, but New Castle records give the date as October 27. It may well be that the surviving passengers of the *Welcome* emitted a desperate sigh of relief at the first sight of land and noted the earlier date with prayerful thanksgiving, and it could easily have taken the ship another three days to negotiate Delaware Bay and River as far as New Castle. The *Welcome* had not been blown off her course, and she did accomplish the voyage in slightly less than two months—a reasonably successful trip, but comfortable shipboard life was still far in the future. The crowded, sleepless, unwashed, often seasick passengers of the *Welcome* had to reckon with an epidemic of smallpox en route that reduced their lists by thirty-one. Those who, like Penn, had once had the disease were immune and could safely tend the stricken. Richard Townsend, one of the passengers, paid tribute to Penn's ministrations, his "good conversation was very advantageous to all the company. His singular care was manifested in contributing to the necessities of many who were sick with the smallpox then on board." And in the midst of so much discomfort and distress at least one child was born.

It is possible, though not certain, that one or two other ships accompanied the *Welcome*. The *London Gazette* of September 2 noted that three ships had sailed out of The Downs bound for Pennsylvania, and a little earlier a letter of James Claypoole stated that three ships planned to go in August. However, the *Jeffreys*, undoubtedly one of these three ships, did not get off until the middle or end of September. The third may have been the *Elizabeth, Ann and Catherine*.

In the sunset glow the *Welcome* furled her sails and dropped anchor before New Castle, and the weary travelers who crowded to the rail caught their first glimpse of the green forested land and the cluster of buildings that made up the most important town on the Delaware. New Castle, although built of the primitive stuff of the countryside, was no doubt very Dutch in appearance. It had its fort, courthouse, weighhouse and cultivated land close by, and in old New Castle records there is a reference to dikes protecting the meadows and another to the building of a windmill toward the northeast end of town. The shoreline was crowded with settlers and coppery-skinned, almost naked Indians, curious over the arrival of any ship. Here papers must be cleared, and Penn showed his deeds to the three lower counties and letters of attorney from the Duke of York to John Moll, Attorney for His Royal Highness, and a few others who came aboard. The Quakers' intent was peaceable, and they hoped for a friendly reception from the many temperaments awaiting them, both aboriginal and European. Their reputation had gone ahead of them through Quakers already living in West New Jersey and on the western side of the Delaware; and when, next morning, the haggard handful climbed over the side to the small boats and were rowed ashore, they found a warm welcome awaiting them.

William Markham, Deputy Governor, and Thomas Holme, Surveyor, were at New Castle to greet their Proprietor and Governor. William Penn was escorted to the fort with great formality where

John Moll and Ephraim Harman, another Attorney for His Royal Highness, surrendered the quiet and peaceful possession of the town of New Castle "with twelve miles circle or compass of the said town" and performed the ceremony of presenting to Penn the key to the fort and a piece of turf with a twig implanted in it and water and soil of the River Delaware. Holme and Markham were among the witnesses who signed the document of surrender. Several days later Markham received possession of the counties below New Castle. The inhabitants of New Castle executed a further document declaring themselves loyal subjects of their new Governor, William Penn; and a representative of the Swedes came forward with a special statement that "they would love, serve and obey him with all they had; that it was the best day they ever had." Penn immediately appointed John Moll, Peter Alricks, Johannes de Haes, William Simple, Arnoldus de la Grange and John Cann to be justices of the peace "for the preservation of the peace and justice of the province, according to law."

New Castle was not the resting place of the new arrivals. They returned to the ship that same day and sailed farther up the Delaware to the village of Upland and went ashore once more. Here Robert Wade seven years earlier had started a Quaker meeting in his home as a result of William Edmundson's visit, and by 1682 a monthly meeting was well established with three member meetings. Robert Wade whose house was on Upland Creek was Penn's host. He had also been host to many of the First Adventurers who had arrived the previous winter on the *Bristol Factor*. Reaching the Delaware in the middle of December, the *Factor* had achieved this point and then frozen in the ice. There was no choice for her passengers but to go ashore on Robert Wade's landing and seek shelter in the little settlement there. The *Welcome* went no farther either.

Since ships are slower than horses and slower than canoes, news of the arrival of the *Welcome* flew up the Delaware ahead of her, and excitement filled the air when her boats were lowered a second time. To the Indians came the Sachem from far away to wait upon their sachems, the Sachem who in his first message had said he wanted only to live with them as neighbor and friend, who had promised them justice, and who had already kept his promise to come among them himself. To the Europeans who were not English came the promise of benevolent rule and capital and facilities to help tame the wilderness that threatened them at their backs. To the Quakers who had come ahead of him he brought the administration they needed, the impetus for the real beginning of their new life.

William Penn stepped ashore at Upland to handle almost single-handed a vast multi-faceted program. To effect it he called upon every variety of training he had ever had—his boyhood on a country manor, his legal training and experience, his familiarity with the administrative problems of kings and courts, his colonial experiences in Ireland, his long training in doing business after the manner of Friends. "In no outward thing have I known a greater exercise," he had said before leaving England, "and I am firm in my faith that the Lord will prosper it." Carried forward by that deep compulsion as he strode into the tasks at hand, he must have been thrilled to discover that the land was richer, better, more promising than the reports he had received. "It is a very fine country, if it were not so overgrown with woods, and very healthy," Markham had written home to his own wife. "Here people live to be above a hundred years of age. Provisions of all sorts are indifferent plentiful, venison especially . . . wild fowl of all sorts; partridges I am cloyed with . . . here are abundance of wild turkeys . . . duck, mallard, geese and swans in abundance . . . fish are in great plenty. In short, if a country life be liked by any, it might be here." Markham had understated the case. Penn found the country's "soil, air, water, seasons, and produce" to his joyful liking. The soil was rich, the vales watered by inland brooks and navigable rivers, the air healthful, the natural produce of the country limitless—black walnut, cedar, cypress, chestnut, poplar, hickory, sassafras, beech, oak, mulberry, walnut; plums, strawberries, cranberries, grapes of diverse sorts, peaches; fish, fowl, elk, ox, deer, beaver, raccoon, rabbits, squirrels, birds, creatures for fur, whales right in the bay, no want of horses, cow-cattle, and sheep and oxen. And he stepped ashore with his deep capacity for sustained enthusiasm and his boundless physical energy to take up the administrative reins and continue to work as he had been working in England for the past year at an intensive rate of speed—traveling vast distances, sleeping only short hours at night, co-ordinating, conciliating, corresponding, making an endless succession of extraordinary decisions.

Upland he renamed Chester at the suggestion, according to legend, of a man named Pearson who wanted it named in remembrance of his home city in England. It was an attractive site, Penn felt, well situated on creek and river, and could some day develop into a city. He turned next to diplomatic relations with neighboring provinces and sent two messengers to Maryland to convey his loving greetings to Lord Baltimore and arrange an appointment to see him. Markham had been trying to conciliate Baltimore ever since his arrival, and now Penn was prepared to take up where Markham had left off. On the second day, October 29, Penn sent out notices that the first court would be held at New Castle on November 2.

The intervening three days, I think, are the time he would have used to journey on up the river and inspect the site selected by his land commissioners for the new city. That it was Penn who chose the name of Philadelphia for his city, taking the two Greek words, *philos* and *adelphos*, meaning love and brother, somewhat as he had coined the word *Philanglus*, I consider true beyond any reasonable doubt even though I have found no positive documentation. It was his dream, and he was the classical scholar. Its site, called Coaquannock by the Indians, which Penn saw as he approached it, on his way up the Delaware in a barge or boat, had long ago been discovered by the agents of the Dutch West India Company as a strategic spot for a landing and trading post. The banks of the Delaware rose in high bluffs above the water and formed the kind of location that Penn had prescribed in his earlier instructions to his land commissioners: "Be sure to make your choice where it is most navigable, high, dry and healthy." Below the bluffs Dock Creek, just as it flowed into the Delaware, widened into a natural pond and haven for sloops and schooners, and near its mouth the beach was low and sandy and formed the landing place that had captured the attention of the Dutch and now captured Penn's. Penn immediately declared it a public landing place for all the inhabitants. Canoes shot out into the water to accompany him as his barge turned in to the shore and was eased up to the wharf on the flat beach. There were already ten houses standing in a row extending north from Dock Creek Pond, some brick, some wood, some unfinished; dominating the group was the historic Blue Anchor Tavern, reputed to be the first house ever built on the Philadelphia site, already ten years old when Penn arrived. It was brick, about sixteen by thirty-six feet, and functioned as post office, ferryhouse, exchange, taproom and inn for trappers and traders. Captain William Dare was its owner in the fall of 1682.

The land commissioners had chosen well, and they had planned well. The city they envisioned lay along the Delaware for more than a mile and stretched back almost two miles to the Schuylkill River. Thus the town would be serviced by two navigable rivers. The streets were planned as Penn had directed—with straight streets running parallel—a wide avenue called High Street (now Market) traversing the length of the city through its center from river to river, and another called Broad Street bisecting it. Where the two thoroughfares crossed a wide area was left for an open park. Some city lots had already been admeasured and drawings had been held on September 19, 1682, for lots on Second Street, Broad Street, Fourth Street, and back street lots, under the supervision of William Markham, Thomas Holme, William Haig and Griffith Jones.

The exact continuity of Penn's first days in America is lacking, but it is logical to assume that he would have continued his trip up the river to inspect the site of his new home purchased for him from the Indians by William Markham. The location of Pennsbury is about twenty-four miles north of Philadelphia on a lovely piece of land where the river turns almost at a right angle, flowing southeast then southwest. Penn was deeply pleased with Markham's choice; the place had what his temperament needed—space and retreat and a commanding view of the surrounding country. Markham had negotiated for it only that summer, and the deed dated July 15, 1682, is the first executed between William Penn and the Indian sachems. Pennsbury Manor was a vast tract, "all that land lying and being in the Province of Pennsylvania aforesaid beginning at a certain white oak . . . over against the falls of Delaware River, and so from thence up" the river for five and a half miles, and "westward to Neshammony's Creek." It had been paid for in currency of both America and England and in merchandise: 350 fathams of wampum, (a fatham or fathom was six feet), 300 gilders, 20 white blankets, 20 fathams of "strawd waters," 60 fathams of duffields (coarse woolen fabric), 20 kettles, 20 guns, 20 coats, 40 shirts, 40 pairs of stockings, and quantities of hoes, knives, glasses, shoes, pipes, scissors, combs, tobacco, two anchers (an ancher is about ten gallons) of rum, cider, beer.

He planned a lovely home for himself and Guli, and construction may even have been started before he arrived. The house and outbuildings standing there today are a conscientious recreation of the one he built. Three-storied, of red brick with tile shingled roof, and primfronted, it looks through its casement windows at the river down a long, tree-lined walk that led in his time to steps at the water front where his boat or barge that took him to and from Philadelphia could tie up. The main house is sixty feet wide and forty feet deep with floors of hand-hewn planks. There are three rooms across the front, the great hall being the center one, and the other two smaller ones being parlors. Their walls are wood paneled below and plastered above, and each has its fireplace framed with delicate tiles. Behind them are three more rooms: one is the dining hall that connects with the kitchen wing, and another is the center room which contains the stairway leading to the second and third floors. The flower gardens, herb gardens, dipping well and bakehouse are there, and so is the brewhouse with its great iron cauldrons set into brick tables over ovens. Behind the manor house is a large stone barn with rows of horse stalls.

Penn, Markham and Holme were all at New Castle on November 2, to convene the first court, and Penn made a formal declaration and reaffirmation of his intent. He particularly resolved, he told the gathering, to settle land titles to everyone's satisfaction, and he therefore requested them to bring to the next session of the court all their patents, surveys, grants and claims so that they could be reviewed, adjusted and confirmed. He asked the magistrates to inspect all town plots and let him know what vacant room was still to be found. Until fitting laws and regulations could be enacted the residents would be governed by the existing laws of the province of New York wherever they did not conflict with the laws of England.

In November Penn went on a diplomatic mission to New York, where he was officially received by Anthony Brockholls, Commander-in-Chief and Governor pro tempore, who read over the two deeds to the three lower counties which Penn presented for inspection. On November 21, Brockholls wrote to the two attorneys, Moll and Harman: "We being fully satisfied (after seeing the indentures) of the said William Penn's right to the possession and enjoyment of the premises . . . . give you our thanks for your good services done in your several offices and stations, during the time you remained under His Royal Highness's government, expecting no further account than that you readily submit and yield all due obedience and conformity to the powers granted to the said William Penn. . . ." But to Sir John Werden at Whitehall, Brockholls wrote in a more confidential tone: "I received yours of 24th August past, the 4th December, but too late to assist or serve William Penn in giving possession of what His Royal Highness has been pleased to grant him . . . am ready to obey all his Royal Highness's commands, and serve his interest, but fear what is left of his province not able to defray the charge."

On his way back to Pennsylvania across New Jersey Penn stopped at Elizabeth Town to see the new Governor of the recently acquired East New Jersey, Thomas Rudyard. Rudyard had just arrived in America on the thirteenth of November, and he and everyone working with him felt the need of a conference with Penn. "The people in general were not a little satisfied with thy late visit," Rudyard wrote to Penn afterward, "and bear thee a very reverent respect. And by thy inoffensive obliging carriage thou laid the foundation for an amicable compliance on their part to the Proprietors, that the work cannot prove so difficult as hath been imagined. . . ."

The Great Treaty, a favorite item of scholastic debate, that Penn is supposed to have held with the Indians, must have occurred shortly after his arrival in America, and the most likely time for it seems to be right after his return from New York and New Jersey and before his visit to Lord Baltimore in December. Was it at Shackamaxon? What was its exact date? Was it a peace conference or for land purchase? Did it really take place? Scattered evidence and tradition both support the conclusion that there certainly was such a Great Treaty, probably the largest gathering that Penn ever held with the Indians. Where it took place is not particularly important, but Shackamaxon was then just north of the site of Philadelphia and is now in the Kensington section of the city; the "Treaty Elm" stood near the home of Thomas Fairman at about the intersection of Columbia and Beach streets. Although no transcript of proceedings comes down to us, the Indians had their own way of keeping records—in their keen and accurate memories—and they themselves are said to have kept the memory of the conference alive for almost a century. The Indians preferred to hold their conferences out of doors, and Penn would of course have respected their taste in this as he did all their other customs. Voltaire, a man in his twenties when Penn died, wrote of the Great Treaty in his *Dictionnaire Philosophique* as an absolute fact and called it the "only treaty between those nations and the Christians which was never sworn to and never broken." As for the purpose of the Great Treaty, the Quaker message is a peace message, and Penn's first effort would automatically have been to establish peaceful relations with his new neighbors and guarantee to them the peaceable intent of the immigrants who had already arrived and the many more who would follow. Not until the following June is there any record of an actual land transaction between him and the Indians. They were sorry such things took so long, one of the chieftains told Penn, but some of their young people and owners of land had not been as ready as he. They apparently did not move in matters concerning the whole tribe without tribal unity.

What a magnificent scene such a treaty would have made, with the tall, centuries-old trees there to shelter it. So important an occasion would have called for the finest feather headdress. The Quakers would have arrived in their unadorned yet complex European attire. Tradition again speaks and says that Penn wore a blue sash for the event, and this is entirely believable, since his high-level diplomatic training would have taught him the importance of a distinctive item of dress for the highest ranking chieftain of his people in the eyes of the Indians, as well as the courtesy to the Indians of that special gesture.

Penn himself in a letter the following summer to the Free Society of Traders in London showed clearly that he had had many conferences with the Indians by that time: "Every King hath his council; and that consists of all the old and wise men of his nation; which, perhaps, is two hundred people. Nothing of moment is undertaken, be it war, peace, selling of land, or traffic, without advising with them; and, which is more, with the young men, too. It is admirable to consider how powerful the Kings are, and yet how they move by the breath of their people. I have had occasion to be in council with them, upon treaties for land, and to adjust the terms of trade. Their order is thus: The King sits in the middle of an half moon, and hath his council, the old and wise, on each hand; behind them, or at a little distance, sit the younger fry, in the same figure . . . it was the Indian custom to deliberate and take up much time in council before they resolve."

The Delawares would have been the chief attenders at the Great Treaty, since they dwelt in the Delaware Valley, and a few Susquehannas may have come in from the west. The Delawares, rightly called the Lenni Lenape, were tall and broad-shouldered, narrow-waisted, regal in their manner. They went almost naked in summer except for moccasins and a breechclout; they added leggings and a blanket or skin around the body and across one shoulder in the winter; their weather-brown skin was carefully greased with bear's fat as a protection against insects. The heads of the young men were shaved all except the coarse black hair of a tuft on the top, left as a challenge to their enemies. Their art was beadwork, their medium of exchange wampum made of fishbone, their weapons the tomahawk and bow and arrow, their transportation the unshod horse and the canoe made by hollowing out the trunk of a tree with fire and a sharp stone. They ate meat and cooked vegetables, corn, whole or ground, but hunting and fishing were their chief means of livelihood. Tobacco was their only stimulant before the arrival of European influence. Their home was the wigwam, fashioned like an inverted bowl of sapling poles covered with bark. "Their language is lofty, yet narrow; but, like the Hebrew, in signification, full; like shorthand, in writing, one word serveth in the place of three, and the rest are supplied by the understanding of the hearer: imperfect in their tenses, wanting in their moods, participles, adverbs, conjunctions, interjections. *I have made it my business to understand it, that I might not want an interpreter, on any occasion;* and I must say, that I know not a language spoken in Europe, that hath words of more sweetness, or greatness in accent and emphasis, than theirs," Penn the master of Latin, Greek and French was able to report in less than a year.

The ease with which Penn, who had never before traveled beyond the European Continent, was able to understand the Indians is remarkable. Perhaps the starting point was mystical, since the Indians were natural-born mystics, and Quaker and Indian concepts of the divine being were similar. A further point could have been the similarities in social relationships, the Quaker and Indian habit of patient group deliberation, of allowing the wisest and most elderly to have the greatest voice in secular affairs without ignoring the wishes of the younger. Beyond these points, though, their social patterns differed. In the matter of land ownership, for instance, the Indian concept was communal, while the new Pennsylvania settlers most of whom were Whig-inclined were moving strongly toward the concept of private property. But even this proved no barrier to Penn, although it did disturb some of the other settlers when they found they could not have individual deeds from the Indians guaranteeing their land titles. Penn came among the Indians himself, as he had promised, and met them in their own land and let them set their own standards of negotiation. When he found that the exchanging of gifts was a part of Indian diplomacy, he exchanged gifts with them. If they wanted to proceed slowly to their land sales, he let them set their own rate of speed. When he found that among Indians the word of a chieftain was his bond and contract, he had no adjustment to make. Socially, they took him to their hearts at once, because he visited in their homes, ate their food in their way, and joined in their games and sports with such vigor and skill that he bested competing warriors younger than himself. The day soon came in Pennsylvania when an Indian could pay a white man no higher compliment than to tell him he was like William Penn.

Chester became the temporary capital of the new province, and there the first meeting of the first Assembly was held on December 4, 1682, in response to sheriffs' writs issued in each of the six counties into which the province had been divided—Bucks, Philadelphia and Chester counties in Pennsylvania, and New Castle, Kent and Sussex (formerly Whorekill) in Delaware. On the first day committees of election and privileges and "for justice and grievances" were appointed, and on the second day Nicholas More, already President of the Free Society of Traders, was chosen chairman. The second day was devoted to rules of procedures and discipline of the legislative group, and a committee was sent to the Governor "humbly to desire him to honor the house with a transmission of his constitutes" (the proposed laws). On the third day a "petition is presented for an act of union betwixt the freemen of the three lower counties . . . and the freemen of the province of Pennsylvania, that as one united province, they may be endowed with the same privileges of law and government." (This union proved to be an all too brief honeymoon.) The petition was unanimously approved, given three readings, and sent to the Governor for his approval. The next petition to be approved—one to naturalize the Swedes, Finns and Dutch—had been sent to the Assembly by the Governor. The balance of the session was devoted to the study of the Constitution and laws.

As for the Great Charter, Constitution, or *Frame,* designed by Penn in England, this first gathering of freemen respectfully—however, unanimously—requested a few revisions to which Penn graciously yielded. The changes they requested quite obviously arose out of the difficulties of the native situation, that could not have been anticipated three thousand miles away: "the fewness of the people, and their inability in estate, and unskilfulness in matters of government, will not permit them to serve in so large a council and assembly," and they asked that for the time being three from each county serve as a council and six from each county an assembly, with quorum and other requirements adjusted. With a few other minor changes the new Assembly declared "their most hearty acceptance of the said Charter."

The body of forty laws, or Great Law, was expanded to sixty-nine. A Preamble was added pertaining to the glory of God, and liberty of conscience became item number one. Part of the increase in items was due to the expanding of Penn's single article on offenses against God into fifteen separate articles. Other provisions were added which had no doubt been omitted only through haste. The structure of the court system was described in detail and the right of appeal added. They defined the freeman the same as Penn had described him but added for officeholders a prescribed declaration of fidelity and obedience to William Penn, his heirs and assigns, as Proprietor. They added a law allowing the secular courts to grant divorce (an ecclesiastical matter in England) in the event of adultery. Because of the scanty population they felt it necessary to drop Penn's original provision of allowing a man to hold only one public office at a time.

On December 7, the fourth day, William Penn appeared in person before the General Assembly to bestow upon the situation all the dignity and solemnity that it deserved, having until that time tactfully withheld the weight of his personal influence. Some of the men present understood what was happening, but many more had never participated in such an event before and in addition had spent the better part of their lives in the wilderness. These latter must be educated to it, and no more gracious way to teach than through the manner and mien of a man thoroughly at home in both courts and parliaments, a man who could bring them the kingly bearing of a confident administrator. Penn assumed the chair, addressed the gathering on a religious theme, and then proceeded to sign the bills that awaited him: those uniting the counties, naturalizing the non-English European residents, and approving the revised Charter and Great Law. He was enacting the closing scene of the first General Assembly, and from it he would move directly to another dramatic scene, his visit to Lord Baltimore in Maryland.

As William Markham had prepared the way for Penn's negotiations with the Indians, so he had made the first diplomatic overtures in America to Charles Calvert, the third Lord Baltimore. Since a potential difference about the Maryland-Pennsylvania border had been evident from the time of the earliest conferences in London, Markham gave Maryland a high priority rating on his list of responsibilities, and toward the end of August, a scant two months after his arrival, he journeyed to Maryland armed with Penn's letter of introduction and a letter from King Charles addressed to Baltimore.

Markham, fresh from an English climate, ought not to have attempted the journey into Maryland in August, for he highlighted the occasion by succumbing to the heat, and Baltimore took him to his own home and gave him nursing care for three weeks. On parting, he and Baltimore agreed to meet again in October "in order to take observation for the ascertaining the fortieth degree of northern latitude"; Markham promised Lord Baltimore "that he would send to New York to borrow of one Colonel Lewis Morris there a sextile of six or seven foot radiis, being the only fit instrument that could be heard of."

Maryland records question the authenticity of Markham's illness, and they may be right. Markham had probably been stricken with more than the August heat upon discovering the complexity of the border question and decided to delay matters until the arrival of his chief. He suffered such a severe relapse on his return that the question of the bounds had to be postponed until the following spring. One serious attack on his health could have been the discovery that the fortieth degree of northern latitude was going to fall farther north than anyone had realized. A second could have been learning that Penn had written a letter to some residents of the Chesapeake Bay area telling them to pay no more taxes to Maryland since they were now within his province. Penn's letter, which considerably upset the Maryland landholders, may have thrown a monkey wrench into Markham's preliminary negotiations. It had been addressed to men named J. Frisby, August Herman and others, sent directly instead of through Markham, and was dated September, 1681, so that it would have arrived around November, after Markham's return for Maryland. Frisby is observed in Fox's *Journal* as living on the western shore of Chesapeake Bay, well down into Maryland. Herman was a prominent personality in Maryland, active in her colonial development, and an extensive owner of land in the eastern part near New Castle. The question Penn must have inspired in the minds of Marylanders was: "How much more territory does Penn have than we realize?" It was a real question, for Penn was very high in favor at Whitehall; and the answer seemed to depend upon the location of the fortieth degree. Reports were even circulating in Maryland that the fortieth degree would come down as far as Poole's Island in Chesapeake Bay.

Faced with the problem of collecting taxes from those who had been told to stop paying them, Baltimore wanted a speedy settlement, and in May, 1682, he wrote to Markham suggesting that they meet on the tenth of June at August Herman's plantation. But when June 10 rolled around an uprising in Virginia (plant-cutting riots) that threatened the tobacco crops of Maryland made it impossible for Baltimore to leave the Potomac region, and he sent commissioners to Herman's in his stead. After a few days they came back with a curious—and encouraging—report. Markham, it seems, had not put in an appearance either, and an express dispatched to him had returned with the information that Markham was away in New York on some business or other. They had waited several days for Markham to no avail. Then, since they were so close to New Castle, they decided to push on and visit the town. By a stroke of luck there was a sloop in the harbor with Colonel Lewis Morris's new surveying instrument aboard, ready to be delivered to Markham. Eagerly they begged the use of it and took a reading. The town of New Castle, they were pleased to discover, stood at "39 degrees 40 odd minutes" north latitude.

Letters flew between Markham and Baltimore. Markham requested a second appointment, and Baltimore agreed to be at Herman's plantation some time in September. True to his word, Baltimore set out in the fall, almost a year after his first meeting with Markham, and while Penn was on the high seas bound for America. He reached Elk River only to learn that Markham was again gone on business up the Delaware. Since Herman's place was too small to accommodate him and his twenty-odd companions, Baltimore like Mohammed decided to go to the mountain, and he reached New Castle on the twenty-first. After waiting three days at New Castle, and feeling confident that Markham had received his letters, he went on up Delaware Bay to Upland. Markham, it turned out, had gone to Burlington; so Baltimore moved right in to Captain Markham's own lodgings. Markham could not escape him there! When Markham's boat turned in at Upland Creek, its occupant registered frank surprise to see Baltimore and his party waiting. Their conferences began at ten next morning, Baltimore confident, Markham with a "disordered countenance." Baltimore asked for the new instrument he heard Mr. Penn had sent him. It wanted some small glasses, he was told. Then what about the instrument Colonel Lewis Morris had sent? That was brought forth and set up and the reading at Upland was 39 degrees 47 minutes and five seconds. This concluded the conference. Before leaving Upland next morning, the third Lord Baltimore declared his position:

"You are sensible, Captain Markham, that by an observation taken yesterday, that this plantation is in thirty-nine degrees forty-seven minutes and some seconds, and must therefore be sensible that I am here about twelve miles to the southward of the degree of forty, which is my north bounds, as the same is Mr. Penn's south bounds. Therefore, afore you and afore all the rest here present I lay claim to this place, and as far further as the degree of forty will reach."

For his only answer, Markham escorted Baltimore to the waiting boat, and although there were promises exchanged of future conferences and future surveys, none of them occurred until Penn's arrival a month later.

No wonder Penn was so prompt to dispatch messengers to Baltimore, and no wonder he did it immediately after his first conference with Markham. The fortieth degree lay just north of the site chosen for Philadelphia! By the time Penn had returned from his trip through New York and New Jersey his messengers had returned from Maryland, and four days after the adjournment of the first General Assembly Penn set out for West River in Maryland and met Lord Baltimore at the house of Colonel Thomas Taylor in Anne Arundel County, on Wednesday, the thirteenth of December.

A shorthand recording of the conference made by Baltimore's attendants and a brief summary sent by Penn to the King's Privy Council tell essentially the same story. Penn immediately presented a letter from the King which instructed Lord Baltimore to make his measurements "two degrees north from Watkin's Point, the express south bounds in the patent [of Maryland] and already so settled by commissioners between Virginia and Maryland . . . according to their final computation of sixty English miles to a degree. . . ."

This initial conversation in American between Penn and Baltimore was long, strained and inconclusive. Baltimore maintained that the contents of the King's letter contradicted the terms of his patent and insisted that there was no better way to find the fortieth degree than by taking an observation with a sextant. Penn offered to measure northward two degrees fifty-five minutes from the Capes, since they had been reputed to be at about thirty-seven degrees and five minutes. Baltimore turned a deaf ear. Then what about measuring from thirty-seven and a half?

"It is other discourse that I expected to have heard from you at this time," replied Baltimore testily.

Obviously the whole Baltimore-Penn border dispute arose out of ambiguously drawn documents based on inaccurate maps and insufficient surveys. Baltimore had been given two degrees of territory which, if measured from Watkin's Point would fall short of the fortieth degree, yet the fortieth degree was certainly mentioned in his patent. Penn had been given three degrees from a point twelve miles north of New Castle which was thought to be the location of the fortieth degree but was not. For that matter Penn's three degrees, if measured from the fortieth, would have brought his northern bounds up in the neighborhood of the present city of Syracuse.

Baltimore injected into the conference yet another phase of the dispute: "I desire to be informed by you whether you have purchased the Duke's pretentions to Delaware."

Baltimore's patent had specifically stated that he was being granted "parts of America not yet cultivated and planted"—that is—by Europeans. So there was the additional question to be answered: Who owns Delaware? That question devolved upon the further question: Who settled there first? If the Dutch were there before Baltimore received his grant, then it was part of the Duke of York's grant and could properly be deeded by the Duke to Penn. There is said to have been a Dutch colony founded in 1631, the year before the Maryland Charter was issued, at Zwaanendale near the present Lewes. It was a tiny settlement of some thirty-odd who were completely wiped out by an Indian attack. David de Vries found the burned cabins and murdered remains a few months later, but none had survived to testify. The next settlement was established by the Swedes near Wilmington, but not until four years after the Maryland Charter.

Penn did not want to complicate the discussion with the Delaware question; he replied, "This leads to other discourse. I would willingly proceed first to the ascertaining the bounds between us."

"The certain bounds betwixt us must be the fortieth degree of northern latitude as I have already shewn you by my grant," said Baltimore.

But Penn insisted that the King's letter showed clearly that Baltimore was to have two degrees, bearing in mind that two degrees from Watkin's Point would fall comfortably below Philadelphia. Baltimore insisted that the fortieth degree be located by on-the-spot survey.

"I told him, it was not the love, nor need, of the land, but the water; that he abounded in what I wanted, and access and harboring, even to excess," Penn later reported to the Lords of Trade and Plantations. Penn's point was clear: it was the Delaware Bay and river facilities that he needed. Baltimore had the lovely sheltered and deep Chesapeake Bay all to himself, out of which to export his tobacco and import his manufacturies from the mother country.

Nothing accomplished, Penn at last returned to Chester.

As a man rises above the level of his fellows into new ideas, outstanding achievements, marked leadership, so do his enemies rise around him; Penn began immediately to attract the tearers-down and the critics, and they harassed him with increasing intensity for the rest of his life. In Whitehall, of course, there were ever the jealous, the backbiters, malicious schemers and betrayers of confidence; and in the world at large there were the spreaders of false rumors and misinformation. During his first few months in America, gossip spread to an alarming degree in England that he had died and, further, that he had died professing the Church of Rome. It persisted until Philip Ford not only placed a statement in the *London Gazette* verifying the fact that Penn was still very much alive, but wrote a tract as well, called, *A Vindication of William Penn, Proprietary of Pennsylvania, From the Late Aspersions Spread Abroad on Purpose to Defame Him.* Ford added to the tract an up-to-date account of affairs in Pennsylvania.

Even within the ranks of Quakerdom there were some who distrusted his intent. Among the Quakers who made Penn unhappy with their lack of confidence was one Jasper Yeates who complained that Penn was not reserving political power in Pennsylvania to the Quakers and accused Penn of having selfish motives in founding Pennsylvania. Penn took the time to write Yeates a long and careful letter, because he knew that what bothered Yeates bothered many more. Penn had all along insisted that all freemen in Pennsylvania should participate fully in their own government; many Quakers felt that it would be the better part of wisdom to limit power to themselves. Their fears were intensified when at the first General Assembly they found themselves within one vote of losing control. Two non-Quaker assemblymen had been absent when a vote was taken on a particular issue, otherwise the result would have been reversed. The Quakers considered that too close for comfort, but Penn stood his ground. "If you Quakers had it in your power, none should have a part in the government but those of your own way," he wrote to Yeates. As for any extraordinary personal gain that might accrue to himself out of Pennsylvania, he was prepared to answer that, too. "Had I sought greatness, I had stayed at home, where the difference between what I am here and was offered, if I could have been there, in power and wealth, is as wide as the places are."

There wasn't time to think of greatness; there was only a vast volume of responsibility for other people's lives and welfare; and more ships of settlers were on the way to swell the need. Immediately behind Penn came a wave of immigration, urged on at first by his optimistic hopes and then by his marvelous on-the-spot reports. They came long before there were any accommodations for them and lived as best they could in whatever natural shelters they could find. They camped under the great trees or moved into caves in the high banks along the Delaware. The banks were soft and the caves could be enlarged with digging and new ones could be created. Cave dwellers (Pastorius among them) extended roofs of brush and sod out in front of the caves, contrived primitive stone chimneys and in some cases strengthened the walls with timber. A valiant expedient at first, the caves in later years changed hands and deteriorated into rum dens and brothels to accommodate the seafaring men who came and went at the thriving seaport of mushrooming Philadelphia, until at last an Act of the Pennsylvania legislative bodies was needed to close them.

Penn issued writs for another election at the beginning of 1683 to choose a full Council and General Assembly. He was strict about procedures so that wholesome habit patterns could be established from the outset. "Remember," he wrote to Markham early in February, "that the twelve must be chosen for the Provincial Council in pursuance of the writ, and after that, a petition to me that three, A.B.C., should be for the Council and the other nine for the Assembly. . . . Then the Council will be eighteen, a good number at present, and fifty-four for the Assembly (total of seventy-two); the exact numbers. Also the petition must declare which is chosen for one, two and three years as the third article informs thee in the charter. *Let all that is done be the act of the people and so it will be safe.*"

The exact method of balloting in Pennsylvania no doubt varied from one county to another. Freeholders of a county were called together in a meeting to do their voting. There is a reference in Pennsylvania's *Colonial Records* to the fact that voting in Upland and the three lower counties was accomplished by placing black or white beans in a hat. The paper ballot came into use only gradually in Pennsylvania.

On the tenth day of the first month (March), 1683, William Penn met with his first Council at Philadelphia. Among the members were many already familiar names and a diversity of backgrounds: William Markham from London; Christopher Taylor from Yorkshire; Thomas Holme from Waterford, Ireland; Lacy Cock who was one of the Swedish settlers; John Simcock from Cheshire; John Moll, a very early settler at New Castle; and James Harrison of

Lancashire who was one of Penn's land agents and soon to become his Pennsbury steward.

Out of those earliest sessions and debates in the Council developed a unanimous opinion that the *Frame of Government* needed further amending, and a joint committee of twelve, one from both Council and Assembly, prepared a new draft. The *Frame of Government* dated April 2, 1683, is essentially the same kind of document as its predecessor. Its Preface was expanded to include the three lower counties; the Council was reduced to eighteen members and the Assembly to thirty-six, with memberships to be increased to seventy-two and two hundred respectively in the future. Most of the changes suggested by the first Assembly were incorporated. The Governor gave up his treble vote in presiding over the Council, and the Council relinquished its right to erect courts until the death of the present Governor. Council still was to elect judges, treasurers and masters of rolls, although their term of office was indefinite; and election of sheriffs, justices of peace and coroners was to be done by all the freemen. Four new and interesting clauses were added. One third of the Council with the Governor were empowered to "have the care of the management of public affairs, relating to the peace, justice, treasury and improvement of the province. . . ." To encourage colonization, aliens owning land in Pennsylvania were assured that their heirs could inherit their estates. Inhabitants were given the right to hunt their own lands and any other land not enclosed. Penn guaranteed all inhabitants "the full and quiet possession of their respective lands, to which they have any lawful or equitable claim, saving only such rents and services for the same, as are, or customarily ought to be, reserved to me, my heirs or assigns."

Philadelphia, the permanent capital, was already advanced enough in her growth to be hostess to the new government. Houses and cottages were going up, and by the first summer the number completed was nearly eighty. Another year would see 357 completed and a resident population of around 2,500. Many of the houses were of brick, many were affluent, for not all of the Quakers and others who came were poor by any means. New-born Philadelphia had many advantages that other New World cities had not had.

She had lured many merchants with both capital and experience who set up her trade life at once and got her produce flowing out and her needed manufactured items coming in, who opened well-stocked shops and launched competent ships. Well-to-do Quakers like Samuel Carpenter built lovely homes. Carpenter's home in particular, known as the "Slate Roof House," was so grand as to be an item of conversation and acclaim, and he built in addition a great quay to accommodate ships. Others founded country estates near Philadelphia with extensive orchards and cultivated lands. When Robert Turner came, he brought seventeen servants. Philadelphia rapidly became a cultural center, because she attracted scholars as well and did not have to wait for them to torture their way up out of the primitive soil. Francis Pastorius, George Keith, Thomas Lloyd, and many more had fine classical educations. Since William Penn himself was a tremendous scholar he acted as a magnet for others.

I have been unable to determine the location of Penn's first residence in Philadelphia. On arrival he no doubt stayed at the home of Thomas Fairman at Shackamaxon. In 1684, just before he sailed for England, he made a will covering his American holdings in which he bequeathed to his wife "this lot I live at in Philadelphia." The 1683 schedule showing to whom the first city lots were assigned does not include Penn's name although it does include the names of his children, William, Jr. and Letitia; there are some unassigned lots on the list.

Penn began early to develop friendly relations with the neighboring colonies as correspondence with New Jersey, Virginia and New York shows. New Jersey, of course, was a second administrative responsibility for him, and he kept in constant touch with Rudyard in East New Jersey and the Governor and Council of West New Jersey. Thomas Culpepper, Governor of Virginia, wrote to Penn: "I congratulate your arrival into your new dominion where I hope things will answer your expectations." When Thomas Dongan succeeded Anthony Brockholls as Governor of New York, Penn extended an invitation to him to visit Pennsylvania. "I give you my hearty sincere thanks for kind entertainment," the reply came back. "I am afraid this winter season will not give me leave to see my good friends in your Province and I very much wish for an opportunity to do it. There is no one more resolved and fixed to demonstrate himself ready to do all offices of friendship than I am, being very much obliged by you. . . ." At that time Penn was asking Nicholas Bayard to delve into New York's ancient Dutch records to find evidence of the right of the Dutch to parts of Delaware.

Penn kept his diplomatic life lines with England in constant repair, too.

To Lord Keeper North: "I thank God I am safely arrived, and twenty-two sail more; the air proveth sweet and good, the land fertile, and springs many and pleasant. We are one hundred and thirty miles from the main sea, and forty miles up the freshes. The town platt is a mile long and two miles deep; on each side of the town runs a navigable river. . . . The weather often changeth without notice and is constant almost in its inconstancy."

To Colonel Henry Sydney: "Would be glad I could be of any service to thee, at this distance to be sure I cannot, but neither can distance wear out the impressions, a long and kind acquaintance hath made upon my mind. . . ."

To the Earl of Sunderland: "Ever since he [Sunderland] yielded me the advantage of his acquaintance in France (a time of twenty years' standing, or running rather) I have said, many times, to many people, I remember not to have met a young nobleman promising a sharper and clearer judgment and of closer and better sense, and pardon me if I wish that this occasion may give thee time to prove it yet more abundantly to the world. I was a little elevated with the hopes of a free discourse and censure upon my American enterprise, when it pleased thee to give me to believe I might meet thee some evening at Colonel Henry Sydney's; but some greater affairs diverting robbed me of the advantage I had reason to promise myself from so correct a conversation . . . please to take me and my poor feeble concerns into thy protection and give us thy smiles and countenance and I will venture to say that by the help of God and such noble friends I will show a province in seven years equal to her neighbors of forty years' planting."

To Henry Savile, he laid claims to an old and very worthy acquaintance.

To Robert Boyle, the research chemist, he sent samples of ore and a description of the many medicinal herbs he had found in Pennsylvania.

English Friends were not the least in his heart: "My soul remembers my dear brethren in their afflictions."

And there was Guli in Worminghurst. She had not followed him to America as planned and she would not, at least in the near future, for her health would not permit it. Of the child she had been expecting when he left for America there are only references in correspondence and no known record of its exact birth date, or name. It was born some time early in the month of March, 1683, seven months after Penn's sailing, as a letter written by James Claypoole to Benjamin Furly, dated March 13, 1683, confirms: "Guli Penn is safe delivered of a daughter." Claypoole wrote to Penn on April 1 to say, "The 20th instant my wife and I with George Fox and Bridget Ford came to thy house at Worminghurst where we were very kindly entertained by thy dear wife and stayed there till the 26th then came away. And that morning she and thy four children were in good health."

The visitors had witnessed one week of a brief life span, for the frail spirit was snatched back to its source very quickly. There is a local legend that it is buried at the Blue Idol. Guli herself, in August when she was finally strong enough, wrote to Margaret Fox about the child and the party of loving Friends who had come to Worminghurst:

Dear Margaret Fox:

. . . I received thy dear and tender lines long since when I lay in. Several things prevented me from writing to thee again which I hope thou wilt pass by. I was very weak a long time after my lying-in and it pleased the Lord to take away my little one when it was about three weeks old. It was a mighty great child and it was near dead when it was born which I think it never got over. Dear George Fox came apurpose to see me which I took very kindly and was truly refreshed in his company. I have since had a sore fit of illness, that they call St. Antony's fire in my face and a fever. I could not see very little several days and nights, my face and eyes were so swelled, but it pleased the Lord to raise me up again. I am not wholly come to my strength yet. My eyes are very weak. Thy son and daughter Rouse has been here since to see me. . . . I have had several letters from my husband. He was then very well and Friends there have large meetings at Philadelphia which is the city. 300 at a meeting. . . . I expect to hear shortly what my husband will have me do, whether I shall go this year or not, but fear if he does send I shall scarce be well enough yet to go. . . .

Guli's letter tells of her illness with calm dignity once the emergency has passed, but she was alarmed enough at the time to send a messenger to her oldest and most trusted friend, Thomas Ellwood. Ellwood was being prosecuted at the time by a justice in Rickmansworth for having published a tract against informers, but he explained the urgency of the situation to the justice, that he was "divided betwixt honor and friendship," being bound to appear both before the justice and at Guli's side many miles away. "William Penn's wife . . . lay now there very ill, not without great danger, in the apprehension of those about her, of her life," Ellwood explained. Such was the reputation of the Penns in Rickmansworth, where they had lived for five years, that the justice postponed Ellwood's hearing to a later date so that he could ride to Sussex.

Friends' concern for Guli was pointed up by the fact that she no longer had her mother with her. Mary Penington had died at Worminghurst less than three weeks after Penn's departure for America.

The land—its purchase from the Indians and its redistribution to settlers—was the biggest administrative task in the first years of the colony. Records that still exist of land purchases from the Indians show that negotiations went on intermittently from July, 1682, well into the eighteenth century. During his first stay in America, Penn personally purchased from the Indians most of the river-front land from the Pennsbury tract southward through the three lower counties. The first purchase—Pennsbury—Markham had made in advance of his arrival. The second he made himself in June, 1683, of land between Neshaminy and Pennypack creeks, lying just south of Pennsbury and extending backward into the wilderness for two days' journey with a horse, and taking in the northern tip of the present city of Philadelphia. The third deed was negotiated that same month for "lands on the west side of the Schuylkill River beginning from the first falls of the same all along upon the said river and backward of the same, as far as my right goeth." The fourth purchase, on July 14, 1683, included the site of Philadelphia, the lands between the Schuylkill and Pennypack and between the Schuylkill and the Chester River. There is a deed dated October 18, 1683, for lands between Delaware River and Chesapeake Bay and up to the Falls of the Susquehanna River. By the end of 1683 he had a promise of a sale of the intervening piece between the Christiana and Chester rivers. Many of the deeds had walking or riding clauses in them, but the tract that became famous as the "Walking Purchase" many years after Penn's death, was not bought until the summer of 1686 after Penn had returned to Europe. It lay along the Delaware River just north of Pennsbury Manor. Tracts described in the various deeds often overlapped if chieftains or tribes had overlapping claims; Penn took great care to satisfy them all.

During his first spring in America, William Penn began to push his Indian purchases westward into the Susquehanna Valley. His reason was threefold: he wanted to block off any northward pushes on Baltimore's part; he had in mind a second settlement along the Susquehanna; and he wanted to draw Indian trade through Philadelphia. He was entirely within his Charter in doing so since his grant extended five degrees of longitude westward from the Delaware River.

The Indians of the Susquehanna Valley were Iroquois, often called Susquehannocks, Conestogas or White Minquas. Because of an ancient defeat in war they were subjects of the great Iroquois Confederacy to the north, the Mohawks, Cayugas, Oneidas, Onondagas and Senecas, often called the Five Nations, but they were not members of the Confederacy. The consent of the Confederacy was needed before the Susquehannas could sell their land, since they only occupied it by consent of the one-time victors; and the consent of the New York government was needed, since the Indians had turned over the lands to New York four years before. Some of the members of the Confederacy were willing to consent, some were not; New York certainly was not. The stumbling block was trade, because the trade of the Susquehanna Valley, along with the Five Nations trade, was routed to Albany and hence down the Hudson River to the port of New York. In the fall of 1683 there was a conference at Albany of Penn's agents, the Indians and New York commissioners. The Indians stood pat on their deed to the New York government. Dongan quickly found a temporary excuse for delay—the border dispute with Maryland—and sent word to Albany that "it is for the good and weighty reasons thought very convenient and necessary to put a stop to all proceedings in Mr. Penn's affairs with the Indians until the bounds and limits be adjusted." The Albany commissioners advised Penn's agents that the whole matter rested with Governor Dongan. At another conference in August, 1684, the Onondagas and Cayugas said in effect, "Penn has spoken to us here . . . by his agents, and desired to buy the Susquehanna River, but we would not hearken to them nor come under his government." Penn did not try to force the situation but quietly persisted until he had won over both Governor Dongan and the Indians. The former required fourteen years, the latter eighteen.

Allocating land to settlers proved a less complex diplomatic matter, however voluminous. The original Pennsylvania grant comprised about twenty-eight million acres. To the First Purchasers up to October, 1682, went 875,000 acres. From October, 1682, until 1701 some 83,000 more were distributed. Much of the first granting of land to the settlers had been made in England as to quantity and priority, and the principal task in America was selecting the actual sites—lots in the city of Philadelphia and tracts in the countryside. In March, 1682, a year after the date of the royal Charter, Penn gave Ford a list of more than 450 purchasers, and it includes many familiar names: Ford, Rudyard, Claypoole, Springett, Markham, Burnyeat, Penington, Ellwood, Lloyd, Lowther, Crispin, Whitehead, Turner, Holme and Penn's children. Land speculation was conspicuously absent in the founding and early years of this colony; most of the purchasers became settlers, and this stabilizing factor contributed strongly to the success of the project. The settlers who came, up to 1700, comprised sixty-eight per cent English, ten per cent Welsh, about ten per cent Irish, five per cent Dutch and Rhenish, with a sprinkling of other backgrounds. A few Scottish settlers came, but most of the Scottish immigrants were drawn to East New Jersey since that was Robert Barclay's particular project. Barclay had become Governor of East New Jersey in absentia, with Thomas Rudyard the on-the-spot Deputy Governor. The close personal friendship between Barclay and George Keith is undoubtedly what influenced Keith to settle there instead of in Pennsylvania. A project was set up and thirty thousand acres purchased in 1686 in Chester County, Pennsylvania, to create a colony for persecuted French Protestants, but the community never materialized. Most of the English and Irish came as individual settlers. The Irish came principally from Ballyhagen, Lurgan, Cashell, Waterford, Mountmellick and Dublin, the greatest number being from Dublin, and settled in Philadelphia, Chester and Middletown.

The Welsh were an interesting—and sometimes troublesome—group. Charles Lloyd (a brother of Thomas Lloyd) and seven others formed a company that purchased ten thousand acres and settled in Merion (now a Philadelphia suburb in Montgomery County), so named because some were from Merionethshire. Charles Lloyd came in advance of the rest of the group about the same time that Penn sailed. A second Welsh company was formed by Edward Jones, who was also from Merionethshire.

The migrations from Holland and the Rhineland, particularly the group that founded Germantown, were the direct result of Penn's two religious journeys through that part of the world. The confusion of the Crefeld and Frankfurt colonizing efforts has given rise to two traditions: that Pastorius founded Germantown and that the first inhabitants of Germantown were German. Neither is true. A group of thirteen Dutch families living in Crefeld were the first, after six of them had purchased through Benjamin Furly early in 1683 eighteen thousand acres in Pennsylvania. They did not organize into a company, although their effort was co-ordinated. Another group in Frankfurt did form a company, called the Frankfurt Company, with Daniel Pastorius as its agent, purchasing fifteen thousand acres, but this second group never sent any colonists. Pastorius was the first to arrive in America, sailing from England in June, 1683, and reaching Philadelphia in August. His own diary records that he dined with Penn five days later and that their new acquaintance flourished through the following year. "William Penn is loved and praised by the people. Even the old vicious inhabitants must recognize they have never seen so wise a ruler," was Pastorius' particular compliment. But Pastorius remained in Philadelphia for two years awaiting the never-to-arrive settlers of the Frankfurt Company, finally asking to be released in November, 1685, as their agent. Meanwhile the Crefeld Quakers, the seed planted by William Ames and nourished by William Penn, journeyed to Rotterdam in June, 1683, where Benjamin Furly had been making arrangements for their passage, and sailed July 24, 1683, on the *Concord* from Gravesend, reaching Philadelphia on October 6. That same month their land was allotted to them, and they began at once to clear it and build their community, choosing the name Germantown. Two years later another Dutch Quaker group migrated from Krisheim and settled in Germantown. Pastorius himself eventually moved to Germantown and became such a prominent figure in the community that his name is inevitably linked with its beginnings. William Penn wrote to Galenus Abrahams in Amsterdam, the learned divine with whom he had once debated, and invited him to come to America, but to no avail. Penn most earnestly wanted Benjamin Furly to come, too, but Furly preferred to negotiate the departure of others, and many left Holland under his guidance.

In March, 1683, Penn acquired some private lands in West New Jersey, by purchasing what remained of Fenwick's one tenth share; and in later years he acquired at least two other New Jersey tracts.

All of the administrative problems of Pennsylvania seemed soluble except the border dispute with Baltimore, and on that Penn was willing to make every effort to reach an amicable conclusion. Markham had delayed and avoided the issue; Penn did not. He sent a messenger to Baltimore in April of 1683 to ask when and where in Maryland it would be convenient for him to hold another conference.

"I wrote him word that I would begin my voyage up the bay about the middle of May," Baltimore relates, "which accordingly I did and being arrived at Saxafras River Wednesday the 23rd of the month I dispatched from thence Mr. John Darnall, one of my chief secretaries, with a letter to Mr. Penn signifying my arrival in that part of my Province; and Tuesday following being the 29th of the same month I met Mr. Penn about eight miles short of New Castle to which place that day I came in company with the said Penn."

"I invited him to the town," Penn takes up the narrative, "where having entertained him, as well as the town could afford, on so little notice. . . . I pressed that we might sit severally with our councils."

Their discussion rehearsed many of the arguments of their previous conference, and then Penn came forward with a fresh proposition: if Baltimore would let him have the Susquehanna River for an inlet, with some land on each side, Penn would then consent to locating the fortieth degree with proper instruments, as Baltimore wished. But Baltimore had obviously no further liking for the debate, for he pleaded ill health and returned home. What was becoming increasingly apparent was the fact that the whole affair would have to be reviewed by the King's Privy Council.

When Penn heard that Baltimore had sent a report to the Lords of the Council he hastened in August to send them one of his own, lest his silence sound like neglect. He had not wanted to trouble the Council with the matter until some conclusion had been reached, but he felt it necessary to advise them that Baltimore had made his narrative of the conferences without Penn's consent and had then promised, "upon his word and honor, that it should go not farther."

Penn addressed another letter to his "Great and Gracious Prince" the King, introducing the man whom he had decided to make his Agent Extraordinary in London, according to the requirement in his Charter, his kinsman, William Markham. Markham sailed home for England armed with letters commending him to the good care not only of the King but such men as the Earl of Rochester, Lord Sunderland, Colonel Henry Sydney and others.

Colonel George Talbot, who was Surveyor-General of Maryland, paid a courtesy call upon Penn, and the report of their conversation reveals that Baltimore had promised Penn another conference in September, but "when he came up the bay never to send to me to meet him, but take observations and run a line without giving me the least notice." And there were other petty differences revealed in the conversation, too—paying rents, Indian hunting rights, encouraging or discouraging settlers to live here or there—that showed the border dispute was rapidly becoming a personal conflict between the two proprietors.

It began to look as though Penn would have to return to England himself to settle his difference with Baltimore. "He hath searched the Dutch records but what he hath in them to his advantage I know not. My Lord Baltimore is going for England and I believe if you would go over it would not be to your disadvantage," Governor Dongan had advised Penn as early as the previous May. Going home could well mean going home to a highly tense and still dangerous political situation. "I suppose you'll hear Lord Russell is beheaded and others . . . and two more were tried either Thursday or Wednesday last. What their doom is I know not and Essex cut his throat in the Tower," Penn's sister, Margaret Lowther, wrote to him early in August. Algernon Sydney's execution was only a few weeks away. These deaths were the culmination of the efforts of the Duke of Monmouth, Charles II's illegitimate son by Lucy Walters, to seize the throne. A weak and vain young man, Monmouth could easily be sold the far-fetched idea of inheriting the throne by those who wished to ride in his train, and the famous plots known as the Insurrection Plot and Rye House Plot stirred public tempers and Royalist wrath to a level which allowed both Russell and Sydney to be convicted by grossly unfair trials.

In September Baltimore commissioned Talbot to go to Philadelphia and demand of William Penn "all the part of the land, on the west side of the said [Delaware] River, that lyeth to the southward of the fortieth degree, northern latitude, according to an east line, run out from two observations the one taken the 10th of June 1682 and the other, the 27th of September, 1682." Talbot's demand was received by the new Deputy Governor of Pennsylvania, Nicholas More, since William Penn was in New York visiting with Governor Dongan; but the reply to Baltimore came from Penn, upon his return from New York. The demand was abrupt and unprecedented, Penn declared, and no deputy in Pennsylvania had the power to conclude away his Pennsylvania inheritance. Further, no lines had as yet been run; if Baltimore had run one he had done so as an intruder and without warrant.

Tensions continued to gather. Penn accused Baltimore of forbidding the inhabitants of New Castle to pay him quitrent. In December Baltimore wrote to William Blathwaite at Whitehall asking to be heard in person before the Lords of Council regarding his right to Delaware. He hoped, he told Blathwaite, to be there the latter end of May (1684). "And if my unkind neighbor William Penn or his agents are able to make out that there were Dutch seated at Delaware before my patent for Maryland was granted I will then make it plainly appear that such Dutch were usurpers."

The situation reached the point of violence in the disputed area, and the plantation owners were harassed with letters and invaded and beset by sheriffs and mercenaries. Early in 1684 an invasion party from Maryland seized by force several plantations in the lower counties, and Pennsylvania sent a request to Baltimore that the dispossessed persons be reinstated. Later Talbot went with three musketeers to the houses of the widow Ogle, Jonas Erskin and Andreas Tittle, near New Castle, threatening them with eviction and confiscation if they did not yield obedience and pay rent to Maryland. In April Penn gave instructions to John Simcock, William Welsh, the Surveyor-General of Delaware, James Harrison and John Cann to go to the lower counties and seize and hold for trial some local men, at least one sheriff among them, who had been collaborating with Baltimore and suffering Baltimore's "emissaries to go up and down the country to seduce people from their obedience." Colonel Talbot's next move was to arrive with a body of armed men upon Ogle's land, within five miles of New Castle, erect a fort, breastwork and palisades, and establish a military force there. The President of the town of New Castle gathered together his sheriff, magistrates and some citizens and went immediately to the fort to demand an explanation for the warlike proceedings. Talbot ordered the visitors to stand off, and they found themselves looking down the barrels of guns and muskets. Wisely, they withdrew, and the garrison continued to menace the town, promising to fire upon anyone who attempted to demolish the blockhouse.

The whole unfortunate matter would have to be taken to the top, and Penn began to make serious preparations for returning to England. He sent a long, detailed letter to the Earls of Rochester and Sunderland telling the up-to-date story of the lower counties, and another to the Duke of York telling him particularly about Baltimore's garrison near New Castle, as well as Baltimore's recent departure for England. "I am following him as fast as I can, though Colonel Talbot, since his departure, threatened to turn such out by violence, as would not submit to him, and drive their stock for arrears."

John Purvis, captain of the ship *Duke of York* wrote to Penn from the Rappahannock in Virginia on May 21: "The Lord Baltimore and his family passed this river mouth about six days since in an English fly boat . . . and is now with the Lord of Effingham who [it] is supposed will stay most part of this week through and then the first fair wind he sails for England." Purvis hoped that Penn would sail with him the end of May, but that was not to be; Penn had too many details to attend to before he could turn over the reins to anyone else, even temporarily.

Keeping Pennsylvania on a paying basis and keeping himself and his family solvent were already beginning to be the most distasteful parts of his task, and yet it had to be faced as well as understood. "Loving Friends and Tenants," he wrote to the settlers in New Castle, Chester, Philadelphia and Bucks counties in November, 1683, "I kindly salute you and wish you heartily well. I have sent the bearer, James Atkinson, to gather in my quitrents among you, and you must not take it hard that I press you in this matter, for you know that I receive neither custom nor taxes but maintain my table and government at my own cost and charges, which is what no governor doth besides myself. This makes me endeavor to get in my own dues for my winter supply. I expect you will all strive to answer me herein and so engage the kindness of, your friend and landlord, William Penn." A few months later, when the shortage of currency in America began to be apparent, he said, "Let the planters give me credit for being willing to take my quitrents in tobacco at two pence per pound, as also for this that I being a governor upon my own costs hitherto, and separated from the greatest comforts of my life—my wife and children—for the good of all. I hope my half of my quitrents to supply me with bread will not be made a reason of rebellion by men in their wits that love their lives and estates." He had plunged his whole life and fortune into America, and his family's with it, and yet over the years that fact would be forgotten to a shameful degree by those who had benefited most.

Above all else, William Penn was a Friends' minister, and the building of meeting houses, organization of monthly and quarterly meetings, the strengthening effect of an eloquent minister at meetings for worship, were all part of his task. To meetings that he could not reach in person he sent spiritual epistles. A yearly meeting had been established at Burlington in 1681. By 1684 it would be meeting in the city of Philadelphia, and alternating from then on between Philadelphia and Burlington.

Since government was "a part of religion itself," Penn often turned to his Society for help in making the government a success. "God hath brought us hither, and we are yet among the living. He hath a work for us to do here, though the spiteful and envious will not believe us. O! that we may be faithful to the measure of grace received, that the evil-minded may be disappointed. Friends, keep in the sense of that which first visited you and kept you, and He that was with you to bless you in your native country, will be with you and bless you and yours, and make you a blessing to them that you are come among. . . ."

The Quakers had discovered almost upon arrival that the Indians whom they had come among were already being shamefully exploited by Europeans with strong drink. Alcoholic beverages did not occur in the Indian culture pattern until they were introduced by the white man, and the Indians were unable to adjust to them. Sober, they were extraordinary, sensitive people of high integrity; drunk, they were helpless dupes. Jasper Danckaerts in his journal of a visit to America some three years earlier was forced to observe when he reached Elizabeth Town, New Jersey, "I must here remark, in passing, that the people in this city, who are almost all traders of small articles, whenever they see an Indian enter the house, who they know has any money, they immediately set about getting hold of him, giving him rum to drink, whereby he is soon caught and becomes half a fool. If he should then buy anything, he is doubly cheated, in the wares and in the price. . . . They do not rest until they have cajoled him out of all his money." Rum had been part of the purchase price in the early New Jersey transactions and in the first deed that Markham executed with the Indians, but it was never a part of the purchase price in any subsequent deeds that Penn negotiated. As soon as the evil became evident Markham forbade the sale of rum to the Indians, and Penn confirmed it on arrival. In the ensuing years, it became an ever increasing concern of the Friends. The peaceful relationship with the Indians of mutual trust and honor and good will that Penn and the rest of the Quakers had succeeded in establishing must be maintained; upon it could rest the success or failure of Pennsylvania.

The administration of his government he left in the hands of his Provincial Council, with Thomas Lloyd as President. Thomas Lloyd, a substantial and gifted Quaker who had brought his family from Wales, was entrusted with the care of the Great Seal as well. James Harrison became the steward of Penn's household at Pennsbury. "My desire is," Penn told Harrison, "and I offer to the consideration of thee and thy wife . . . that thou shouldst be the steward of my household to oversee servants, building and what relates to the place where I live, to receive, pay, take and put away servants . . . thy wife to overlook the maids . . . with the charge of linen and plate. . . . I shall allow you a group of chambers and a horse and give you besides meat, drink, washing and lodging, forty pounds the first year and fifty ever after. . . ." The Harrisons apparently were pleased with the offer, for Harrison's commission to the post is dated August 15, 1684. Instructions for layout and construction of the manor house and outbuildings had largely been made but more would come later from England.

To Ralph Smyth, his gardener at Pennsbury, Penn left a long list of instructions: "Get the courtyards paled and gates like Philadelphia in the places I have appointed, before, behind and on each side of the house, more than which need not be, save one against the gate that goes across the waterside court into the garden. Let the land in the water court be leveled, and steps made of brick covered with stone, or stone such as by waterside, covered with quarry stone. Set out the garden by the house, plant sweet herbs, sparro grass, carrots, parsnips, artichokes, salatin, and all flowers and kitchen herbs there. Let a peach tree be planted between every apple tree. Let all the peaches about the grounds in Indian fields be saved, making a barrel of wine or two, and dry the rest, save that a few be preserved when almost ripe. . . . Get the walks to the house in the courts graveled. . . . Let handsome steps be made at the waterside. . . ."

When these matters had all been provided for, he could at last turn his full thoughts toward home. There many more waited for him who loved him and needed him. His phlegmatic brother-in-law, Anthony Lowther, had begun to respond weakly to Penn's appeals to come to America: "I am sorry that we are at so great a distance, and if wishing inwardly would bring us together it would have been before now, without your leaving Pennsylvania, for which place on your account I have more inclinations than for any other part of the world except poor England. . . . I am rather by custom or nature of so inactive a temper that I am altogether unfit for any undertaking that shows the least of difficulty in it." Lowther's letter had also shown a beginning interest in Quaker doctrine: "I am sure I now think there is something besides riches to make one happy."

Penn wanted to gather his whole family together around him in America, his sister, Margaret, and her husband and children, his own wife and children. Guli must come. He needed her presence and dignity at Pennsbury as the letter he sent to her from Philadelphia just ahead of himself shows:

Philadelphia, August 6, 1684

My most dear G. Penn:

Being now to leave this part of the world, and ready to come to thee, not knowing how the Lord pleaseth to deal with me in my passage, lest the sea be my grave and the deeps my sepulchre, I write unto thee, as my beloved one, the true and great joy and crown of my life above all visible comforts, always valued by me, and honored above women, I do most dearly salute and embrace thee with thy dear children, praying the God of our many and rich blessings to be with you and that He would preserve you from the evil that is in the world, and among those that profess a faith that is above it, faithful to His blessed Truth and in constant communion with the faithful remnant that keep the testimony of Jesus with zeal and fidelity to the end. The Lord crown you with His life, love and heavenly presence, lead you not into temptation but deliver you from evil and bless you with the mercies of His chosen both here and hereafter.

I have herein inclosed my will as to this place, the rest being settled already. Again does my soul embrace thee and thine and forever shall our spirits live together where no tears nor troubles shall divide or separate or grieve us, which is our country and lasting dwelling place, and blessed will you be if here you be strangers and sojourners as were our fathers Abraham, Isaac and Jacob. Dearly I bid thee farewell and my children, whom breed in the fear of the Lord and in the strict way of His holy Truth, and the Lord God Almighty bless, keep and be with you forever. I am

Theirs and thine
in that which is not of this dying world,
WILLIAM PENN

The will referred to in this letter left "this lot I live at in Philadelphia" to his wife while she lived and then to his daughter, Letitia. Guli was also to enjoy Pennsbury until his son Springett came of age, and it would then be his manor. To his son William he gave a lot running all the way from the Delaware to the Schuylkill on the southern side of town plus ten thousand acres on Schuylkill, four hundred on Delaware, five thousand in each county, and twenty thousand on the Susquehanna. To Letitia went other lots in Philadelphia, one on Schuylkill and two on High Street, and all the land from the creek to the falls north of Pennsbury as far as the land of James Hamilton, five thousand acres on Schuylkill, ten thousand in each county and ten thousand on Susquehanna. William and Letitia each received one hundred pounds yearly forever out of his quitrents, and the rest of his rents went to his wife until Springett reached his majority. Guli was given an additional ten thousand acres when and where she pleased. Fifty thousand acres were set aside to be parceled out to poor families; in Philadelphia County ten thousand acres each were set aside for a school and hospital and a like amount on Susquehanna for similar uses. There were smaller land bequests to each of the servants who had come with him and to those who had stayed with his wife during his absence.

Shortly before Penn's departure from Pennsylvania, a letter came from Stephen Crisp, elderly Friends' minister, that expresses the weight of Quaker sympathy that was with Penn at the time:

DEARLY BELOVED IN THE LORD:

My soul salutes thee in the fellowship of that life that reigns over death and darkness in which is the kingdom we seek. . . . I hope thou will bear this my style of writing to thee; my spirit is under great weight at the writing hereof, and much I have in my heart, because I love thee much. I cannot write much at present, but to let thee know I very kindly received thy letter, and was glad to hear from thee, and always shall; and my prayer to God is for thee, and you all, that you may be kept in the Lord's pure and holy way; and above all for thee, dear William Penn, whose feet are upon a mountain, by which the eyes of many are upon thee; the Lord furnish thee with wisdom, courage and a sound judgment; prefer the Lord's interest and He will make thy way prosperous.

The ketch *Endeavour*, which had brought with her more new residents, was to take Penn home, and before she unfurled her sails, he wrote a final message "For Thomas Lloyd, James Claypoole, J. Simcock, Christopher Taylor and James Harrison, to be communicated in meetings in Pennsylvania and the territories thereunto belonging among Friends." It is the letter that contains his prayer for Philadelphia and the pledge of his complete personal dedication. "My love and my life is to you, and with you; and no water can quench it, nor distance wear it out, or bring it to an end. I have been with you, cared over you and served you with unfeigned love; and you are beloved of me, and near to me, beyond utterance."

During Pennsylvania's brief life of less than three years, fifty sail of ship had brought settlers from England, Wales, Ireland, Holland and Germany to swell the incumbent European settlements to some seven thousand persons. The city of Philadelphia alone had more than 350 dwellings and a population of 2,500, and the value of her lots had quadrupled. Wharfs and their accompanying warehouses were accommodating the ships of the world, a great yearly fair took place in the city to which the livestock and products of the province were brought, Philadelphia's booming trade was already challenging Boston's prosperous supremacy, and twenty other townships had been set up.

So far Penn had kept his province from the evil that would overwhelm her. He had given her a government that rested upon her people's desires and could be changed and adapted to their changing needs, and he had stayed with her long enough to see her economic life lines well established. He had united her many kinds into a single community, and guided them into keeping faith with their own peaceable intent. When he reached England he would be able to report happily and gratefully to Stephen Crisp, "not one soldier, or arms borne, or militia man seen, since I was first in Pennsylvania."

For God's sake, let us sit upon the ground
And tell sad stories of the death of kings:
How some have been deposed; some slain in war,
Some haunted by the ghosts they have deposed.
——Shakespeare, *King Richard II*

16. The Turning Tide

"I ARRIVED from America the sixth of October, 1684, at Wonder, in Sussex, being within seven miles of my own house," says a fragment of Penn's autobiography.

His reunion with Guli was a precious first consideration over which he lingered for several days before going up to London. To find her and the children well was the reassurance that he needed most. By the time he was able to return to America he would take her with him, and soon letters began to go to James Harrison at Pennsbury telling him to expect more servants, three carpenters and another gardener, to build "a kitchen, two larders, a wash house and room to iron in . . . a brew house, in it an oven for baking and a stable for twelve horses. . . . I would have the back door a two-leaved one and the front made from tip to bottom. . . . I would have a rail and bannisters before both fronts. . . . I hope the barge is kept safely from wind, weather. . . . I desire that a pair of handsome steps be made at the landing. . . . The partition between the best parlor and the great room the servants used to sit in should be wainscoted with double leaved doors. The door had best be large between the other parlor and with-drawing room. . . . I will send this fall divers seeds and plants. . . ." All comforts that Guli would want and need at Pennsbury and many no doubt suggested by her. His estate in England as well needed some of his time. Guli's long illness had forced her to neglect many details, more than Thomas Ellwood could have tended to for her—the gardens and orchards of which Penn was so fond, the forests and roads about the estate.

"After some days of refreshment, I went to wait upon the King and Duke, then both at New Market, who received me very graciously, as did the Ministers very civilly. Yet I found things in general with another face than I left them: sour and stern and resolved to hold the reins of power with a stiffer hand than heretofore, especially over those that were observed to be State or Church Dissenters, conceiving that the opposition which made the government uneasy came from that sort of people, and therefore they should either bow or break."

Penn had returned to a Tory England. Her King, "resolved to hold the reins of power with a stiffer hand," was still ruling without a Parliament and would do so until his death. Civil liberties achieved through so much hardship over so many years of strife were wiped away; all printed matter was completely censored, and an anti-Tory pamphlet could mean a gross trial before a corrupt court and packed jury. Charles still yearned to avow his secret Catholicism, still basked in the financial sunlight of the French King, and bore down on every kind of dissenter in England since most of them were of the Whig strain.

Penn had only to meet his King to realize two things: first, an easily corruptible man had been so far corrupted by personal power at home that his interest in a colonial border question three thousand miles away had been obscured; second, the King's health was obviously failing which further decimated his concern for Penn's problems. Even if the Penn-Baltimore hearings before the Privy Council could have been guided by an able and vigorous King they would have dragged on for a considerable time; now there was no knowing how long they would take. The case had been delayed to await Penn's arrival, and to make matters worse one of Penn's staff had carelessly left behind the York papers relating to Dutch possession of the river and bay which Penn called "the ground and very strength of my coming." The day after his arrival home Penn had to send a hasty request to James Harrison to post them to him aboard the next ship. "I am now here with my finger in my mouth," he told Harrison. "He would not have done me a worse injury nor Baltimore a greater service if he had had the bribe of ten thousand to do it." It meant that the case could not even be heard for many weeks.

With so many delaying factors at work to keep him in England longer then he wanted to stay, Penn had time on his hands and to spare, and so he cast about him for useful tasks. The fact that so many of his close friends were Whigs placed him in an ambiguous position: "finding myself narrowed in this manner, that one day I was received well at Court as Proprietor and Governor of a province of the Crown and the next taken up at a meeting by Hilton or Collingwood, and the third provoked and informed of for meeting with men of the Whig stamp." He could neither remain idle nor betray his own convictions, yet he did not want to jeopardize the case for his province either, since Pennsylvania offered a greater solution for more people than any other single thing.

"Upon the whole matter, I found no point so plain, so honest, so sensible, that carried such weight, conviction, and compassion with it, and that would consequently find an easier reception and more friends than *Liberty of Conscience, my old Post and Province.*"

Among the 1,460 Quakers who had been swept back into prison in forty counties of England and Wales by the unfortunate turn of affairs in England and the many more out of prison suffering impoverishment from continuous fines, there was a wide choice of opportunity for a man who wanted to be their champion. Three months before Penn's arrival in England George Whitehead, Alexander Parker and other Quaker leaders had presented Charles II with a petition for mercy, protesting that the recent plot against the King and his brother was being made an occasion to persecute them; but having seen the internal picture at Whitehall, Penn did not choose to apply to Charles for any general amnesty. Instead, he "sought out some bleeding cases, which wasn't hard to do," and began with the case of Richard Vickris of Bristol, a prominent man in that city being used as a scapegoat. Persecutions were particularly bad in Bristol at that time. Vickris was a personal acquaintance of long standing, a man to whom Penn had written a special letter of comfort before sailing to America. Vickris was now under sentence of death because, as a Quaker, he could not take the oath under any circumstances, and thus the suspicions of treasonable plotting had fallen upon him. Even though illness and corruption had made Charles a difficult person to deal with, Penn's relationship with the Duke of York was unspoiled, and so he took Vickris's case to the

King's brother. "Upon my assuring them he [Vickris] would live peaceably under the government, the Duke promised to press the King in his favor, who grew harsh and very tender to be spoken to upon that head . . . the Duke was as good as his word. He was pardoned."

Penn was most alive within himself, most vital, most aware of the significance of living when he could justify his convictions by some deed like snatching a man from the gallows or any other evil snare. "The ancient love and path of life," he called it in a letter to Margaret Fox, and a conviction justified once could be justified over and over again. The suffering was so widespread he need not pause a moment. Even in Ireland the Friends were feeling the pressure once more. He had already written to the Lord Deputy of Ireland from Philadelphia appealing for clemency and had drawn a kindly reply from the Earl of Arran who wrote, "I intend to remain some time in this kingdom, and I will do good offices to your brethren, for I must confess I ever had more charity for them than for other dissenters."

Even though he still bore in mind Pennsylvania's priceless destiny, Penn decided to try an oblique approach to the King, and he wrote a piece called *True Interest of King and Kingdom* and sent it to him in manuscript. Let the King review his own reasoning; let him see that he was splitting his own kingdom in half, that the cleavage lines were growing deeper and would eventually serve to ruin one party or the other. Penn, still the Old Testament Prophet, could see the future with clarity and accuracy! He warned Charles "to look upon past things as a King, and not as a man, without passion, and not suffer his own resentment or his ministers' flatteries, interests or revenges to carry him further than was good for his interest."

What the fate of that manuscript was, or whether the King ever read it, I do not know; but all history knows that King Charles died four months after Penn's arrival back in England. A stroke felled the dissolute, vengeful monarch and seventeenth-century medical techniques—"they opportunely blooded and cupped him, and plied his head with red-hot frying pans"—speeded up his demise. Before he breathed his last a priest was brought to his private chambers to administer the last rites of the Church of Rome. The effect of the accession of James to the throne was immediate on both sides of the ocean. He was an honestly avowed Catholic, and although he proclaimed that he would maintain the established church and state and further announced elections for a new Parliament, he and his Queen went "publicly to mass," thereby bringing back to the surface all the hates, fears and doubts that had been smouldering since the crushing of the Whig movement. A deeply Protestant England cocked her rebellious head to get a better view of her new monarch, and the social forces that had made Monmouth's presumption and the Rye House and Insurrection plots possible began to come back into focus.

William Penn believed James to be a genuinely tolerant man, even though he was a less able politician than his brother, and his own friendship had always been closer with James than with Charles. Through James he had been able to effect Fox's release form Worcester prison, and through James he had very recently saved Vickris from the gallows. James had agreed readily to the Pennsylvania grant and had relinquished to Penn the three lower counties. Penn wrote out of a deep good faith when he addressed this letter to James:

GREAT KING:

Suffer in the crowd a most dutiful and affectionate subject to condole the loss of a wise and gracious brother, and to congratulate thy fair accession to the imperial crown; in which the providence of God hath so conspicuously appeared, that it hath added a divine to an unquestionable natural right; in the use of which, I do with humble heart beseech almighty God to give the King the wisdom of Solomon, and the mercies of David, that his administration may tend to God's glory, the general good, and his own immortal honor. I have only to pray leave to hope that the King's wonted grace and favor, will receive no abate from his greater power to show it, to his most faithful, loving and obedient subject—

WILLIAM PENN

Penn now had private access to a King with whom he could speak with even greater candor and directness than in the past, and he did so even before the coronation. "He declared he concealed himself to obey his brother, and that now he would be above-board; which we like the better on many accounts. I was with him and told him so," Penn wrote to Thomas Lloyd in Pennsylvania. "But, withal, hoped we should come in for a share. He smiled, and said he desired not that peaceable people should be disturbed for their religion." Dissenters could look to the new King with great hope for an ease of their sufferings, but, as Penn cautioned Lloyd, "till his coronation, the 23rd [of April] . . . no hopes of release; and, till the Parliament, no hopes of any fixed liberty." Three weeks after the coronation James issued his first limited declaration on behalf of liberty of conscience, curbing the greedy activity of informers and taking the worst edge off of persecutions then going on.

Moving rapidly back into a position of high favor in Court, Penn used all his political prowess and suddenly improved advantage to further Friends' interests and the welfare of countless individuals who came to him for help. He sent Markham back to Pennsylvania as his personal secretary and Secretary of the Province and Territories. Realizing that this same set of circumstances, together with the demands on his time by the Baltimore dispute (delayed by Charles's death), would require him to spend a great deal of time in London, he took lodgings in Kensington in a magnificent old mansion known as Holland House. Set upon a gently rising hill in a stretch of natural forest to the west of London, the Jacobean manor house with its rows of pointed arches, its cloistered courtyard, had been the home of the Earls of Holland off and on since the earliest years of the seventeenth century. Its building had begun in Elizabeth's day. Penn engaged a suite of rooms in the house, and Guli and the children remained in Worminghurst. From his headquarters at Holland House Penn devoted his efforts to solving his border dispute and to promoting his "old post and province." Petitioners wrote letters pleading that he intercede for them at Court, or they flocked to Holland House in person begging for his help. Often when he came out of the door of a morning there would be as many as two hundred gathered in the courtyard, hoping for an audience.

The worsening times drove them to Penn's doorstep like small craft fleeing before a storm, for James soon began to show his true

Stuart colors. The King had no real love for Protestants in his heart; his brief gesture toward the Quakers had been the act of a man easily influenced by whoever sat near him at the moment, of a morally weak man bent momentarily in the right direction by one morally strong. The persecution of Protestant dissenters in England and Scotland during the first year of James's rule—designed to win to James's side the support of Church of England leadership and to punish Whig opposition—reached a degree of hysterical cruelty which, Trevelyan declares, could have meant the ultimate extermination of non-conformists. Titus Oates, onetime witch-hunter of Roman Catholics, was apprehended, tried for perjury, and sentenced to be imprisoned for life after a deadly flogging, and to be displayed once a year in the stocks. The Parliament that James convened in May, corruptly elected and carefully packed, was heavily Royalist, and gave little indication that it would approve any legislation designed to encourage liberty of conscience. The time was ripe, thought the shortsighted Protestant extremists, for that long-needed uprising. Argyle landed on the western shores of his native Scotland in May to raise the insurrection there, and in June Monmouth returned from exile in Holland to land in western England and begin his military advance toward Bristol. Their attempts were quixotic and short-lived, quickly brought to an end by the King's better trained troops. That same summer Monmouth contributed his troublesome head to the axe of Jack Ketch, and Jeffreys circulated through western England with his Bloody Assize.

Penn's political position had never been more delicate, and in it he proved himself a superb diplomat. He was able to express to James his opposition to the King's approach to England's affairs, even to save twenty of Monmouth's followers from the gallows or transport into bondage, and at the same time not to lose James's personal approval of his Pennsylvania project. William Penn dared not lose Pennsylvania. Pennsylvania was the only solid hope there was at that time for Protestant dissenters on the Continent as well as in the British Isles. During the Monmouth uprising in England, the Krisheimers were packing up to flee from the Palatinate. The blood of Jeffreys' assize had not dried when Louis XIV revoked the Edict of Nantes in France, and the Huguenots who were able to escape to England brought harrowing tales of terror with them. "In France, not a meeting of Protestants left; they force all, by not suffering them to sleep, to conform; they use drums or fling water on the drowsy till they submit or run mad. They pray to be killed, but the King has ordered his dragoons to do anything but kill. . . . Such as fly and are caught, are executed or sent to the galleys to row," Penn wrote to Harrison in Philadelphia.

According to Gilbert Burnet, the seventeenth-century historian, Penn witnessed the burning at the stake in London of a woman Anabaptist, Elizabeth Gaunt, who had been convicted on the most dubious evidence of having sheltered a rebel in her home; he watched while she drew the straw closer about herself so that her burning would be accomplished more speedily, and while she conducted herself with such courageous martyrdom that the spectators were moved to tears. He also witnessed the execution of Cornish, a London merchant of strong Whig convictions whom the Royalists had been licking their chops over for some time. And Burnet reports Penn as the author of the deeply compassionate remark that the King was "much to be pitied, who was hurried into all this effusion of blood by Jeffreys' impetuous and cruel temper."

His almost constant attendance at Court and his personal friendship with James naturally brought upon Penn the malice and slander of guilt by association, and the rumors began to fly that he had declared himself a Papist and was going openly to mass. " 'Tis enough for me 'tis false," was Penn's natural reaction, but when a volume of pro-Catholic verses were published with the initials W.P. on them the rumors persisted with such vigor and the circumstantial evidence was so strong against Penn that at last he had to write an epistle to the Quakers, *Fiction Found Out*. In it he denied authorship of the verses and reaffirmed his faith in Friends' principles. A little later he had to devote considerable time and thought to a correspondence with Dr. John Tillotson, a man destined to become Archbishop of Canterbury, who eloquently misrepresented Penn's views. The exchange of letters which Penn began in the kindliest tone possible proved fortunate, and it ended in an apology from John Tillotson.

A tiff between William Penn and Robert Barclay marred the late summer and fall of 1685. As Barclay viewed American affairs, Penn had grown too ambitious for territory, and not only wanted to add West New Jersey to Pennsylvania, but was considering trading East New Jersey to the Duke of York in exchange for it—a plan that never materialized. "Thee knows best what is proper for thee to do," Barclay wrote rather testily to Penn, "as to securing thy own or enlarging it by the accession of West Jersey (as I hear they have petitioned it should be). . . . I am of the mind that thy surrendering thy share of East Jersey in order to that (in case thou do so) is no good policy but rather to stave off annexation from New York, at all that, that topic may never take place, otherways the same unjust appetite will recur again and East Jersey will not satiate it. . . ." A month later he wrote again, cautioning Penn to "avoid the ambition and envy of others who will scarce rest until all be upon the level, lest that province that can boast of privileges beyond them should thereby overgrow them . . . compliments to princes are often forgot, and seldom have the desired effect. . . ." Not until the beginning of the next year were feelings healed between the two ministers.

As soon as the dust of the Monmouth uprising settled and the situation in Whitehall came back into its own kind of focus, Penn could hope for a resolution of his Maryland border quandary. On August 17, 1685, he wrote happily to Philadelphia, "I have been at Windsor and the King has ordered my business with Lord Baltimore to be heard forthwith, and I am now going to the Lords of Plantations to set a day, this day week I suppose will be the time." On September second he and Baltimore both appeared before the committee of the Privy Council, and from then on their appearances were frequent. "Penn produced divers proofs . . . that the country was inhabited by Swedes and Dutch before the date of the Lord Baltimore's patent." On November 13 the committee made a report to the King and his Court at Whitehall: they had found that the land intended to be granted to Baltimore was only land uncultivated and that the land in dispute was inhabited and planted by Christians before the date of the Lord Baltimore's patent, a distinct colony from that of Maryland. They therefore recommended that "for avoiding further differences the tract of land lying between the river and bay of Delaware and the eastern sea on the one side and Chesapeake Bay on the other be divided into equal parts by a line from the latitude of the old Cape Hinlopen to the fortieth degree of northern latitude" giving the half lying on the Delaware River to Penn and the half on Chesapeake to Baltimore. His Majesty approved the recommendation, and thus what is now almost the identical north-south boundary between Maryland and Delaware was settled.

So much for that portion of the dispute. Next would come the east-west line between Pennsylvania and Maryland.

These first hearings were so encouraging that at the end of October Penn had sent further instructions to James Harrison regarding Pennsbury, and dispatching another gardener and a carpenter, "There comes a Dutchman, a joiner and carpenter, that is to work 150 days as I take it and pay me five pounds or seven pounds that country money there [the pound was worth less in the colonies] for seven pounds sterling lent him by me here. Let him wainscot and make tables and stands for some of the rooms but chiefly help on with our outhouses, because we shall bring much furniture." Penn probably planned to bring much of the contents of the Worminghurst house with him when he and Guli and the children came to Pennsylvania.

The urgency to return to America increased as reports circulated in England of dissension within the ranks of the Pennsylvania legislators—animosities ill becoming the backgrounds of the men he had left in charge of the colony's affairs. "Cannot more friendly and private courses be taken to set matters to rights in an infant province whose steps are numbered and watched; for the love of God, me and the poor country, be not so governmentish; so noisy and open, in your disaffections. Some folk love hunting in government itself," he cautioned them; and again, "If anything be amiss let it be by more hidden and gentle ways remedied. An infancy of government can hardly bear the shakes a riper age may and sometimes as a last remedy must endure. . . . The noise of some differences that have been in the Province have reached these parts with no advantage to the reputation of the country."

The problem of collecting quitrents needed his personal attention as well. "I have spent 3,000 pounds since I see London besides the bills I paid, that became due since I arrived." As for income on his Irish lands, "The Roman Catholics are mostly in power in Ireland, lands fallen there half." King James was building his support in Ireland with the Earl of Tyrconnel as his Lord Lieutenant. Penn had therefore to depend upon Pennsylvania income for his personal needs. "I am sorry that the public is so unmindful of my exercises and expenses as to be so very slow in aiding me in my public services. What it has cost me I am ashamed to tell . . . I entreat thee to stir them up in it."

Penn began to feel that social conditions in Philadelphia needed his personal attention. Since the population of Philadelphia was not entirely Quaker, her moral tone could not be completely controlled. A rapidly growing seaport, Philadelphia was attracting transients of every background and temperament with their complement of quick profit-takers alert to the possibilities with inns, ordinaries and kegs of rum. "There is a cry come over into these parts," Penn wrote to his magistrates, "against the number of drinking houses and looseness that is committed in the caves." His letter urged that the system of licensing already on the books be enforced so that the number of drinking houses could be controlled and that the empty caves be used to accommodate poor families. "Whatever you do, let virtue be cherished."

Mounting patronage in the new government was beginning to trouble him, particularly when he learned that ten or twelve pounds had been spent to entertain one guest. Let them "move slowly in their offices without bottles of wine and treats," he instructed Lloyd. None knew better than Penn how rapidly the patronage virus could develop into graft.

Letter after letter went out from Penn at Kensington giving administrative instructions to those in America. He wanted all vacant land surveyed as deep into the country as possible. He wanted the courts to administer justice with greatest care. He wanted the piece of land northeast of his house cleared and planted and his mares and their colts well cared for. The Pennsylvania government must be careful of its diplomacy with New York colony, especially where New York's declining trade was concerned. He sent pamphlets on liberty of conscience. He frequently dispatched another adventurer with a letter of introduction: John Saxby, "a bred scholar, capable of teaching the Latin, Greek, writing and arithmetic very well. . . . I desire you to encourage and employ him. He has an accurate short way of teaching the Latin which is very valuable." James Bradshaw, "a kinsman of mine," who was to have the Clerk of the Council's place when it became vacant. Penn hoped to be with them all in the spring. His family would be able to go since Guli's eighth child, Gulielma Maria, was born at Worminghurst, November 17, 1685.

Yet, Penn was certainly needed in England as much as in America, especially by Friends. If there was any hope of persuading the King to repeal the penal laws or release Friends from prison, the hope lay in Penn's intimate position in Court, an advantage so personal that it could not conceivably be turned over to an agent or exploited effectively from a great distance. And, too, while in England he was personally available with advice to those who wished to transplant themselves to America. He published a new and up-to-date tract on the subject, dated Worminghurst, December 12, 1685, A *Further Account of the Province of Pennsylvania and Its Improvements.* When he did leave England, Philip Ford would act in his stead on Pennsylvania matters.

That he still trusted Philip Ford implicitly is indicated in a letter that he wrote to Thomas Lloyd about this time: "I would have you forthwith take care and order Philip Ford's city lot as his 1000 acres an 102 foot front on Delaware and back to the 4th street. The like on Schuylkill in the place before allotted near the Society, and his 150 or 60 acres in the suburbs to be laid out the very next of all that is not taken up. For he deserves of the whole country to be preferred, that for the good of it has neglected the advancement of his own." Thus his blind faith in his steward caused him to become more and more deeply involved in debts. On arrival home in England in 1684 he had still owed the old debt of £2,851/7/10; and in spite of sales of Pennsylvania lands amounting to eight thousand pounds, that original debt had greatly increased. When Ford presented Penn with new statements of account, Penn again signed them in good faith. Urged on by his wife, Ford persuaded Penn to make him a further grant of lands as security for the additional debt, and although Penn was reluctant to do so at first, he finally consented, since Ford assured Penn that the deeds were merely to be regarded as collateral and that he would never use them to impair Penn's rights in Pennsylvania. Penn signed a document dated June 10, 1685, which gave Ford three hundred thousand additional acres, including Pennsbury, Springettsbury, a manor in Chester, if Penn did not pay him five thousand pounds by March 21, 1687, and further executed a double indemnity bond of ten thousand pounds to guarantee performance of the covenants.

While he awaited further hearings on the second phase of his dispute with Baltimore, Penn and other Quaker leaders in London watched the gathering of national tensions as James increased his standing army, eased more and more Roman Catholics into public office, made Jeffreys of the Bloody Assize Lord Chancellor and prorogued his Parliament. The cautionary advice Penn had given Charles against splitting England into two camps with shortsighted persecution had to be forcefully repeated to James; and though Penn had ample opportunity to drive his urgent reasoning home in private sessions with the monarch, he chose further to implement his efforts with a tract, *A Persuasive to Moderation to Dissenting Christians, in Prudence and Conscience: Humbly Submitted to the King and His Great Council.* "Moderation is a Christian duty, and it has ever been the prudent man's practice," is the substance of Penn's message. "For those governments that have it in their conduct have succeeded best in all ages." He drove his point home by needling James in a tender spot: Look at Holland and her "superlative clemency and industry." In Holland lived Mary, James's Protestant daughter by his former wife Anne Hyde, married to the Protestant William III of Orange, and next in line to the English throne.

In the spring of 1686, King James issued a pardon to Quakers, and for this Penn personally deserves a high degree of credit as well as for James's two general Acts of Indulgence which followed in the next two years. Nearly thirteen hundred Friends walked out of prison and rejoined their families, as a result of Penn's persistent influence. "My *Persuasive* works much among all sorts," he wrote to Harrison in April, "and are much spoke of. I have been thrice taken at meetings, but got off." And the Quaker historian, Gough, wrote, "It was a great consolation at their ensuing annual meeting in London [London Yearly Meeting] to have the company of so many valuable Friends, whose faces had not been seen there for many years, having been immured in prison, some of them, twelve or fifteen years and upward, for no crime but endeavoring to keep a good conscience toward God." Penn viewed the Quaker amnesty as something wonderful that God had wrought. "The King shows himself merciful to all. Meetings very full and living . . . if it goes well with England it cannot go ill with Pennsylvania." The time consumed in waiting for the Baltimore dispute to be settled had been well spent indeed.

"I am going for Holland," he wrote very soon after the pardon, and it is generally conceded that he went as James's personal emissary. King James appears to have given him the task of waiting upon his son-in-law the Prince of Orange at his Court in The Hague and obtaining his approval of Toleration and the removal of the Tests designed to bar Catholics from public office in England. With what a deep sense of satisfaction he must have gone—Penn, who had long since risked his reputation espousing an across-the-boards toleration!

A record of Penn's conferences at The Hague comes down to us from Gilbert Burnet in *The History of My Own Times*, in a rather unfriendly and frankly envious tone. Bishop Burnet had come to Holland with the idea of making it his home and he was at the Court of the Prince of Orange when Penn arrived. He describes Penn as "a talking vain man, who had been long in the King's favor, he being the Vice Admiral's son. He had such an opinion of his own faculty of persuading, that he thought none could stand before it, tho' he was singular in that opinion. For he had a tedious luscious way, that was not apt to overcome a man's reason, tho' it might tire his patience." Penn had two or three long audiences with William, Burnet relates, and the Prince gave his approval of a toleration of both Catholicism and dissenters provided it passed through Parliament, but he could not consent to a canceling of the Tests. The Dutch had not yet forgotten the tragic and costly war they had fought to throw off the Spanish Catholic yoke; and the

Prince felt that, while conscience was only subject to God, the Tests guaranteed the security of the Protestant faith. But, Penn persisted, James was ready to secure toleration by a solemn and unalterable law, if the Test Acts were repealed. The Edict of Nantes had been an unalterable law, perpetual and irrevocable, William retorted, and now it was gone.

After the audience with Penn, William III turned to Burnet, who had a more realistic understanding of the Stuarts. Burnet's advice to William III, among other things, was to put the fleet of Holland into good condition.

Penn left The Hague and reached Amsterdam some time before the sixth of August and remained there for the Yearly Meeting. "Dear William Penn has also been here and we have had such great meetings as never before," said Peter Hendricks. Penn's reputation in Holland was extraordinary by that time, and the Hollanders were as eager to hear of the Pennsylvania colony from his own lips as he was to tell them. His friendship with Willem Sewel is thought to have begun at this time and that he stayed at Sewel's home in Amsterdam. Sewel, who wrote the first definitive history of the Friends, was at that time translating Penn's *Further Account of the Province of Pennsylvania* into Dutch and he later translated *No Cross, No Crown.* The two men corresponded in Latin after Penn's 1686 visit, and six of Sewel's letters to Penn still exist.

There is a brief note left by Roger Haydock that Penn traveled from Holland up the Rhine, and another that he attended a meeting at Sneek in Friesland. He met Henry Sydney by appointment either at Arnham or Amersfort [a letter from Sydney expressed a preference for Arnham], and he was in Rotterdam. Beyond that little or nothing is known of his activities in Holland and Germany in 1686. He was back in London on September 15.

"I have had a blessed service in Holland and Germany," said Penn at the conclusion of his continental trip.

He found an accumulation of mail from America that was considerably less gratifying, giving him an account of the "scurvy quarrels" there; and he found a list of bills to be paid and still no quitrents to meet them or his other mounting expenses. As for the rest of the Baltimore dispute, it was going to drag on for an interminable length of time. Guli had given up all hope of ever seeing America, and while Penn looked forward to going yet another spring he admitted, "I count myself a prisoner here."

"I shall hardly know the province when I come among them," he wrote with a touch of poignance to Thomas Lloyd.

Penn had to depend upon the news that was sent him from America, and too often complainers and anti-Quaker gossip spreaders were more willing to write than those who could have reassured him. The quarrels within the small circle of government men in Philadelphia were only a fragment of the total picture of the growing, prospering colony, but tales of their disaffections were spread in England with sufficient glee to discourage new settlers. One quarrel in particular related to the Free Society of Traders and its President, Nicholas More. More was a provincial judge and a member of the Assembly as well, and the conflict between him and the government reached such a pitch of intensity that the Assembly impeached him for malpractice and a list of misdemeanors in his public offices, sending their findings, ten articles in all, up to the Council. He twice ignored orders to appear before the Council to answer the charges, with the result that he was ordered to cease from acting in his public offices until he did appear. More himself wrote to Penn urging him not to give too much credit to the evil reports. How untrue the accusations were he would find out when he came to Pennsylvania. "You make mention of your coming to us again with your family, a thing so much desired by all in these parts, and more particularly by me." Penn himself may even have set off the proceedings against More, for some time in 1686 he had written to the Council, "The Society is a great reproach to the Province, and in nothing more than not sending an account of the debt and credit which I stayed there so long and let so often for, and saw effected; that itself was mislaid or lost or designedly kept back after all that pains, so that my own credit, that I saw it and the total of debt 6,000 odd hundred pounds and the credit 9,000 odd hundred pounds, was all that had to rest upon, and certainly merchants and traders that trust not themselves, but their books, had little reason to give me that respect. Pray call the

President or Chief Officer before you on my complaint, order him to transmit a faithful account. . . ." Apparently the stockholders in London were beginning to ask for a reckoning on the profits that were not coming in. After receiving Nicholas More's letter, Penn wrote to Thomas Lloyd: "This quarrel about the Society has made your great lions heard hither. . . . I could wish Dr. More and P.R. would have been softened. . . ."

A few wrote to Penn in an effort to reassure him. More himself had told him of the augmenting abundances in the colony, the abounding crops and other foodstuffs and the good prices received for them, "good fresh pork in our market at two pence half-penny per pound, of this country money, which is an English two-pence; beef at the same rate; the last is this year; and butter for six-pence per pound; wheat four shillings per bushel; rye three shillings . . . Indian corn seven groats and two shillings. . . . Barbados potatoes is now become a dish with us. . . ."

His steward reported that "the gardener is brisk at work. The peach trees are much broken down with the weight of the fruit . . . our barn, porch and shed are full of corn." Robert Turner did the same; so did Thomas Holme, James Claypoole and David Lloyd, Clerk of the Peace for Philadelphia County.

But what good all this abundance if those who were blessed with it could not work peaceably together? How long would it last if the members of the Council and Assembly neglected to attend meetings and shrugged their shoulders at their responsibilities? How much real comfort was there in hearing reports of so much abundance when those who enjoyed it would not even send him his rightful share and were indifferently allowing him to run himself and his family into debt?

"It almost tempts me to deliver up to the King and let a mercenary governor have the taming of them . . . the Charter is over and over again forfeited, if I would take advantage of it. Nay, I hear my name is really not mentioned in public Acts of State, nor the King's, which is of a dangerous consequence to the persons and things they have transacted, since they have no power but what is derived by me, as mine is from the King. . . ."

As for his quitrents, then worth at least five hundred pounds a year, he could not get a penny, and when they were added to his other losses he was six thousand pounds out of pocket. "I do desire thee to let no more mention be made of the supply," he told Harrison. "I will sell the shirt off my back before I will trouble them any more. I shall keep the power and privileges I have left, to the pitch, and recover the rest as their misbehaviors shall forfeit them back into my hands. For I see I am to let them know, that 'tis yet in my power to make them need me, as much as I do their supply . . . nor will I ever come into that Province with my family to spend my private estate, to fill up and discharge a public station, and so add more wrongs to my children. This is no anger, though I am grieved, but a cool and resolved thought."

It was mighty close to anger, though, and written in a moment of despair and discouragement, even revealing a streak of petulance in his nature that may have been a legacy from his mother.

That some revision in the administrative setup in Pennsylvania was necessary he had to realize, and while he pondered the problem he sent a stop-gap appeal to Harrison: "I beseech thee as a brother and as thou and the rest must answer it to God, a few of you get together, thyself, Thomas Lloyd, A. Cook, J. Simcock, T. Janny, William Yardley, etc. and see what is wrong, and in God's name exhort, and in the King's name and mine as his governor charge at peril, that a better course be taken to end or prevent such disputes. One speaks so ill of t'other that I should be at a stand who to write to. . . ."

Meanwhile, he set out on a ministerial journey through the northern counties of England, leaving the end of November and traveling during most of December in a circuit—covering Friends' meetings in Derbyshire, Nottingham and Yorkshire, and going on out to the Cleveland Hills country to visit his sister and brother-in-law at Marske. From there he went over to the west, to Westmoreland and Lancashire, the birthplace of Quakerism; and while the precious evidence is lacking to prove the assumption, he would certainly have paid his respects to Margaret Fox at Ulverston and bring her the news not only of Truth's progress but the woman's news that she wanted of his wife and children. He came down through Manchester, where such a large meeting assembled to hear his message that they overflowed J. Alcock's house and courtyard. From there he worked his way homeward through Cheshire, Staffordshire and Warwickshire.

By the time he had returned to his headquarters at Holland House, commuting back and forth between Kensington and Windsor in the Kensington coach, he had decided on a course of action for Pennsylvania. He appointed his "trusty and well beloved friends," Thomas Lloyd, Nicholas More (so recently impeached), James Claypoole, Robert Turner and John Eccles, or any three of them, to act as Commissioners of State, the group functioning in the capacity of Deputy Governor; and in a letter dispatched from Worminghurst and dated February 1, 1687, he gave them some stern instructions. They were to remind the Provincial Council of its responsibilities, "for I will no more endure their most slothful and dishonorable attendance, but dissolve the *Frame* without any more ado." They were to allow no disorders either in Council or Assembly. Past proceedings of both bodies were to be examined for breaches of Charter. Penn abrogated all actions of the Assembly in his absence, ordered the Assembly dismissed and called anew, and the qualifications of all members of both houses carefully examined to make certain that they were in accord with the Charter. "Be most just, as in the sight of the all-seeing, all-searching God; and, before you let your spirits into an affair, retire to Him . . . that He may give you a good understanding and government of yourselves in the management thereof."

On April 14, 1687, James issued his first Declaration of Indulgence, releasing thousands of dissenters of every hue from prison and granting genuine freedom of worship throughout the country. It was England's first experience with total toleration, and Penn's love for his monarch must have been extremely deepened by it. The Quakers, so often petitioners for mercy, this time drew up at their London Yearly Meeting in May an address of thanks to the King and made Penn head of their deputation to Windsor. Penn's presentation speech and the King's address of acceptance have both come down to us. "Now, since the King's mercy and goodness have reached to us throughout the Kingdom of England, and Principality of Wales, our general assembly from all those parts met at London, about our church affairs, has appointed us to wait upon the King, with our humble thanks, and me to deliver them; which I do by this address, with all the affection and respect of a dutiful subject."

"Gentlemen," replied the King, "I thank you heartily for your address. Some of you know, I am sure you do, Mr. Penn, that it was always my principle that conscience ought not to be forced; and that all men ought to have the liberty of their consciences. And what I have promised in my declaration, I will continue to perform as long as I live; and I hope before I die, to settle it so that after-ages shall have no reason to alter it."

In the same year Penn published *Good Advice to the Church of England, Roman Catholic and Protestant Dissenter, In Which It Is Endeavored to be Made Appear That It Is Their Duty, Principles and Interest to Abolish the Penal Laws and Tests.* His name did not appear on it, but on the title page was the Latin inscription, "Beati Pacifici"—Blessed are the Peacemakers—and in the Preface the clue, "Yet if thou wouldst know the author, he is an Englishman, and therefore obliged to this country and the laws that made him free."

During the summer Penn went on another strenuous ministerial journey through Berkshire to Gloucestershire, reaching Bristol at fair time in July, and there he was able to draw what John Whiting, a Bristol Friend, called in his *Memoirs* "mighty meetings, notwithstanding the late persecution in that city." He visited nearby Chew and had an opportunity to see Richard Vickris. He went on to the northwest of England, through Worcestershire and Shropshire to Cheshire. In the city of Chester his path crossed that of King James who was also on a tour of the country. "I had two meetings on a first day at Chester in the tennis court [tennis was originally played indoors] where was above a thousand people while the King was there." From Chester Penn turned southward once more, passing through Staffordshire and Warwickshire to Oxford, arriving on September 3, the same day that James arrived there. Penn was in the city of Oxford only three days, just long enough to become involved in a ruinous altercation between the university and the King, particularly Magdalen College and the King. The seats of learning in England were Protestant, Oxford and Cambridge in particular trained the clergy for the Church of England. Overlooking the fact entirely that Oxford was deeply Royalist, James proceeded to cut himself off from her support and from the support of other universities as well by attempting to Romanize them. His quarrel with Magdalen developed when he tried to force on the college a president of his own choosing, and expelled the Fellows of the college when they resisted. The Fellows, knowing Penn to be both an Oxford alumnus and a friend of the King, laid their case before him; and he reached the conclusion that the King had violated the charter of the college and helped the Fellows compose a letter to the King expressing these views. The King resisted Penn's advice to his own undoing. When Penn left Oxford on the fifth of September, he was still involved in the dispute, but he was never able to make James aware of his own folly. From Oxford Penn went through Hampshire to Sussex and so to Worminghurst. "I am straightened being just come home weary," he wrote to James Harrison on the eighth of September.

The tide of the times rushed on at an accelerated rate of speed, and the politically sensitive James felt the waters of Protestant revolt swirling around his ankles. His Declaration of Indulgence was not a law properly processed through Parliament; it could be interpreted as illegal since it controverted such laws as the Test Act. But James was a self-willed, shortsighted man, lacking his brother's astuteness, and while the honesty of his religious convictions is to be admired his political wisdom is not. In wooing the support of non-conformists and in attempting to Romanize the universities he had alienated the vast Anglican majority. The following April, 1688, he issued his second Declaration of Indulgence, reaffirming the contents of the first, and promising that Parliament would be convened in November. He proceeded further to precipitate his own ruin by ordering the second Indulgence read and distributed in the churches throughout the land, thus forcing an examination of its legality. Seven bishops of the Church of England petitioned James to withdraw the order, and James, responding like a man possessed, ordered their arrest and trial on a charge of seditious libel. The English public had not been too deeply stirred by a fine point of legality, but the affront to the dignity of the church fanned its already kindled excitement into flame, and the birth of a son to James's second wife, the Italian Princess, Mary of Modena, was fresh fuel. A Prince of Wales meant a Roman Catholic succession to the throne; it meant that William and Mary of Orange had been eliminated, that mere patient waiting would no longer guarantee the security of Protestantism in England.

The day the Prince of Wales was born, according to Burnet, Penn rushed to the King and begged him to set the bishops free and accept the wise appeal in their petition. James turned a deaf ear to his good friend.

Penn had chosen the dangerous summer of 1688 to move his whole family to the home of a Mr. Charlwood Lawton, less than two miles from Windsor Castle, because national affairs held him so close that trips to Worminghurst had become impossible.

The extraordinary and dramatic trial before the King's Bench Court of the seven bishops drew throngs of concerned and fascinated spectators. They nodded their heads with deep gratification when the jury finally returned with a verdict of not guilty. The stubborn King had turned the affront upon himself, and the last shred of England's confidence fell away from him. That same day William of Orange received a secret invitation from Whig, Church and Tory leaders to enter England with troops and help them overthrow the government.

Penn, true to the dictates of his own conscience, remained loyal to James; if James was to be pitied during the Bloody Assizes, he was more to be pitied now as gossip even declared the Prince of Wales to be a hoax, sneaked into the palace in a warming pan. The last few desperate efforts that James made to mollify his subjects as news filtered into England of military preparations in Holland followed the lines of earlier advice reiterated to him by Penn and other moderates, but by then they were the foolish hindsight of a foolish king. James learned too late to distinguish between friend and sycophant. In November William landed with his forces at Torbay, James and his Queen and infant son fled to France, and William Penn was left in the acutely dangerous position of having espoused the losing side.

I know my enemies and their true character and history and their intrinsic value to this or other governments. I commit them to time with my own conduct and afflictions.

——Penn in a letter without address in 1692

17. "I Am a Man of Sorrows"

WILLIAM POPPLE, Secretary of the Board of Trade and Plantations, who trusted Penn and recognized his suddenly difficult situation, wrote him at length to point out that his persistent association with James now left him wearing a Jesuit label by implication. He tabulated the accusations arising around Penn: "that you have been bred at St. Omer's in the Jesuits' College; that you have taken orders at Rome, and there obtained a dispensation to marry; and that you have since then frequently officiated as a priest in the celebration of the mass at Whitehall, St. James's and other places." Penn had enemies of high rank, Popple warned him, who would be only too happy to make the most of such gossip and urged him to apply some remedy. " 'Tis fit I contradict them," Penn said in a long, gracious reply; yet, if his "constant zeal for an impartial liberty of conscience" laid him open to such dangers, he must continue the risk. "For these are cornerstones and principles with me; and I am scandalized at all buildings which have them not for their foundations. . . . I love England; I ever did so; and that I am not in her debt. I never valued time, money or kindred, to serve her and do her good. No party could ever bias me to her prejudice, nor any personal interest oblige me in her wrong."

Penn felt confident that when the last twenty years of his life were examined England would realize this, but soon another warning came from Willem Sewel in Amsterdam, who was making a passionate defense of Penn's reputation there:

"The things which are rumored about you in this part of the world in the discourse of almost everyone have sometimes struck me with a sad horror, although I never doubted the sincerity of your heart; but I always feared for you because of your enemies, who have usually interpreted your best counsel in the worst way. Not without grief have I perceived also that there are many here who have rejoiced in secret over your ill fortune."

Penn turned his attention to his province and her mounting administrative problems. Since he was out of favor at Court, and Pennsylvania had lost her royal patron, he could no longer press his suit against Baltimore. On the other hand Baltimore as a Roman Catholic was enjoying even less favor in government circles than Penn. So for the next few years the border dispute between the two proprietors was shelved. A document drawn the day before James II fled shows clearly that the King had intended to add the three lower counties to William Penn's grant and raise them to the rank of province; that document, never executed, would no doubt have been followed by other favorable territorial decisions.

Penn could, however, attempt to solve the internal confusions in Philadelphia, and had taken a major step in that direction the previous July by appointing a deputy governor. Penn would much have preferred the Quaker Thomas Lloyd, but Lloyd begged a respite from public office, and Penn finally settled upon Captain John Blackwell. "Since no Friend would undertake the Governor's place, I took one that was not, and a stranger, that he might be impartial and more reverenced. He is in England and Ireland of great repute for ability and integrity and virtue."

Blackwell, living in Boston at the time of his appointment, was a dyed-in-the-wool Puritan, a veteran of the English Civil Wars, who had been appointed by Cromwell to the posts of Treasurer at War and a Receiver General for Assessments. The Restoration transplanted him to Dublin, and from Dublin he had ventured to America. Wherever he lived he rose rapidly in public office, particularly in posts calling for financial ability; and in Boston he had been trying to establish a Bank of Credit to cope with the currency shortage when Penn asked him to become Lieutenant Governor of Pennsylvania. Actually, he appears to have sought the post through oblique overtures made by his wife who happened to be traveling in England and made it a point to meet Penn, but when he received the commission he was frankly startled. "I retired myself and spread it with my case before the Lord, casting myself under some consternation," he told Penn, and hoped that Penn would not repent his choice. He was to receive an annual salary of two hundred pounds to be derived from quitrents, maybe three hundred if the people of Pennsylvania were willing to grant it.

Blackwell's career as Lieutenant Governor was short-lived, brought to a quick end by the hostility he met and seemed to have a faculty for creating. He set out for New York and traveled across the Jerseys, reaching Pennsbury on December 15, 1688, where he began to anticipate the chilly welcome awaiting him. There was no one at Pennsbury but the gardener. Resting there two days he went on to William Penn's residence in Philadelphia. Still no deputation to honor the new Governor. Further, the house was very much occupied by William Markham who was not at home. Blackwell established himself in the council room (the Council usually met at Penn's house) and waited, and as soon as Markham, Lloyd and others began to appear his administration problems were under way. He had difficulty in obtaining a quorum to hold Council meetings, difficulty in obtaining records, difficulty in persuading Lloyd to attach the seal to papers that required it. The cleavage line soon developed between William Markham and a group supporting Blackwell, and the opposition led by Thomas Lloyd. Markham's compassionate attitude toward Blackwell grew out of his devotion to Penn; he knew Blackwell's presence was an effort at a solution to the confusions in the government. When Blackwell met with the Assembly in the spring the hostility had already spread to their ranks. Among other things, the Assembly refused to obey an earlier order to abrogate laws passed in Penn's absence. To complicate matters, instructions had been received from Whitehall in April to make preparations for war with France, and the heavily Quaker group could not reach an agreement on such an action.

Blackwell's own personality contributed something to his failure as Lieutenant Governor. He was an old soldier fed on the sword-and-open-Bible doctrine. "Rule the meek meekly, and those that will not be ruled, rule with authority," Penn had told him, and Blackwell took the instructions at face value, striding into an untidy situation and taking hold with a firm and experienced hand. He found himself confronted by the terrible meek, Quakers who never committed acts of violence or raised their voices in anger, men without arms who were worse than the mosquitoes that rose in clouds from the New Jersey swamps, who resisted not yet yielded not and hit him with every passive resistance device they could contrive. To them was added the large minority of non-Friends in the government who heartily resented the sudden catapulting of an iron-handed administrator into their midst and were not restrained by any non-violent doctrine. Blackwell had a further disadvantage in his American post: he lacked strong backing. In government posts in England he had had the support of Cromwell; in Pennsylvania his backing came from a proprietor whose monarch had fled for safety to the Continent.

Penn's errors in judgment were at fault, too. He ought not to have chosen so militant a man to deal with a predominantly Quaker situation; and he ought not to have cued Blackwell with such severe administrative instructions. Blackwell was to see that things were transacted in the Proprietor's name by the style of the patent; he was to collect the laws and send them to Penn for careful scrutiny, to make certain that impartial justice was administered, to extinguish feuds between persuasions, to supervise the Commissioners of Property over land not yet settled and land settled but whose obligations were indifferently complied with. The sheriffs in their respective counties were to be charged with the receipt of rents and fines and give security for them to the Receiver General. Penn expected Blackwell to accomplish singlehanded all that the commission of five had failed to do. "We hear Captain Blackwell carries a high and mighty hand over Friends and that Thomas Lloyd and he are much at difference," was a spot of Bucks County gossip. Blackwell failed because Penn handed him down from the top, after he himself had set the pace and pattern with his own formula: "Let all that is done be the act of the people so it will be safe." By the time Blackwell arrived, the democratic habit patterns had had six years to become set.

Penn's poor judgment may be pardoned at least in degree when we consider the pressure he was under in England. The incredible accusations and virulent gossip of which Popple had warned grew more dangerous, until, under a cloud of guilt by association with the deposed King, Penn was apprehended in December, 1688, in Whitehall and brought before the Privy Council for questioning. He reiterated to them his love of England and the Protestant religion. Of course, he admitted freely, James was both his and his father's friend, but he had never done more than advise James in his own best interest. The Lords had no evidence against Penn, but they made him post a heavy bail to guarantee his appearance at their next term.

On February 27, 1689, two months after Blackwell had arrived in Philadelphia, the King's Privy Council issued a warrant for William Penn's arrest "upon suspicion of high treason." He and all of his letters, writings and papers were to be brought before the Earl of Shrewsbury for examination. Shrewsbury and Nottingham were the King's Principal Secretaries of State. William and Mary had just been proclaimed joint rulers of England; and, while they spelled the end of feudalism in England and the beginning of modern times and soon made genuine toleration a legal fact, James was still very much alive to threaten them, and James's friends were liable to close and constant scrutiny.

As soon as he learned of the warrant Penn wrote to Shrewsbury: "I thought it would look rather foolish than innocent to take any notice of popular fame, but so soon as I could inform myself that a warrant was out against me, (which I knew not till this morning) it seemed to me a respect due to the government, as well as a justice to myself, to make this address, that so my silence might neither look like fear nor contempt; for as my innocence forbids the one, the sense I have of my duty will not let me be guilty of the other. That which I have humbly to offer is this:—I do profess solemnly in the presence of God, I have no hand or share in any conspiracy against the King or government, nor do I know any that have; and this I can affirm without directing my intention equivocally. And though I have the unhappiness of being very much misunderstood in my principles and inclinations by some people, I thought I had some reason to hope this King would not easily take me for a plotter, to whom the last government always thought me too partial. In the next place, as I have behaved myself peaceably, I intend by the help of God to continue to live so, but being already under an excessive bail, (where no order or matter appeared against me,) and having, as is well known to divers persons of good credit, affairs of great consequence to me and my family now in hand that require to be dispatched for America, I hope it will not be thought a crime that I do not yield up myself an unbailable prisoner, and pray the King will please to give me leave to continue to follow my concerns at my house in the country, which favor, as I seek it by the Lord Shrewsbury's mediation, so I shall take care to use it with discretion and thankfulness."

That letter was written in March; the conspiracy referred to materialized into James's arrival in Kinsale and progress to Dublin with troops where he was welcomed by cheering throngs and joined by Tyrconnel. Public hysteria was far from ended, and Penn was wise to avoid arrest as "an unbailable prisoner"; but he appears not to have gone to Worminghurst immediately, for he and Guli were in London the first week of April and attended a meeting in Gracechurch Street with Stephen Crisp and George Fox. George Fox's health was failing, and he was so wearied and weakened by the effort of speaking at length in the meeting that he had to retire to Henry Gouldney's house to rest. Penn and Guli and several other Friends visited with him there until he felt strong enough to go on to his night's lodging.

On June 22, 1689, Lord Nottingham authorized a "strict and diligent search for William Penn, Esq., and him having found you are to apprehend for suspicion of high treason or treasonable practices, and to bring him in safe custody before me to be examined concerning such matters as shall be objected against him relating to the premises and to be further dealt with according to law." Two days later the King's Council appointed Nottingham, Shrewsbury and six others to act as a special committee for "examining and committing to prison such persons, they shall have cause to suspect, to be guilty of high treason or treasonable practices."

By the twenty-eighth of June Penn had left the dangerous London scene and had written to Lord Halifax telling him of his arrival in Sussex and asking for his lordship's protection.

On the Continent England's Protestant Revolution had already had a widespread impact. "Europe looks like a sea of trouble—wars all over it like to be this summer," Penn had written to Pennsylvania in the spring, and a few weeks later England was formally at war with France, precipitating the question of military preparedness upon Blackwell and the Pennsylvania Assembly. In Ireland the Jacobite war was working its havoc, and Penn's lands there once valued at twelve or thirteen hundred pounds a year were now worth not one penny to him, and as the shadow of the treason charge darkened over his head he was rapidly descending down the spiral to utter poverty.

In Pennsylvania Blackwell's administration went from bad to worse. Doubly embarrassed by non-payment of his salary and the inflated price levels in Philadelphia, Blackwell turned sharply upon the Philadelphia merchants who were buying cheap abroad and selling high at home. Such a policy, he felt, would in time depress the economy. This forthright attitude threw Samuel Carpenter, one of the wealthiest of the Quaker merchants and a member of the Council, into Thomas Lloyd's camp. Blackwell further let it be known that he thought the Navigation Acts ought to be more strictly adhered to. Quakers dealt too shrewdly for comfort, he did not mind observing, as he searched in vain for the merciful side of their Christian dispositions. By June he wrote to Penn in despair: "I now only wait for the hour of my deliverance; for I see 'tis impossible to serve you in this place." His Englishman's soul hated the climate, too. The summer was hot to the point of suffocation, and "hosts of mosquitoes are worse than armed men; yet men without arms worse than they." In September Penn wrote Blackwell of his decision to relieve him of his unsavory post, but he was not yet free to leave Pennsylvania. No, indeed! Captain Blackwell was a man of integrity and financial ability. "I have made thee my Receiver General of the Province. . . ." Blackwell could have the dubious privilege of trying to collect quitrents.

Some time during the latter part of 1689 Penn moved his family to Hammersmith, an historic village on the Thames, now a borough of London, flanked on its eastern side by Kensington and the Holland estate. It is quite likely that he had given up his apartment at Holland House for the time being, although he did return to it later; for his own letters during the winter of 1689-90 are date-lined from Hammersmith. There personal grief was added to declining personal fortunes, and the youngest child, four-year-old Gulielma Maria, died November 20, 1689, and was laid to rest in the Jordans burial ground alongside of the first-born Gulielma Maria and the twins.

A letter which Penn wrote a year later suggests that he was questioned before the Privy Council committee more than once, and the arrest warrant of the previous June must have been set aside at one of these hearings, because at the end of 1689 he was planning to leave England. "I purpose in a few months to set forward to you," he wrote to his Commissioners of Property. There was nothing else to hold him, certainly. His dispute with Baltimore was shelved. Protestant dissenters had their toleration law. If they wanted anything more at Whitehall, he no longer had the influence to command it. Withdrawal from the English scene could be a wise move for the safety of himself and his whole family; he could be of greatest service to the greatest number of people if he were in Pennsylvania to unravel the predicament aggravated by Blackwell's appointment; and the new scene might have a tonic effect on Guli's waning strength and overtaxed courage.

Meanwhile Blackwell was making an effort to collect quitrents, inspired no doubt by the fact that his own salary was at stake, and Robert Turner gave him some help. The two men collected more indifference than cash, and after a few weeks of fruitless effort Blackwell handed the Receiver General's post to Robert Turner and departed for Boston, having borrowed his boatfare from Turner. Robert Turner was someone upon whom Penn depended a great deal through the years. "I advise thee for thy own and province good to constitute under thee no single person here," Turner advised him. "It's aspired at that some might work their will, if thou dost; expect great discontent amongst the people, and a disuniting of the upper and lower counties, which since Blackwell went much appears; the now Frame of Government people like best except thyself in person." The Pennsylvania government was back in the hands of the Council and awaited Penn's arrival.

None could have anticipated the length of that vigil, as Whitehall began its cat-and-mouse treatment of Penn. An order dated June 24, 1690, appears in the Privy Council Register committing Penn to the custody of the Chief Governor of the Tower of London, "being charged with high treason, in abetting and adhering to their Majesties' enemies." But the royal Proclamation issued under Queen Mary's name ordering the arrest of a long list of persons including William Penn, is dated July 14, 1690: for having "conspired together and with divers other disaffected persons, to disturb and destroy their government, and for that purpose have abetted and adhered to their majesties' enemies in the present invasion, for which cause several warrants for high treason have lately been issued out against them, but they have withdrawn themselves from their usual places of abode." When he realized he was suspected of hiding, Penn wrote to Lord Nottingham:

As soon as I had heard my name was in the Proclamation, I offered to surrender myself, with those regards to a broken health, which I owe to myself and my family; for it is now six weeks that I have labored under the effects of a surfeit and a relapse, which was long before I knew of any particular mark of the government's displeasure; and it is not three days ago that I was much fitter for a bed than a surrender. I shall not take up time about the hardships I am under, nor the defense of myself. Though I was never asked for where I dwelt, before I saw my name in the Proclamation. But since the government refused bail, and does not think fit to trust me, I shall trust the government, and submit my conveniency to the state's safety and satisfaction. Therefore I do by this humbly beg to know, when and where I may wait upon thee, and it shall be, God willing, punctually observed by

Thy faithful friend,

W. P.

William III was in Ireland from June 24 to the end of August, executing his military triumph over James's Catholic forces, and the arrest was carried out in the white heat of anti-Catholic sentiment. William Penn was placed in the Tower of London, as he had been in his youth, but this time for less than two weeks. On August 15 he and a long list of others were released on bail and ordered to appear "in the King's Bench on the first day of Michaelmas Term next."

Philip Ford, with his keen sense of timing, moved in on Penn's distressed and embarrassed situation once more. Three years earlier, in April, 1687, Penn had signed another account of more than five thousand pounds and guaranteed it with a mortgage of six thousand pounds on the province of Pennsylvania and Delaware for five thousand years, together with a double indemnity bond. In August and September, 1690, a series of documents were executed between Penn and Ford that can only be explained by the fact that Penn wanted to protect Quaker interest in Pennsylvania in the event he was found guilty of treason, beheaded and his estates forfeited. On August thirtieth Penn relinquished to Philip Ford all the equity of redemption in the foregoing mortgage; on September first Ford assigned over to Thomas Ellwood the same mortgage "in trust to attend the freehold and inheritance of the premises." Ford and Penn held long, intense conferences over the fate and safety of Pennsylvania, and Ford began to play upon Penn's concern for those who depended on him. Penn had many enemies, he pointed out; it would be wise for him to protect both the province and his family by making an absolute conveyance to Ford. The whole thing would be kept private, Ford promised, known to none but Penn, himself and Bridget. In fact, Ford would not even mention it in his last will and testament. And so, trusting Ford implicitly and not knowing what the results of his impending treason trial would be, Penn, on September 3, 1690, conveyed the entire province and territories to Philip Ford without defeasance (right to have the deed defeated or rendered void).

No record of a Penn trial appears in the indices of the court of King's Bench, but in December, 1690, Penn wrote to Markham, Turner and Carpenter, "I was cleared at Westminster again the 28th 9th month [November]." The "trial" may have resolved itself down to another committee hearing. In any event Penn was free to resume his former life, his plans for returning to America and expanding his colonial development.

A tract came out in 1690, no doubt written by Penn since its narrative is in the first person, entitled, *Some Proposals for a Second Settlement in the Province of Pennsylvania.* Negotiations for the Susquehanna Valley were not yet resolved, but William Penn was confident enough of his westward expansion to have already envisaged a second settlement, "about fifty miles west from the River Delaware, as appears by the common maps of the English Dominion in America. There I design to lay out a plat for the building of another city, in the most convenient place for communication with the former plantations on the East, which by land, is as good as all ready, a way being laid out between the two rivers very exactly and conveniently, at least three years ago; and which will not be hard to do by water, by the benefit of the River Schuylkill, for a branch of that river lies near a branch that runs into Susquehanna River." As in the case of Philadelphia, town lots were to go to each purchaser, but quitrents were not to begin for five years. Letters of inquiry were to be directed to Philip Ford.

Penn could go to George Fox, who had tasted so deeply of the frustrations of imprisonment, tell him he was once more free to go on working in the movement and that he was arranging to take more settlers to America, and watch the aging face light up. It was perfectly apparent to those closest to Fox that his work was done. Every effort taxed his strength. About six weeks after Penn was cleared at Westminster, Fox attended a meeting for worship at the Gracechurch Street Meeting House. He had had a strenuous week before that Sunday morning, with Quarterly Meeting, a midweek morning meeting, Meeting for Sufferings and two other worship sessions. On Sunday he told Friends that he felt better than he had in a long time, but by late in the afternoon he became ill, cold and shivering, and took to his bed, at Henry Gouldney's in Whitehart Court. During the next three days he failed rapidly, and soberly other leaders and his closest associates—Whitehead, Penn, Crisp—came to his bedside. "The seed of God reigns over all, and over death itself," Fox told them, and at last he "slept sweetly."

To William Penn fell the responsibility of sending the heartbreaking news to Margaret Fox in Ulverston, and he wrote to her that same evening,

London, 13th of 11th Month, 1690
[January 13, 1691]

DEAR M. FOX:

With the dear remembrance of my unfeigned love in Christ Jesus I am to be the teller to thee of sorrowful tidings as I may call it in some sense, which is this, that thy dear husband and my beloved and dear friend G. Fox, has finished his glorious testimony this night about half an hour after nine, being sensible to the last breath. O he is gone and has left us in the storm that is over our heads, surely in great mercy to him, but as an evidence to us of sorrow to come. He was as living and firm fourth day last was a week at Gracechurch Street and this last First Day (being the day before yesterday) but complained after meeting of [being] inwardly struck and lay ever since at H. Gold. [Henry Gouldney's] where he departed. My soul is deeply affected with this hasty great loss, surely it portends to us great evils to come. A prince indeed is fallen in Israel today.

I cannot enlarge, for I shall write several tonight, and it is late. The Lord be with thee and thine, and us all, Amen. I am thy faithful and affectionate friend

WM. PENN

Present: Robert Barrow, James Taylor, John Vaughton, John Field, John Butcher, Samuel Waldenfield and myself. George Whitehead and Stephen Crisp were here about two hours since. He died as he lived, a lamb minding the things of God and his church to the last in an universal spirit.

For the memorial service, Gracechurch Street Meeting House was filled to overflowing, with latecomers assembling in the courtyard. More than four thousand are said to have been present, and the most eloquent ministers were there to speak—James Parke, Robert Barrow, Ambrose Rigge, George Whitehead, Stephen Crisp, William Penn. A great crowd followed the coffin to the burial ground near Bunhill Fields, and there Willian Penn and a few others spoke again.

But Whitehall could not leave Penn alone at even so somber an occasion, and at the very grave of Fox he would have been served with an arrest warrant had the officer not arrived too late. On the fifth of February, 1691, Queen Mary issued a proclamation ordering the apprehension of the Bishop of Ely, William Penn and James Grahme, for having "designed and endeavored to depose their Majesties and subvert the government of this kingdom, by procuring an invasion of the same by the French, and other treasonable practices, and have to that end held correspondencies and conspired with divers enemies and traitors, and particularly with Sir Richard Grahme, Bart. [Viscount Preston in the Kingdom of Scotland] and John Ashton, Gentl., lately attainted of high treason. . . ."

The Secretary of State had already issued an order granting Penn a convoy for his voyage to America, and a company of adventurers had begun to assemble around him. Now the hopes of them all had to be dashed again.

The trouble had arisen this time in Ireland upon the testimony of a man named William Fuller, who was himself later convicted and sentenced for perjury, but on whose evidence at the time an indictment of high treason was found against Penn by the grand jury of Dublin. Penn described it as "the most extraordinary case that has been known; for that law by which Englishmen are tryable absent, here or there, is because a subject of these dominions may commit treason abroad where he cannot be tried; but that an Englishman in England walking about the streets should have a Bill of High Treason found against him in Ireland for a fact pretended to be committed in England, when a man cannot legally be tried in one county in England for a crime committed in another—and the others are at ease that were accused of the same fault. . . ."

Penn decided to go into retirement until he could find a way to clear his name, and his whereabouts for the next three years were known only to his most trusted friends and his family. There was no alternative to a temporary hiding; his and his family's fortunes had been caught in a tidal wave set in motion by revolution. Guli showed marked signs of the strain she was under as their fortunes declined, and sixteen-year-old Springett was far from robust. Penn could not help them from within the Tower, neither could he administer the affairs of Pennsylvania from such an address. Realizing how his less-than-forthright course of action must seem to Friends, most of whom did not understand the machinations of Whitehall as he did, Penn sent an epistle to London Friends dated May 30, in time for the Yearly Meeting: ". . . My privacy is not because men have sworn truly, but falsely, against me; 'for wicked men have laid in wait for me, and false witnesses have laid to my charge things that I knew not'; who have never sought myself, but the good of all, through great exercises; and have done some good, and would have done more, and hurt no man; but always desired that truth and righteousness, mercy and peace, might take place amongst us. Feel me near you, my dear and beloved brethren, and leave me not, neither forsake, but wrestle with Him that is able to prevail against the cruel desires of some; but we may yet meet in the congregations of His people, as in days past, to our mutual comfort. . . ."

A similar letter went to Thomas Lloyd as President of the Council in Philadelphia, this one datelined London.

There are two pieces of circumstantial evidence that point to the fact that Penn may have gone over to France in the summer of 1691. A letter dated September 16, from Robert Harley to Sir Edward Harley observed that "William Penn got safely into France last week." On the eighteenth of the same month a contemporary diarist, Narcissus Luttrell, said, "William Penn, the Quaker, is got off from Shoreham in Sussex and gone for France." James had returned to France after the failure of his coup in Ireland, and there were many in his Court at St. Germain who could have testified to Penn's innocence, even furnished him with documents. That Penn was in France for at least a short while is entirely plausible.

He was back in England at the beginning of 1692, appealing to individuals in high places to intercede for him with the King. One of these was Henry Sydney, by now elevated to Earl of Romney. Sydney had written to the King on January 20, regarding Lord Preston who had been apprehended, convicted and sentenced to be executed, and was apparently the only witness the Crown had against Penn. "Lord Preston is very unwilling to lose his life," Sydney wrote. "I think he will do you more service than his head is worth and therefore I am suspending his execution. He will, if he obtain his pardon, be a good evidence, and what he can say against Lord Clarendon, the Bishop of Ely and Mr. Penn (which he will be ready to do) is of great importance. We cannot find the Bishop nor Mr. Penn. . . . Mr. Penn is as much in this business as anybody, and two of the letters are certainly of his writing, and if we can catch him it will so appear." Penn may not have known of this action of Sydney's when he wrote to him, asking him to carry his address to the King. Penn felt he owed it to the King, to his friends and to himself to present his circumstances to the King's sense of justice and goodness. "Lay my case before him," he pleaded with Sydney, "and God almighty dispose him to regard me and mine, under our present great and pressing difficulties. . . ." Penn begged of his King, "allow me to live quietly anywhere, either in this kingdom or in America . . . and that the King may be secured that I will make no ill use of his favor . . . it will perhaps serve the King more than making me and my poor family unhappier than we are. . . ."

A reply soon came back that the King had taken a tolerant attitude.

"Let me be believed," Penn wrote again to the King through Romney, "and I am ready to appear; but when I remember how they began to use me in Ireland upon corrupt evidence before this business, and what some ill people have threatened here, besides those under temptation, and the providences that have successively appeared for my preservation under this retirement, I cannot, without an unjustifiable presumption, put myself into the power of my enemies. Let it be enough, I say, and that truly, I know of no invasions or insurrections, men, money, or arms, for them, or any juncto or consult for advice or correspondency in order to it. Nor have I ever met with those named as the members of this conspiracy, or prepared any measures with them. . . ."

In February William Penn sent his brother-in-law, Anthony Lowther, to Sydney with the message that he wanted to see Sydney if he would promise to let him go and return unmolested. "I sent him word I would, if the Queen would permit it," said Sydney. "He then desired me not to mention it to anybody but the Queen." And so a rendezvous was arranged, and Lowther led Sydney to William Penn's hiding place. Sydney was startled on meeting Penn.

"I found him just as he used to be, not at all disguised, but in the same clothes and same humor I have formerly seen him in."

The two men held a long discourse, and Penn assured Sydney, according to Sydney's report to King William, that he was a "true and faithful servant to King William and Queen Mary, and if he knew anything that was prejudicial to them or their government, he would readily discover it. He protested, in the presence of God, that he knew of no plot, nor did he believe there was any in Europe, but what King Louis had said, and he was of opinion that King James knew the bottom of this plot as little as other people. He said he knew that you have a great many enemies, and some who came over with you, and some who joined you soon after your arrival, he was sure were more convertible against you, and more dangerous than the Jacobites."

"There is not one man amongst them," Penn told Sydney, "that hath common understanding to the letters that were found with my Lord Preston."

Penn asked for the privilege of seeing the King, feeling that he could persuade the King of his sincerity and innocence. If he could not have the audience, he told Sydney, then he would be obliged to quit the kingdom, something he could already have done twenty times if he had pleased. Apparently the audience was not granted; the King was engrossed in his war on the Continent and in his successful efforts to subdue Scotland.

Penn had earlier appealed to Archbishop Tillotson to "pray speak to the King and press him to let me live safely and easily and I do promise by the help of God to live very peaceably"; and to Lady Renelagh (Orrery's sister), asking her to intercede with Queen Mary.

In June he wrote to Lord Nottingham:

My noble friend:

The motions or success of the government have not been the measure of my addresses; for I have humbly made them, with all possible sincerity of a peaceable disposition, for many months together.

But, I would hope, the more prosperous conditions of your affairs, should soften your minds to the unhappy among whom, I am sure, I have not been the least. And hearing you incline at this time to make such easy, forgive me if I say, it will hardly consist with the Queen's goodness to distinguish me from the rest; and yet if continuing my many misfortunes could give her any real satisfaction, I would be the less solicitous to be delivered from them.

I do not capitulate, but if I am cautious, they will easily excuse it that know how much the unkindness of some people makes it absolutely necessary to me.

I can never forget the handsome reception at Whitehall I found upon my last surrender; and I have only waited such another opportunity, and if this be that, I am to be sure very ready to lay hold of it, if it please thee to give me leave to hope so, and let not, pray, the vulgar opinions of my sentiments or obligations, have any longer prevelancy to intercept my deliverance that have lain so long and so singularly under the displeasure of the government and incredible hardships by it, because I am sure I shall never misuse the liberty I humbly crave.

But there was to be another year and a half of doubt, worry, suspense and humiliation with one trial rapidly mounting upon another. His estates in Ireland were put up among the estates of outlaws, even before he had been convicted, to be leased for the Crown. News from America increased the heartbreak with every packet of letters that arrived.

The cleavage lines in the Council had continued to deepen. At one point the Council passed a resolution disallowing the actions of six of its members who were accused of meeting separately and conducting Council business without notifying the rest of the Council. At another point a further schism began to develop between the upper and lower counties, and seven members for the lower counties (three of them of the above offending six) issued a declaration regarding the form of government they preferred for the province: most preferred the mode of five commissioners, second in their preference was being ruled by a commission of the Council, and least agreeable to them was having a deputy governor. Such a division could, and eventually did, lead to a splitting off of the three lower counties from the rest of the province. The most newsworthy and most reliable letters came from Robert Turner.

The Maryland Province was faring even worse. There the Protestant revolution had precipitated internal sectarian disputes to the point of an armed insurrection, and the Maryland Assembly was forced to petition the Privy Council to take Maryland under its protection. In June, 1691, Maryland became a royal province. The same thing could happen to the province of a proprietor suspected of treason, and the dissensions within Pennsylvania together with her reluctance to give military aid in the war against France did not improve her outlook.

At last in September, 1691, when Penn received two separate packets of mail from the two factions in Philadelphia, he replied to the entire Council out of the depths of his clear-sighted fear, frustration and despair with a letter that could not have helped but touch the most callous:

FRIENDS:

I have received your divided packet which show your divided government and surely the cause of it will early or late meet with its reward wherever it lies. In the meantime your division has torn me to pieces and opened those wounds that malice gave me here, and time and patience had closed up and almost cured. No public frowns have given me that trouble or concern, and I am grieved that what I thought the highest mark of a lowly and loving mind has had no better effect. What is next to be done to gain you or quiet you, to persuade you to your own interest before your disorders spoil you and devour the country? You cannot imagine what use is made by all sorts and especially those at the helm of your divisions. O friends I came to you in love. I left you in love and with resolutions of returning to you with all that was dear to me in this world and my letts and disappointments the righteous God knows were neither what I desired nor could overcome, but the course you take will ever make it impracticable. I am a man of sorrows and you augment my griefs, not because you don't love me, but because you don't love one another. . . . Cannot you bear a little for the good of the whole at least till it please God to bring me among you? One party complains of a surreptitious council, the other of an incompetent election of a deputy. . . . I call upon you all, my loving friends . . . to hear what I say and to remember your Governor, your friend and your affectionate one, too, asks this at your hands.

Again Penn turned to Thomas Lloyd, President of the Council, and persuaded him to become Deputy Governor; but the lower counties protested the appointment. In a further attempt to heal the rift between upper and lower counties, Penn then sent two commissions, one appointing Thomas Lloyd Deputy Governor of Bucks, Philadelphia and Chester counties, and the other making William Markham Deputy Governor of New Castle, Kent and Sussex. Early in 1692 he received the gratifying report, signed by Lloyd, Markham and fifteen others, that his two deputies were "concurring amicably at this time to act as one general government in legislation. . . ." "I long with many more that love thee to hear of it [his good welfare] and of thy liberty and arrival here," Robert Turner further assured him. In June, 1692, when Turner advised him that the dual governorship had joined them to some extent but was not proving practical, and that he thought they would be better off under one government of five persons or of President and Council, Penn followed his advice and once more appointed a five-man commission, one of whom was Turner.

Penn then approached his American Friends, who owed so much of their safety and freedom to his planning, with a proposal to solve his pressing financial problem: his "very great expenses in King James's time . . . and great losses in this King's time, the one being at least £7,000, and the other above £4,000 sterling and £450 per annum totally wasted in Ireland." He asked that a hundred persons in town lend him £100 each for four years free of interest, for which he would give his bond to guarantee repayment. He was confident, he assured them, of getting passage to America in that period, and when he came hundreds of new settlers would come with him. He never received the loan.

The Crown was developing other plans for Pennsylvania, implemented in large measure by England's long, bloody rivalry with France for dominance of both Europe and America. The first of her colonial wars, known as King William's War, forced her to give stricter attention to her American holdings than she had in the past. The French had spread all through the Mississippi Valley, fanning out into the Northwest, the Great Lakes region and the St. Lawrence Valley. Better colonizers on the whole than the English, the French were winning Indian allegiances all along the way. The New England colonies and New York were directly involved in King William's War, and Pennsylvania came within its orbit by having demands made on her for troops and supplies. The predominantly pacifist temper of Pennsylvania created a weak frontier, and so the Crown moved in on her embarrassed Proprietor and Pennsylvania's internal strifes, and took the colony under its protection, appointing Benjamin Fletcher, already Captain General and Commander-in-Chief of New York, as Captain General and Governor-in-Chief of Pennsylvania.

Fletcher arrived in Philadelphia in April, and at first glance his task did not seem too hard, for President Lloyd and his associates courteously surrendered the administration to him. But when he called the Assembly into session and presented to them the importance of raising troops and funds for war supplies to meet the rising French menace, he began to sample Blackwell's recent experience. Fletcher's basic plan was to sweep aside the Charter and laws of Pennsylvania and unite the province with New York, New Jersey and Connecticut under a single government. The legislators were ready for him and jealously declared that the Charter granted them by Penn was still in force. A letter soon came from Penn cautioning Fletcher to "tread softly and with caution" as the soil and government belonged to him and his royal Charter was still very much in effect. And so Pennsylvania wrestled with her unwelcome Governor every step of the way, until at the end of his short career he commented sadly, "My door was never shut, but it was avoided, as if it were treason for the speaker, or any other representative, to be seen in my company during your sessions."

A theological dispute, the sort that will always torment religious sects, developed during the period just preceding Fletcher's appointment, and since weighty Friends in religious circles were often also prominent government men the religious split was reflected in government affairs. The Scottish Quaker, convert-martyr-minister, George Keith, was the instigator. He was one of the New World's outstanding scholars, a gifted and much loved man. That he in his later, most dignified years, could turn contentious to the point of creating a split in the Society came as a grievous shock to many Friends. Perhaps too much scholasticism was the real cause; as the Labadist in Holland had once said to Penn, "Let not the learning of this world be used to defend that which the spirit of God hath brought forth; for scholars now coming among you, will be apt to mix school learning amongst your simpler and purer language, and thereby obscure the brightness of the testimony." Keith began to conceive of Christianity along more literal and fundamentalist lines in his later years, to the extent that he eventually returned to the Church of England. But before his return he drew a whole segment of Friends away from the main body into separate meetings with his eloquent argument that Friends denied the outward Christ.

For those looking for any opportunity to find fault with the Friends, particularly the Pennsylvania Friends, the Keith controversy was tailor-made, and it added one more burden to the sorrowing Proprietor's lot. When his trusted friend Robert Turner joined the Keithites, Penn could only say to him in a letter written in November, 1692, when he himself was attempting to bring his case before the King: "Before this sad news came from you, in my illness that I had about three or four months ago, I charged my children that they never [trusted] to hearken after notions and speculations, nor be drawn from the common communion." Keith's case finally reached the Yearly Meeting for Pennsylvania and Jersey where after careful thought he was read out of membership. He then took his case to London Yearly Meeting which, after many days of deliberation, upheld Pennsylvania's stand.

The three years that Penn spent in seclusion afforded him for the second time in his life a period of withdrawal, meditation and introspection, and during this second withdrawal he wrote several pieces. *Immediate Revelation Considered and Explained* is part of a Preface to the works of Robert Barclay, and at about the same time Penn wrote a Preface to the works of John Burnyeat. *Just Measures: Being an Epistle of Peace and Love* is a short essay addressed with a "deep sense and sorrow" to Friends troubled by the question of how far they should go in having a church discipline.

His prose of this period is free of the haste and urgency found in the tracts written during the 1670's; Penn was writing to fill an internal as well as an external need, and so the two most remarkable works are those that grew out of his deepest Quakerism: *An Essay Towards the Present and Future Peace of Europe*, and *Some Fruits of Solitude, in Reflections and Maxims Relating to the Conduct of Human Life.*

"He must not be a man, but a statue of brass or stone, whose bowels do not melt when he beholds the bloody tragedies of this war, in Hungary, Germany, Flanders, Ireland and at sea; the mortality of sickly and languishing camps and navies, and the mighty prey the devouring winds and waves have made upon ships and men since '88," are the opening words of the *Peace* essay. As for those who *are* men of brass and stone, Penn pleads with them to see the great profits in peace—trade, manufacture, building, industry, charity and hospitality—all devoured by war. The essay reflects the persisting influence of Grotius when it says that peace is achieved by justice and there is a need for a morality in the relationships of nations just as much as of individuals. Peace is derived from justice, justice is derived from government, and government is derived from the consent of society. "Now if the sovereign princes of Europe, who represent that society . . . would agree to meet by their stated deputies in a General Diet, Estates or Parliament, and there establish rules of justice for sovereign princes to observe one to another; and thus to meet yearly, or once in two or three years at farthest, or as they shall see cause, and to be styled, The Sovereign or Imperial Diet, Parliament or State of Europe; before which Sovereign Assembly, should be brought all differences depending between one sovereign and another, that cannot be made up by private embassies, before the session begins; and that if any of the sovereignties that constitute these imperial states shall refuse to submit their claim or pretensions to them, or to abide and perform the judgment thereof, and seek their remedy by arms, or delay their compliance beyond the time prefixt in their resolutions, all the other sovereignties, united as one strength, shall compel the submission and performance of the sentence, with damages to the suffering party, and charges to the sovereignties that obliged their submission."

As the author of that farsighted plan, Penn has sat at the council tables of world peace ever since. With it he did as he had done in creating the Pennsylvania community: he gathered together the most advanced and creative thinking of his period and projected it forward into time. Penn was not the first to suggest an international sovereign government; he simply made once more a practical application of legal, social and moral theories. The idea of a supranational organization to maintain peace began to develop at least as far back as the sixth or seventh century; in the thirteenth century Dante wrote of governing nations by law; and in the fourteenth Pierre Dubois designed an actual system for governing a federation of states. Penn refers in his essay to Henry IV of France who, with the aid of his chief adviser Sully, designed a plan for the union of the Christian world known as the Grand Dessein of Henry IV. "I will not then fear to be censured, for proposing an expedient for the present and future peace of Europe, when it was not only the design, but Glory of one of the greatest princes that ever reigned in it."

The *Peace* essay was published in the year 1693, anonymously for safety's sake, with the same Latin maxim that had appeared on his *Good Advice to the Church of England:* Beati Pacifici.

Some Fruits of Solitude, often called merely *Reflections and Maxims,* is a collection of fine cameos of wisdom covering every conceivable phase of living. It could have been produced only in long, lonely hours of solitude, where the naturally gregarious soul dwelt upon his wife whose health was failing, the son approaching his majority, the daughter and the younger son in their adolescence, the comfort and sustenance of meeting for worship that he had to forego, the lost fellowship of those Friends who had fallen away from him because they did not understand.

He was still in correspondence with Willem Sewel in Amsterdam, and during the summer of 1693 he sent Springett on a trip to the Continent bearing a gift and letter for Sewel. Sewel replied: "Greetings, well beloved Friend. Your letter was delivered to me through your son, along with the gift which, although I did not at all desire it, nevertheless could not but be very gratifying." Springett returned to England in a few weeks as a letter from Sewel dated October 27 indicates:

To SPRINGETT PENN, ZEALOUS IN THE LIBERAL ARTS:

Your letter in which you state that you had returned to your own country, I received, honored youth, and gladly learned of your safe return; but not so the news of the illness of your mother, for whose better health I earnestly pray, and whom I esteem highly although she is personally unknown to me, for I am more than convinced from things which I have heard here and there, that she is a woman of unusual type. But does any love of the Italian and Dutch tongues still linger with you now? And have you made any progress in them? Or do you still give more attention to Latin eloquence? . . . Of course, the pursuit of letters, or of the Muses (who they say are maidens) has some unknown incentive, by which we are impelled to higher things not reluctantly, but with the greatest alacrity. . . . Good literature should be cherished in such a way that we regard it rather as a solace in its season, and not spend a whole life-time working on it to such an extent that care for other things which are of greatest importance seems despicable to us and utterly worthless; a fate which I fear falls to the lot of many. But why do I say these things to you, whose father is truly pious and prudent, a man who has not failed to sow in you good seeds of virtue, walking before you with his own illustrious example. Continue, therefore, as you have begun and apply yourself to the reading of the best Latin authors, so that you can finally report a harvest of your work not to be despised. Farewell.

Before the end of 1693 Penn's persistent appeals to high-positioned friends and their efforts on his behalf began to bear fruit. On December 11 Penn was able to write to Thomas Lloyd and others: "It hath pleased God to work my enlargement, by three lords representing my case." The Lords Rochester, Ranelagh and Sydney waited themselves upon the King and made their personal plea for a fair hearing. Penn's case, they told the King, was not only hard but oppressive, based on the testimony of imposters. They had known Penn for some thirty years and had never known him to do an ill thing, but many good offices. If Penn had any intention of plotting against the present government, he would have gone abroad for the purpose long since. King William agreed with them. He, too, had known Penn personally, and as far as he was concerned Penn could go about his business freely. Then, the three appellants asked, would His Majesty not instruct the Secretary of State, Sir John Trenchard, to convey his opinion to Penn in an official manner. King William agreed, and Henry Sydney, closest to Penn of the three, was assigned the task of carrying the King's message to the Secretary. Sir John Trenchard was himself a man who owed much to Penn, for a few years earlier when Penn was high in Court favor, Penn had carried him in his own coach to Windsor and presented him to King James. Sir John received Penn in his home and gave him the news he had waited three years to hear: Penn was as free as he had ever been and as long as he lived quietly and prudently would remain unmolested. "The Lords spoke the twenty-fifth of November, and he discharged me on the thirtieth," said Penn's letter to Lloyd.

William Penn with his old impetuosity hurried immediately to the Friends' meeting at the Bull and Mouth, there to settle happily into one of the seats and let the fellowship flow over him, rising at last to speak as of old on Truth's account. His confident reappearance in meetings for worship was a bit shocking to many Friends, and Thomas Lower wrote to his mother-in-law at Swarthmoor on December second, "Yesterday at Bull and Mouth meeting appeared Will Penn, his pardon being granted some days before. . . . Friends thought he would first have appeared amongst them and have given them some satisfaction privately touching the scandal brought upon Truth and Friends by his long absconding and the matters laid to his charge and not to have appeared in the offering of his gift before he had been reconciled to them he had given offense unto; but his appearing first to preach in a public meeting before reconciliation looks too triumphant, and high, and is not well resented amongst some Friends here."

But that rebuke was posted to Ulverston in Lancashire, and Penn had posted with Springett, his almost constant companion in these trying days, to Guli, Tishe and Bille.

He knew what awaited him. Guli had been seriously ill for six months. "My wife is yet weakly; but I am not without hopes of her recovery, who is of the best of wives and women."

Two letters which Penn wrote datelined from "Hodsdon," one in December, 1693, and one in February, 1694, have given rise to the legend that Gulielma and the children lived in the hamlet of Hoddesdon, Hertfordshire, during the three years of Penn's hiding, but there is no better documentation of it. Penn was not always an accurate speller, and so his letters could have been written from Hoggeston in Buckinghamshire or Hodson in North Wilts. There is one piece of circumstantial evidence to support the Hoddesdon theory: both Springett Penn and his father attended Monthly and Quarterly Meetings in Hertford in 1693 and 1694, only about three miles from Hoddesdon.

The hiding and arrest warrants at last ended, William Penn could sit at Guli's bedside wherever she was. Gulielma was fifty, but many lived beyond that age; Penn himself was only a few months younger, and he felt no nearness of death. Ancient friends came to her bedside, where she lay growing weaker and more resigned, to encourage her with their advanced years. To one of seventy-five Guli said, "Thou and I to all appearances are near our ends." To another of sixty-five she said, "How much older has the Lord made me by this weakness than thou art?" To enter that sickroom and look upon the face he had loved so long, still beautiful while it wasted away, to know that much of the wasting had been caused by their reversed fortunes, to wish that he could endow her with some of his own ample energy—these were Penn's experiences when he returned to Guli.

"I submit to His Holy Will," Guli murmured.

He would have stayed by her side constantly day after day, but she would not allow him to neglect his meetings.

"O go my dearest! Don't hinder any good for me. I desire thee go. I have cast my care upon the Lord. I shall see thee again."

She asked to see her children one day, and when they assembled she said to them, "Be not frighted children, I do not call you to take my leave of you, but to see you, and I would have you walk in the fear of the Lord, and with His people in His Holy Truth."

As January passed and February advanced, relatives came to see her, and Penn remained close to the house. On the twenty-third of February, 1694, about three hours before she died, she asked all to withdraw but her husband, and Gulielma and William spent their last half hour alone together, "in which we took our last leave, saying all that was fit upon that solemn occasion." She sank rapidly from then on, and members of the family came back into the room to watch her breathe her last in her husband's arms, her head upon his bosom.

"She was an excelling person, both as child, wife, mother, mistress, friend and neighbor," was his eulogy for her.

Gulielma Springett was laid to rest in the Jordans burial ground, alongside of four of the five children she had lost, and William Penn gathered up his remaining family and returned to Worminghurst in Sussex. The great, rambling manor house would seem quite empty now.

I would persuade myself thou art of the same mind, tho' it is hard to make thee say so.
——Penn in a letter to Hannah Callowhill, 1695

18. *Middle-aged Suitor*

PENN EXPERIENCED another serious illness after Guli's death, and he needed many weeks to recover his resiliency. In a letter from London to Samuel Carpenter and others in Philadelphia at the end of April he described himself as not yet out of danger. He and Guli had begun and created a single life together, a life that in turn was a segment of the greater life of the Society; her death had brought it to a close. Guli's quiet, patient, self-effacing temperament had been a perfect complement to his, and although he did remarry, the texture of the second marriage was quite different from the first. The second, although it was certainly another love match, lacked the mutual growth of the first. Gulielma Springett had shared in the creation of his Quaker personality, and had experienced only one lengthy separation from him—his first American sojourn. The role of the second wife was one of devoted service to an already established public figure, often in absentia.

As Penn recovered slowly from the shock of losing Guli, he turned quite naturally to those about him for consolation. Springett, already nineteen and heir to the proprietorship, offered deep solace; father and son were almost constant companions. Springett would soon be old enough to go to America as his representative. In Friends' affairs there was further solace. The Yearly Meeting in London in 1694 was the first Penn had attended in a long time, and he served with George Whitehead, William Mead and thirteen more on the committee appointed to draw up the epistles that would go out to Friends all over the world. His preface to George Fox's *Journal*, reprinted as *A Brief Account of the Rise and Progress of the People Called Quakers*, published the same year, was probably written during his period of convalescence. And, much to Margaret

Fox's satisfaction, the journal of Penn's travels in Holland and Germany in 1677 was published around the same time.

The hope of recovering his colony, now that he had been exonerated, combined with returning health to set the tireless, energetic Penn back into motion, and he turned his keen diplomatic talents upon Whitehall once more. His powerful, high-ranking friends were still there, and Pennsylvania was presenting England with a dilemma that perhaps Penn could solve better than the still incumbent Governor Fletcher. The war with France continued to confront the colonies with threats from the French and French-loyal Indians, and to meet the threat England needed men and money from Pennsylvania as well as from Virginia, Maryland, Connecticut, New England, New York and Rhode Island. Pennsylvania, it was estimated, could furnish two thousand men, and her cash quota of the total cost to the colonies for maintaining six hundred men and their officers at Albany was fourteen hundred pounds. By the time Penn applied to the Crown to have his colony restored, it was quite apparent on both sides of the ocean that he was the best possible administrator for Pennsylvania—if he could be persuaded to a moderate stand on military preparedness.

In King William's absence, Queen Mary received Penn's petition, and she turned it over to her legal advisers and the Privy Council Committee on Trade and Plantations. The government needed to turn Pennsylvania back to the Proprietor's care, but the golden opportunity to drive a hard bargain was not wasted. Penn had to make two promises: to return to Pennsylvania and administer it in person, and to contribute troops and money toward the mutual defense of the English colonies against the French. They did try to be lenient: his quota was not to exceed eighty men or their equivalent cost. It was a hard choice for a Quaker, but his only alternative was to see the colony continue under an arbitrary military rule; so Penn assured the royal advisers that he did intend "with all convenient speed to repair thither and take care of the government and provide for the safety and surety thereof." In a royal grant, dated August 20, 1694, issued by King William and Queen Mary, the administration of the province and its territories was restored to William Penn.

Why did he not go to America at once? Why did another five years pass before he set foot on the colony's rich soil? One reason at least was financial, and he already knew he could not hope to borrow from wealthy Philadelphians. He began to contemplate a trip to Ireland to examine and salvage his estates there, meanwhile continuing William Markham as Deputy Governor, an office he had been filling under Fletcher. There were fewer old dependables in the colony for Penn to turn to than in the past. Death had removed Thomas Lloyd, and Keith was absconded into apostasy. It was all right, though; the day was not far off when Springett would move into government affairs and assume responsibilities in his father's behalf. Springett was not so husky nor so tireless as his parent, but he was a lad whose soul ran deep and in whom his father saw "the seeds of many good qualities rising in him that made him beloved," a lad who possessed humility, plainness, tenderness and many of Guli's sweetest traits.

The Society had recovered from Penn's abrupt return to its ranks, and his prestige as a minister was gradually being restored. His spiritual gifts had been enriched by grief and adversity, and his volatile temperament subdued by the passing years. In the autumn, taking Springett with him, he set out on a trip through the meetings of western England—Wilts, Gloucester, Somerset, Devon and Dorset—drawing large crowds of the devout and the curious as news of his approach spread before him. "Since it hath pleased God and the King to give me my liberty, I have been willing to visit my friends before my going for America, and in those places especially where I have suffered most in my character, by common fame, stirred up by ignorance or prejudice, that if it were possible I might do my profession, person and posterity that right of appearing another and better man than I have too often been represented." He reached Bristol toward the end of November, and out of that city he visited Chew where Richard Vickris lived, Clareham and Wrington where he dined aboard a Bengal ship in King Road. Westbury and Devizes were next, and then he returned to Bristol, remaining for about two weeks in the city where his father had been born and lay buried in St. Mary Redcliffe. Large gatherings of Quakers waited upon him in Bristol and crowded around him after each meeting.

Among them was the thirty-year-old, unmarried daughter of a linen draper who must have been a little nonplused at the sudden, frank attention he paid her, and startled to realize that his extended stay in Bristol was, at least in part, on her account. It could not be, of course; he was twenty years older than she, much higher in station and far weightier in the Society than she or any member of her family. He would leave Bristol—and forget—and she must do the same.

Penn did not forget Hannah Callowhill for a moment from then on, but it took him a goodly while to persuade and convince her that this new phenomenon in both their lives not only could be but must be. Hannah was the daughter of Thomas Callowhill and Hannah Hollister, and they had been living on High Street in Bristol when she was born on April 18, 1664. They were economically substantial people though they did not think in terms of the grandiose style of living to which Penn was accustomed, and they were a leading family in local Quakerdom. Penn was no stranger to Bristol Friends. He had been there in 1681 to see the *Bristol Factor* and her passenger list off to America, and again in 1687 when his and King James's itineraries had crossed in Chester and Oxford. It is most likely that he had known the Callowhill family for some time, including Hannah, who had been seventeen when he was launching the Pennsylvania project; but it was on this trip through the western counties that he looked upon Hannah for the first time as someone distinct from the others.

His tour took him to Wells, Somerton, Bridgwater, Sherborne, Dorchester and Exeter, and from Exeter he went all the way up to Gloucester. Local magistrates had prevented his appearance there when he was conveniently near by in Bristol.

In the middle of January he was back in London and soon after that in Worminghurst. Scarcely was he home than the woman in his daughter Letitia knew how it was with him, though she decided to keep it to herself for a while. Best not make him self-conscious about the heart pinned to his sleeve.

Penn did not allow the Callowhills to forget him, and letters began to travel the post roads between Bristol and Worminghurst. With an obvious thoroughness he courted the whole family. To

Hannah's mother in June he sent a very particular recipe for drying fruit. Apparently the subject had been thoroughly exploited in conversation with her, and upon his return he had gone to some lengths to find the recipe for her. There were many such available from Spain or Portugal, but he wanted for her the one he had sampled himself in Toulouse, France, and at last he had obtained it from the Earl of Leicester. And, he added, "give my endeared love to thy dear husband and virtuous daughter." Over the ensuing months Thomas Callowhill was encouraged to avail himself of Penn's advice on legal and real estate matters or any other problems arising out of the responsibilities of husband and father.

That Penn's dreams were racing ahead of him once more shows clearly in a letter to Robert Turner and Thomas Holme when he treated at length the two problems about which a potential bridegroom must concern himself—income and a home. "I long to see you; but my impediment you know, and if I cannot be assisted I must do as I can." He goes on at length in strong language about those in America who thwart and censure him instead of trying to help; he speaks once more of the quantities of money owed him for lands and rents of which he has seen not a penny; and—the unkindest cut of all—Pennsbury has been allowed to run to rack and ruin. "My face is now turned towards Ireland; when that journey is over (for I have not seen my estate since I had it, 24 years and an 1/3) I bend towards you with divers families, I may say many, and some considerable, and some persons you will be glad to see there."

In the balance of the letter Penn gives them the news of Friends in England. He has just come from Yearly Meeting in London where George Keith was finally disowned. Keith "licks up the very vomit of T. Hicks and J. Faldo, and never did one go from us that carried fewer with him. . . . His rudeness to me has been beyond compare after all my tenderness with him."

Penn was referring to a "painful meeting" between himself and Keith at Ratcliffe the previous February, and to Keith's later behavior in meetings for worship, where he was becoming so disgruntled and contentious that he was disturbing the meetings with his frequent rantings. One meeting actually arose and left the room in order to put an end to Keith's angry outbursts. Said a non-Friend who visited one of these gatherings, "Why do they suffer him to disturb their meetings thus, to spoil a good sermon and a good prayer thus? I wonder at Mr. Penn's patience, that he did not fling him over the gallery."

Friends flourished in spite of these internal problems. This same year the first Yearly Meeting was convened at Bristol, and it was a "precious one."

Bristol itself had become a precious place as far as Penn was concerned. A legacy of love letters tells us so.

10th of 7th month [September] 1695

MOST DEAR H.C.:

My best love embraces thee, which springs from that fountain of love and life, which time, distance nor disappointments, can ever wear out, nor the floods of many and great waters ever quench. Here it is, dearest H, that I behold, love and value thee and desire, above all other considerations, to be known, received and esteemed by thee. And let me say, that the loveliness that the tendering and blessed Truth hath beautified thee with, hath made thee amiable in my eye above many, and for that it is my heart, from the very first, has cleaved to thee. Did I say above many, ay, above all, and that is my confidence in this thing at all times, to myself and others. O let us meet here, most dear H! the comfort is unspeakable, and the fellowship undesolvable. I would persuade myself thou art of the same mind, tho' it is hard to make thee say so. Yet that must come in time, I hope and believe; for why should I love so well and so much when I am not well beloved? Take it not amiss. I have no other way of converse. Let my letters have some place if I deserve any, tho' I hope thou art sensible of me in that in which we can never be separated; but the time draws near, in which I shall enforce this subject beyond all scruple. Yet till then I must tell thee, and ever that thou art most entirely beloved of

Thy unchangeable friend,

W. P.

To "enforce this subject beyond all scruple," Penn went on another speaking tour through the west of England; its route took him to Bristol, almost as the crow flies. With him were Springett, Tishe and Bille. Melksham in Wiltshire was his most prominent stop on the way to Bristol, and he reached it some time in October. There he attended a public debate between John Plympton, a Baptist, and John Clark, a Quaker. It was a nostalgic thing to witness; he had debated many a Baptist in his younger years, and older seasoned ministers had sat back and watched him handle the discourse upon the universality of grace, on baptism, the Last Supper, the Resurrection. Now he found himself in that seasoned role, listening while Clark handled these subjects, knowing that Clark realized he could depend upon him to step in if help were needed. Not until evening did Penn speak. No doubt feeling that the meeting had gone on long enough and that it needed to be brought expertly to a close, Penn rose to give his testimony to the Truth. The effect of his personality upon a public gathering had lost none of its spellbinding power, and his declaration, Besse says, the audience "received with singular attention; and he concluded the meeting with a prayer."

And so to Bristol, where he lodged at the home of Richard Snead. The reappearance of the hearty, affable, impulsive, persuasive Penn with his Cavalier's grace upon the Bristol scene speeded his courtship to a quick triumph, and the consent he could not win from Hannah by mail was accomplished in a very few days in person. He did not arrive much before the first of November, and on the eleventh he and Hannah appeared before the Men's Meeting, Thomas and Anna Callowhill present, and made the first declaration of their intention to wed. William Penn was asked to bring a certificate from his own Monthly Meeting in Sussex, and Charles Harford and Richard Snead were appointed to inquire into their clearness to wed.

Four days later Penn was in Wells, seventeen miles south of Bristol, speaking to a great assembly in the main hall of an inn. His notoriety combined with recollections of his earlier visit to the place, drew a crowd that overflowed the inn and filled the street outside. In order to be heard both indoors and out, Penn preached from a balcony. It was not hard for petty officials, still hostile to the Quakers but frustrated by the Toleration Act, to interpret such an incident as an unlawful and riotous assembly; and when informers rushed to them with the testimony that the place was not properly licensed, the Mayor issued an arrest warrant for Penn, and officers reached the scene with it while the meeting was still in progress. Rudely they seized Penn, rudely refused to let him finish his sermon, roughly they dragged him before the magistrates, and gently were they defeated when shown the proper certificate for the meeting. Hannah could realize then, if she had not grasped the fact earlier, that life with William Penn would never be dull.

Pennsylvania's administrative problems had pursued Penn to Bristol. His concession to the Crown to furnish men or money for military defense had not been well received by his Provincial Council, and they had point-blank refused to send either to New York. "Now our case is this," Penn pleaded with them, "here we pay to carry on a vigorous war against France; that is the whole Title of the Acts, and so it is collected by the Commissioners of it; and Friends here admire at the difficulty of the people there to pay; saying, it seems to contradict us here; especially since it may be given under the style of peace and safety or to defray the exigencies of the government, and deposit it in such hands as may keep Friends clear from the breach of their testimony, and the country from such complaints as may overset the government again, or contradict Friends here, that pay much more barefacedly. Others there will give besides Friends and others pay as well as Friends. It is a mixed thing and for mixed services."

Among Friends there has always been a variation in views on the peace testimony, from those absolutists who follow the Sermon on the Mount exactly and will not participate in any military activity to those moderates who see wisdom in military defense. Penn had grown gradually into the moderate school; he believed in a positive, creative approach that set up circumstances in which peace could survive; his peace-loving colony was one, his proposed world government another.

Penn's plea for co-operation was contained in a letter dated November 5 to Turner, Carpenter, Phineas Pemberton, David Lloyd (another Welshman, thought to be a cousin of the late

Thomas Lloyd) and four others. Dwelling on the last paragraphs of his letter, Penn reflected upon Springett. In him lay the real solution for Pennsylvania. "I hope in the Lord to see you," he told his Council, "and in the meantime perhaps you may see my son, a man grown, and he will bring requisite countenance and what I hope you will be pleased with."

On the twenty-fifth of November, 1695, William Penn and Hannah Callowhill appeared before the Bristol Men's Meeting to make their second declaration to wed and to hear Snead and Harford report favorably on their clearness.

Hannah was a deeply shy person, but while she was in Penn's company most of her shyness dissolved. During his second Bristol visit it seems to have dissolved sufficiently to allow her to recommend a saline purgative for whatever complaint he confided to her. He tried it devotedly as soon as he reached home on December 6:

By this, dearest H, thou wilt know that yesterday, about noon, we got, through the mercy of God, safely home, if I may truly call any place so where thou art not. I found all well, which to be sure is more than I can say for myself, till I hear it is well with thee. . . . I left so much of my heart there, that it is very improperly said that I am here. However, it is not in the power of time or place to weaken or any accidents to alter the deep and religious as well as natural affection that lives in my heart to thee. Springett, Tishe and Bille give thee and thy relations their respects, to whom dearly salute me. . . . I this day took salt, and hope thou dost not forget it. I fear you have a flood. Dearly farewell.

But when Penn had left Bristol and Hannah was left without the stimulation of his company, she suffered a reaction. He had visited a whirlwind of excitement upon the stately and modest Callowhill household, with his three children reflecting his own disposition, and as the dust of his visit finally settled, Hannah experienced doubt, a failing self-confidence, and even a mild illness that could well have been an emotional reaction. A rapid succession of letters from Penn during December, January and February assured and reassured and advised.

It is no small satisfaction to me that I can make my solemn appeals to the Lord, who from my youth, has been my God, concerning the rise and spring of my love to thee, in reference to that near concern between us. That it was not what others said of thee to me (though that gave me a general liking and esteem for thee, as a deserving Friend) but what mine own eyes saw and beheld, in the openings of the divine life and love of God, once and again, when my soul was in the best frame and sense of Him; and that before I did in the least suspect any such thing was in the thought or wish of any Friend whatever. And it is not less my joy, dearest H, that after my most recollect considerations, in my present solitude, of what has past, in order to accomplish that near relation between us, I can say my heart is the same; yea, that my love is renewed daily toward thee, and with that confidence, comfort and pleasure, that I am sure the Lord is with me in it. Neither distance, nor absence, nor any other thing, hath had any power to lessen it. . . .

In that same letter he expresses his alarm for her illness:

Thine delicately writ came safely, as well as acceptably to hand. I wish it had brought me better news of thy health, for that is dearer to me than my own, but in order to it, thou must take advice of those that are learned and able in that distemper, and not rely too much upon thy own opinion, which is never the part of discreet patients to do. I hope time, the good air, and a good God will accomplish the cure to restore thee to thy former vigor and strength again. I am indifferent well, for one that sleeps so little, only my nose frequently upon blowing bleeds a little. . . .

In a postscript he adds a remedy:

Pray use milk or wine, sack, as thou doest tother liquor, and it will do; be sure it dry of itself, and apply the cover to this as directed, very hot to the eyes, and it is good for the sight. . . .

After Hannah has entered Penn's life we begin to accumulate many news notes on his personality. The above letter reveals the fact that he could do with very little sleep, a trait common to highly energetic persons; and to Hannah we are indebted for the information that he sometimes wore calico drawers and in the house a long dressing gown made of "huffe" and lined with another fabric, lightweight and warm.

Not only had Penn capitulated completely to Hannah's warm and loving nature, but so had his children. On returning to Worminghurst, Letitia wrote to Hannah as quickly as her father:

Worminghurst 12—10 Month [December]—95

DEAR AND RESPECTED FRIEND:

Please to give me leave to salute thee with that true love and esteem which I am sure thou deservest from me, and which I hope I shall always be ready to pay thee, for I desire thee to believe that though I am not much in words and less in writing, I have great pleasure in thinking how easy and happy I shall be in the enjoyment I promise myself of thy company, which I can truly say I prefer before any other settlement. And if I may be so bold, I must tell thee that at my father's first coming from Bristol ten months since, though I kept it to myself, I perceived which way his inclinations was going, and that he had entertained an inward and deep affection for thee, by the character he gave of thee, and pleasure he took to recommend thee for an example to others. And therefore I was not a little desirous to see Bristol for thy sake, and I am sure I was not disappointed, for ever since my esteem for thee has increased, and my father's design been more and more pleasant to me. And what my brother told me he said to thee in my name was but a little of that respect and duty I shall, I hope, be always ready to show to thee; and what I cannot express in words I shall endeavor my deeds shall supply. . . . My brothers present thee with their respects, and I desire thou wilt please to give theirs with mine to thy father and mother. . . .

Penn's sister, Margaret Lowther, added her efforts to the courtship and sent Hannah a gift of a pot of chocolate.

Penn's letters to Hannah far outnumbered hers to him, probably because words came so easily to him. His to her, he admitted, were often "writ with more haste than was fit," but hers, he assured her, were "excellently writ." "While others are muddling in the world, my desires are to converse with thee, in that which is above it, and since time and distance forbid it in another way, let me be acceptable to my dearest H in this only way that is left me; for there is nothing in this world so desirable or pleasant to me, and if thou canst but see and reach me where I live and love, I am satisfied, it will be so with thee. For this I loved thee, and in this I love and honor thee, and forever embrace and am united unto thee."

He had made his first declaration to wed before Horsham Monthly Meeting on December 11, five days after returning to Worminghurst, and at the Men's Meeting of January 8, 1696, he made his second declaration by mail. "To this meeting did our dear friend William Penn send a few lines under his hand wherein he signified his intention of taking Hannah Callowhill to be his wife and the several Friends appointed to inquire concerning his clearness from all others on the account of marriage did signify that they find nothing . . . so this meeting hath ordered a certificate to be sent to the Friends of the city of Bristol to which the said Hannah Callowhill doth belong." Springett Penn was there in person, and he no doubt presented his father's letter.

Penn himself was not well enough to attend, for by January, when plans were being made for this third trip to Bristol for the wedding, illness struck the Worminghurst household as well as the surrounding community, with symptoms that read very much like grippe. Letitia seems to be the only one who did not succumb to it, but Penn was laid up for weeks, and so were his two sons. The weather had been particularly bad and the season "so rude" that Penn had been unable to get up to London until the roads improved, so rude indeed that it aided and abetted the epidemic. Fifteen-year-old Bille began with a hoarseness, and Penn began to feel unwell about the same time. Bille, he told Hannah, "is lively, yet tender. I have cut off his hair." There were gifts on their way to the Callowhill household: three gallons of French brandy "one of which pray present to thy mother" and two pounds of chocolate from Hannah's betrothed, three small pots of venison "of her own manufacture" from Letitia who regretted her pig-brawn was not yet ready. As plans for the wedding and for the house where it was to be held were nearing completion, the illness that began in Bille's throat grew worse. The betrothed couple had planned to wait two months, but the two stretched into three. On January 19 Penn wrote: "If Bille grows stronger, I think to be at London next week." Two days later the situation changed to: "I cannot say my boy is better, for he is a little worse; I fear he got cold First Day while I was at meeting but hope it will pass off again. He complained today of his side, but it is now easy. . . . I am not so well as I could wish, and am much fallen away, which is the best part of it."

Now this is the only clue I have found anywhere to support the tradition of Penn's obesity, a slim bit of circumstantial evidence. It could well be that he merely acquired the heavy-set look of a man in his fifties and worried about how a bride twenty years younger would view it. Added to it was the gnawing little worry that Hannah might not fully understand the need for delay in his coming to Bristol. "I intend as fast as I can, to make thee my most dear wife, and to love, prize and tender thee above all my worldly comforts. . . ."

His fears were as groundless as Hannah's, fostered by the post service that took two days and sometimes mislaid a letter. Hannah wrote compliments about his sister's cooking, concerns for his and his children's illness and welfare. Her brevity was disconcerting, and he begged to hear at least twice a week.

By the end of January Penn was able to report: "My dearest H, know that I am through the Lord's goodness, better, so well, that nothing but my poor boy's weakness stays me from the orchard. His fever is mercifully abated, but his looseness apt to return, which debilitates him much, and endangers the return of the fever." Hopefully, his and Hannah's letters began to contain once more the multitude of practical details. The house was in preparation for their arrival. Penn would bring his own manservant and Tishe her maid, who would help with the housework as well and ease the burden on the other servants being provided at Bristol. There was a bit of a tiff over the carriage that was to bring the bride and groom back to Worminghurst. He had in mind a "chariot for four to sit in, and harness for four horses upon occasion . . . all to be plain without and within, only the lining velvet of an olive color." There was to be another for her. "Thine is not yet lined. What wilt thou have and what color? Let me know by the next pray. If cloth complete, calamanco hair or silk plush or velvet . . . please thyself every way." But Hannah wanted to hire a more elegant affair that was being made available to her, and Penn put his foot down. "I am determined to keep my old plainness, that have kept about nine or ten in my time, and have determined either to have a cloth or calamanco. . . . I'll tell thee a short story; a man of quality sitting down at table at the lower end, some formalists in breeding . . . mightily pressed him to sit higher that they should be ashamed to be seen to sit above one so much above them. At last, he, to stop their troublesome civilities, told them that wherever he sat was the upper end, and so much for that affair about the hiring of the coach."

Hannah responded with growing warmth and trust to this incredible lover who had been catapulted into her life. He was so frank and so full to her that it is apparent by the implications in his own letters to her that she was being drawn rapidly out of herself, and she began even before his arrival for the wedding to be a mother to his children. She wrote to Bille, who was "at best at a stand," to tell him that she loved him, and Penn rushed back to her the assurance that she was absolute mistress of his entire household. Before she had time to reply to that the post galloped up with another:

I cannot forbear to write where I cannot forbear to love as I love my dearest Hannah, and if that be a fault, till she ceases to be so lovely, I need no apology for it. Receive then my dearest heart, the embraces of the best love I have, that lives and flows to thee every day, with continual desires for thy felicity every way; more especially in the best things, which sets all to rights, and gives a peace above the little and low interruptions of this world. Suffer not anything of it to disturb or abate thy satisfaction, but feel thy peace bottomed upon that which is unchangeable. O meet me there mine own dearest, in thy retired walks and recesses from the world, and let our fellowship be enlarged in that nobler relation, which time cannot dissolve. . . .

Did she surely understand that it was the illness of himself and his children that kept him from her? Did she feel any aversion to his years and character, he asked frankly. He apparently had received an extremely delicate letter from her confessing the fear she felt of the marital experience she was about to enter upon, and her distrust of her own competence and knowledge. The lovely delicacy of his reply was no less than hers:

Since thou went for living to the Lord, as thy husband, thou thus marryest Him in me. As our case is not common, so if the rest be not in the common road, we ought less to wonder. Perhaps it was not begun so weightily in thy mind as it will end; or thou mightest also foil those beginnings, thou now desirest to see more of the progress of and can't easily get at them. I shall oblige thee when I get to town, but want of longer familiarity, and inward and intimate freedoms before it came to the push, with natural shyness and an averse education to that way of life, certainly disjointed things at first; and that bone, by time, I don't doubt but it shall effectually set. I have faith, yea assurance of it, and if thou hast not at last too much I will hazard thy having too little. However, dearest and best friends we shall ever be, and a life of Truth and tenderness and devotion I hope we shall live. . . .

There was another difference to be overcome. Hannah did not want to live in Worminghurst; the house was too big, too ostentatious, and most important of all, too isolated. Hannah liked city life; she wanted to make her home in a little house in Bristol near her family. Penn on the other hand liked the seclusion and the perspective of the open countryside at Worminghurst, and he loved the big, old house.

"I like a city less than a little house," he wrote as he thought of his expansiveness cramped and crowded into tiny rooms, and he promised that he would make any alterations she wished. "Worminghurst is a pleasant place, but more by nature than art. The house is very large, but ugly, and yet has convenient room enough for twelve or twenty people more than our and your family; but greatness is least of my thought. What thou concludest with, I will; the Lord's love and presence and answering Truth and service of it is what I pray may ever lead and prevail with us. For the chimneys, it is the worst part of the character, yet if for us, Tishe and G. H. [probably a housekeeper] and my sons, and one for strangers, it may serve."

The illness that found its leisurely way through the Penn family did not reach Springett until February, giving him a troublesome cold that would not respond to treatment. Penn hoped to set out for Bristol on February 25 and reach Bristol on the twenty-eighth. He and Bille had regained their strength and were ready, but Springett's cold grew more ugly and developed into a cough. Springett was the most fragile member of the family, the one least able to throw off a chest ailment. Upon eighteen-year-old Tishe's shoulders fell the responsibility of the household, and her energy nearly matched her father's. In the midst of caring for three sick men she found time to assist at the delivery of a child in one of the neighboring houses. She did have to leave the letter writing to her father, though, and any messages for Hannah went into his letters. "Tishe is well and is divided between fear and duty. She thinks she ought to write and fears it may be troublesome. . . . Tishe desires thee to excuse her sending her white curtains unwashed. She had not time, I pressing her, and promising to excuse it, overlook her outside. It was a gift of her mother's, and she never made it up before. The curtains are to come no lower than the bedstead at bottom, the counterpane reaching the ground, serves for lower valance."

Although Springett's cold and cough proved far graver than anyone realized, it did not prevent the entire Penn family and their servants from reaching Bristol for the wedding, and on the fifth day of March, 1696, Hannah Callowhill and William Penn joined hands in the Friends' marriage ceremony and mutually promised to live together as husband and wife in love and faithfulness according to God's holy ordinance until by death they should be separated. After the bride and groom wrote their names, sixty-six other guests signed the marriage certificate, which gives a small estimate of the size of the gathering. Three Penington names appear to suggest that Guli's relatives approved his second marriage; Springett, Letitia and William, Jr., all signed it; so did Thomas and Anna Callowhill;

and there were other names dear to Penn—Richard Snead, Richard Vickris, John Whiting, John Vaughton and Henry Gouldney in whose house Fox had died. Penn had succeeded—at least temporarily—in persuading Hannah that Worminghurst would be the best of all possible homes for them, and he took her back there after the wedding.

Capable Hannah entered the household just in time to support William Penn through one of his most difficult losses. She came home with the ailing and coughing Springett and assumed her nurse's place beside his sick bed.

"Don't thee do so, let them, don't trouble thyself so much for such a poor creature as I am," Springett protested, but the protest was not convincing and she continued to minister to his needs.

His strength failed rapidly until he realized that he could not recover, and he began to speak with wisdom far beyond his twenty-one years.

"I am resigned," he told the family gathered around him.

And another time to his father, "All is mercy, dear father; everything is mercy."

He called to his side the sixteen-year-old brother who was so much less sensitive, so much less responsive to good discipline. "Be a good boy, and know there is a God, a great and mighty God, who is a rewarder of the righteous. . . . Have a care of idle people and idle company, and love good company and good friends." And like all deathbed advice and dying wishes, it overwhelmed the lad, at least for the time being.

Resigned to God's desires, yet filled with the will to live, Springett rose one day for a coach drive in the open air with his father, and when he returned to the house exhausted by the effort he said, "Really, Father, I am exceeding weak; thou canst not think how weak I am."

The next day he must have gone for a drive again, because William Penn says in his memorial to Springett that they were about twenty miles from home, perhaps at an inn, when Springett asked his father to close the door and hold a little meeting for worship with him, "like a precious ointment for his burial." Then Springett expressed the desire to die at home, and Penn took him back to the house. His father asked him if he wished to be remembered to his friends at Bristol, London and elsewhere.

"Yes, yes! My love in the Lord, my love to all Friends in the Lord."

He called each to his side—father, sister, brother—and asked them to kiss him goodby.

"Let my father speak to the doctor," he said, and he closed his eyes and was gone.

"Breathing his last on my breast, the 10th day of the 2nd month [April] between the hours of nine and ten in the morning, 1696," wrote William Penn.

It was a crushing blow to lose that eldest, most promising son. "God is God, and good," Penn had said at the loss of Guli, lest even his grief seem to dispute divine will; with the same spirit of resignation he told of his loss of Guli's counterpart: "So ended the life of my dear child, and eldest son, much of my comfort and hope, and one of the most tender and dutiful, as well as ingenious and virtuous youths, I knew, if I may say so of my own dear child; in whom I lost all that any father can lose in a child, since he was capable of anything that became a sober young man; my friend and companion, as well as most affectionate and dutiful child."

Consoling letters came from many, and two in particular—from Robert Barclay, Jr. and Willem Sewel—are noteworthy. Barclay had been unable to attend Springett's burial, and Penn, already so deeply hurt by the loss of his son, took offense. Barclay still valued Penn's respect and friendship, he wrote; he had come from London expressly to attend the burial, but when he met Penn at George Boles thought "thee conveyed it with so much straightness and indifferency that my company might rather be burdensome than otherways." Barclay humbly desired to know of Penn's continuing love for him. The news of Springett's death took a while to reach Sewel, and his letter did not leave Amsterdam until August. It was "not without sensible grief" that he had learned of it, "but it needs must be a very great comfort to thee in thy sorrow that though his death might seem premature it was accompanied with a safe and glorious departure."

In the year of Springett's death William Penn published a tract called *Primitive Christianity Revived; in the Faith and Practice of the People Called Quakers,* and in 1696 there also came out a small book called *The Harmony of Divine and Heavenly Doctrines Demonstrated in Sundry Declarations on Various Subjects Preached at the Quaker Meetings in London by W. Penn, George Whitehead, Benjamin Coole and Samuel Waldenfield.* It is a little known but highly valuable volume of nine spontaneous sermons taken down in shorthand; six of them are Penn's delivered at Gracechurch Street, Wheeler Street and Devonshire House.

Penn turned his attention to that extraordinarily healthy child, Pennsylvania, which was surviving parental mistakes, unsympathetic foster parents, hostile neighbors, wars and wealth. Fletcher had upset the patterns badly in Pennsylvania by disregarding the provisions of the Charter, and the war with France had further done so. Now in this year of Penn's marriage and Springett's death the war was still going on and there had come to light a second Jacobite plot to invade England with French aid, which excited anti-Jacobite and anti-Catholic feelings and made the war against France seem more justified than ever. Pacifist ranks of Quakerism were deeply disturbed by it on both sides of the ocean. Markham was doing his best to persuade the Pennsylvania Assembly to support Penn's guaranty of military assistance to the Crown, but he seemed to be proceeding in Fletcher's footsteps in assuming a careless attitude toward the provisions of the Charter.

After his reappointment Markham had met with the Assembly in September, 1695, and assured them that he would uphold their privileges and rights. Under those circumstances they had listened sympathetically to his plea for military aid and had passed a bill assessing estates in the province for the support of the government, but it was "not expressly appointed for any other particular use." That was as far as their consciences would allow them to go. Incensed by their attitude, Markham abruptly dissolved both houses, and let a whole year go by before he issued writs for another election. His arbitrary action had shocked the legislators, and when the new Assembly convened it met in a ruffled and determined mood, presenting Markham with a remonstrance several pages long. Not only did they review the circumstances of their dissolution, but there had been a second bill, they reminded him, the New Act of Settlement, which he had rejected. The New Act was really a revised *Frame of Government* designed to restore their rights and privileges lost under Fletcher and to make a few more necessary amendments. Now that their wrath was up, they turned it full force upon Markham. The New Act must come first, before he could hope for any further co-operation from them.

Penn had originally placed the power in the people, and the base of popular power was spreading. Markham had to yield to the social phenomenon. The new *Frame of Government* which Markham was forced to grant was dated November 7, 1696, and was to remain in effect until William Penn's arrival in America. Its biggest innovation was the new power of the Assembly to prepare and propose bills for the Council and Governor. Enabled by a similar law passed in England earlier, it allowed the affirmation instead of the oath.

That same year a Board of Trade had been set up in Whitehall, properly called the Board of Commissioners for Promoting the Trade of the Kingdom and for Inspecting and Improving the Plantations in America and Elsewhere; and one idea arising from this new body was for a unified military command of the American colonies with a captain general appointed by the King. Penn immediately saw great possibilities in a co-ordinated administration, and in February, 1697, presented to the Board of Trade his own plan for a union of the colonies. It reflects much of the thinking to be found in his earlier proposal for a world government. He suggested that two deputies or representatives be appointed by each province to meet in a congress about once a year "to debate and resolve of such measures as are most advisable for their better understanding and the public tranquillity and safety. . . . Their business shall be to hear and adjust all matters of complaint or differences between province and province." There were so many current problems that could be solved by such a congress: persons fleeing from one province to another to escape debt or justice, injuries in point of commerce, mutual defense. Of course, the plan smacked too much of self-government to hope for any kind of reception.

Still gnawing away quietly at Penn's interests in Pennsylvania was Philip Ford. The difficult situation in which Penn had allowed Ford to entangle him seemed for a while to be easing, although his debt to Ford had mounted to more than ten thousand pounds, because he had approved additional accounts. However, Penn had reserved the liberty of inspecting the entire accounts and the words "errors excepted" had appeared in the subscribing language. In 1696, when Ford received from Penn a general release and subscription to the accounts, he executed in Penn's behalf a document dated September 29, 1696, agreeing and promising "that if hereafter any material error shall be found in the said account to his prejudice . . . in such case the said shall be made him good notwithstanding the said general discharge." Under the same date he also executed in Penn's favor an Indenture of Defeasance, agreeing to reconvey to Penn the mortgaged estates if Penn by March 30, 1697, paid him the ten-thousand-pound account due.

But when March 30, 1697 rolled around, Penn was no closer to having ten thousand pounds than he had been six months earlier, and Ford reappeared with a new scheme. "The Parliament having laid a tax on monies at interest [foreign], the said Philip Ford, under a pretence, as he said, only of saving the money from being taxed," Penn related in later years, "did frequently urge me to save him that money by a show of releasing the equity of redemption . . . and that it might look of the better face of taking a lease of the premises for three years, though upon his urgent request I made him a mortgage of the whole in usual form with condition of redemption about six months before, which was in the year 1696. I then not so much as suspected the baseness and extortion of the account." In short, Penn naïvely entered upon a *sub rosa* agreement with Ford. He conveyed the premises to Ford and Ford rented them back to Penn for three years at an annual rental of £630, the interest on the ten-thousand-pound debt compounded semiannually at three per cent. They agreed between themselves that this was to be only a mortgage, that the arrangement should be kept secret so that it would not hinder land sales in America, that Ford would never demand payment beyond what Penn could raise from the province, and that Ford would give Penn a deed containing the right of redemption. It was Penn's understanding that he was making Ford his trustee. An indenture dated April 1, 1697 transferred the province to Ford, and about ten days later Ford executed a "deed-poll containing a clause for the redemption of the premises."

William and Hannah Penn planned to make Pennsbury their permanent home. There could no longer be any reason other than financial why Penn could not keep his promise to the King and now deceased Queen to administer the colony himself: so, to this end, his oft-mentioned trip to Ireland to salvage his estates there, became a fact in 1698. The Treaty of Ryswick the previous September had ended the war with France, and the sea lanes were once more relatively safe for travel. Penn first moved Hannah to Bristol, much to her delight.

One of the traveling companions that Penn chose for the trip was Thomas Story, a young lawyer in his late twenties from Justice Town near Carlisle, convinced eight years earlier. Story had met Penn for the first time on his way to London Yearly Meeting in 1693. As other Quaker leaders had once fired the imagination of young Penn, it ultimately became his turn as a stable, middle-aged member of the Society to inspire those younger than himself. "At that time," says Story in his *Journal*, referring to the first meeting with Penn, "I contracted so near a friendship in the life of Truth and tendering love thereof in many tears, as never wore out till his dying day." Story later called Penn, "that great minister of the Gospel, and faithful servant of Christ . . . who abounded in wisdom, discretion, prudence, love and tenderness of affection, with all sincerity, above most in this generation; and indeed I never knew his equal."

Story led Penn into an extraordinary incident shortly before they sailed for Ireland. Story had learned that the Czar of Muscovy, eventually to be known as Peter the Great, was in London, and employing a distant relative of the Barclays. Story leaped at the opportunity of bringing to the Czar's attention Robert Barclay's *Apology*, and he and Gilbert Molleson, another Barclay relative, went to the Czar's residence, "a large house at the bottom of York Buildings." Lucky far beyond their hopes, they were ushered into the presence of the Czar. Peter was interested in their ideas and didn't seem to notice that they left their heads covered. What good were they to any kingdom, the Czar wanted to know, if they would not bear arms? They explained their non-violent doctrine to him at length, and after he had paced the floor thoughtfully for a while they offered him a copy of Barclay's *Apology* in Latin. But after the interview they learned that he could not read Latin, only Russian and High Dutch. Here Penn, the European traveler, took up where Story had left off. He, Whitehead and some others went to Deptford, where the Czar had gone to learn shipbuilding, and delivered more Quaker literature in High Dutch. Penn saw Peter not once but twice.

Peter at that time was still in his impressionable twenties; he took Penn very seriously and never forgot the Friends. "If thou wouldst rule well, thou must rule for God; and to do that, thou must be ruled by Him," Penn advised Peter. Fifteen years later, when Peter the Great found himself in Friedrichstadt, he inquired after the Quaker meeting and expressed a desire to attend. Soldiers were quartered in the meeting house, he was informed. Then remove the soldiers and put the house back in order for the Quakers, were his orders.

The Czar left England on the twenty-first of April, and on the twenty-ninth William Penn, Thomas Story and John Everett sailed from Holy Head in the Isle of Anglesea, an extreme western tip of Wales, reaching Dublin Bay about twenty-four hours later.

It was a kind of native's return. In Ireland, too, Penn had been a colonizer; as one of the young convinced he had been a traveling minister, a champion of conscience, a rescuer of Friends from prison. His arrival was a conspicuous event to Friends and non-Friends alike, and throngs of people of "all ranks, qualities and professions" came to the Friends' meetings at which he spoke, and Thomas Story assures us that Penn fulfilled their every expectation. Penn visited meetings in the area of the harbor before going on to Dublin, and because a shipload of friars bound for France was in the harbor at the time, the rumor began to circulate that Penn had preached among the monks and converted some of them. He and his companions reached Dublin on the sixth of May, in ample time for the half-yearly meeting. The curious continued to crowd in, and many who came to be amused remained to be convinced; among his challengers were Catholic and Baptist clergy. Outstanding among the Baptists was John Plympton, a journeyman woolcomber, who rushed into print with an attack that went so far as to call Penn a willful and desperate liar. Penn went candidly to the Baptists and asked them if this was their work, and they shook their heads. No, that had been Plympton's personal doing. Replying to Plympton in kind, as was his wont, Penn wrote *Gospel Truths Held and Briefly Declared by the People Called Quakers.* Plympton bounced back with A *Quaker No Christian* to which Penn, Everett and Story wrote *The Quaker a Christian* and reprinted a portion of Penn's *Primitive Christianity Revived.*

"As William Penn's travels through the nation at that time made the envy of the priests to boil against the Truth and us, the Bishop of Cork wrote a book against the above sheet entitled *Gospel Truths.*" Penn replied to it in September when he was back in Bristol.

Meanwhile he, Story and Everett journeyed southward through Wicklow and Wexford counties, a route that would take them to Penn's estates in County Cork. They held a good meeting at Lambstown on the way and reached the city of Wexford on June first, returning to Lambstown for the night. From there the three wrote a letter to the London Yearly Meeting. "And now, dear brethren, know that the Lord hath brought us well into this kingdom of Ireland, and given us many large and blessed opportunities in several parts." Truth was prospering in Ireland, they were happy to report, and Friends there showed "simplicity, gravity and coolness, in managing their church affairs." They pushed on southward as far as Ross and were about to board a boat to cross the river to Waterford when Truth's prosperity was threatened by a dozen dragoons who dragged them from the boat. Seeing some responsible persons nearby, Penn realized that they must have ordered the incident and he spoke to them at once:

"What! Are you gentlemen and officers, and will stand here and suffer such insolence in your open view?"

Their horses had also been seized, they soon discovered, under a post-Jacobite law forbidding any Papist to own a horse worth five pounds five shillings or more. There had to be valuable time lost going before the magistrates and arguing their case, but when Penn finally reached Waterford he wrote to the Lords Justices of Ireland about the incident, who promptly clapped the offending officers into confinement. Several weeks later when the same officers appealed to Penn to help them recover their freedom, he mercifully interceded successfully with the Lords Justices for their release.

Penn and his companions went on through Clonmell and Youghall and into the barony of Imokilley where Penn spent three days looking over his lands, listening to stories of narrow escapes, of personal tragedies, of conscripted grain and cattle, of badly disciplined troops quartered on the people, of roving bands of plunderers. The Jacobite war had added one more tragic phase to Ireland's fierce history, and Penn's lands, temporarily confiscated on the strength of Fuller's testimony, were described by Penn himself as "almost ruined." He did not stay long enough to make surveys and establish new tenants, no doubt because he knew he could not garner enough to do him any real good. Pennsylvania had to be the solution, the only remaining solution, to his economic plight.

From Shanagarry Penn went up to Cork and spent a full week in the city of his convincement, devoting much time to Friends' meetings there and in neighboring communities, and paying a visit to the Lord Shannon at Shannon Park. He made the sad discovery in both Cork and later in Dublin at the Yearly Meeting, that within the Society Truth was suffering at the hands of some members of its own ministry who had set themselves up as small dictators and who greeted the illustrious Penn with envy and malice. The unifying pressure of persecution had been removed. Story calls Penn, without reservation, a man endowed "with the glory and dignity of the Lord," and it was that very glory and dignity which roused such jealousy among high-ranking Irish Friends. They attacked him, "even in the Yearly Meeting, to the great grief of all the right-minded among them," and the young, hero-worshiping Story shares with us his thrill at watching and hearing Penn confound even these attackers. On First Day morning in particular, "we had another very large and much crowded meeting there [Cork]; and the Lord was mightily with William Penn that day, clothing him with majesty, holy zeal and divine wisdom, to the great satisfaction of Friends there, and admiration and applause of the people; even increasing that unsought praise which some did much grudge him."

Charleville, Limerick-on-Shannon near his mother's early home, and Birr all heard William Penn, and at Rosenallis he met once more the venerable William Edmundson, founder of the Irish Quaker movement. Then came Mountmellick, Edenderry, Carlow, Lurgan and Dundalk. Story's adoration of Penn reached a poetic level at one meeting and he described him as full of his message "as a new bottle with new wine; and He who filled him therewith, by him dispensed the same liberally to all that were athirst." Penn and Story parted company for a while and met again at Cashel in County Tipperary. There Story and John Vaughton had been preaching to a large meeting when the Mayor appeared in person to break it up and pull Story down from the platform, and the Mayor it was discovered had been motivated by the Bishop of Cashel. Penn arrived in time to act as arbitrator of the situation, and he soon learned the cause of the Bishop's complaint. On Sunday morning so many of the townsfolk had flocked to the Friends' meeting that the Bishop had found himself preaching to an empty hall. "Which I confess," said the Bishop, "made me a little angry."

From Cashel Penn, Everett and Story returned to Cork and remained there until the nineteenth of August, setting sail in the *Jane of London*, landing in Minehead and arriving in Bristol on the twenty-second. Thomas Story remained with Penn for several weeks after that to assist him in writing his reply to the Bishop of Cork, "transcribing his sheets, searching the Scriptures, etc."

At least we are certain of the name of one of Penn's personal secretaries, and there must have been many more adoring young converts ready to sit at his elbow and lovingly write as he dictated and make the long, tedious copies needed for his printers and his personal records. Penn's collected papers show a wide variety of backgrounds in these young men; some wrote in hands as fine and legible as print, some were only modestly educated as their poor spelling and clumsy penmanship show. Penn had his own reason for choosing each—a small debt that had to be liquidated, a faltering scholar of the faith who needed constant exposure to his teacher, or, like Story and the dispute with the Bishop of Cork, on-the-scene knowledge of the subject. The 1683 list of those to whom lots were assigned in Philadelphia reveals the name of Philip Lehman of Bristol, Gentleman, Secretary to William Penn.

The Penns returned to Worminghurst, in spite of Hannah's obvious preference for Bristol, because Penn's roots were there—his meeting membership, his records and files, his friends, his children's friends—and because it was more convenient to London. But Bristol had proved as attractive to his son as to his wife, and on January 12, 1699, they all gathered in that city once more for the wedding of William Penn, Jr., to Mary Jones. The groom was just under nineteen, and his bride was three years older, daughter of a Bristol merchant. Among the long list of signers on the wedding certificate were Thomas Callowhill, Richard Snead, the parents of Mary Jones, William and Hannah Penn, Letitia, Margaret and Anthony Lowther and their daughter Margaret.

From May 29 to June 2, 1699, Penn was in London attending the London Yearly Meeting, serving with Whitehead, Ellwood and others on the epistles committee, but Pennsylvania claimed the greater part of his thoughts and efforts during those final months before his sailing. Much of his American correspondence in the last few years had been with Robert Turner, Samuel Carpenter and Markham, but Turner's letters had grown scarcer since the Keith controversy. Penn had counseled Turner against Keith so often ("Rob, the ancient, noble, glorious Truth turns against his work and he is fallen in with the dregs of apostacy") that Turner had no doubt grown shy of Penn. But Turner was both close-mouthed and blunt, and for both those qualities Penn valued him highly. Penn could entrust the utmost confidence to Turner, and Turner could rebuke and advise Penn—rebuke him for his own negligence in replying or giving specific instructions at times, advise him to come to America and look after his affairs in person. Out of the occasional long letter that still came from Turner, Penn could anticipate with a high degree of accuracy the problems that awaited him. Many colonists had lost faith in him because they thought the loss of liberties and privileges had occurred with his sanction. "Thou hast left us too much to ourselves and the mismanagement of others," said Turner. "My advice is to thee that thou take speedy care to settle the government." As for the ill-fated quitrents, what few were collected were absorbed into the cost of government; Turner urged Penn to "send some honest man and family if can be to look after thy quitrents and affairs here." On Turner's advice, Penn, two days before he sailed for Ireland, appointed Edward Penington, Guli's half brother, to be his Surveyor-General, dispatching the young man to America armed with a letter to Samuel Carpenter. Alleged violations of the Navigation Acts, illegal trading, privateering and pirates cruising profitably up and down the Atlantic coast were further problems awaiting the Proprietor's arrival.

Trade problems were all closely tied in with the court problem, because of the creation of a Vice Admiralty court. Penn had been given by his royal Charter the power to erect courts and appoint judges. The County courts, some of which were in existence when Pennsylvania was granted to Penn, were continued, and they presided over cases relating to debt, account, slander, trespass and real estate within the county as well as criminal cases. Penn created the Orphans' courts whose chief responsibility was "the estates, usage, and employment of orphans." The Provincial court of five judges sat in Philadelphia and heard appeals from the local courts. During the period that Pennsylvania was under the protection of the Crown, a Vice Admiralty court had been gratuitously set up. It was never appreciated locally. One excuse for a superimposed court with jurisdiction over maritime matters was the problem of piracy. The famous and fearless Captain Kidd, supposed to lurk near Cape Henlopen and deal profitably with Pennsylvania citizens, was one of the pirates. Another excuse was the enforcement of the Navigation Acts that required colonials to deal almost exclusively with the mother country. By the time the Vice Admiralty court spread itself out to all of its cases of marine accounts and debts, loans, bonds, trespasses and crimes arising in such an active trading region, it grossly overlapped the established judicial system.

In February, 1698, Colonel Robert Quary had been appointed Judge of the High Court of Admiralty in Pennsylvania. A staunch Church of England man, heavy-handed, arbitrary, Quary stepped into his post with a bull-necked attitude, taking no pains to conceal his dislike of Quakers, determined to remake the whole trade situation in Pennsylvania to His Majesty's best interest, and an increasingly bitter and tense situation developed around him.

Penn was doing his best to keep Whitehall conciliated until he could reach America, all the while Quary was feeding Whitehall with complaints that Markham was protecting pirates and conniving with illegal traders, that the jurisdiction of the Admiralty court was being flouted and circumvented. "It is the general discourse of this place," Quary at one point pouted, "that Mr. Penn hath greater interest at Court now than ever he had in King James's reign," which was an exaggeration of the case, although Penn's influence was regenerating. Many of his influential friends were still in the government. Sunderland, the expert politician, had returned from temporary exile in Holland and transferred his devotion to William III. Nobody knew better than Penn how fragile and limited a thing his influence at Court under William of Orange was, and it would grow no stronger while Quary continued to complain.

At last in August, 1699, the Lords of Trade sent a formal recommendation to the Lords Justices that, since Mr. Penn was about to repair to Pennsylvania to attend to all irregularities, Mr. Penn be directed in the first place to remove Colonel Markham from his post as Lieutenant Governor, David Lloyd as Attorney General and Anthony Morris as Commissioner of the Peace. It further requested due obedience to the Admiralty court, enforcement of the Acts of Trade, prevention of piracy and the establishment of a militia for the defense of the province. There could be no doubt in Penn's mind as to what was expected of him upon his arrival in America. The government added a farewell kiss: that "with all convenient speed after your arrival there you make report to His Majesty of the state of that province with relation to all foregoing matters."

Penn had a final conference on his personal affairs with Philip Ford on the eighteenth of August, at Ford's home in Islington (now part of London) since Ford was not well enough to come up to London. In spite of all that had transpired, Penn still could not quite comprehend the depth of Ford's villainy. Other London Friends certainly knew Ford by then as something of a bad boy. Six years earlier he had brought to the Six Weeks Meeting a complaint against four members of the Devonshire House Meeting, claiming that they owed him £423/16/6 and producing documents to support his claim. Friends rarely initiate court action, and it was entirely in keeping with their point of view that Ford should bring the complaint to the meeting and that a committee of disinterested members should be appointed to hear arguments, weigh testimony and arrive at a just conclusion. But Ford did not accept their just conclusion. By one technicality, ruse or device after another he kept the matter in dispute for six years, no doubt feeling that prolonged litigation would net him a bigger sum. Meeting after meeting heard the committee's report, urged that the disagreement be resolved for the sake of harmony in the meeting and for the sake of time and energy needed for more pressing problems. Committee members gave up in despair and others were appointed to replace them. Around the second year of the dispute Ford took it into a public court, and Friends begged him to drop his lawsuit and let them settle it for him in the privacy of their own meeting. By the end of the third year the arbitrators of the meeting reported with complete discouragement that they were unwilling to be further concerned, and the meeting pressed Ford to comply with their advice. He would not. New arbitrators were chosen; Thomas Ellwood was one of them, William Mead another. In the fifth year of the controversy Ford began to be tractable. Still it took another year, and the matter finally ended with entire submission on both sides, on the twenty-fifth of August, 1699, a week after William Penn's visit to Islington. How much Ford gained financially by dragging out the dispute with the Devonshire House Friends, I do not know; but he was in a quietly triumphant mood that day at Islington and warming up to more cunning. If Penn seems to have been blind to Ford's worst intent, perhaps it was because Penn still remembered the Ford of more than twenty years earlier, the Ford whose name appears so often in the minutes of the Meeting for Sufferings as having his goods confiscated and having endured other discomforts on Truth's account, the Ford who went with him to Ireland to straighten out his father's estates, the Ford who helped him with the great volume of paper work in setting up the Pennsylvania project.

Penn spent a gracious afternoon with Philip and Bridget Ford, and just before he said farewell to them they withdrew and held a whispering conference. Together they approached Penn. They wanted some money from him before he went to Pennsylvania, Ford said, and he wanted to recover the paper he had executed and given to Penn in 1696. There had been two papers executed September 29, 1696, in Penn's favor: one agreeing to rectify errors in account, the other agreeing to reconvey the mortgaged estates to Penn if certain conditions were complied with. Ford referred to the former. Rather startled by the sudden and last-minute request, Penn explained that he could not lay his hands on it readily, that it was somewhere among his other papers in the house in Sussex. "Then thou must give me another paper to release that," declared Ford, and produced an instrument ready and waiting for Penn's signature.

But why? Penn wanted to know. For mortality's sake, he was told. Ford was ill and Penn was risking his life expectancy in a long ocean voyage. Ford generously told Penn that he trusted him, but he did not know about those who would come after him. He did not want the Penn family to have the power to tear him to pieces.

What should become of his own family in the event of his death, Penn asked, and pointed out that it would be unsafe for his own interests if he discharged the 1696 paper. Further, this new document contained an untruth; it stated that Penn had examined Ford's accounts, and he had not. The ingratiating Ford struck an Oh-you-can-trust-me-and-my-wife attitude and promised Penn that none would ever know what had passed between them. Still Penn was reluctant, and Ford grew angry and declared he must have more money and the instrument or he would prevent Penn's sailing by exposing him both in England and Pennsylvania.

Penn had waited fifteen years for the chance to return to America. The ship was in the harbor with his household goods already aboard; he had agreed to embark on the twentieth, two days hence. Hannah was pregnant with her first child, and delaying the voyage would be unsafe for her. And how would Whitehall take it if he again put off keeping his promise with them? The Crown that had relieved him of his province once could do so again. Penn had to sail as scheduled.

"Hoping some providence might relieve me," Penn tells us, "I subscribed."

His actual sailing date was determined by wind and weather, and the *Canterbury* weighed anchor at Cowes on September 3. Penn sent ashore a last message to Friends, *An Epistle of Farewell to the People of God Called Quakers, Wherever Scattered or Gathered in England, Ireland, Scotland, Holland, Germany, or in Any Other Parts of Europe*, exhorting his whole family and flock of God to carry on and keep faith. "I must leave you, but I can never forget you," he wrote in a tone that suggests he did not really expect to return from this second journey to the western world.

With him were Hannah and Letitia, but not William, Jr., and not Springett.

The voyage took three tedious and monotonous months; and when William Penn set foot once more on Pennsylvania soil and stretched forth his hand to the great crowd assembled to welcome him, it was the first day of December.

> The Proprietary and his family were received with the universal joy of the inhabitants, in general; which was the greater, on account of his known intention to fix his residence among them, during the remainder of his life.
>
> —Proud, *History of Pennsylvania*

19. *Second American Sojourn*

GREAT WAS the excitement along the banks of the Delaware in anticipation of Penn's arrival. Crowds were swelled by those who traveled from the interior and from the rural areas into New Castle, Chester and Philadelphia for a first glimpse of the sails of the *Canterbury*. To many Penn was returning as a long absent friend and source of strength, to others who had never seen him he was a fabulous legend come to life. The ship paused before New Castle on the twenty-eighth, but Penn didn't go ashore there; he stayed aboard until it reached Chester, and there he was rowed up Chester Creek in state and dignity to rise and mount the landing with all the aplomb of the traditional Cavalier—the refreshing touch of elegant manners that frontier life needed. The house of the well-to-do simulated with imports the homes they had left behind, but the wilderness was just at their backs; aborigines not much beyond the Stone Age of their development walked the streets; and the farther away from town one went the more difficult and primitive living became. Here was tonic! A spot from the heart of the cultured world that even the most Quakerly among them could secretly relish.

So great was the excitement, in fact, that some young men who apparently forgot Penn's commitment to gentleness fired two shots from a cannon to welcome him. Two shots called for a third, and one of the men dashed up impulsively and "darting in a cartridge of powder before the piece was spunged" had his "left arm and hand shot to pieces." A ship's surgeon began immediately to amputate the shattered arm, but while he was working some spirits in a basin nearby caught fire and spilled on his apron, setting his clothes on fire. The crowd that milled around and pressed in close for a glimpse of the lurid accident further complicated the situation, but the fire that enveloped the doctor was soon extinguished and he continued with the operation.

"Such is the unreasonableness of envy, and of those that are exercised therein, that some such would gladly have blamed the governor," said Thomas Story. Story, who had come to America a year earlier, had hurried up the river from New Castle to be at Chester when the ship dropped anchor.

Colonel Quary, Judge of the Admiralty court, and his associate John Moore, the court's advocate, were down on the wharf as big as life to give the Governor an ingratiating welcome, and so were a host of their partisans. They were the group who developed into the Church of England Party, opposed to the Proprietary, and who had already sent so many damaging reports to Whitehall against Penn. Perhaps it was these to whom young Story made his slightly bitter reference.

As soon as the confusion and embarrassment died down and the welcome on the Chester wharf was accomplished, Penn and his party returned to the *Canterbury*, and the next morning they proceeded on up the Delaware to Philadelphia, where Governor Markham awaited them.

And thou, Philadelphia, "named before thou wert born," what of thee? In a scant eighteen years your population has swelled to five thousand and you have risen to the rank of second largest city in the New World, outranked only by Boston. Your wide, lovely streets are lined with ample homes—seven hundred in all—most of them brick and graced with balconies and porches; and, as Penn intended, each has its green plot with tall trees and gardens. Penn often cautioned you against cutting too many trees, and now they give you beauty and dignity as well as protection against wind and fire. Your face to the river has large, ample quays to handle your exports of linen, hemp, potash, whale oil, lumber, furs, tobacco and even iron and copper. At Samuel Carpenter's quay, the first and the handsomest, a ship of five hundred tons "can lay her broadside." You have shops that offer every sort of imported luxury. You have a market twice a week, where livestock and produce may be bought and sold, and a great fair twice a year. You have your churches and your schools and your intellectual set, and you are rapidly becoming the cultural center of America. In their true perspective your governmental problems are only a fragment of the whole picture, mere mosquito bites upon your skin that your lusty health throws off with ease, and the unfavorable criticism and cruel gossip about you that have been coming to England fade into the background. Your founder can ride through your streets, Philadelphia, and lay a hand upon his bursting heart. His sufferings, like yours, are as nothing when he sees what God hath wrought of them.

And thou, Pennsylvania? For eighteen years you have given your testimony to the world that it is possible for men of widely differing cultures and temperaments to live side by side in peace and harmony. There are no militia patroling your borders and no bristling stockades protecting your towns. Governments of other colonies have learned to come to you for advice in settling their differences with Indian tribes. Recently a Quaker couple left their isolated cabin full of children for several days to travel into Philadelphia and attend Yearly Meeting. During their absence Indian neighbors kept watch over the children for them. Your peace treaties have endured and will endure as long as your founder lives, and when they finally fail the first violation will not be committed by an Indian.

With Penn on his return to America was a young man of twenty-five, named James Logan, of Scottish Quaker parentage, born in Lurgan, County Armagh, Ireland, a language prodigy who knew Latin, Greek, Hebrew, French, Italian and Spanish, a mathematician, and ultimately an amateur scientist. Logan was beginning to establish himself as a merchant trader between Dublin and Bristol when Penn invited him to go to America as his personal secretary. Fortunately for both of them Logan accepted, Logan to rise from the role of obscure pedant to statesman, Penn to acquire a trusted and devoted assistant as close to him as his own right arm for the rest of his life. Logan's arrival meant that there were two devoted young men to serve Penn in America—Logan and Story—but Logan and Story were to show little devotion to one another, because destiny had cast them, says the legend, in the roles of rival suitors for the hand of Edward Shippen's daughter, Ann. Shippen was Philadelphia's first Mayor.

When Penn reached Philadelphia he waited immediately upon Governor Markham, and then, since it was First Day, he repaired to the Friends' Meeting House at Second and High to deliver the chief sermon and prayer. He established his family and secretary at Edward Shippen's house, a mansion known as the Governor's House on the west side of Second Street a little north of Spruce. In about a month the Penn family moved to the Slate Roof House, Samuel Carpenter's sumptuous home, also on Second Street. Pictures still exist of the Slate Roof House with its modified Elizabethan lines, built in the shape of a U, its two ells shortened and its courtyard reduced to an entryway. At that time it was surrounded by elaborate gardens and a wall and its interior divided into several apartments, making it possible for Penn to live in the stately elaborateness befitting the Governor of so big and prosperous a province.

Penn took hold of the governmental situation immediately and with a firm hand, plunging into a schedule strenuous enough to have tired a man many years younger than himself, and his energy and zeal could still have an electrifying effect on those who worked with him or even stood at the road as he passed by. He was undoubtedly stouter in his fifties than he had been in his thirties, but the forthrightness, the open-faced candor, the faith and perspective were still there. The same Penn had come back to Pennsylvania, the same visionary, the same creative genius, organizer, influencer-of-other-men, peacemaker, great-hearted administrator. Diplomatic letters flowed from his writing table—to Governor Nicholson in Virginia desiring "with all sincerity a good understanding among the governments of the provinces under the Crown" and pointing to the suppression of illegal trade and roving pirates as their most conspicuous mutual problem; to Nathaniel Blackistone, royal Governor of Maryland, respectfully saluting him and expressing pleasure at having "so fair and honourable a neighbor," making specific reference to a physician of Captain Kidd's who pretends to have left Kidd (arrested the previous summer) but whom Penn has clapped into prison; to a member of the New York government, thanking him for his civility in writing first and expressing sympathy that the churlish climate has so badly affected the Earl of Bellomont's gout; to Lord Bellomont, Governor of Massachusetts and New York, commiserating with him and wishing him speedy relief from his discomfort; to the Governor of the Barbados saluting him as a neighbor governor; to the General of Jamaica a few loving observations about Pennsylvania's intent to stamp out piracy and illegal trade; to John Nanfan, Lieutenant Governor of New York, a goodwill item and more observations on their mutual interests.

He began to travel about his province to observe conditions at firsthand, and less than two weeks after his arrival we find him attending the court in Chester with Thomas Story. On the first day of January he held a meeting in Philadelphia of the Provincial Council that had not been convened since the previous May, informing them of the necessity of calling a General Assembly and passing laws to suppress piracy and illegal trade. The next day he was in Haverford visiting with Story among the Welsh Friends. On the third, fourth and fifth he held Council meetings in Philadelphia, devoting most of the time to a problem that had been waiting for him and must be added to those the Crown had visited upon him: discontent with the existing *Frame of Government*. Robert Turner and three others brought in the letter they had originally addressed to Markham complaining that they had lost many of their privileges granted by the original *Frame*. If the Governor would call an election for March 10 next, to choose representatives to Council and Assembly as prescribed by the original *Frame*, they felt the newly elected bodies with the Governor could then work out together the best possible *Frame of Government* for the province. Their proposal was well received, for election writs were issued a week later.

William Penn and Thomas Story spent a week in Burlington in the middle of January, visiting among Friends and picking up the life lines of New Jersey's political affairs.

In the Slate Roof House between three and four in the afternoon on January 28, 1700, John Penn was born. He was known in later years as "the American," the only one of William Penn's children born in the New World. "My wife is safely laid of a boy and both well for their time," Penn wrote proudly to Lord Bellomont. "Their little son is a comely, lovely babe, and has much of his father's grace and air, and hope he will not want a good portion of his mother's sweetness, who is a woman extremely well beloved here, exemplary in her station, and of excellent spirit," was the opinion of Isaac Norris, a member of the Assembly.

Penn's first grandchild had been born at Worminghurst the previous November 10, while he and Hannah were on the high seas, named Gulielma Maria for her late grandmother.

Very shortly after his arrival in America, Penn called the existing Assembly together, and by February 28 he was able to write to the Commissioners of Customs in London that two laws, one against pirates and the other against forbidden trade, had been enacted. Next came the problem of enforcement, since the now imprisoned Kidd had many counterparts. Even when a pirate was captured, what was to be done with the prize cargo? Whitehall wanted pirates shipped back to England for trial, and the King wanted all of the booty. Penn begged to be allowed to keep enough of the booty to pay the cost of policing the coasts and shipping the prisoners back to England. Unlike any other governor, he reminded Whitehall, he was operating his province entirely out of his own pocket.

Any question relating to trade inevitably led straight into that of the Admiralty courts and Colonel Quary. In very olden days England had divided her plentiful coastline into vice admiralties, each with its court that met at least once a year to hear the complaints of seafaring men and mariners living within its jurisdiction, keeping a roll of both men and ships, handling cases dealing with division of captured booty, seamen's wages, bottomry (mortgaging the ship to borrow money), contracts made outside of England, freight, foreign debts, and misdemeanors committed on the high seas—problems not covered by England's common law. After Queen Elizabeth's reign enforcement of the Admiralty laws declined, until some thirty years after her death when an Act of King and Council straightened out jurisdictional problems between the Admiralty and Westminster. But the civil wars disrupted the results. After the Restoration Sir William Batten, Sir William Penn and ninety-seven other petitioners waited upon King and Council for a revitalizing of the laws and clarification of their jurisdiction. The King and

Council of a nation well on her way to eminence as a sea power wisely listened to her top naval men, but in 1700 the problem was still not solved, and Sir William's son had to deal with it in Pennsylvania.

Indigenous resentment toward the Vice Admiralty court was more responsible than any other single factor in fostering the subsequent cleavage lines in the Pennsylvania government. Robert Quary's Church of England Party was opposed by the Assembly Party led by David Lloyd, and both were opposed to the Proprietary interests. The three-way split was highlighted by a test case arising out of conflicting court jurisdiction. A well-to-do merchant named John Adams had arrived from New York before the customs inspection at New Castle with a large, valuable cargo. He lacked a necessary certificate which the navigation laws required, and the King's collector seized his cargo and placed it in the care of the marshal of the Vice Admiralty court. Adams hurriedly obtained the necessary certificate, but when he requested his cargo Quary declined. Adams appealed to Governor Markham with no results. He then appealed to the Philadelphia County court which issued a writ of replevin (writ for obtaining cargo unlawfully detained) in his behalf, and with that in his hand he obtained his cargo. The County court's action in superseding the Vice Admiralty court would have caused trouble enough, but David Lloyd, then Attorney General of the province, and vehemently opposed to Quary, made matters worse by persuading Adams to sue the marshal for damages. Lloyd himself represented the plaintiff and John Moore, advocate of the Vice Admiralty court, the defendant. Lloyd with all his brilliance and histrionics could not win the case, and the court decided in favor of the marshal. The case had just concluded when William Penn arrived, and Lloyd rushed to the Proprietor and asked to be allowed to appeal the case to Westminster. Knowing better than any of the Pennsylvanians how delicate and susceptible to change the London situation was, Penn refused. To pour oil on the local waters, when Quary appeared at the sessions of the Provincial Council to complain against Anthony Morris, the justice who had signed the writ of replevin, and against David Lloyd, William Penn relieved both men of their public posts. Penn's efforts to placate Quary by dismissing Lloyd threw Lloyd into the camp of the opposition as its vigorous and popular leader for many years to come. James Logan later observed that Lloyd was "a man of sound judgment, a good lawyer, but pertinacious and somewhat revengeful."

Walking a tightrope of tensions among his government men, Penn was at the same time guiding the grand committee that had been appointed out of the newly elected Council to consider the *Frame of Government*. The committee could not come to an agreement on the revision of the *Frame*, and in June they passed it back to the Proprietor. "Since you were dissatisfied with the Charter you had, and that you could not agree among yourselves about a new one, I shall be easy in ruling you by the King's letters patent and act of union," Penn told them.

Before the Assembly adjourned it voted Penn an impost upon liquors which they estimated would net him a thousand pounds a year, as an alternative to a bill giving him a three pound tax. "They would seem to come off with flying colors," Isaac Norris wrote to Philip Ford, "but I do not think it worth one half the money."

Shortly after those strenuous June sessions the Penn family fled from the heat of Philadelphia. Pennsbury could not have gone so completely to rack and ruin as Penn had dismally believed, for it served as his home for the rest of his stay in America. Pennsbury was rather remote and difficult to reach; roads where they existed at all were almost impassible, and the only comfortable means of communication was by water, either in Penn's barge or by boat. Hannah became mistress of the lovely red brick mansion, and she and Letitia managed the place with an ample domestic staff. It became a center of hospitality, and its board creaked under the burden of plenitude, just as the board had once creaked at Wanstead; here it held beef, mutton, pork, smoked shad, claret, madeira, ale and cider, Indian corn and English peas, complemented by fine damask linens, silver, and even fragile table china to supplement the pewter. Penn complained in July that his leg was out of order and swelled about the ankle, but it did not prevent him from making frequent trips to Philadelphia. He was down six times in July, eight in August, once in September. James Logan remained at the

Slate Roof House, and acted as his tireless liaison, sending meticulous letters and reports to Pennsbury and carrying out endless instructions that Penn sent him, dealing with everything from governmental details to orders for household supplies.

The Five Nations Indians who lived in the Susquehanna Valley had learned to love and trust Penn. After seven years of patient negotiating with both the New York government and the Susquehanna tribes, Penn finally succeeded in winning from the Indians a deed, dated September 13, 1700, granting him "all the said River Susquehanna and all the islands therein and all the lands situate lying and being upon both sides of the said river and next adjoining to the same extending to the utmost confines of the lands, which are or formerly were the right of the people or nation called the Susquehanna Indians." He had managed to obtain a deed and release from Colonel Dongan in 1696, but he waited for the Indians to capitulate in their own due time.

Penn initiated an important conference of the four colonial governments of New York, Massachusetts, Virginia and Pennsylvania. From the first to the fifth of October, he sat in the company of the Earl of Bellomont and of Colonel Nicholson at New York to further his plan for a union of the English colonies. Blackistone had started out for New York, but illness forced him to turn back. Once the idea of a union had come alive in Penn's mind its virtues were so obvious to himself that he could not resist it, and during the four years that had elapsed since his first presentation of the plan to Whitehall he had accumulated an additional list of new arguments: the value of money could be standardized throughout the colonies, a mint could be set up at New York to alleviate the currency shortage, court procedures could be standardized and cases appealed across borders, criminals and debt-dodgers apprehended, pirates more efficiently dealt with, transfer of land titles made easier, life lines of inter-colonial commerce cleared. Hopefully Penn and the other governors sent a detailed report of their findings to the Lords of Trade. Looking back over the centuries it is almost impossible to understand why Whitehall could not have seen the wisdom of such a proposal, but Whitehall continued her divide-and-rule colonial policy and turned her attention to more immediate concerns—the throne of the defunct Spanish empire was about to fall into the French orbit, and England was rushing into a preventive alliance with Austria, Holland, Brandenburg-Prussia, Hanover, the Palatinate and eventually Portugal. The excellent hopes of the well-intended colonial governors went begging. Penn wrote to Governor Blackistone promising him a copy of their report to Whitehall and inquiring after his health. "I hope this will find the air of Maryland more favorable to thee than that of our river, which at such a time was a great mortification to me. Governor Nicholson was knocked down that night and came but feebly to Elizabeth Town where we halted two and a half days and a night and very low indeed. His weakness continued several days so that it was but once in a day or two we could discourse of anything. However, seven or eight particulars were agreed upon. . . ."

The weather that autumn must have been dismal indeed, for Penn himself finished up in his bed at Pennsbury with a cold and fever. "His sweating last night, something relieved him, but not so as to be capable of going to town without great hazard of his health, which has prevailed with him to stay till tomorrow," Hannah reported to James Logan. Penn was spoiling to be in New Castle where the Assembly was already in session, to continue to placate the hostile Quary and prevent him from making too much trouble in Whitehall, to try to control the perverse David Lloyd who buzzed around Quary's head like a persistent bluebottle, and to consult with Thomas Story who was reading the laws carefully and observing "their shortness and other defects." Hannah's protests could not hold him in Pennsbury long, in the face of so many pressing affairs, and a letter to his "esteemed friend" Colonel Quary of November 11 is datelined New Castle. That Assembly session of nearly seven weeks was wearing, "much teasing, and sometimes almost off the hinges, for they would creak loudly; then we used to sit and reduce ourselves to good order again. Some turbulent spirits would often endeavor to drive it to a pitched battle betwixt upper counties and lower, Quakers and Churchmen. . . ." said Isaac Norris. However, they did manage to compile ninety new laws out of the old ones, and get them into shape to be sent to England for approval, and to vote the Governor two thousand sorely needed pounds.

The split between the upper counties and the three that would eventually comprise the state of Delaware was developing slowly and inevitably, but the battle "between Quakers and Churchmen"—or more specifically the feud between William Penn and Robert Quary—was the big battle of the hour and was finding its way straight to Whitehall in long detailed complaints from both men. Quary accused Penn of allowing illegal trade in his province, of not enforcing the acts passed against it by the Assembly, of appointing water bailiffs of his own thereby invading the jurisdiction of the Admiralty court, of failing to establish a militia, of making friends with the French Indians. He complained of the £2,000 outright and the additional annual income in taxes that the Assembly had voted Penn; he gleefully exploited the hostility between upper and lower counties, reopened the wound of the Maryland dispute by questioning Penn's right to govern the three lower counties. As for the Pennsylvania courts, a murderer had been pardoned here, a jury had proceeded illegally there. Really a broadside! Penn replied with an experienced writer's skill. That the government was permitting illegal trade was news to him; he wanted proof of any neglect in enforcing laws against it. As for the water bailiffs, Penn had appointed them because Quary was away from his Admiralty court post for months at a time attending to his own trading affairs. There was as much militia in Pennsylvania as there had been in Colonel Fletcher's day, and anyone who knew these vast stretches of wilderness knew no militia could defend it anyway. "I never, to my knowledge, invited or entertained one French Indian in my life; but discouraged Frenchmen, employed by Colonel Quary, or his customers, from trading with *our* Indians." Penn's services to the King and his personal losses in operating Pennsylvania made a long paragraph in answer to the complaint about the small amounts allowed him by the Assembly, so did the charge about his right to govern the three lower counties. To the "foul charge" about justice, the records of the county were open to inspection. Another set of complaints from Quary; another set of replies from Penn, followed by a special set of specific complaints against Quary as a judge of the Vice Admiralty court. Quary was unacquainted with civil law, and thus did not even know when cases brought before him properly belonged in the common law courts. Quary himself had become a great merchant in the province, which rendered him highly partial in such matters, and he had shown deliberate favoritism to some merchants and undue harshness to others. It was another kind of tract battle, and the tracts grew more virulent as one followed another.

Penn convened his Council at New Castle on October 14, 1700, feeling no doubt that such a gesture would have some healing effect upon the attitude in the lower counties, and on the third day when the entire Assembly and Council met together he urged upon them the importance of drawing up a *Frame of Government* and a body of laws "without which society cannot subsist." The Council then sat in almost continuous session, except for First Days, through the balance of October and the entire month of November.

In the midst of the political tribulations there flashed another ray of private happiness, a family news note from Worminghurst to warm and gladden the heart of a harassed statesman who secretly felt his resilience flagging a little and his schedule circumscribed by a developing susceptibility to ill health. Another child was born to William Penn, Jr.'s wife on February 10, 1701—a "brave boy"—a new Springett to take the place of the lost heir. John, the American, had just passed his first birthday, and Hannah wrote of him to Elizabeth Taylor (a daughter of Richard Vickris) in London: "My dear little boy grows bravely; he's very pleasant and lively, much like his father, in whom he takes great delight, is well beloved of his sister, and indeed proves a great comfort and diversion to us all. I have suckled him myself hitherto but think of weaning him in a little time. He has fine teeth and can go alone very well if he pleases." So there were to be two sets of children growing up together—Penn's and his son's.

Penn made a personal journey down through the lower counties in April, 1701, all the way into Sussex, where he discovered that the lines setting off the three lower counties from Maryland ordered by Whitehall in 1685 had not yet been run. Some of his tenants in Sussex had been forced off their lands by "some in authority in Somerset County in Maryland, as the affidavits which accomplished this express, and in a manner too that was an aggravation of the breath of good neighborhood and no line run or order from home to back it," he wrote to the Governor of Maryland. "I beg you therefore that since delay of running of the line lies not at my door I may not suffer by it."

Ford's son, Philip Ford, Jr., appeared on the Philadelphia scene in the late spring of 1701, and was entertained in the home of Isaac Norris. With youthful arrogance he called upon William Penn and demanded the "rent" due his father under the terms of their lease. If it were not paid, he declared, the lease would be published; Penn managed to pacify him. But the real purpose of his trip was to establish contact for his father with Penn's most potent enemies in America—David Lloyd and Robert Quary. That accomplished, he sailed for home.

A deep and abiding source of comfort to Penn was the unshakable faith and trust that existed between himself and the Indians, and it lasted as long as he lived. That same April, chieftains of the Susquehannas—Conestogas, Shawnese, Potomacs and Onondagas—with many companions, some forty Indians in all, met with William Penn in Council in Philadelphia for another peace treaty. The text of their Articles of Agreement reaffirmed their friendship and trust and they agreed never to injure or defraud one another. The Indians promised to respect the laws of Pennsylvania and to remain loyal to the Crown. Penn (and his heirs and successors) agreed to protect the Indians against trade abuses, to allow the Potomac Indians to settle anywhere along the Potomac River that they wished within the bounds of Pennsylvania and the Conestogas along the Susquehanna. In witness whereof the Indians presented Penn with five parcels of skins and Penn gave them the equivalent in English merchandise.

In June Penn returned the diplomatic gesture by traveling to the Susquehanna Valley to visit them.

"I am just come home from Susquehanna," Isaac Norris wrote to a friend on June 21, "where I have been to meet the Governor. We had a roundabout journey, having pretty well traversed the wilderness. We lived nobly at the King's palace on Conestoga, and from thence crossed it to Schuylkill, where we fell in about thirty miles up from hence."

Penn even became an impartial mediator of wars between Indian tribes, one such incident occurring immediately after his trip to Susquehanna. He wrote to Nanfan of New York about it on July 2: "I find the sachems of our Indians (that I am told make at least 1,000 fighting men) take it well and resolve to quit their war with the Carolina Indians and refer themselves to me upon all differences with the Indians in the governments under the Crown of England."

Some time during his second summer in America Penn broke his shin; he refers to it in a letter to James Logan from Pennsbury dated July 17; but he was in Philadelphia for Council meetings the end of June, the fourteenth and twenty-sixth of July, and the entire first week of August, so it could not have incapacitated him too much. On the twenty-third of July he wrote to Logan from Pennsbury to tell him that he and Tishe both had colds and fever, and that Hannah was coming to Philadelphia with a document that could not be trusted to a lesser messenger.

Penn was beginning to receive disturbing news from abroad which he could peruse with both hindsight and foresight and realize how closely it would touch upon the security and welfare of the province. War in Europe would mean war in America, because the chief combatants were England and France, two of the three big colonial holders in the New World, and that would mean terrific pressure on Pennsylvania for military aid. When England was at war, her capital filled with ruthless self-seekers, men greedy after profits, personal glory, influence; and once launched upon a war she had to sublimate every resource and every good to winning. For some time a trend of thought had been developing in Whitehall favoring the royal province over the proprietary form, and that made fertile soil for Quary's complaints and for the machinations of others who hated Penn. If England decided to consolidate her efforts, she might well snatch Pennsylvania back and place the province under a governor appointed by the Crown. Virginia, New Hampshire and New York were already royal colonies, and Massachusetts had been made so only ten years earlier. The Maryland proprietorship had been suspended in 1692 and a governor appointed by the Crown. Could not the Crown realize how economical it was to establish colonies at the cost of others? "I only wish myself twenty years younger and no Englishman. I would hope to enjoy the fruit of my labor and receive the return of my deep and sinking experience. For instead of enriching me it pays not the debt the Crown owed my father, but involved me in twenty thousand pounds sterling to bring it to pass." Perhaps Pennsylvania's real crime was her prosperity.

The trend began to solidify into an actual bill before Parliament to bring the proprietary governments under the Crown. Penn's colony was to be taken away from him "without a trial," and the excuses for doing so were plentiful. Pennsylvania had an "independent government"; she allowed piracy to go unchecked; her Proprietor made judicial appointments that infringed upon the jurisdiction of the Admiralty; she was carrying on secret trade via the Dutch island of Curaçao. Quite obviously Penn could best serve Pennsylvania's interest by being in London and appearing in person to answer such charges; but he *wasn't* in London, and even without a broken shin he couldn't get to London in time for the present session of Parliament. Penn did the next best thing; he began to write letters to England—a long report to the Lords of Trade refuting each accusation and promising to come and negotiate in person the affairs so important to himself and his family. "We renounce all independency both as our duty and security. . . . As for piracy, I know myself to be so innocent that I think myself meritorious instead of culpable." Regarding the Curaçao trade, a sloop had come up from there carrying illegal goods (claret, iron, linen cloth) and had transferred her cargo to a shallop that came but from Jersey and wasn't searched when she put in at a private wharf. Colonel Quary was informed of it at the time, but didn't do anything about it until six weeks later when the goods had passed to the hands of honest persons. Penn sent personal appeals to every high-ranking person he could think of—the Earl of Dorset, the Duke of Devonshire, the Marquis of Normanby, the Duke of Somerset, Lord Jefferys, Lord Pawlett, Sir Hennage Finch, Colonel Depeister, Lord Romney. "I have heard of the unfair treatment some have given me in my absence which I am apt to think one word from the King . . . would alter," Penn told Romney. "I was thus attacked in King James's time and when he came to know the ruin it would prove to me and my family he cried out God forbid. He would never be the author of such a cruelty. . . . I will depend upon the King's justice and goodness . . . at least I pray for time, since it is too long and dangerous a journey to remove presently as well as that it hath all the dishonorable appearance here, to be tossed thus about, both to Indians and Europeans."

The sudden unfortunate turn of events could not be kept from anyone, Indian or European, and the alarm and dismay at the prospect of losing Penn as Proprietor with all the guarantees that went with him was widespread in Pennsylvania. By September his impending return to Europe was official knowledge, for on the sixteenth he presented his Assembly with a formal address explaining the necessity of it: enemies of the prosperity of Pennsylvania were taking advantage of his absence. In less than a week the Assembly had prepared and presented to him an address or memorandum of twenty-one concerns. They wanted persons of integrity appointed to public office; they wanted the security of their property titles, an instrument from Penn guaranteeing their estates, efficient confirmation of future land grants, a safe depository for ancient documents and many other points. Penn replied promptly, agreeing to almost every item, and assuring them that some of their fears were groundless. He would execute the instrument they asked, and he fully intended to appoint those "in whom I can confide . . . and I hope they shall be of honest character."

In order to raise money for the voyage he instructed James Logan to "dispose of many good patches [of land] that else I should have chosen to have kept as everybody's money."

He wanted Hannah and Letitia to remain in America, but Hannah flatly refused. She had had quite enough of the New World. He could not prevail upon her to remain, even though he pointed out that all he had "to dispose of in this world is here for daughter and son and all the issue which this wife is like to bring me." If anything remained to be salvaged from his Irish or English estates it would go under the laws of England to the only surviving son of his first marriage. Letitia appeared ready to return to England, too, and she requested of the Philadelphia Monthly Meeting a letter certifying that she was "clear of any engagements" to wed. There had been some gossip around about herself and William Masters of Philadelphia that she apparently wanted to clear up, and the letter which Philadelphia gave her left no room for doubt that she "hath behaved herself very soberly, and according to the good instruction which she hath received in the way of Truth." She was "well-inclined, courteously carriaged, and sweetly tempered . . . a diligent comer to meetings."

Before his departure, the Delaware tribes, from "near a hundred miles around," gathered at Pennsbury "to settle our future good understanding," and to review their former covenants with Penn. All was done "in much calmness of temper and in an amicable way," and in reply to Penn's assurances of good faith one of the chieftains stepped forward to speak. They had never broken a covenant with any people, and he struck his hand on his head three times to show that they did not make covenants there but in their hearts, and he struck his hand on his heart three times. After they had settled their business there was an exchanging of gifts and then a long, friendly conversation on their religious beliefs. It's interesting that at this conference Penn used an interpreter; perhaps pressure of events had not allowed him to keep up his original study of the Indian language, particularly during the fifteen years he was in England.

Since the Maryland proprietorship had been suspended, feelings between Lord Baltimore and William Penn had lost their bitterness and the two men were almost friendly. Penn attended Friends' Yearly Meeting at Tredhaven, Maryland, in October 1701; to one of its meetings for worship came Lord and Lady Baltimore and several companions, and they and Penn conversed graciously together.

The imminence of his departure served to stimulate his legislative bodies to conclude a great many unfinished items of business, the most important of which was the new *Frame of Government*, or *Charter of Privileges*. Its final form, as approved by Council and Assembly, was signed by Penn on October 28, 1701. The most important single factor in the new Charter was the complete shift in emphasis from the Council to the Assembly. As in the 1696 interim Charter, laws once initiated by the Council and approved by the Assembly, now were created by the larger more representative body. Freedom of conscience had been the leaven working in the loaf for nearly twenty years, and there had been a continuous growth toward more self-government with an ever increasing participation of the people in the creative branch of the government.

The city of Philadelphia received its first Charter at this same session, permitting it to have its own city administration.

Penn appointed Andrew Hamilton to be Lieutenant Governor of Pennsylvania. Hamilton was a proprietor of East New Jersey and had been Governor of both the Jerseys. James Logan became Secretary of the Province and Clerk of the Council.

William and Hannah Penn, Letitia, and the infant John were aboard the *Dolmahoy* on November 3, and from the ship Penn sent a final set of instructions to James Logan. "Use thy utmost endeavors in the first place to receive all that is due me. Get in quitrents; sell lands according to my instructions. . . . Thou mayst continue in the house I lived in [in Philadelphia] till the year is up. Pay off my notes . . . discharge all my debts. . . . Thou must make good to Colonel Hamilton, my Deputy Governor, two hundred pounds per annum . . . write to me diligently . . . send all the household goods up to Pennsbury, unless thou inclinest to keep sufficient furniture for a chamber to thyself. . . . For thy own services I shall allow thee what is just and reasonable, either by commission or a salary. But my dependence is on thy care and honesty."

They were making a winter crossing and could expect strenuous usage from the sea, but their ship's quarters were of the best. Penn contracted with the captain for the "free use of the whole great cabin of the ship," for a charge of fifty guineas and three pounds per head for all but the baby.

Another returning to the crowded city of London with her noises, cross-currents and tight-strung nerves. The older Penn grew the more he preferred the peace to be found in wide open countryside, but such peace was a luxury to be laid aside when he was personally responsible for so many destinies. If Pennsylvania passed out of his hands, the Friends would lose their refuge and liberty of conscience its capital. And while he was about it—during those trying diplomatic waits for audiences and hearings—there would be an abundance of other cares to which he could attend: affairs of his children, grandchildren, and two sets of inlaws, Friends' meetings that needed ministry—and Philip Ford.

Never was there any person more barbarously treated or baited with undeserved enemies. He has been able to foil all attacks from public adversaries, but 'tis his fortune to meet with greatest severities from those that owe most to him. One would think there was almost a commission granted, as one against Job, for his trial.

—James Logan to Thomas Callowhill, August 13, 1706

20. *Penn versus Ford*

"We had a swift passage—twenty-six days from the capes to soundings, and thirty to Portsmouth, with five of the last days clear for observation, before we came to the channel. The captain very civil and all the company. Tishe and Johnne, after the first five days, hearty and well, and Johnne exceeding cheerful all the way."

The only thing that went wrong, Penn went on in his letter to James Logan, was that his tender leg had received a rub about four days before coming into the Channel, which laid him up in town for a while, but it was now better. Hannah was going to her father in Bristol and taking Johnne with her. She was by then within two months of another delivery and no doubt wanted to be with her family when her second child was born. As for his grandchildren, they were "a sweet girl and a Saracen of a boy." William the Younger was another matter, of a lesser fiber, his father had returned home to discover; twenty-two, yet woefully immature and irresponsible. To Logan Penn covertly described the lad as "very serviceable, but costly." There was a return of the Cavalier in William, Jr., a longing for surface luster and the plumes and ruffled cuffs his father had renounced. He was to be the next Proprietor, and so his father drew him into Pennsylvania's affairs as soon as he arrived back in England, but as Penn watched this only surviving son of his first marriage, he had to realize that he lacked the depth to operate effectively without parental supervision. In 1702 Penn was willing to defend him as "serviceable but costly," though he knew in his heart that "serviceable" was not enough to administer a province and "costly" would be impossible on Pennsylvania's quitrents. Pennsylvania was a mistress who demanded of her highest Sachem brilliance, insight, prescience, tact, dignity, humility, fortitude, faith and a great fund of energy both physical and spiritual. William, Jr., like so many sons of the great, was considerably less of a man than his father, and in another few years would forfeit the Founder's confidence altogether. Meanwhile, the aging Penn dared not do otherwise than shoulder the full responsibility for the proprietorship himself.

"Nothing yet done in my affairs, but my coming I do more and more see necessary," he observed in January.

There had been nothing done partly because England was in a turmoil of war preparations. The Grand Alliance had not yet declared war on France, but it was only a matter of weeks. France had already violated the treaty that ended the last war with England by seizing Dutch fortresses in the Spanish Netherlands and by recognizing the son of the deposed James II as King of England. And there had been nothing done partly because the first parliamentary bill against the proprietaries had been quashed, and those who plotted to ruin the proprietaries had to lose a certain amount of time engineering another bill up through the House of Commons. "Our foolish and knavish enemies" was Penn's way of describing them, and to further their ends they had called Colonel Quary home to England to aid them with his on-the-spot knowledge of Pennsylvania's internal politics.

William Penn once more chose Kensington as his residence so that he would be within convenient distance of Whitehall, and Tishe remained with him for a while. Her presence was fortunate for him and convenient for her, because he came down with a fever for a few days near the end of January and needed her care, and she could be near the man she intended to marry, William Aubrey, a merchant of White Lyon Court, London.

Thomas Penn, the Founder's second child of his second family, was born at the home of his grandfather, Thomas Callowhill, in Bristol on March 9, 1702. Nothing could bring home more acutely to a parent the peril of his economic situation than another child whose future must be provided for.

"Hasten over rents, etc. all thou canst, for many call upon me for old scores, thinking I have brought over all the world with me," Penn wrote to James Logan. "The war is likely, and goods bear a price. Deer skins and bear skins, tobacco—" And in June: "Never had poor man my task—neither men or money to assist me. I therefore strictly charge thee that thou represent it to Friends there that I am distressed for want of supply; that I am forced to borrow money, and add debt to debt instead of paying them; besides my uncomfortable distance from my family. . . . My wife hitherto is kept by her father, whence she is coming next week to Worminghurst, on my daughter's account, in likelihood to marry."

Faithful Logan! None had ever taken hold more earnestly of the proprietary interests than he; none had ever tried harder or come closer to succeeding in collecting quitrents and conveying them to England than he. But the root of the financial problem lay in the economic patterns of the times. Pennsylvania, like other English colonies, suffered from a shortage of currency, and during the first decade of the eighteenth century the shortage grew more and more acute. "The country, even where willing, cannot pay for want of money," Logan explained carefully to Penn, "and for the same reason the subscriptions are very much behind, not for want of good will, but for want of some way to bring it into my hands, for all our trade is now by discount and transfer of debts." Logan immediately called upon his own earlier experiences as an international merchant and tried to buy bills of exchange, drawing upon English merchants for credit. But bills could not be bought with produce which was all the colonists had to offer; nothing but hard, cold cash would do. Penn instructed Logan to send produce, and Logan began to ship beer, flour, bread, pork, tobacco, skins. Some of the cargo arrived safely. It seemed like a solution. Optimistically Logan purchased on Penn's behalf a part interest in the brigantine *Hopewell* and in another ship called the *Industry* (or *Cantico*). But the world was at war; the high seas were alive with danger. The *Industry* was soon captured, and the *Hopewell's* cargo "barbarously fooled away" by an unreliable crew. What cargoes were successfully shipped did not yield enough to meet Penn's mounting costs.

Comforting Logan! At last there was someone in America who

never tired of writing home, meticulous, detailed and trustworthy accounts about every facet of life in Pennsylvania, letters filled with the minutiae of information that Penn needed for his peace of mind. "All things have gone very smooth and easy since thy departure. . . . The thousand acres was, last week, cut off from thy tract in East Jersey . . . having had three hundred pounds bid for it. . . . That lump of scandal, George Keith, has left us for Virginia. . . . They misinform who say the place [Pennsbury] goes to ruin. . . . There comes now a full copy of all the laws in force, under the great seal, by order of the Council. . . . Edward Penington's decease, of the smallpox, of which I suppose thou hast heard by Isaac Norris, cast us much back. . . David Lloyd carries on smooth, but is the same at heart. . . . Philadelphia town being above half the inhabitants, two-thirds of those I believe are no Friends, which brings town and country, as I judge, near upon a balance, the greater part of the country being Friends. . . . Governor Hamilton acquits himself well by an easy carriage, but dare strain nothing for want of approbation. . . . The town mill goes well. . . . Old Peter died last week at Pennsbury. . . . Thomas Story is returned from his northern tour. . . . A fever alone, and a fever and ague, rages amongst us here very violently; the fever is not at all mortal, but is exceeding afflicting. . . . The mournful news of the King's death, of which we first heard last week, will, I fear, strike a great damp on business. . . ."

Any damp caused in Pennsylvania by the death of William III was highly temporary, for with the accession of Anne to the throne Penn emerged once more into the bright rays of royal clemency. Anne was English, and a Stuart; James II had been her father, Charles I her grandfather. And Anne was a tolerationist; her reign was one of Whig supremacy, of free intellectual growth, of expanded empire, of a strengthened Parliament. The opening years of the eighteenth century in England belonged to Addison and Steele, Alexander Pope, Daniel Defoe, Jonathan Swift. Literary satire pecked away at the religious dogmas and passions of the seventeenth century; doubt gained new stature as an intellectual virtue; the thinking of such men as John Locke gave the individual new values; public ethics and political morality shed their radical garbs and became respectable.

Queen Anne promised England that she would maintain the Act of Toleration, and in the first year of her reign she was waited upon by a delegation of Quakers headed by William Penn; they brought from their Yearly Meeting "the humble and thankful acknowledgment of the people commonly called Quakers." The Queen's generous response to Penn was: "Mr. Penn, I am so well pleased that what I have said is to your satisfaction, that you and your friends may be assured of my protection."

With the sudden change in the political picture, Penn was not certain whether to remain in England or return to America. "I have had the wisest men in England, and of the greatest, to advise with . . . that love me, and all say, stay a while; be not hasty." Penn's energies were waning; it wasn't hard for him to put off a long sea voyage. There were times when even the journey from Worminghurst to London was too much, as he wrote to the Lords of Trade early that summer, "I was too infirm to stand an hour or two with legs as feeble as mine are well known to have been. . . . I came but three nights ago to my family and neither the condition of that nor my own health allow me to post up."

He had returned to Worminghurst for Letitia's wedding. She and William Aubrey had made their first declaration to wed before the Horsham Monthly Meeting of July 8, 1702, and their second declaration on August 12, and Letitia had given her monthly meeting the letter from Philadelphia regarding her clearness there. The letter from Philadelphia proved fortunate foresight, because William Masters turned up at Worminghurst and tried to claim that she was engaged to him. All James Logan said of it in a letter to Letitia was: "We exceedingly long, dear mistress, to hear of you, and especially to be put out of doubt about thy marriage, which is commonly reported here, if so, I wish thee happiness, and shall say no more." To Letitia's brother he was more detailed, and William, Jr., wrote back: "I was much surprised at what you wrote to me about my sister's engagement to W. Masters, but we find little in it, for she has been at the meetings, and he was here, but could prove no engagement, so it passed the meetings, and she is to be married the day after tomorrow." And a little later to someone else: "William Masters, whatever grounds he had for it in Pennsylvania, made a mighty noise here, but it lasted not long."

The wedding, which took place August 20, 1702, brought the whole Penn family together for a while, but not for long. Tishe was soon gone to her own home, Penn was planning to send William, Jr., and his family to America, and Hannah was going to Bristol for the birth of her third child. Want of funds had forced Hannah to return to Bristol; Pennsylvania's affairs forced Penn back to London; and out of his loneliness he sought consolation once more at his writing table. *More Fruits of Solitude* was the result, published in the year 1702.

Philip Ford had died in January, 1702, almost immediately after Penn's return, and at the time it seemed that the only problem arising out of his death was the increased amount of administrative detail that Penn had to handle himself. But Ford had betrayed an old promise to Penn not to mention in his will the Pennsylvania arrangement they had made; he drew up a new will shortly before his death providing that his Pennsylvania interests should be sold for the benefit of his wife and children unless Penn paid a sum of more than eleven thousand pounds plus all arrears of rents within six months. The bereaved widow, Bridget Ford, as her husband's executrix and as one of the trustees of the Pennsylvania holdings, descended upon Penn, and in April at her dwelling in Water Lane, London, there occurred another ugly argument with several present. Bridget Ford wanted Penn's approval of accounts from April 1, 1697, to April 1, 1702. When he read the statement, he found that it included an acknowledgment of "rent" on the premises. The lease and conveyance which he had executed to her husband in 1697, Penn reminded Bridget, had been merely to save her husband taxes and he would not sign the statement unless it was clearly understood that the word "rent" was not to be construed to make her title absolute. Penn further insisted that he was reserving the right to examine the accounts and to make objections to errors. Bridget Ford and the company expressed their complete contentment. On this basis Penn executed the document.

But Bridget Ford's vindictive attitude and the betrayal of trust revealed in the will of Philip Ford forced Penn at last to realize how very grave his position was, and he confided in legal counsel—Henry Gouldney (host to Fox at the time of his death) and Herbert Springett, the late Guli's uncle. With Penn they went through his mountainous collection of papers and found sufficient statements of account from Ford to show that the fantastic balance claimed to be due him from Penn was fraudulently arrived at. The Fords had charged interest on advances and none on receipts; they had charged eight per cent when the legal rate was six; they had compounded interest upon interest; they had charged Penn with exorbitant agent's commissions; and throughout the accounts were a multitude of isolated bookkeeping items that were highly irregular. Even with so much evidence against them, the Fords struck a confident attitude. Bridget, her son Philip, and her two daughters would neither reason nor compromise; they wanted their full due; the document which Penn had executed to the late Philip Ford was a deed, and it gave them clear title to Pennsylvania. If Penn wanted his province back, he must pay.

Troubles never come singly. Penn's financial circumstances were growing rapidly worse, with a mountain of debt piling up. His son-in-law, Aubrey, was becoming abusive over unpaid dowry. His weak son was growing more dissolute. When the incorruptible proprietor of a province has passed his prime, the temptation to corrupt his heir is irresistible. The political picture in Pennsylvania was developing deeper cleavage lines. David Lloyd, who had fortified the resistance against Blackwell and later made the Admiralty courts his target, had become the personification of opposition, with James Logan for his nemesis. Lloyd, whose influence had been strong both in obtaining the Charter of 1696 from Markham and the *Charter of Privileges* from Penn in 1701, was really a man of much wider vision than Logan, but his assaults on Logan were highly vindictive and often petty. Logan's devotion to Penn and the proprietary interests was deeply personal, and because he was so trusted and trustworthy he enjoyed increasing personal power. He was, for instance, in complete charge of all land transactions and of all trade with the Indians. Quary, at least, had been reduced to the role of pest. Upon the accession of Queen Anne he was replaced by Roger Mompesson as Judge of the Admiralty and remained in Pennsylvania as Surveyor-

General of Customs. Thus the Pennsylvania political picture resolved itself into a duel between two extraordinary personalities—David Lloyd, Speaker of the Assembly, and James Logan, Secretary of the Province and Clerk of the Council.

Penn felt secure with Queen Anne. She had resisted Quary's efforts to discredit him in her sight, and she had approved the appointment of Hamilton as Lieutenant Governor after William III had declined to do so. He saw in her a real solution to Pennsylvania's financial and governmental problems, and on the eleventh of May, 1703, he petitioned the Lords Commissioners for Trade and Plantations to resign the government of his province to the Crown in exchange for a cash settlement, preservation of the laws and civil rights in the province, and "some few privileges that will not be thought, I believe, unreasonable." The Commissioners were interested, but they did not like Penn's terms, and left it to him to offer better ones. Logan was sympathetic to the surrender of the government to the Crown and impatient with Penn's desire to preserve the liberties of people who so little appreciated them. Increasing confusions and conflicts in the Pennsylvania government, as far as Logan was concerned, had arisen because Penn had granted too many privileges to people "who neither knew how to use them nor how to be grateful for them." He wrote frankly to Penn: "Were the government mine, I would as soon give it gratis as keep it, and I must say thy strange attachment to it is to me most unaccountable."

Meanwhile, Governor Hamilton had died, and Penn proposed John Evans to take his place, describing Evans to the Lords of Trade as a man with "a liberal education, been abroad and knows the world very well, is sober, discreet and of a good understanding for his time. No merchant, and so no temptation that way; no soldier, but has been in Flanders and observed the discipline of the troops. . . . Not in debt but lives like a gentleman upon his estate here. He is a single man, neither voracious nor extravagant and a known zealous member of the Church of England." But Evans was only twenty-six, a highly social fellow, with no understanding of colonial problems, destined to prove a very sorry choice indeed, although he received royal approval without any difficulty.

On July 30, 1703, at the home of Hannah's parents at Bristol, Hannah Margarita Penn was born, third child of the second marriage. "They [the two Hannahs] with my two sons, were lately well, and so am I, I bless God, at present," Penn told Logan. A third grandchild, William III, had been born at Worminghurst just the previous March.

Hannah Penn was growing frankly discontented with her long separation from her husband. By October of 1703 she was still in Bristol; her sons—John going on three and Thomas a year-and-a-half—scarcely knew their father; her daughter of nearly three months he had not seen at all.

She wrote to him on the thirteenth of October:

My own dearest,

Because I am ready to hope thou wilt put an end to this way of converse, ere another can come to thy hand, I am therefore willing to make use of this post to carry thee my dearest remembrances, and to tell thee, I cannot with any satisfaction endure thy absence much longer; and therefore I hope thy next will bring me the joyful account of thy coming to me since I am so constrained to abide from thee, or else we would not have lived so long apart as already we have done, and yet the many mercies I do enjoy I must not forget; but desire to be reverently thankful for that of our health, which through the goodness of our great preserver is continued, in a good measure to us all. My mother has not her ague as we feared, nor our little girl any fit since the first, but pretty well again; Johnne well and hearty, so Tomme when I last heard and myself pretty well, as is my father, cousins, etc. all desire to salute thee but none so dearly as her that with great patience as well as great satisfaction is

Thine own H.P.

It was his poverty, Penn tried to explain to her, that prevented their reunion, poverty caused by the slow motion of things where he was and by the continuing war. He was planning to let lodgings for them in or near London, he promised, with the services of a cook and maid. Besse tells us that about this time Penn moved to "Knightsbridge over against Hyde Park Corner," and this location of his lodgings is confirmed by two of his own letters datelined from Hyde Park.

Penn still thought longingly of the day when he would return to Pennsbury; his letters to Logan contain occasional instructions for its care. Pennsbury was a rich estate that could support itself, and there in quiet, secluded dignity its creator planned to finish out his days. His son William, whose trip to America was at last materializing, was going to live in Pennsbury meanwhile.

"We shall be exceedingly glad to see Master William here," Logan had assured Penn, "and, for my part, never be wanting in anything that may tend to thy or his interest and honor." Penn sent some specific instructions to Logan for his son's guidance. "Possess him, go with him to Pennsbury, advise him, contract and recommend his acquaintance. No rambling to New York, nor mongrel correspondence. . . . He has wit, kept the top company, and must be handled with much love and wisdom; and urging the weakness and folly of some behaviors, and the necessity of another conduct from interest and reputation, will go far. And get Samuel Carpenter, Edward Shippen, Isaac Norris, Phineas Pemberton, Thomas Masters, and such persons, to be soft, and kind, and teaching; it will do wonders with him, and he is conquered that way. Pretends much to honor."

William Penn, Jr., did not take his wife and children with him to America. Instead he set out on the same ship with the new Lieutenant Governor, John Evans, and the two young men arrived in Philadelphia on the second of February, 1704. In a very few days those who were charged with the care of Penn's heir began to understand his personality. "It is his stock of excellent good nature that in a great measure has led him out into his youthful sallies when too easily prevailed on," Logan told Penn. His amiability seemed to register well enough at first. In March a group of a hundred Indians, nine chieftains among them, called on him at Pennsbury and presented him with nine belts of wampum to ratify their peace treaties, and he received them with proper hospitality. But by the end of that same summer the reports coming to England about him grew more and more discouraging.

In August Isaac Norris wrote to a friend: "William Penn, Junior, quite gone off from Friends. He, being in company with some extravagants that beat the watch at Enoch Story's, was presented with them [in court]; which unmannerly and disrespectful act, as he takes it, gives him great disgust, and seems a waited occasion. He talks of going home in the Jersey man-of-war next month. I wish things had been better or he had never come." Penn and some companions had got into a street brawl with the night watch and the case had actually come into court. His raucous companions were so incensed by the "presentment of thy son by the grand jury to the mayor's court," Logan told the Proprietor, "that they have in the night time committed some disorders in the streets, in which himself, I think, has been no ways concerned."

A Council proclamation for the suppression of vice resulted from the incident, and the Proprietor heard from the Secretary of the Province again in September: "Mr. William, incensed at the barbarous treatment he received from the corporation in that act of theirs, thought himself obliged no longer to keep any measures with such as, making more than ordinary pretences to religion, could so little observe any rules of decency with him, or gratitude and respect to their founder; and, therefore, to show he would have no more communion with men of that temper, indulged himself in the same freedom others take, upon a visit to Lady Cornbury made to this place, while his lordship sat at Burlington, and so seems resolved to continue." Lord Cornbury was Edward Hyde, a grandson of Clarendon; he was Governor of New York and the Jerseys which had been united and made a Crown colony in the first year of Anne's reign. The Proprietor's son could not have found himself a lady to call upon who possessed more dangerous political potential than Lady Cornbury.

Young Penn quite naturally grew short of cash in America, and he sold his Schuylkill manor for £850.

Even David Lloyd, opposed though he was politically to the proprietary viewpoint, felt sufficient personal esteem for the Founder of Pennsylvania to write: "I suppose you will have a more ample account by others of the condition this poor Province is brought to by the late revels and disorders which young William Penn and his gang of loose fellows he accompanies with are found in, to the great grief of Friends and others in this place."

There were many in Philadelphia with less integrity than Lloyd, who were ready to exploit a foolish young man.

Penn had returned to Bristol with Hannah, where on November 7, 1704, her next child, Margaret, was born, and from Bristol Penn wrote sorrowfully to James Logan: "If my son prove very expensive I cannot bear it, but must place to his account what he spends above moderation, while I lie loaded with debt and interest here, else I shall pay dear for the advantage his going thither might entitle me to, since the subscribers and bondsmen cannot make ready pay, according to what he has received, for his land there. So excite his return, or to send for his family to him; for if he brings not wherewith to pay his debts here, his creditors will fall foul upon him most certainly."

"Let me take the freedom to request thee to be very tender toward him in thy resentment," Logan urged, "lest those he has already conceived from the abuses put upon him should by any addition precipitate him into ruin; he has much good nature, wants not very good sense, but is unhappy chiefly by indiscretion. 'Tis a pity his wife came not with him. There is scarce anything has a worse effect upon his mind than the belief thou hast a greater regard for thy second children than thy first."

William, Jr., returned to England at the end of the year and reached Worminghurst in January, 1705, full of airy, garrulous ambitions for himself—a career in the army or navy, perhaps, or a seat in the legislature. Upon arrival he had drawn a "bill for ten pounds to ride two hundred miles home." His father met him halfway between London and Worminghurst, and they spent only three hours together. Those hours must have been as filled with strain and heartbreak as the few hours the Founder had once spent with Sir William Penn to tell him that he had chosen a different way of life, that he was casting aside all the opportunities for the future that his father had worked so hard to create.

"O Pennsylvania! what hast thou cost me? Above thirty thousand pounds more than I ever got by it, two hazardous and most fatiguing voyages, my straits and slavery here, and my child's soul almost. . . ."

William Penn fell ill immediately thereafter, revealing the telltale symptoms in a letter to an acquaintance in Ireland. "Pardon this abrupt scribble, 'tis the third I have writ since a stroke of illness that has much affected my head."

Evans's administration in Pennsylvania was proving almost as discouraging as his son's disaffections. Vain, insensitive to the political atmosphere, Evans seemed to go out of his way to lose the esteem of Pennsylvanians, and consequently to lose it for the proprietary interests and make James Logan's task even harder than it was. William Biles rose in the Assembly to say, "He is but a boy; he is not fit to be our Governor. We'll kick him out; we'll kick him out." Immediately upon adjournment, Governor Evans brought an action against Biles for two thousand pounds, and David Lloyd, Speaker of the House, promptly came forward as Biles's attorney. The court action went against Biles, although it was reduced to three hundred pounds, but the reaction went against the Governor. Not long after that Evans flew straight into the face of the increasingly hostile Assembly by trying to force the establishment of a militia with a cheap public hoax. The war with France, still going on, had everyone on edge. One day, while crowds attended the fair in Philadelphia, a messenger rushed into town with the alarming "news" that a French fleet was on its way up the river. Dramatically the Governor sent warning messages out all over the province and himself rode on horseback through the streets with a naked sword in his hand, calling for volunteers for a militia. The panic was severe while it lasted; many fled, some burned their effects or hid them in wells, and many did join up, although Proud assures us that only four Quakers were inveigled into bearing arms.

Through it all Penn was still negotiating with the Privy Council for the surrender of his province to the Crown. "My surrender of government is before the Lords," he wrote to Logan from Hyde Park in April, 1705. "I can do no more; and what with the load of your unworthy spirits there, and some not much better here, with my poor son's going into the army or navy, as well as getting into Parliament, through so many checks and tests upon his morale as well as education; with the loads of debt hardly to be answered, from the difficulty of getting in, what I have a right to, of twice their value, which is starving in the midst of bread, my head and heart are filled sufficiently with trouble. Yet the Lord holds up my head. . . ."

By then the Fords had been harassing Penn almost constantly for three years. Bridget Ford, as executrix, actually brought action against him at common law for twenty thousand pounds in the court of Exchequer at Westminster. By petitioning the Chancellor, Penn was able to stop that proceeding with an injunction. The Fords then took action to have Penn's right of redemption canceled and the Pennsylvania lands sold under the terms of the late Ford's will. Actually, they were forcing Penn to bring action against them in Chancery, where they were confident they could compel the sale of Penn's Pennsylvania interests and extinguish Penn's right and equity of redemption.

Friends of Devonshire House Meeting rallied to Penn with compassion and appointed a committee of arbitration to consult with both Penn and the Fords in an effort to straighten out their hopeless tangle. But Ford's widow and children reacted just as the late Philip Ford had done years earlier toward a committee of arbitration; they refused to refer the matter to the meeting. Friends admonished the Fords "to forbear" from legal action; the Fords refused. The meeting then adopted a minute, dated December 26, 1705, reading the Fords out of membership, and declaring it "is the judgment of this meeting, that William Penn cannot be denied his liberty now to make his defence in law, as he shall see meet."

Logan was close to heartbreak over the situation that was just being fully revealed to him, and told Penn of a letter from Philip Ford to Lloyd, Norris and others "informing them that in March, 1697, his father had purchased of thee the Province of Pennsylvania and Territories in fee, and on the first of April, following, had granted thee a lease of it for three years, at the rent of £630 per annum, which term expired the first of April, 1700, and that since that time thou hadst been but tenant at will." Logan was appalled to learn that Penn had given the Fords a deed. "This unusual method of giving security is strangely surprising to all kinds of men; our enemies make reflections upon it very disadvantageous . . . and thy friends who were rallying now, more than for a long time before, are extremely grieved."

The Fords had already been spreading their base and had been corresponding with David Lloyd, Colonel Quary, Isaac Norris and others in America. Shortly before the Devonshire House decision, powers of attorney arrived in America from the Fords making Lloyd, Norris and one other their attorneys. Isaac Norris declined the privilege of joining the Ford camp and made it clear to young Ford that he was an honorable political opponent of the Proprietor, not a personal enemy. "I write to thee as a friend," he rebuked Philip Ford, Jr., "as well as being incited thereto by my respect to the Proprietor, requesting thee to pursue it with as much temper and respect to him, as well as regard to the quiet of the whole country, as the thing will bear, remembering that thy father was his friend from the beginning, and he is."

Penn never denied that he owed the Fords some money; he simply maintained that their charges were exorbitant. The accounts when finally analyzed showed that Ford had received £17,859 on account for Penn, and had paid out £16,200, leaving a net receipt by Ford of £1,659, not including commissions. This credit balance he had run up to a £14,000 debit. Penn's counsel found that the overcharges amounted to £9,697, leaving a real debt to Ford of £4,303. Penn was willing to settle for that amount, but the Fords, confident that they were protected by the deed which they held on the province, forced the case into Chancery. Penn's attorneys were highly confident of a favorable decision from the court, since they had so much evidence of fraud, but Logan was not. Some of the accounts were too many years old. "As to Ford's business, I wish thou may not be disappointed and counsel deceive thee . . . I much fear the result in Chancery, and am apt to believe thy relief must be from the House of Lords, if to be obtained anywhere."

Hannah had returned to Bristol once more while Penn remained in London, and at the home of her parents their fifth child, Richard, was born, January 17, 1706. But it was apparent to her and her husband that the Ford case would hold Penn in London a long time, while it worked its tedious way through Chancery. So, as soon as she was able, she gathered up her brood once more and rejoined him, this time at Ealing, about two miles from Brentford and some eight miles west of London. It was in the part of London's countryside that Penn had always favored, lying just west of Kensington and Hammersmith.

The case dragged on for more than three years. "A Chancery suit is a dreadful curse as now managed," Logan wrote to William Penn, Jr., "and if thy father end it not himself, who was the actor in it, I much fear the consequences." It meant one more increment to Penn's mounting personal debt. The deep embarrassment Penn felt because of the amount of help he had to receive from his father-in-law never showed more plainly than in January, 1707, when the Ford case was a little more than a year old. At that time Penn signed over to Thomas Callowhill a perpetual annuity of forty-six pounds that the Crown had recently granted him, arising out of certain Pennsylvania excise duties collected by the Crown.

On February 26, 1707, another child, named Dennis, was born to Hannah and William Penn, in their home at Ealing, making a total brood of six. Penn was by then sixty-two; he could not hope to see them all through to adult life. The oldest at the time of Dennis's birth was only seven.

In a will he had drawn two years earlier he had made an appeal to William, Jr., to consider the welfare of these children of the second marriage. Under the law all estates descending from Sir William Penn and Sir William Springett would go to William Penn, Jr. That included all of the Irish estates and any land in England that Guli had owned, no doubt including the house at Worminghurst. Penn was only free to leave his Pennsylvania holdings to Hannah and her children. "If my son William will let my younger children . . . into my father's estate in Ireland, viz, the lands west of Cork . . . then I give him two-thirds of my Pennsylvania estate and to be styled the chief Proprietary." If William did not respond to this appeal, then he could count on but one third of Pennsylvania.

In November, 1707, father and son agreed to sell Worminghurst to James Butler of Mistelgrove in Sussex and Henry Penrise of London. The place brought £6,050, in spite of the fact that £2,000 of timber had been cut from it, and the entire amount was "applied towards payment of the debt now running thereupon." The place had run down considerably under his son's care, and the father was quite frank about his daughter-in-law's unjustifiable fondness for so large and costly a house, "who has cost me more money than she brought, by her unreasonable and for that reason imprudent obstinacy for dwelling there, to which she could have no pretence either by family or portion, but by being my son's impetuous inclination; and I wish she had brought more wisdom, since she brought so little money, to help the family."

The Lords of the Privy Council were still considering and weighing terms under which they would accept surrender of the province, and from time to time Penn was called into conference, "to bring him to such terms as should be most advantageous to Her Majesty's service." It was the opinion of the Lords that the "large and ample privileges, immunities and liberties" originally granted to Penn by Charles II were "capable of being extended to the diminution of the Royal Prerogatives of the Crown, and which if reunited to the Crown from whence they were originally derived, by a voluntary surrender of the said Charter, would be of great use and benefit," and would improve royal authority over the province, make more speedy administration of justice possible, and make more efficient enforcement of the Trade Acts possible. They admitted that Penn had vastly improved the tract he had been granted and had thereby greatly increased Her Majesty's revenue, "as appears by the accounts of the Custom House, at the same time badly impairing his own private fortune." However, they still felt that such surrender "ought to be absolute and unconditional, including a renunciation of all right, claim and pretention." Penn, they reported, was in a ready disposition to do this, and they left the amount of the payment to Penn to be determined by "Her Majesty's grace and goodness."

From Pennsylvania came the sad news that the hostile feelings between Logan and Lloyd had reached such a pitch that David Lloyd was spearheading impeachment proceedings against Logan. A set of fourteen articles of impeachment was presented to the Governor and Council by the Assembly, accusing Logan of some extraordinary offenses, such as tampering with the wording of the Lieutenant Governor's commission, usurping the rights of the Commissioners of Property, requesting quitrents before they were due, denying land patents to several persons who were entitled to them, ordering resurveys on land after the two-year period for taking them up had expired whereas the Queen had repealed the act allowing this, withholding information about Penn's plan to surrender the government to the Crown, holding the Surveyor-General's job himself since the death of Penington, delaying recording of laws passed by the Assembly, detaining some land patents after they had passed the seal, and more. Logan immediately drew up answers to each of the points and sent them to Penn in England. Some of them he labeled ridiculous, many were outright falsehoods. As Penn knew, the Lieutenant Governor's commission had been written in England and he had nothing to do with it. David Lloyd was against land patents drawn in the Proprietor's name and style and preferred to have grants made by common deeds drawn by such as the grantees would employ. Had he told the House about the impending surrender of government, they might have stopped the supply of money. He was handling the Surveyor-General's post because no other person had been appointed and he had made not one farthing from it. He only kept laws long enough to make the necessary copies for England and for the counties. He detained patents until what was due upon them was paid, and no honest man would ask otherwise.

Governor Evans hedged on the idea of impeaching James Logan, using a legal technicality that he and the Council did not have the right to sit upon impeachments, but he agreed to hear the complaints against Logan. While the Assembly persisted and the Governor delayed, information began to circulate in Pennsylvania about the list of accusations made against Logan, until at last Logan himself asked the Governor and Council to make a due inquiry and give him a speedy hearing to clear his reputation. But Governor Evans never took any action.

Early in 1707 Isaac Norris, whom the Fords had failed to recruit, came to England and spent a year and a half with Penn, absorbing some of the burden of Pennsylvania's administration, consulting with the Fords in an effort to work out an arbitration of the case, going to court and observing the Penn-Ford case in progress.

"Last fourth day I was at the hearing of Ford's business before the Lord Chancellor," said Norris in a letter dated May 17, 1707, "which was not a full trial, but an examination or trial whether the accounts should be opened . . . the Lord Chancellor declared he was sorry he could not consent, for there had been so many settlements of accounts and assurances by deeds of various kinds upon it, that he would rather pay the money than set the precedent which would render all business uncertain and endless. Howbeit, he did as good as declare his opinion, that it would not go beyond a mortgage. I suppose another trial soon, and the Proprietor thinks to draw it into the House of Lords. I have some hope still that the whole may be lumped if the money can be but raised. I have not been wanting, and thought I had brought Philip to consent to an arbitration, but he went from it by his mother's refusal."

Logan's prediction was coming true. Penn had approved so many accounts over the years without examining them and had signed so many documents that Chancery refused to examine the accounts themselves, and the case devolved upon the question: Did the Fords have a good deed to the province? They certainly thought they did, because they had already sent orders to their attorneys in Pennsylvania to stop any further payments of rents to the Proprietor's agents and to collect them for the Fords instead. Encouraged by the Court of Chancery's decision not to examine the accounts that would have revealed so much fraud, the Fords then brought suit in Common Pleas against Penn as their tenant, claiming that he owed them back rent on the province.

By November, 1707, Norris was making gloomier observations: "His business with B. Ford, 'tis expected, will come to trial this Term. Everybody fears the law will go against him, notwithstanding the great injustices done him in the accounts."

And on November twenty-ninth: "I have now only to add that last fifth day the special verdict at common law, for the rent, as they call it, on the lease, went against William Penn . . . believe in a few days he must yield up, or abscond till the next term, when the principal will be determined in the Chancery, and he must appeal to the House of Lords. . . . I presume that thou understands that this execution is upon a judgment at common law for rent, as they call the interest on their money, because they had an absolute deed of sale."

Penn neither yielded nor absconded; determined not to pay the unjust charge of nearly £3,000, he chose a third course, that of going about his business as usual. On January 7, 1708, he attended a meeting at Gracechurch Street and sat with Henry Gouldney and Herbert Springett in the gallery. In the midst of the meeting, bailiffs appeared, under orders from the Fords, and attempted to arrest him. Exasperated beyond measure by this most recent piece of Ford effrontery, Gouldney and Springett tried to reason with the bailiffs to prevent the gross indignity to Penn. William Penn would surrender himself up later in the day, they promised. The bailiffs withdrew, and a few hours later William Penn, sixty-three, failing in health, fleeced over the years of the resources with which to pay even just debts, voluntarily reported to the Fleet, London's famous debtors' prison, and once more became a prisoner for conscience's sake.

Isaac Norris was still in London, and he went immediately to Penn. "He has commodious lodgings, and we hope is pretty easy. I have been several times to see him, and he sent for me this evening. The Fords might have saved themselves some reflections if they had forbore such an aggravation, as taking him at meeting, for as soon as this term came on the bail must have surrendered him, and he would have became a prisoner of course."

He had only to remain within the rules of the Fleet, not actually within its lurid confines, and he took lodgings in nearby Old Bailey. Very shortly after entering, he dismissed Evans and appointed Charles Gookin as Lieutenant Governor of Pennsylvania.

Once more Hannah Penn gathered up her children and took them to Bristol, planning to return alone to London. In Bristol, the first week in February, 1708, Hannah Margarita Penn, aged four and a half, died, and not until May did Hannah feel equal to the trip to London. Once back, she must have lived very close to the prison, for their seventh and last child, another Hannah, was born in Ludgate Parish the following September 5, probably while Penn was still a prisoner.

Friends had been rallying long since to Penn's aid as more and more of them had an opportunity to examine Ford's bookkeeping methods. The insolence of the Fords in actually invading a meeting with bailiffs solidified their efforts and brought more Friends volunteering their aid. Many besides Friends wanted to help Penn; even the Lord Chancellor who sat upon the case displayed an increasingly sympathetic attitude. The Fords' persistent refusal over the years to compromise by so much as a farthing and their mounting arrogance as they won one legal victory after another worked in Penn's favor. Their forcing a respected national figure into debtors' prison proved a boomerang. "No better way than this to bring them to terms," was Isaac Norris's opinion, and in the long run he was right, although the Fords grew bolder before they eventually wavered.

Feeling quite cocky that their deed had been upheld, the Fords at last overplayed their hand; they petitioned the Queen to issue a new Charter granting the Pennsylvania government to them. "That the like might be to Governor Philip or to Governess Bridget now!" was a caustic Norris quip.

The government of Pennsylvania had never been part of the case, as the Fords were to learn very quickly. Norris sat in on the hearings before the Lord Chancellor the end of February, 1708, and sent his observations to James Logan: "The Lord Chancellor . . . declared positively that the equity of redemption still remained in William Penn and his heirs . . . told the Fords they were too early to ask such a thing of the Queen, if it would ever be proper; and as to taking the Government, that could not be, for it would not be decent—to use his own words—to make Government ambulatory; stated, 'suppose the Queen should, as they desired, proclaim the Government, then perhaps, a year, or year and a half, or two years hence, Mr. Penn might, by himself or Friends, pay the whole money demanded, if recovered, or might, in the meantime, have his plea of abatement to the accounts granted, which he would not say was impossible. . . .' He spoke more fully and handsomely than I can repeat and, in a word, their petition was laid aside, and the Queen will be advised not to answer it."

After that alarming rebuff the Fords displayed their first willingness to arbitrate, and by May Penn was talking of possible terms. "The Fords seem to embrace an accommodation, and several Friends and others not of our profession interpose to mediate it. Seven thousand pounds looks to be the sum. To be sure, eight thousand will do it effectually; and tho' I don't like my friends' method, yet it will do, I hope, at last, in which my poor recovering Father Callowhill comes in for a thousand pounds for his share; so that I hope to regain my property and pay them by way of the Government, or what arises there [surrender to the Crown]. The Lord Treasurer I hope will lend me seven thousand pounds and receive it at New York, for the service of the Government, or for us, and give me seven years to pay. . . ."

As soon as his financial skies began to clear, Penn's hopes began to flower, and he talked once more of going to America. Pennsbury still waited for him, and for his wife and children. "I hope next spring, if not next fall, to set forth."

By early September he was able to say "My business is agreed with the Fords, and writings in hand for ratification." The compromise settlement was for seventy-six hundred pounds, a far cry from fourteen thousand. It did not come from the Lord Treasurer as he had at first hoped, but sixty-six hundred of it was raised by Friends, Henry Gouldney, Joshua Gee, Silvanus Grove, John Woods, Thomas Callowhill, Thomas Oade, Jeffery Pennell, John Feild and Thomas Cuppage, to whom Penn executed a fresh mortgage, "without naming that base family therein."

I take history then to represent to us, as in a glass, the whole world at one view, or as if the dead were returned, to report to us the actions done in their time; it is a sort of pre-existence, making us to have always lived, or to have lived and had knowledge before we were born. For, by story, we at once see all ages together in their customs, governments, policies and declensions; a most edifying and profitable scene of life, to be the heirs of so much knowledge and experience, as this mighty view affords us.

——Penn in a Foreword to a contemporary history by Sir Bulstrode Whitlocke, 1709

21. *Peace*

THERE WERE too many years and too many trials to look back upon, and too little energy remained to be squandered upon bitterness. With tranquil dignity William and Hannah Penn picked up the threads of their life once more. "Neither he nor my daughter sinks under it, but from the Divine Providence have support to their spirits," Thomas Callowhill had said during their darkest hours. Hannah's stability had been a priceless asset through the twelve years of their marriage, and she was calmly prepared to go on with what remained. Grief was not quite done with them. On January 24, 1709, the infant Hannah died at Kensington and was buried at Jordans with Guli's children. During the early part of 1709 Hannah returned once more with her children to her father's in Bristol and Penn took lodgings in London until he could find his wife and children a permanent place to live.

To Hannah from "Tishes" June 25, 1709, he wrote in a hand that had become more scrawly than in the past with large, uneven letters indicating poor hand control, though no palsy:

MINE DEAREST H.:

I bless the Lord I can tell thee I am pretty well and much affected with thy very kind letter of last post, and humbly pray the almighty God to keep us to His eternal kingdom, and while here make us happy in our meetings together to our mutual comfort again and again. I send thee by Arthur Thomas one pound of chocolate and one half of coffee and a bottle of Hungary water. . . . I am just going for Colchester . . . son Penn, with or after me. . . . I dined at my good sister's upon little dishes the other day. . . . So, my own dearest, I embrace thee and my dear lambs beyond words.

W. P.

To Hannah from Buckingham Court on July 9, 1709:

This is to let mine own dearest know that hers is, through the Lord's mercy, pretty well, and rejoices that her most acceptable letter told me so of her and ours. . . . I go tomorrow to Edgeworth, with many friends, my old way to Rickmansworth, the first of this earth. I have chid R. Bull's about the coffee, and they desire it back to change. I cannot be with thee till this day week at soonest, because I would end with this wicked town and stay that away a month or two. . . .

To his wife from London on the fourteenth of the same month:

It is not with a little trouble that the enjoyment of mine own dearest is thus deferred; for ten days ago and more I purposed to have been with her, but those that I fear never care whether I see thee or not detain me, and I cannot say that I have no interest therein. Scores of guineas have melted since I saw thee, there is no enduring it any longer, but I waive much till I see thee, but I see my course positively and clearly to which I hope for my dearest H's compliance. It will be fourth day next before I can get away and intend by the two days' coach. I have been today with Cousin Poole at the house by Croyden, which is by [situation] in its privacy as good as thirty miles off, and yet is but eleven. . . .

The prospective house in the above letter was not their final decision, and Penn continued in the midst of house-hunting to write to his family from London. To seven-and-a-half-year-old Thomas at Bristol on October 22, 1709:

My dear boy:

I was glad of thine yesterday, but tell thy dear mother that to get your letters at fourth hour post days, is a great favor, for nearer eight or nine at night has several times been the earliest here as thine came last night. I salute you all, thy dear and beloved mother, and you my dear children and so the family with you, but especially your grandfather and grandmother, with that family and our kind relations and friends at Bristol. Know that through the Lord's mercy I am pretty well and bless the Lord that you are so . . . and I charge thy brother Johnne and thee to follow your book two hours in the forenoon and two hours in the afternoon, and do readily what you are bid and you will comfort your dear mother, and your poor father to hear you do so. I sent thy mother so full a letter last post that I shall write the less now, but let her know that this week and next I have thoughts of going both for Rochester and for Reading, both on Truth's account to one and on our account to the other. . . .

And to John, going on ten, in December:

MY DEAR CHILD:

I was much pleased with thy letter, and [wish] thee for writing of it, and I desire to be thankful to the Lord you are all so well as thine tells me you are, that thy dear mother is better, thy grandfather so, too, and can walk abroad so well. If they eat and sleep well, they will quickly be so, and that you my poor dear children are so tenders my heart to the Lord, our common preserver. . . . Know I dined today at thy good Aunt Lowther's, who and Cousin Margaret salute you all; so C. Lawton and thy brother Penn who dined there with me, also thy sister Penn where we called. . . . Let her [Hannah] know my physic worked six or seven times which I took in the city, where I lay four nights, and came to this end last night. . . . Let mother send me my calico drawers and dark jersey and colored stockings per first opportunity. . . . Take care of thy little horse daily and don't ride alone, nor in the dirt without thy sashoons [stuffed leather pad bound about the leg inside of a boot] to fill the feet of the boot, to keep thee dry and warm. Remember what I say and I desire both thou and brother Tomme may have as strong and thick shoes as friend Kippen made for

Arthur at his coming away, and then you may go in the wet and dirt more safely. . . ."

At last on December twenty-fourth to his wife, with news about a possible house at Twyford, near Reading:

MY DEAREST HEART:

That night I writ last to thee, about three or four in the morning, I waked so so but by six or seven in the morning I felt myself a little feverish . . . and stayed at home all day yesterday, and to-night had a good night's rest, and breathed freely. And now have been up three hours, being twelve o'clock, and ready to go and take the air to R. Kirton's and stay two or three nights, the town being broke up at this time from business. I intended for Rochester, but Jos. Taylor and Is. Tompson are gone, and to Reading; the coaches because of the time were all full or I had gone thither this morning. But what allays my disappointment is that a coll [an inexperienced young gentleman] is in hand with that house by Twyford, which will lose it us I fear; D. B. says it stands on a noble large dry gravelly green and clean ways about it; and that they that told me otherwise did it to hinder me from seeing it. I now wait for Dr. Matthews' letter and one from Henley [on Thames]. There is no loss and I like Henley as well as Reading almost, but for the post, better. I am also looking about Maidenhead, for that at Staines [in Middlesex] is out of the way though fifteen miles nearer than London. . . .

To Hannah in a letter from "My lodgings" on January 17, 1710:

As I greatly rejoice to hear by my dearest's obliging letter, she and hers are in a good measure of health, so I bless our great and good God that I can tell her and hers I am at worst, so so, pretty well, and only want the sweet enjoyment of their company to complete the temporal comfort of dear relations, which no man sets a greater value upon than myself. . . . I am sorry thou has put off our meeting beyond our dear little American's birthday, but if it must be so for the reason suggested, I hope the first of next month will be the day of their setting forth at farthest. . . . I hold my resolutions, the Lord willing, to meet thee at Reading, if not Newberry. Fail not, if it be possible. The Bear at Newberry and the Cardinal's Cap at Reading. As for horses, I'll do what I can, and take the best measures, but pray send for Nic at College Green and try him for four and a postilion to Newberry, for four do after that in the stage coaches. . . . I purpose, God willing, to be at Reading next first day and there I think to be off or on about the house D. B. writ to me about. . . . I shall find out a place to receive you, at Reading or Kensington, or London. Tedington house is now to be let, but out of the way two or three miles, and letters must come by way of London. . . .

A letter from Penn on February 4, 1710, is addressed to Hannah at Richard Marchants, Shopkeeper in Bath, where she had apparently taken her children. Two-year-old Dennis, the baby of the family since the infant Hannah's death, had produced some "symptoms" and may have occasioned the trip to the watering place. This time it was Penn who was impatient of the separation:

If you are well come on, in the fear and love of God, twenty miles a day at least, till you meet me or I you, of which you shall hear every opportunity by post or coach and nothing but what I can't avoid or which will make thee easy to be done, shall ever hinder me from meeting thee at Reading at least. . . .

These plans failed, too, for on February 7, his letter to Hannah suggests her reluctance to travel in bad weather:

It is with great concern that I receive so many disappointments which I hope is to fit and prepare us to embrace one another the more thankfully to the Lord, when he gives us the mercy of meeting together; though I desire thee not to stir the poor children, unless fit for it, at any rate . . . stay if thou art pleased, till better, or leave them and Sarah, come with Johnne and Petty and the maid, if thou pleasest. 'Tis cold, I confess, but clean straw, or hay and glasses up will be warm, and I hope you have clothes for the weather, and pray let not Johnne ride on horseback in deep dirty or windy places, only now and then for diversion. . . .

The home that Hannah and William Penn were finally reunited in was at Ruscombe near Twyford in Berkshire. The train from

London to Oxford passes through Twyford just before it reaches Reading. The countryside there is quite flat and even today has a wooded look. Nearer Reading the land becomes undulating and beyond Reading it grows hilly. No trace of the Ruscombe house remains, but it must have been huge because it accommodated not only Hannah and William Penn, their five children and a domestic staff, but William, Jr.'s wife and children besides, since the Founder's namesake had proved himself an improvident husband. Ruscombe was probably not to Hannah's taste, but the kind of big rural manor house she had learned to expect from her imaginative husband.

Settled once more in the peaceful English country with his family gathered around him, Penn continued to negotiate for the sale of his government to the Crown. It seemed the wisest possible course. Governor Gookin was as unsuccessful as his predecessors in getting along with the Assembly. Isaac Norris saw "no room to expect much effectual business." "'Tis a certain sign you are strangers to oppression," Penn wrote to the Assembly. When he founded the colony, he reminded them, he had expected solid comfort from the many hundreds of people who benefited; he had "endeavored to form such a model of government as might make all concerned in it easy." When the first model had proved inadequate, he had allowed revisions. They had the guarantee of fixed elections, a representative assembly enjoying extraordinary privileges. But now the Assembly was trying to usurp the executive powers of the Governor. "The frame of every government ought to be regular in itself, well proportioned and subordinate in its parts, and every branch of it invested with sufficient power to discharge its respective duty for the support of the whole. . . . Nothing would be more destructive to it than to take so much of the provision of executive part of the government out of the Governor's hands and lodge it in an uncertain collective body." And he had personal reasons for feeling that he was justified in doing what he planned to do. "The attacks upon my reputation, the many indignities put upon me in papers sent over hither into the hands of those who could not be expected to make the most discreet and charitable use of them . . . resolves passed in the Assemblies for turning my quitrents, never sold by me, to the support of the government, my lands entered upon without any regular method . . . my private estate continually exhausting for the support of that government, both here and there, and no provision made for it by that country; to all that I cannot but add the violence that has been particularly shown my secretary. . . ."

James Logan had arrived in England in the spring of 1710 to be with Penn for about two years, to give him a firsthand account of affairs in Pennsylvania and to relate his parting experience with David Lloyd. The articles of impeachment against Logan, never quashed and never properly investigated, still hung fire. In the fall shortly before sailing for Europe, Logan had sent the Assembly a long paper of self-vindication, but Speaker Lloyd paid no heed to it at the time. Not until Logan was ready to sail for Europe did Lloyd summon him before the Assembly with his proof, and on the day he was to go aboard ship David Lloyd issued an arrest warrant, "charging the sheriff to take James Logan into his custody, and to detain him safely in the county jail of our Lady the Queen, until he shall willingly make his submission to the satisfaction of this House." Only because Lieutenant Governor Gookin countermanded the arrest order, was Logan able to leave as he had planned. He remained in constant attendance upon the Proprietor and his affairs for two years.

By February, 1711, satisfactory surrender terms began to materialize. The Lords of Trade reported to the Queen on Penn's proposed terms, pointing out the many advantages that would accrue to the Crown, and left the amount to her personal consideration. Penn offered to settle for twenty thousand pounds paid to him over a period of seven years. The Lords urged that such surrender be absolute and that Penn renounce all right and claim or pretention whatsoever.

That spring Penn suffered an attack of illness while he was in London; it is thought to have been a mild stroke, and he described it as being "ill of a fever." He was sufficiently alarmed by it to draw a new will, one in which the Pennsylvania government would not be in danger of falling into the hands of his profligate son. Under the terms of this latest will—drawn in London at the time of his illness and confirmed at Ruscombe May 27, 1712—the government of Pennsylvania was to be placed in the hands of two trustees: Robert Harley, who was Earl of Oxford and Earl Mortimer, and at the time Lord High Treasurer of England, and Will Earle Poulet whom I have been unable to identify. All of the Pennsylvania lands, tenements and hereditaments went to Penn's second family, to his sister Margaret, to Thomas Callowhill, Gilbert Heathcote, Samuel Waldenfield, John Feild, Henry Gouldney in England, and Samuel Carpenter, Richard Hill, Isaac Norris, Samuel Preston and James Logan in America. His three grandchildren and his daughter Letitia were to receive ten thousand acres each in America. Hannah was his sole executrix, and to her he left all of the American rents and all of his personal estate.

Meanwhile the Crown had agreed upon surrender terms, although Whitehall could not resist the opportunity to cut the price from the twenty thousand pounds suggested by Penn to twelve thousand. At Penn's request they advanced him a thousand pounds immediately, while the Lord Treasurer perfected the agreement.

It was never to be. On the fourth of October, 1712, while William and Hannah Penn were visiting at Bristol, Penn suffered another stroke. He was writing a letter to James Logan, who had returned to America. There were four full pages and the start of a fifth, its first word "She . . ." appearing in the lower right-hand corner of the fourth, when the hand holding the quill was suddenly stopped, wilted by paralysis, and the great mind lost consciousness.

Hannah wrote the next page herself:

Bristol, 13th 8br [October] 1712

Lo. Frd.:

The inclosed my poor husband wrot, but had not time to finish before he was taken with a second fit of his lethargich illness, like as about six months ago at London, which has been no small addition to my late most severe exercises. But it has pleased the Lord, in the midst of judgment, to shew us mercy, in the comfortable prospect of his recovery; though as yet but weak. And I am ordered by the doctors to keep all business from him till he is stronger; and yet, loath to lett what he has wrot be left behind, I therefore thought best to send it, tho unfinished, for thee to make the best use of; there being several things of moment. And I pray thee use thy utmost diligence to settle things and returns for our comfort and quiett of those that dwell near to the Lyon. I ought to say more in answer to thine intended for my dear, deceased father, but time and trouble forbids my inlarging, only pray show thy regards thou had to him, by thy diligence for his poor, helpless little offspring. I am called on in haste the wind coming fair; so conclude this hasty scraule with my well wishes to thee and love to my good and kind friends that ask after me.

From thy real frd, H. PENN

Penn was by then able to scrawl a message on the next page:

I am through the Lord's mercy pretty well. I had begun another sheet but not above more than the inclosed, but being upon six and I suppose the time ready for the boat, send thee this and may yet more. This goes not yet. So farewell, and persue former earnest orders and thou will oblige this real friend. Dr love to all my friends

Wm. PENN

Hannah took him back to London toward the end of January, 1713, "by easy journeys"; and he rallied himself sufficiently to attempt to resume his public affairs. But the noises and tensions of the capital city were too much for him, and he returned exhausted to Ruscombe. "He just reached home, when he was seized by the same severe illness that he has twice before labored under," Hannah told James Logan. From then on to the end of his life he was dependent on the care of others.

The great soul had completed its course, had won its release from all worry and pain. Those who came to his bedside found Penn "pretty well in health, and cheerful of disposition, but defective in memory . . . nor could he deliver his words so readily as heretofore." On First Day morning he felt well enough to ride in his carriage to Meeting for Worship at Reading, where he and his family had been attending since taking the house at Ruscombe, and he actually was able to speak "several sensible sentences."

Thomas Story returned from America to look once more upon his idol, to see the sweet, childlike face that had once been so forceful, to hear a few disconnected words from the once brilliant orator. "His memory was almost lost, and the use of his understanding suspended; so that he was not so conversable as formerly, and yet as near the Truth, in the love of it, as before. . . . When I went to the house I thought myself strong enough to see him in that condition, but when I entered the room and perceived the great defect of his expressions, for want of memory, it greatly bowed my spirit, under a consideration of the uncertainty of all human qualifications, and what the finest of men are soon reduced to."

Story remained in Europe, traveling among the meetings in England and the Continent, returning occasionally to Ruscombe, giving Hannah Penn what help he could, since she must now guide Pennsylvania's affairs.

In 1715 Hannah described Penn as "near as usual. He was at Reading Meeting this morning and in himself fine and comfortable as he generally is, blessed be the God of all our mercies." During the summer she took him to Bath, hoping that the curative waters would help him. "Thy poor father holds through the Lord's mercy as well as at home. He drinks about a quart of the Bath water and has a good stomach after it," she wrote home to her sons.

William Penn in his closing years continued in what Besse called "a gradual declension," and on July 30, 1718, between two and three in the morning, he died, to be buried at Jordans with Gulielma and so many of his children.

"He was learned without vanity, apt without forwardness, facetious in conversation yet weighty and serious of an extraordinary greatness of mind, yet void of the strain of ambition as free from rigid gravity as he was clear of unseemly levity. A man, a scholar, a Friend, a minister, surpassing in superlative endowments whose memorial will be valued by the wise and blessed with the just." Thus reads the Testimony of Reading Quarterly Meeting.

And he is more. He is eternally our contemporary, holding before us the finest traditions of Anglo-Saxon law, showing us the fruits of liberty of conscience, pointing the way to lasting freedom through individual dignity and endowing us with the example of a workable peace among men. William Penn speaks to the condition of our times.

Notes

For the sake of brevity I have used the following abbreviations to indicate a few of the sources that occur frequently in the Notes:

HSP	Historical Society of Pennsylvania
FHL	Friends House, London
PRO	Public Record Office, London
CSP	Calendar of State Papers, Great Britain
JFHS	Journal of the Friends Historical Society
Penn Mag	Pennsylvania Magazine of History and Biography

All sources referred to are in the Bibliographies, pages 427-44.

The legend of John Locke's influence on William Penn in designing the Pennsylvania government

I have found no verification of this legend. It is true that Locke was lecturing at Oxford when Penn was a student there, but an examination of their published diaries and letters, the Penn manuscripts and Locke manuscript letters at the British Museum and at the Bodleian Library (letters written by Locke and index of letters to Locke) through 1682 revealed no correspondence or acquaintanceship between the two men. Locke's political writings were not published until 1689, long after Pennsylvania was founded.

Slavery in early Pennsylvania

The Pennsylvania province never had a large slave population, although many of its families, the Penns among them, owned slaves. The Quakers always took a humanitarian attitude toward their slaves and felt a continuously growing concern for their welfare. Friends were the first to teach Negroes to read and write, and among the first, indeed, to search their Christian consciences regarding the institution of slavery itself. The abolitionist movement really had its beginnings in a little Quaker meeting in Germantown in 1688. Its voiced disaffection was sent up through the monthly, quarterly and yearly meetings and gradually found its way into more and more hearts, until seventy years later when the Philadelphia Yearly Meeting (by then the largest in the world) united to declare itself forever opposed to the buying, selling or keeping of slaves. The provincial government adopted a succession of laws controlling the slave trade and providing for the welfare of Negroes who were imported. In March, 1700, William Penn himself laid upon the Philadelphia Monthly Meeting his personal concern for Negroes and Indians, urging Friends "to be very careful in discharging all good conscience towards them in all respects." One of the direct results was the creation of meetings for worship for both groups. In a letter to Hannah Penn some three years after the Proprietor's death, James Logan said, "The Proprietor in a will left with me at his departure hence gave all his negroes their freedom, but this is entirely private. However, there are very few left." The "will" referred to is not Penn's final will at the Principal Probate Office in London.

Chapter 1: GENTLEMAN COMMONER

Biographical information and quotations relating to Penn's father from Granville Penn unless otherwise indicated. Earliest biographical material on Penn from Aubrey's *Brief Lives* and Besse's *Journal of His Life.*

Page 9 Description of house on Tower Hill quoted from *Extract of a Survey Ordered by Parliament of All the Possessions of Charles Stuart,* PRO; copy in FHL. Penn's birth date from Aubrey and Besse; his baptism is recorded at All Hallows Barking, as October 23, 1644. Other genealogical information from Coleman and Howard M. Jenkins. Father's marriage date from register of St. Martin's Church.

Page 10 "Penn being Welsh . . ." letter of Penn to Robert Turner, March 5, 1681, HSP.

13 "under great misery . . ." from Fox's *Journal.* Information that Penn had smallpox at three and lost his hair contained in a letter from George Fox to Henry Sidon, May 25, 1677, copy in Penn's hand at FHL; published in JFHS, Vol. 6.

14 There is a letter from Penn in Philadelphia to John Aubrey, June 13, 1683, in the John Locke collection at the Bodleian to indicate an acquaintanceship between Aubrey and Penn.

17 "cobblers and weavers . . ." from Godfrey Davies.

21 Episode of West Indies trip and father's arrest supplemented from Clarendon.

22 "Lord Broghill, with his lady . . ." CSP, Domestic.

23 The Harvey Manuscript (also known as Huntley Manuscript) published in full in JFHS, Vol. 32; original MS at FHL. "A black of his father's . . ." Harvey MS.

26 Date of Penn's enrollment at Christ Church from the college records.

CHAPTER 2: A YOUTH OF EXCELLENT GENIUS

30 "hellish darkness . . ." from Penn's 1677 *Journal.*

31 Latin poem from *Epicedia Academiae Oxoniensis . . . MDCLX,* HSP.

32 Episode of viewing Coronation in Cornhill from Pepys.

36 "persecution at Oxford . . ." from Penn's 1677 *Journal.* Expulsion from college from Christ Church records; "bitter usage" and "whipping, beating . . ." from Penn's 1677 *Journal.*

38 Quotes describing Paris life from *A View of Paris.* A letter from Penn to Spencer as Earl of Sunderland, July 28, 1683, verifies Penn's association with Spencer in France in 1663, HSP.

40 Quotes *re* sword episode from Penn's *No Cross, No Crown.*

CHAPTER 3: THE PLAGUE YEAR

Incidents with Pepys family from Pepys' *Diary;* father's biography from Granville Penn.

47, 48 Penn's letters to father of April 23, 1665, and May 6, 1665, in Janney; incident of Penn's conversation with King from second letter.

49-51 Material on Plague from Bell, Pepys and Evelyn.

CHAPTER 4: THE YOUNG CONVINCED

Information about Penn's father and Irish land grant as well as incident of Penn's military service from Granville Penn.

53 "and desire you to send . . ." Granville Penn.

54 Penn's letter to father, July 4, 1666; father to Penn, July 17, 1666; father's instructions to Penn *re* new post, Granville Penn.

54-55 Material on Fire from Bell and Pepys.

55 Peg Penn's wedding from Pepys.

56 Penn's visit to Cork and hearing Loe from Harvey MS.

57 "Being ready to faint . . ." from Penn's 1677 *Journal.*

58 Incident of disturbed meeting and Cork arrest from Harvey MS. Penn's conversation with Mayor in Penn's letter to Orrery, 1667, HSP.

59 "Religion which is at once . . ." from above letter.

60 Letters from father, October 12, 1667, and October 22, 1667, HSP. Penn's testimony at time of Coale's death in Coale.

61 "Oh, England . . ." from Coale. My statement that Sir W. Penn purchased Wanstead house based on A. C. Myers and on evidence that house remained in family after Sir W. Penn's death.

Pages 61-63 Penn's and Coale's return to London, visit to Wanstead, quarrel between Penn and father, second quarrel at the tavern, Harvey MS.
64 "About the year 1668 . . ." Besse's *Journal of His Life.* Father's ill health and impeachment from Granville Penn, Pepys and CSP.
65 Penn's meeting with Guli, being cut off from estates, from Harvey MS. Biography of Gulielma Springett from Hodgkin. "A match of providence's making . . ." Penn to wife and children, August 4, 1682, HSP.

Chapter 5: DEAR GEORGE FOX

Fox biography from his *Journal,* Sewel, and Braithwaite's *Beginnings;* related quotations from Fox *Journal.*

70 "Oh, Derby . . ." from Sewel.
72-73 "the greatest religious leader . . ." from Godfrey Davies. Fox's interview with Cromwell from Sewel.
75-76 Interviews with Buckingham and Berwick from Penn's *Fragments of an Apology,* HSP *Memoirs,* Vol. 3.
77 Death of Loe in letter of Penn to I. Penington, October 17, 1668, FHL, Sewel, and Penn to "G.S.," 1668, HSP.
78 Quotations pertaining to Vincent episode from Penn's *Sandy Foundation;* letter to Vincent of October 31, 1668, HSP.
81 Arrest warrant of December 12, 1668 in Penney's *Extracts.*
82 Tower conditions from Fox letter to Sidon, May 25, 1677 (see notes to chapter 1): December 24 permit to Cooke in Penney's *Extracts.*
83 "recant in Common Garden . . ." in Penn letter to "G.S.," December, 1668, HSP; "Thou mayst tell my father . . ." from the same.
84 "Though I knew him not . . ." from Penn's Foreword to Coale.
86-87 Father's petition to Council in *Archaeologia,* Vol. 35: Penn's July 1 letter to Arlington in Penn's 1726 collected works.
88 Date of Penn's release from *Archaeologia,* Vol. 35.

Chapter 6: AMONG THE IRISH FRIENDS

Most of the information in this chapter comes from Penn's *My Irish Journal;* I am indebted to Isabel Grubb's scholarly notes in that volume and to the exhaustive survey she made of Penn's land holdings in Ireland. Biographical material on Thomas Ellwood from Ellwood's *Journal.*

97 "It is the duty of a magistrate . . ." letter to Desmynières, probably November 5, 1669, HSP (Isabel Grubb questions authenticity of this letter in Penn's *My Irish Journal*).
103 "So soon as I received . . ." Broghill (Orrery) to Penn, May 18, 1670, HSP. "My brother Broghill . . ." O'Bryan to Penn May 19, 16(70), FHL.
104 "I wish you had well done . . ." father to Penn, April 29, 1670, HSP.

Chapter 7: FOR ALL THOU ART PENN'S SON

105-06 Letter of John Gay to Penn, July 23, 1670, Elizabeth Bowman to Penn, July 16, 1670, *re* Margaret Fox, and Gulielma to Penn *re* Penington's imprisonment, July 16, 1670, *Penn Mag,* Vol. 70, with annotations and interpretations by Dr. Henry J. Cadbury, who questions Bowman's veracity *re* M. Fox's pregnancy.
106 Text of Coventicle Act from Sewel and Whitehead *Journal.*
107-08 Incident of Fox's arrest from Fox's *Journal;* Whitehead's arrest from his *Journal.*
110 Penn's arrest warrant, HSP.
111 Penn's letter to father, August 15, 1670, from Janney.
Entire proceedings before the Lord Mayor from *The People's Ancient and Just Liberties Asserted* (see comment to page 134).
Information *re* four jurymen's case from CSP, Domestic; a pamphlet *The Case of Edward Bushel,* etc. and *The Phenix,* Lincoln's Inn.

Pages 123-24 Sir John Vaughan's opinion from *The Phenix,* Lincoln's Inn.
124-25 Penn's two letters to father from Newgate from Janney.
125-26 Father's dying words from Penn's *No Cross, No Crown;* date of father's death from Granville Penn.
126 Father's last will and testament from Principal Probate Office, Somerset House, London; Wanstead inventory an HSP MS.

Chapter 8: NEWGATE AFTER ALL

Dispute with Ives from Besse's *Journal of His Life* and from Ellwood's *Journal.*

128 Penn's letter to Vice Chancellor from Besse's *Journal,* etc.
129-32 Penn's arrest at Wheeler Street and second trial before the Lord Mayor from Besse's *Journal,* etc.; text of mittimus in Besse's *Journal,* etc.
132 Description of conditions in Newgate from Ellwood *Journal.*
134 The tract, *The People's Ancient and Just Liberties Asserted,* was first printed in 1670 and did not bear Penn's name; since it is a transcript of proceedings of the trial, it was probably brought out by a group of Friends; another tract called *The Second Part of the People's Ancient,* etc., a transcript of a trial of Thomas Rudyard and others, rather bears this out.
Penn's letters to Parliament and R. Lany in his 1726 collected works; *Right Marriage* and *An Holy Triumph* are HSP MSS.

Chapter 9: THE LOVE OF MY YOUTH

Penn's journey to Holland and Germany reconstructed from references in his 1677 *Journal,* minutes of Monthly Meeting at Friedrichstadt 1663-1700 at Friends House, London, and seven letters: Penn to Labadists, October, 1671, and November 24, 1672, HSP; Penn to Dr. Haesbert, November 22, 1672, HSP; Penn to Friends and People of United Netherlands, June, 1672, HSP; Penn to Friends in Holland and Germany, September 1, 1673, in his 1726 collected works; Penn to Inhabitants of High and Low Dutch Nation, September 9, 1671, HSP; Penn to Princess Elizabeth, 1676, in his 1726 collected works.

139 "A trumpet sounded . . . ," HSP.
140 Biography of Haesberts from unfinished manuscript on Quakers in Holland by William I. Hull in possession of Swarthmore College, and from Quaker documents in the Town Archives of Emden (Vol. I/416) published in Vol. 10-1921 of the Upstalsboom Papers, translated by Miss Hildegunde Nuth.
144 Date of Penn's arrival in Harwich and informer's letter in Penney's *Extracts.* Penn's stay in Suffolk based on letter of Penn to "My dearly beloved Friends and Brethren," Suffolk, 15-9 Mo. (November) 1671, HSP.
144-45 Quotations from above cited letter.
145 Penn's and Gulielma's declaration to wed in Howard M. Jenkins. Fox letter to Penn at Tilleringreen May 24 (1671), HSP; year of this letter uncertain.
146 Wedding certificate in Howard M. Jenkins.
147 "good, wise, chaste . . ." letter of Penn to Robert Turner, February 27, 1694, HSP.

Chapter 10: ON TRUTH'S ACCOUNT

148 "I am at peace . . ." Penn to Netherlands, June, 1672, HSP.
149 Biography of Barclay from Wragge. "I have often remembered . . ." Barclay to Penn March 6, 1674, HSP. Epistle of London Yearly Meeting of May 26, 1673, signed by Barclay and Penn in *Letters of Early Friends.*
149-153 Penn's journey through Kent and Sussex based on his *My Journey on Truth's Account Through Kent, Sussex and the Skirt of Surrey Begun the 11th-7th Mo. 1672 and Ended 4th-8th Mo. 1672,* an HSP MS, published in *Penn Mag,* Vol. 68, with Dr. Henry J. Cadbury's notes.

Page 153 Letter to Dr. Haesbert, November 22, 1672, and to De Labadie, November 24, 1672, HSP. Reeve and Muggleton incident from Besse's *Journal of His Life.*
155 Birth and death of Gulielma Maria from original Quaker records, FHL. Death of Richard in Howard M. Jenkins.
158 Penn's letters to Fleming, Holland and Germany, Mary Pennyman, HSP.
159 Fox's arrest from Fox *Journal.*
160 Penn's mother's letter *re* Fox confirmed by letter of Ellis Hookes to Margaret Fox, January 9, 1674, *Letters of Early Friends.* "You, Mr. Fox . . . ," Fox *Journal;* definition of praemunire from Blackstone.
161 Penn's visit to Duke of York from his *Fragments of an Apology,* HSP *Memoirs,* Vol. 3.
162 Birth and death of twins from Quaker records, FHL.
162-63 Baptist controversies from Besse's *Journal of His Life,* Sewel and Penn's tracts as indicated.
164 "It was managed with much levity . . ." Penn to Fox, September 5, 1674, FHL; "To whom is my love . . ." Fox to Penn, August 28, 1674, HSP. "That your coming thither . . ." Penn to Maryland Friends, his 1726 collected works.
164-65 Penn's two letters to Fox *re* Duke of York: former not dated in Janney, latter September 5, 1674, FHL.
165 Fox to Penn, November 25, 1674, HSP. "If thou think that my coming . . ." Margaret Fox to Penn, November 25, 1674, HSP.
166 "If thou canst effect . . ." Fox to Penn, October 10, 1674, HSP. "The King knows not . . ." Penn to Fox, December 1, 1674, *Letters of Early Friends.* "Dear William, I shall not strive . . ." Fox to Penn, September 30, 1675, HSP. "My wife is toward . . ." Penn to Fox, Hodgkin. "My wife is well . . ." Penn to Fox, December 10, 1674, Howard M. Jenkins and Hodgkin. Date of Springett's birth from Quaker records in Friends House, London, but date may possibly be Old Style which would make it 1676 according to present calendar. "Many lawyers came . . . ," Fox *Journal.*
169 "As concerning Friends buying . . ." letter from Coale to Fox, Bowden.
170, 172-73 Texts of *Concessions* from Samuel Smith.

CHAPTER 11: THROUGH HOLLAND AND GERMANY

Penn's journey through Holland and Germany based directly on his 1677 *Journal,* with supplementary material from Haistwell.

176 Indenture dated June 3, 1676, in the Close Rolls, PRO, London. "The said William Penn having . . ." an undated comment in an old letter book, HSP.

CHAPTER 12: THE SEED OF A NATION

197 Penn's reference to "my dear wife . . ." from Besse's *Journal of His Life.* His letter to Margaret Fox about Springett and Guli, January 8, 1678, HSP. Letter referring to his illness the same. Letter from Elizabeth in Penn's 1726 collected works.
198 Birth of Letitia from Quaker Records, FHL. Penn's speeches before House of Commons committee in 1726 collected works.
199 John Gratton letter, December 19, 1678, HSP.
203-07 Penn-Sydney campaigns from Ewald, Janney and Dixon.
205 "Visions, seditions . . . ," Grego.
206 Penn's letter to Sydney, Janney.
208 Birth of Penn, Jr., from Quaker records, FHL.
209 "after the government at home . . ." Penn to Romney, September 6, 1701, HSP.
210 "I perceive . . ." Penn to Henry Sydney at The Hague, British Museum. Penn's petition to King, Hazard; "The Lord Sunderland was one . . ." Penn to Spencer, July 1683, HSP.
211 Letter from Sir John Werden, October, 1680, Hazard. "as very much to prevent . . ." Werden to Blaythwaite, November 23, 1680, HSP. "He is willing that twelve . . ." Werden to Lords of Trade, December 3, 1680, Hazard.
212 Description of Baltimore's northern limits in Hazard. Meeting of February 23, 1681, PRO Acts of Privy Council, Colonial Series.

Page 213 Narrative of processing royal Charter from *Mystery of Pennsylvania Royal Charter,* N.B. Wainwright, *Penn Mag,* Vol. 73, and Mood article, JFHS Vol. 32. Text of royal Charter in Proud.

214 "men of universal spirits . . ." Penn in his *Some Account.*

215 Penn's letter to Robert Turner, March 5, 1681, HSP.

Chapter 13: THE FRAME OF GOVERNMENT

216 Charles II's April 2 declaration, Hazard. "You are now fixed . . ." Penn's letter to inhabitants of Pennsylvania, April 8, 1681, Hazard. "The bearer is a gentleman . . ." Penn to Baltimore, April 10, 1681, *Penn Mag,* Vol. 6.

217 Penn's commission to Markham, April 10, 1681, Hazard. Date of Penn's resignation from New Jersey trusteeship from *The Proprietors of . . . New Jersey,* J. E. Pomfret, *Penn Mag,* Vol. 75.

218 "This I can say . . ." Penn to Turner, Sharp, etc., April 12, 1681, HSP. "I do judge William . . ." Claypoole Letter Book, HSP.

219 Text of *Certain Conditions* in Proud.

220 Penn's instructions to Harrison, August 25, 1681, Hazard.

221 "Now I neither have . . ." Barclay to Penn, August 19, 1681, HSP. "Since my last . . ." Barclay to Penn, October 10, 1681, HSP. "Mine eye is to . . ." Penn to Thomas Janney, August 21, 1681, HSP.

222 Ship departures from CSP, Hazard and Claypoole Letter Book at HSP. "My sincere love . . ." Penn to Markham, October 18, 1681, HSP.

223 Penn's letter to Indians of same date, HSP.

224 "I shall not I think . . ." Penn to Janney, August 21, 1681, HSP. "William Penn is extraordinary . . ." Claypoole Letter Book, HSP. Date of Penn's election to Royal Society, courtesy of the Society. Information about Free Society in Proud.

225 Penn's instructions to Holme, April 18, 1682, in Hazard. Penn's instructions for building Philadelphia in his letter to his land commissioners, September 30, 1681, Hazard.

226 Letter to Penn from Sir William Petty, August 14, 1682, HSP.

227-30 Text of *Frame of Government* and *Laws* in Proud.

231 Death of mother from Howard M. Jenkins and an undated letter of Penn's to a friend in Clarkson.

232-34 Penn's letter to wife and children, August 4, 1682, from 1760 copy addressed "To the Printer" from Oxfordshire, HSP.

234 Letters to three children, August 19, 1682, HSP.

235 "Stephen! We know one another . . ." Penn to Crisp, Janney, n.d. Incident of near arrest in summer of 1682 from first edition of Fox's *Journal.*

236 Delaware grant, Proud.

237-38 Two Penn-Ford incidents from Penn's *Bill of Complaint,* December 23, 1706, PRO.

238 Information *re Welcome* from Vaux article in *Friends Historical Association Bulletin,* Vol. 21, Claypoole Letter Book at HSP, Cadbury article on *Early References* in *Penn Mag,* Vol. 75, records of The Welcome Society of Pennsylvania, and Hazard. Penn's *An Epistle Containing* is an HSP MS.

Chapter 14: "NO CROSS, NO CROWN"

The language of this chapter is almost entirely Penn's own. It is intended to clarify the ideas of his most important tract which is by today's standards difficult to read.

Chapter 15: A PEACEABLE PEOPLE

245 Penn's arrival dates from Penn's letter to Lords of Trade, August 14, 1683, Proud, and Hazard. "good conversation . . ." *Testimony of Richard Townsend,* Proud.

246 For material on *Welcome* see notes to chapter 13.

246-47 Conference on board ship and reception at fort from Moll's account in Hazard.

247 Swedish statement in Vaux article, *Friends Historical Association Bulletin,* Vol. 21. Trip to Upland and Robert Wade in Hazard.

Page 248 "In no outward thing . . ." Penn to Thomas Janney, August 21, 1681, HSP. "It is a very fine country . . ." Markham to wife, December 7, 1681, *Penn Mag,* Vol. 6. Penn's description of country in his letter to Free Society, August 16, 1683, Proud.

249 Renaming Upland and first court notice, Hazard. Description of Philadelphia site from Scharf and Westcott and Glenn article on *Blue Anchor* in *Penn Mag,* Vol. 20.

250 First drawings for city lots in Hazard. Pennsbury deed, HSP MS. and Penna *Colonial Records,* Vol. 13.

251 First court, Hazard.

252 Penn's mission to New York, Brodhead. "We being fully satisfied . . ." Brockholls to Moll and Harman, November 21, 1682, Hazard. "I received yours of 24th . . ." Brockholls to Werden, Hazard. "The people in general . . ." Rudyard to Penn, January 13, 1683, FHL.

252-53 Story of the legendary Great Treaty taken chiefly from Vaux article *A Memoir* in HSP *Memoirs,* Vol. 1, Fisher article *A Memoir* in HSP *Memoirs,* Vol. 3, and Stone's article *Penn's Treaty* in *Penn Mag,* Vol. 6. Voltaire's comment on Treaty can be found under *Quakers* in his *Dictionnaire Philosophique* (1764): *C'est le seul traité entre ces peuples et les Chrétiens qui n'ait point été juré et qui n'ait point été rompu.*

254 Penn to Free Society, August 16, 1683, Proud.

255 Penn's athletic prowess with Indians an undocumented legend in both Watson's *Annals* and Janney.

256-57 First Assembly from Hazard.

257-62 Conferences between Markham and Baltimore and between Penn and Baltimore from Hall.

258 Penn's letter to Frisby, *et al.,* September 16, 1681, HSP.

260 Penn's letter to Privy Council (Lords of Trade), August 14, 1683, Proud.

261 King's letter to Baltimore, August 19, 1682, HSP.

263 Ford's statement in *London Gazette* and text of *A Vindication* in *Penn Mag,* Vol. 6. Penn's letter to Yeates, February 5, 1683, HSP.

264 "Remember that the twelve . . ." Penn to Markham, February 5, 1683, HSP.

264-65 First Council meeting, *Colonial Records,* Vol. 1.

266 "I congratulate your arrival . . ." Culpepper to Penn, December 23, 1682, HSP. "I give you my hearty . . ." Dongan to Penn, December 3, 1683, *Penn Mag,* Vol. 25.

267 "I thank God . . ." Penn to North, July 24, 1683, *Penn Mag,* Vol. 52. "Would be glad . . ." Penn to Sydney, July 24, 1683, HSP. "Ever since he yielded . . ." Penn to Sunderland, July 28, 1683, HSP.

267-68 His letters to Savile and Boyle in *Penn Mag,* Vol. 6.

268 "My soul remembers . . ." Penn to "J.A.," November 29, 1683, FHL. Claypoole to Furly, March 13, 1683, Claypoole to Penn, April 1, 1683, HSP.

268-69 Guli's letter to Margaret Fox, August 20, 1683, is a copy at Friends House, London, with the notation in John Abraham's writing, "A letter to my dear and honour'd grandmother Margt Fox from Wm Penn's first wife. . . ."

269 Ellwood's visit to Sussex from his *Journal.*

269-70 Many original Indian deeds are owned by the Historical Society of Pennsylvania, and texts of all deeds referred to in this chapter are published in *Colonial Records,* Vol. 13, and Penna *Archives,* Vol. 1.

270-71 Narrative of Susquehanna Valley purchase from Penna *Archives,* Vol. 1, *New York Colonial Manuscripts,* and several HSP MSS.

271-73 Analysis of immigrating groups from Pomfret article in *Penn Mag,* Vol. 80, Hull's *Penn and Dutch Quaker Migration,* Myers' *Immigration of Irish,* and Hazard.

273-76 Penn-Baltimore conferences see notes earlier in this chapter.

274 Penn to King, August 13, 1683, to Rochester, July 24, 1683, and to Sunderland, June 14, 1683, FHL; to Sydney, July 24, 1683, HSP.

275 "He hath searched . . ." Dongan to Penn, May 1, 1683, HSP. "I suppose you'll hear . . ." Margaret Lowther to Penn, August 4, 1683, FHL.

277 "I am following him . . ." Penn to York, June 8, 1684, FHL. "The Lord Baltimore and . . ." Purvis to Penn, May 21, 1684, HSP. "Loving Friends and tenants . . ." Penn to settlers, November 9, 1683, HSP. "Let the planters give . . ." Penn to Symcock, April 2, 1684, HSP.

278 "God hath brought us . . ." Penn to Society of Friends, 1684, Janney.

279 "My desire is . . ." Penn to Harrison, August 15, 1684, HSP.

279-80 "Get the courtyards . . ." Penn to Smyth, about 1684, HSP.

280 "I am sorry that we . . ." Lowther to Penn, August 5, 1683, FHL.

280-81 Penn to his wife, August 6, 1684, HSP. Penn's will, HSP.

282 "Dearly beloved in the Lord . . ." Crisp to Penn, May 4, 1684, in *Letters of Isaac Penington.* "My love and my life . . ." Penn to Lloyd, *et al.,* August 16, 1684, HSP.

283 "Not one soldier . . ." Penn to Crisp, February 28, 1685, in *Letters of Isaac Penington.*

Chapter 16: THE TURNING TIDE

Page 284 "I arrived . . ." Penn's *Fragments of an Apology,* HSP *Memoirs,* Vol. 3. Penn's instructions to Harrison in letters to him of March 18, 1685, May 19, 1685, and July 11, 1685, HSP. "After some days . . ." from Penn's *Fragments.*

285 "the ground and very . . ." Penn to Harrison, October 7, 1684, HSP.

286 "finding myself narrowed . . . ," "upon the whole matter . . ." and Vickris case from Penn's *Fragments.*

287 "The ancient love . . ." Penn to Margaret Fox, October 29, 1684, FHL. *True Interest of King and Kingdom* described in Penn's *Fragments.* "They opportunely blooded . . ." Penn to T. Lloyd, March 16, 1685, Janney.

288 "Suffer in the crowd . . ." Penn to James II, February 7, 1685, HSP.

288-89 "He declared . . . fixed liberty." Penn to T. Lloyd, March 16, 1685, Janney.

291 "In France not a meeting . . ." Penn to Harrison, October 25, 1685, HSP.

292 Two letters from Barclay to Penn, September 12 and October 9, 1685, in Grant. "I have been at Windsor . . ." Penn to [?], August 17, 1685, HSP. "Penn produced diverse . . ." September 2, 1685, minutes of Committee on Trade, HSP. "for avoiding further . . ." November 13, 1685, same source.

293 "There comes a Dutchman . . ." Penn to Harrison, October 25, 1685, HSP. "Cannot more friendly . . ." Penn to T. Lloyd, *et al.,* August, 1685, HSP.

294 "I have spent 3000 . . ." Penn to Harrison, n.d., HSP. "The Roman Catholics . . ." Penn to Turner, April 24, 1686, HSP. "I am sorry that the public . . ." Penn to Harrison, July 11, 1685, HSP. "There is a cry . . ." Penn to magistrates, July 26, 1685, HSP.

295 "a bred scholar . . ." and "a kinsman . . ." Penn to T. Lloyd, *et al.,* 1685, HSP. "I would have you . . ." Penn to Lloyd, October 6, 1685, HSP.

295-96 Ford material from *Bill of Complaint* (see notes to chapter 13) and an HSP MS (Penn vs Ford).

296 "My Persuasive works . . ." Penn to Harrison, April 24, 1686, HSP.

297 "I am going for Holland . . ." Penn to [?], about April, 1686, HSP.

298 Peter Hendricks' letter to Longworth, September 9, 1686, in unfinished Hull MS (see notes to chapter 9). "I have had a blessed . . ." Penn to Harrison, September 23, 1686, Janney.

299 "I count myself . . ." Penn to Harrison, November 7, 1686, HSP. "I shall hardly know . . ." Penn to T. Lloyd, February 1, 1687, HSP. "You make mention . . ." More to Penn, September 13, 1686, *Penn Mag,* Vol. 4. "The Society is a great . . ." Penn to Council 1686, *Penn Mag,* Vol. 33.

300 "This quarrel . . ." Penn to T. Lloyd, February 1, 1687, HSP. "good fresh pork . . ." More's letter above. "the gardener is brisk . . ." Harrison to Penn, October 3, 1686, HSP. "It almost tempts me . . ." Penn to Harrison, November 7, 1686, HSP. "the charter is over . . . resolved thought" Penn to Harrison, January 28, 1687, HSP.

301 "I beseech thee . . ." Penn to Harrison, November 20, 1686, HSP.

302 "for I will no more endure . . ." Penn to Provincial Council, February 1, 1687, HSP. "Be most just . . ." from the same.

302-03 Interview with King James from Sewel and Besse's *Journal of His Life.*

303-04 Trip through western England from letter to Harrison of September 8, 1687 and from Whiting.

Chapter 17: "I AM A MAN OF SORROWS"

306 Popple letter and Penn's reply, Janney.

306-07 "The things which are . . ." Sewell to Penn, December 20, 1689, Hull's *Sewel.*

307 "Since no Friend . . ." Penn to "Dear Friends," December 30, 1689, HSP.

307-08 Biographical material on Blackwell chiefly from N. Wainwright article, *Penn Mag,* Vol. 74.

309 "We hear Captain . . ." E. Blackfan to Phineas Pemberton, September 6, 1689, HSP.

310 Penn's arrest warrant February 27, 1689, PRO.

310-11 "I thought it would look . . ." Penn to Shrewsbury, March 1, 1689, Janney.

311 Lord Nottingham order of June 22, 1689, PRO.

312 "Europe looks like . . ." Penn to Friends, March 2, 1689, Janney. Value of Irish lands from letter of Penn to Governor and Council, September 15, 1690, HSP. "I

now only wait . . ." Blackwell to Penn, June 24, 1689, HSP. "I have made thee my receiver . . ." Penn to Blackwell, September 25, 1689, HSP.

Page 313 Death of Gulielma Maria from Quaker records, FHL. "I purpose in a few . . ." Penn to Commissioners, December 29, 1689, HSP. "I advise thee . . ." Turner to Penn, May 24, 1690, HSP.

314 Tower order of June 24, 1690, PRO. "As soon as I had . . ." Penn to Nottingham, July 31, 1690, FHL. August 15, 1690 release, PRO.

315 Information on Ford from *Bill of Complaint* (see notes to chapter 13) and HSP MSS (Penn vs Ford). "I was cleared . . ." Penn to Markham, *et al.,* December 4, 1690, HSP.

317 Penn to Margaret Fox, January 13, 1691, a copy by Cornelius Fry *circa* 1760, FHL.

317-18 Penn's near arrest at Fox's funeral mentioned only by Besse in *Journal of His Life.*

318 Proclamation of February 5, 1691, PRO. "the most extraordinary case . . ." Penn to [?] 1692, HSP *Memoirs,* Vol. 4.

319 "My privacy is not because . . ." Penn to London Yearly Meeting, May 30, 1691, in his 1726 collected works. Robert Harley letter and quote from Luttrell diary from PRO.

319-20 Sydney's letter to King, January 20, 1692, PRO.

320 "Allow me to live . . ." and "Let me be believed . . ." Penn to King, 1691, Janney.

320-21 "I sent him word . . . with my Lord Preston." Sydney to King, February 27, 1692, PRO.

321 "pray speak to the King . . ." Penn to Tillotson, October 31, 1691, HSP.

321-22 "The motions or success . . ." Penn to Nottingham, June 12, 1692, HSP.

323-24 "I have received your divided . . ." Penn to Friends, September 11, 1691, HSP.

324 "concurring amicably . . ." T. Lloyd, *et al.,* to Penn, April 6, 1692, HSP. "I long with many . . ." Turner to Penn, June 15, 1692, HSP. "very great expenses . . ." Penn's request for loan to "Dear Friends," February 4, 1693, HSP *Memoirs* Vol. 4.

326 "Before this sad . . ." November 29, 1692, Penn to Turner, HSP.

328-29 "Greetings, well beloved . . ." Sewel to Penn, 1693, in Hull's *Sewel.*

329 Sewel's letter to Springett Penn, October 27, 1693, in Hull's *Sewel.* "It hath pleased God . . ." Penn to Lloyd, December 11, 1693, HSP.

330 "Yesterday at Bull and Mouth . . ." Lower to Margaret Fox, December 2, 1693, JFHS Vol. 9.

331 "My wife is yet weakly . . ." Penn to Lloyd, December 11, 1693, HSP.

331-32 Guli's death from Penn's *Account of the Blessed End* in his 1726 collected works.

Chapter 18: MIDDLE AGED SUITOR

333 Penn's illness in his letter to Carpenter, *et al.,* April 24, 1694, HSP.

334 Royal grant of August 20, 1694, HSP.

335 "the seeds of many good . . ." from Penn's *Sorrow and Joy,* his 1726 collected works. "Since it hath pleased . . ." Penn to magistrates of Gloucester, January 3, 1695, HSP. Penn's trip to Wilts, etc., Whiting *Memoirs.*

336 Hannah's birth date from Friends' records, Bristol, England. Her biography from Howard M. Jenkins. Early Quaker aversion to "reproductions of the creature" robs us in the case of Hannah Callowhill, as in that of Penn himself and of his first wife, of any certainty as to her appearance.

337 "give my endeared . . ." Penn to Anna Callowhill, June 28, 1695, HSP. "I long to see you . . . ," "My face is now turned . . ." and "licks up . . . ," Penn to Turner and Holme, June 20, 1695, HSP. "painful meeting," Braithwaite who cites letter of Gouldney to Barclay, February 28, 1695, in *Reliquiae Barclaianae.*

338-48 All of Penn's love letters to Hannah Callowhill and Letitia's letter to Hannah of December 12, 1695, are HSP MSS.

339-40 Trip to Melksham and Plymptom's debate and arrest warrant from Besse's *Journal of His Life* and Whiting *Memoirs.*

339, 341 Declarations to wed, Bristol Monthly Meeting minutes.

340 "Now our case is . . ." Penn to Council, November 5, 1695, HSP.

343 Margaret Lowther's gift, Penn letter to Hannah, January 2, 1696, HSP.

344 Penn's declarations, Horsham Monthly Meeting minutes.

344-45 Narrative of Penn family illness from Penn's letters to Hannah.

348 Penn's and Hannah's wedding certificate, Jenkins.

Pages 349-50 Narrative of Springett's death from Penn's *Sorrow and Joy,* his 1726 collected works.

350 Barclay's letter to Penn, April 20, 1696, HSP; Sewel's letter to Penn, August, 1696, Hull's *Sewel.*

351-52 Assembly's remonstrance to Markham and November 7, 1696 *Frame,* Proud. Penn's *Plan for a Union,* HSP *Memoirs,* Vol. 6.

353-54 Ford material from *Bill of Complaint,* HSP MSS and Shepherd (see notes to chapter 13). "did frequently urge . . ." and "deed-poll containing . . ." Penn to Logan, February 7, 1706, HSP *Memoirs,* Vol. 10.

354-55 Meeting with Czar from Story and Whitehead journals.

355-58 Journey through Ireland from Story *Journal.*

359 William Penn, Jr.'s wedding, Howard M. Jenkins. "Rob, the ancient noble . . ." Penn to Turner, December 25, 1696, HSP.

359-60 "Thou has left us . . ." Turner to Penn, June 26, 1697, HSP.

361 "It is the general discourse . . ." Quary to Lords of Trade, May 10, 1699, HSP. "with all convenient speed . . ." Lords of Trade to Penn, September 12, 1699, HSP.

361-64 Conference with Ford at Islington from *Bill of Complaint* and Penn letter to Grimbole Pauncefort, September 7, 1706, HSP. Earlier Ford lawsuit from minutes of Six Weeks Meeting, FHL.

Chapter 19: SECOND AMERICAN SOJOURN

365-66 Cannon incident from Story *Journal.* Quary's presence at wharf, Logan to Penn, Jr., September 25, 1700, HSP *Memoirs,* Vol. 9.

366-67 Material on Philadelphia from Penn's *A Further Account,* Scharf and Westcott, and Bridenbaugh.

368-69 Penn's diplomatic letters all HSP MSS. His travels with Story from Story *Journal.*

369 Birth certificate of John Penn, HSP. "My wife is safely . . ." Penn to Bellomont, January 30, 1700, HSP.

370 "Their little son . . ." Isaac Norris to Jeffry Pinnell, March 6, 1701, HSP. Birth of grandchild, Howard M. Jenkins. Penn to Commissioners of Customs, February 28, 1700, HSP.

371 Adams test case from Lewis's *Courts, Penn Mag,* Vol. 5.

372 "Since you were dissatisfied . . ." Penn to Council, *Colonial Records.* "They would seem . . ." Norris to Ford, June 13, 1700, HSP *Memoirs,* Vol. 9. Penn's residence at Pennsbury from Penn-Logan letters, HSP; his trips to Philadelphia from *Colonial Records,* Council minutes.

373 Deed with Susquehannas, September 13, 1700, *Archives,* Vol. 1.

373-74 Conference of governors from following HSP MSS: Penn to Blackistone, October 10, 1700; Penn to Bellomont, October 10, 1700; Penn to Lord Sommers, October 22, 1700; Penn to Lords of Trade, December 8, 1700.

374 "His sweating last night . . ." Hannah Penn to Logan, November, 1700, and "much teasing . . ." I. Norris to Zachary Taylor, December 8, 1700, HSP *Memoirs,* Vol. 9.

375-76 Quary's complaint and Penn's reply, HSP *Memoirs,* Vol. 9.

376 Birth of second grandchild, Howard M. Jenkins. "My dear little boy . . ." Hannah to Elizabeth Taylor, March 6, 1701, British Museum.

376-77 Penn's journey to Sussex in his letter to Blackistone, May 23, 1701, and to "Honored Friends," May 17, 1701, HSP.

377 Ford, Jr.'s visit to America HSP (Penn vs Ford) MS, Shepherd, and a footnote by Deborah Logan, HSP *Memoirs,* Vol. 10. Indians to Philadelphia from *Colonial Records.* Penn's trip to Susquehanna Valley, Isaac Norris to Daniel Zachary, June 21, 1701, HSP *Memoirs,* Vol. 9.

378 Penn as mediator among Indians, his letter to Nanfan, July 2, 1701, HSP. Broken shin from his correspondence with Logan, HSP.

378-79 "I only wish myself twenty . . ." Penn to Charlwood Lawton, August 18, 1701, HSP.

379 "We renounce all independency . . ." Penn to Lords of Trade, August 27, 1701, HSP. Penn's personal appeals to high-ranking persons are all HSP MSS.

380 Assembly's twenty-one concerns and Penn's reply, Proud. "dispose of many good patches . . ." and "to dispose of in this world . . ." Penn to Logan, September 8, 1701, HSP.

381 Letitia's certificate from Philadelphia Monthly Meeting in Friends Arch Street

Centre. Visit of Delaware tribes to Pennsbury from Richardson *Journal* and Penn letter to Bellomont, n.d., in old letter book, HSP. Penn's visit to Tredhaven from Richardson *Journal.*

Pages 381-82 Charter of Privileges and Philadelphia Charter texts in Proud.

382 "Use thy utmost . . ." Penn to Logan, November 3, 1701, HSP. Penn's agreement with captain of *Dolmahoy,* HSP *Memoirs,* Vol. 9.

CHAPTER 20: PENN VERSUS FORD

383 "We had a swift . . . ," "a sweet girl . . ." and "serviceable but costly . . ." Penn to Logan, January 4, 1702, HSP.

384 "Nothing yet done . . . ," "our foolish and knavish . . ." the same. Birth of Thomas Penn, Quaker records, FHL.

385 "Hasten over rents . . ." Penn to Logan, February 3, 1702, HSP. "Never had man . . ." Penn to Logan, June 21, 1702, HSP. "The country even where . . ." Logan to Penn, May 7, 1702, HSP.

386 "All things have gone . . . great damp on business," Logan to Penn, December 2, 1701, May 2, 1702, May 7, 1702, June 18, 1702, August 13, 1702, September 11, 1702, HSP; May 11, 1702 and May 28, 1702, HSP *Memoirs,* Vol. 9.

387 Queen Anne incident from Sewel and Gough. "I have had the wisest . . ." Penn to Logan, June 21, 1702, HSP. "I was too infirm . . ." Penn to Lords of Trade, April, 1702, HSP. Letitia wedding Horsham Monthly minute book, FHL. "We exceedingly long . . ." Logan to Letitia, August 14, 1702, HSP *Memoirs,* Vol. 9. "I was much surprised . . ." Penn, Jr., to Logan, August 18, 1702, HSP.

387-88 "William Masters, whatever . . ." Penn, Jr., to Logan in footnote, Deborah Logan, HSP *Memoirs,* Vol. 9.

388-89 Incident of Bridget Ford from *Bill of Complaint* (see notes to chapter 13). Explanation of Ford accounts from HSP MS and letter of Penn to Logan, February 7, 1706, HSP.

389-90 Lloyd vs Logan, Lewis's *Courts, Penn Mag,* Vol. 5, and Sharpless.

390 Queen approves Hamilton, Penn to Lords of Trade, December 2, 1702, HSP. Penn's petition to Lords of Trade, May 11, 1703, British Museum. "who neither knew . . ." and "Were the government mine . . ." Logan to Penn, August 22, 1705, HSP. "a liberal education . . ." Penn to Lords of Trade, July 8, 1703, HSP.

391 Birth of Hannah Margarita from Quaker records, FHL. "They with my two . . ." Penn to Logan, August 27, 1703, HSP. "Because I am ready . . ." Hannah to Penn, October 13, 1703, HSP.

392 "We shall be exceeding . . ." Logan to Penn, May 7, 1702, HSP. "It is his stock . . ." Logan to Penn, February 15, 1704, HSP.

392-93 "William Penn, Junior quite gone . . ." Isaac Norris to Jonathan Dickenson, September 27, 1704, HSP.

393 "Presentment of thy son . . ." Logan to Penn, October 3, 1704, HSP. "Mr. William incensed . . ." Logan to Penn, September 28, 1704, HSP.

393-94 "I suppose you will . . ." David Lloyd to George Whitehead, October 3, 1704, HSP.

394 "If my son prove . . ." Penn to Logan, November 2, 1704, HSP. "Let me take the . . ." Logan to Penn, November 22, 1704, HSP. "O, Pennsylvania!" Penn to Logan, n.d. HSP *Memoirs,* Vol. 9.

395 "Pardon this abrupt . . ." Penn to Edward Southwell, Secretary of State for Ireland at Dublin, February 20, 1705, HSP. Evans administration and lawsuit from Penn-Logan correspondence, HSP. French fleet hoax, Proud. "My surrender of government . . ." Penn to Logan, April 30, 1705, HSP.

396-404 Ford Case from *Bill of Complaint* (see notes chapter 13), HSP MSS (Penn vs Ford), Shepherd, and Penn-Logan correspondence, HSP.

396 Devonshire House minute, HSP *Memoirs,* Vol. 10. "informing them that . . . extremely grieved." Logan to Penn, July 13, 1705, HSP.

397 "I write to thee . . ." Isaac Norris to Ford, Jr., August 29, 1705, HSP *Memoirs,* Vol. 10. "As to Ford's . . ." Logan to Penn, 1706, HSP *Memoirs,* Vol. 10.

398 "A Chancery suit . . ." Logan to Penn, Jr., August 12, 1706. Penn's 1705 will, HSP.

398-99 Sale of Worminghurst, Covenant of Indemnity of November 22, 1707, and agreement between father and son, HSP; letter of Penn to Logan, May 18, 1708, HSP.

399 Penn's letter *re* his daughter-in-law to Logan, July 8, 1707, HSP *Memoirs,* Vol. 10. "to bring him to terms . . ." Lords of Trade to [?] February 5, 1707, HSP.

399-400 Logan's impeachment, HSP *Memoirs,* Vol. 10, and *Colonial Records,* Vol. 2.

Pages 400-01 "Last fourth day . . ." Isaac Norris to Richard Hill, May 17, 1707, HSP.

401 Ford suit in Common Pleas, Isaac Norris to Logan, July 14, 1707, HSP *Memoirs,* Vol. 10. "His business with B. Ford . . ." Norris to Moore, November 7, 1707, HSP *Memoirs,* Vol. 10. "I have now only . . ." Norris to Richard Hill, November 29, 1707, HSP *Memoirs,* Vol. 10.

402 Penn's arrest, January 7, 1708, Norris to Joseph Pike, January 27, 1708. "He has commodious . . ." the same. Death of Hannah Margarita and birth of Hannah at Ludgate, Quaker records, FHL.

403 "That the like . . ." and "The Lord Chancellor . . ." Norris to Logan, March 6, 1708, HSP *Memoirs,* Vol. 10.

403-04 "The Fords seem to embrace . . ." Penn to Logan, May 3, 1708, HSP.

404 "I hope next spring . . ." Penn to Logan, May 18, 1708, HSP. "My business is . . ." Penn to Logan, September 11, 1708, HSP *Memoirs,* Vol. 10. New Pennsylvania Mortgage, October 7, 1708, HSP.

Chapter 21: PEACE

405 "Neither he nor . . ." T. Callowhill to Logan, March 23, 1707, HSP. Death of Hannah from Quaker records, FHL.

405-09 All letters between Hannah and William Penn and Penn's to his sons are HSP MSS.

410 "no room to expect . . ." Norris to Penn, December 2, 1709, HSP. "Tis a certain . . . shown my secretary," from Penn's *Serious Expostulation,* HSP.

411 Logan's self-vindication, arrest warrant, and Governor Gookin's countermand, Proud. Penn's surrender of government, report to Queen by Lords of Trade, February 13, 1711, HSP.

411-12 Penn's final will, Principal Probate Office, Somerset House, London.

412-13 His last letter, October 4, 1712, and Hannah's of October 13, 1712, HSP.

413 "He just reached home . . ." Hannah Penn to Logan, February 5, 1713, HSP.

414 Story's visits to Ruscombe from his *Journal*. "near as usual . . ." Hannah to Thomas Story, February 27, 1715, FHL. "Thy poor father . . ." Hannah to one of her children from Bath, May 11, 1715, HSP. Reading Quarterly Meeting Testimony from Quaker minutes at Reading.

Bibliography

Manuscript Collections

The Historical Society of Pennsylvania, Philadelphia, Pa.
American Philosophical Society, Philadelphia, Pa.
Friends Historical Library of Swarthmore College, Swarthmore, Pa.
Friends' Arch Street Centre, Philadelphia, Pa.
Library of the Society of Friends, Friends House, London.
The British Museum, London.
Public Record Office, London.
The Bodleian Library, Oxford.
Friends Meeting House Library, Dublin.

Published Records

The Friends' Library (14 volumes), Philadelphia, 1844, containing the Journals and Memoirs of John Audland, John Burnyeat, Edward Burrough, John Camm, William Edmundson, Thomas Ellwood, John Richardson, Thomas Story, George Whitehead.

Letters, etc. of Early Friends, London, 1841.

Original Narratives of Early American History:

Hall, Clayton Colman, Editor, *Narratives of Early Maryland 1633-1684.* New York, 1910.

James, Bartlett Burleigh and Jameson, J. Franklin, Editors, *Journal of Jasper Danckaerts 1679-1680.* New York, 1913.

Myers, Albert Cook, Editor, *Narratives of Early Pennsylvania, West New Jersey and Delaware 1630-1707.* New York, 1912.

Memoirs of the Historical Society of Pennsylvania:

Heckewelder, Reverend John, *An Account of the History, Manners and Customs of the Indian Nations, Who Once Inhabited Pennsylvania and the Neighboring States.* Volume 12.

Lawton, Mr. Charlwood, *A Memoir of Part of the Life of William Penn.* Volume 3.

Logan, Deborah, *Some Account of the Honorable James Logan.* Volume 9.

Penn, William, *Fragments of An Apology for Himself,* Volume 3 (copied from the original autographs in the library of the American Philosophical Society). Penn's title on manuscript: *Something Begun Toward a History of My Life from '84.*

Penn, William, Correspondence between William Penn and James Logan 1700-1750. Volumes 9 and 10.

Du Ponceau, Peter S. and Fisher, J. Francis, A *Memoir on the History of the Celebrated Treaty Made by William Penn with the Indians Under the Elm Tree at Shackamaxon in the Year 1682.* Volume 3.

Vaux, Roberts, A *Memoir on the Locality of the Great Treaty Between William Penn and the Indian Natives in 1682.* Volume 1.

Colonial Records of Pennsylvania. Minutes of the Provincial Council of Pennsylvania. Published by the State. Philadelphia, 1852.

Pennsylvania Archives, Selected and Arranged from Original Documents in the Office of the Secretary of the Commonwealth, by Samuel Hazard. Philadelphia, 1852.

Proceedings of the New Jersey Historical Society, July 1934.

Kemmerer, Donald L., *The Suffrage Franchise in Colonial New Jersey.*

Documents Relating to the Colonial History of the State of New Jersey (Archives) edited by William A. Whitehead. Newark, 1881.

Journal of the Legislative Council of the Colony of New York 1691-1743.

Great Britain, Public Record Office:

Calendar of State Papers, Domestic.

Acts of the Privy Council, Colonial Series.

Books and Pamphlets

Aubrey, John. *'Brief Lives,' Chiefly of Contemporaries, set down by John Aubrey, between the years 1669 and 1696.* Edited by Andrew Clark. Oxford, 1898.

Ball, Sir William. *Lincoln's Inn, Its History and Traditions.* London, 1947.

Barclay, Robert. *An Apology for the True Christian Divinity Being an Explanation and Vindication of the Principles and Doctrines of the People Called Quakers.* Philadelphia, 1908.

Barker, Ernest. *The Politics of Aristotle.* Oxford, 1946.

Bauchard, Raoul. *Histoire du Saumurois du XV au XX Siècle.* Saumur, 1941.

Beard, Charles A. and Mary R. *A Basic History of the United States.* New York, 1944.

Bell, Walter George. *The Great Fire of London in 1666.* London, 1920.

———. *The Great Plague in London in 1665.* London, 1924.

Besant, Walter. *London in the Time of the Stuarts.* London, 1903.

———. *London, North of the Thames.* London, 1911.

Besse, Joseph. *A Collection of the Sufferings of the People Called Quakers.* London, 1753.

———. *A Journal of His* [Penn's] *Life.* See: Penn, William, *A Collection*

Bishop, Cortlandt F. *History of Elections in the American Colonies.* New York, 1893.

Blackham, Colonel Robert J. *Wig and Gown, The Story of the Temple, Gray's Inn and Lincoln's Inn.* London, n.d.

Blackstone, William. *Commentaries on the Laws of England in Four Books.* Chicago, 1899.

Blaze de Bury, The Baroness. *Memoirs of The Princess Palatine, Princess of Bohemia.* London, 1853.

Bond, Beverley W., Jr. *The Quit-Rent System in the American Colonies.* New Haven, 1919.

Bowden, James. *The History of the Society of Friends in America.* London, 1850.

Bowrey, Thomas. *Diary of a Six-Weeks' Tour in 1698 in Holland.* London, 1927.

Brailsford, Mabel Richmond. *The Making of William Penn.* New York, 1930.

Braithwaite, William Charles. *Beginnings of Quakerism.* London, 1912.

———. *The Second Period of Quakerism.* London, 1919.

Bridenbaugh, Carl. *Cities in the Wilderness, The First Century of Urban Life in America.* New York, 1938.

Brinton, Daniel G. *The Lenape and Their Legends.* Philadelphia, 1885.

Brittain, Vera. *Valiant Pilgrim, The Story of John Bunyan and Puritan England.* New York, 1950.

Brodhead, John Romeyn. *History of the State of New York.* New York, 1859.

Buchan, John. *Oliver Cromwell.* Boston, 1934.

Budgell, Eustace. *Memoirs of the Lives and Characters of the Illustrious Family of the Boyles.* Dublin, 1754.

Burnet, Bishop Gilbert. *The History of My Own Times.* London, 1724.

Butler, James. *The Life and Character of James Butler, Late Duke, Marquis and Earl of Ormond.* London, 1729.

———. *The Life of James, late Duke of Ormonde.* London, 1747.

Cadbury, M. Cristabel. *Robert Barclay, His Life and Work.* London, 1912.

Campbell, Douglas. *The Puritan in Holland, England and America.* New York, 1899.

Chalmers, George. *Political Annals of the Present United Colonies, From Their Settlement to the Peace of 1763.* London, 1780.

Chancellor, E. Beresford. *The Pleasure Haunts of London.* London, 1925.

Clarendon, Edward, Earl of. *The History of the Rebellion and Civil Wars in England.* Oxford, 1843.

Clark, G. N. *The Later Stuarts 1660-1714.* Oxford, 1949.

Clarkson, Thomas. *Memoirs of the Private and Public Life of William Penn.* Philadelphia, 1813.

Clinch, George. *English Costume.* London, 1909.

Clowes, G. S. Laird. *Sailing Ships, Their History and Development.* London, 1930.

Coale, Josiah. *The Books and Divers Epistles of the Faithful Servant of the Lord Josiah Coale.* 1671.

Cobbett, William. *Parliamentary History of England* (selected volumes).

Coleman, James. *A Pedigree and Genealogical Notes from Wills, Registers, and Deeds of the Highly Distinguished Family of Penn, of England and America.* Bloomsbury, 1871.

———. *Reprint of William Penn's Original Proposal and Plan for the Founding and Building of Philadelphia in Pennsylvania, America, in 1683.* London, 1881.

Craig, Maurice. *Dublin 1660-1860.* Dublin, 1952.

Cronau, Rudolf. *Three Centuries of German Life in America.* Berlin, 1909.

Cusack, Mary F. *A History of the City and County of Cork.* Dublin, 1875.

Davies, C. M. *The History of Holland and the Dutch.* London, 1851.

Davies, Godfrey. *The Early Stuarts 1603-1660.* Oxford, 1952.

Dixon, W. Hepworth. *A History of William Penn Founder of Pennsylvania.* New York, 1902.

Drogheda, Countess of. *The Family of Moore.* Dublin, 1906.

Eagleton, Clyde. *International Government.* New York, 1948.

Evelyn, John. *Diary of John Evelyn.* Edited by William Bray, Life of the Author and a New Preface by Henry B. Wheatley. London, 1906.

Ewald, Alex. Charles. *The Life and Times of the Hon. Algernon Sydney.* London, 1873.

Falkiner, C. Litton. *Illustrations of Irish History and Topography, Mainly of the Seventeenth Century.* London, 1904.

Faust, Albert B. *Francis Daniel Pastorius and the 250th Anniversary of the Founding of Germantown.* Philadelphia, 1934. (Pamphlet)

Fay, Sidney Bradshaw. *The Rise of Brandenburg-Prussia to 1786.* New York, 1937.

Fellow, W. A. *The Present State of the United Provinces of the Low Countries.* London, 1671.

Ferrar, John. *A View of Ancient and Modern Dublin, with its Improvements.* Dublin, 1796.

Fox, George. *The Journal of George Fox.* A Revised Edition by John L. Nickalls. Cambridge, 1952. Also the First Edition of 1694, edited by Thomas Ellwood.

———. *The Short Journal and Itinerary Journals of George Fox.* (This volume includes the *Haistwell Diary.*) Edited by Norman Penney. Cambridge, 1925.

Fraissinet, Marc. *Essai Sur La Morale D'Amyraut.* Toulouse, 1889.

Freeman, Edward A. *The Growth of the English Constitution from the Earliest Times.* London, 1872.

Frost, James. *History and Topography of the County of Clare.* Dublin, 1843.

Garber, John Palmer. *The Valley of the Delaware and Its Place in American History.* Philadelphia, 1934.

Gentleman, A. *A View of Paris, Written by a Gentleman Lately Residing at the English Ambassador's at Paris.* London, 1701.

Godfrey, Elizabeth. *A Sister of Prince Rupert, Elizabeth Princess Palatine and Abbess of Herford.* New York, 1909.

Goebel, Max. *History of Christian Life in the Rhenish-Westphalian Protestant Church.* Coblenz, 1852.

Gorsline, Douglas. *What People Wore.* New York, 1952.

Gough, John. *A History of the People Called Quakers from Their First Rise to the Present Time.* Dublin, 1790.

Grant, Mrs. Colquhoun. *Quaker and Courtier, The Life and Work of William Penn.* London, 1907.

Green, John Richard. *History of the English People.* New York, 1882.

Grego, Joseph. *A History of Parliamentary Elections and Electioneering in the Old Days.* London, 1886.

Grubb, Isabel. *Quakers in Ireland 1654-1900.* London, 1927.

Gummere, Amelia Mott. *The Quaker, A Study in Costume.* Philadelphia, 1901.

Haistwell, Edward. See: George Fox, *The Short Journal.*

Hall, Clayton Colman. *The Lords Baltimore and the Maryland Palatinate.* Baltimore, 1902.

Harris, Walter. *The History and Antiquities of the City of Dublin.* Dublin, 1766.

Haverfield, F. *Ancient Town-Planning.* Oxford, 1913.

Hayes, George Passmore. *Robert Barclay, His Life, Works and Position in the History of Quaker Thought.* An unpublished manuscript, 1927. Property of Swarthmore College.

Hayman, Rev. Samuel. *The New Handbook for Youghal.* 1858.

Hazard, Samuel. *Annals of Pennsylvania from the Discovery of the Delaware 1609-1682.* Philadelphia, 1850.

Hiscock, W. G. *A Christ Church Miscellany.* Oxford, 1946.

Hobhouse, Christopher. *Oxford as It Was and as It Is Today.* London, 1939.

Hodgkin, L. V. *Gulielma: Wife of William Penn.* London, 1947.

Holdsworth, W. S. *A History of English Law.* London, 1926. (Selected volumes.)

Hughes, T. Harold and Lamborn, E. A. G. *Towns and Town-Planning Ancient and Modern.* Oxford, 1923.

Hull, William I. *Benjamin Furly and Quakerism in Rotterdam.* Swarthmore, Pa., 1941.

———. *William Penn, A Topical Biography.* New York, 1937.

———. *William Penn and the Dutch Quaker Migration to Pennsylvania.* Swarthmore, Pa., 1935.

———. *Willem Sewel of Amsterdam 1653-1720, the First Quaker Historian of Quakerism.* Swarthmore, Pa., 1933.

Hurst, Gerald. *A Short History of Lincoln's Inn.* London, 1946.

Ilchester, The Earl of. *The Home of the Hollands 1605-1820.* London, 1937.

Janney, Samuel M. *Life of William Penn, with Selections from his Correspondence and Autobiography*. Philadelphia, 1851.

Jenkins, Howard M. *The Family of William Penn, Founder of Pennsylvania, Ancestry and Descendants*. Philadelphia, 1899.

Jenkins, J. Gilbert. *A History of the Parish of Penn*. London, 1935.

Jenks, Edward. *A Short History of English Law*. Boston, 1912.

Jones, Rufus M. *Quakers in the American Colonies*. London, 1911.

Jones, W. T. *Masters of Political Thought, Machiavelli to Bentham*, Volume 2. New York, 1947.

Kull, Irving S. *New Jersey, A History*. New York, 1930.

Latrobe, John H. B. *The History of the Mason and Dixon's Line*. Before the Historical Society of Pennsylvania, November 8, 1854. (Pamphlet)

Learned, Marion Dexter. *The Life of Francis Daniel Pastorius, The Founder of Germantown*. Philadelphia, 1908.

Lee, Robert W. *Hugo Grotius, Annual Lecture on a Master Mind*, Henriette Hertz Trust of the British Academy, 1930. (Pamphlet)

Lloyd, Arnold. *Quaker Social History 1669-1738*. London, 1950.

Lunt, Dudley. *The Bounds of Delaware*. Wilmington, 1947.

Lysons, Rev. Daniel. *The Environs of London*. London, 1795.

Mallet, Charles Edward. *History of the University of Oxford*. New York, 1924-27.

Meadley, George Wilson. *Memoirs of Algernon Sydney*. London, 1813.

Méteyer, L. J. *L'Académie Protestant de Saumur*. Paris, n.d.

Morphew, J. (Editor) *The Phenix: or, A Revival of Scarce and Valuable Pieces*. London, 1707.

Morris, William O'Connor. *Ireland 1494-1905*. Cambridge, 1909.

Mullinger, James Bass. *Cambridge Characteristics in the Seventeenth Century*. London and Cambridge, 1867.

Myers, Albert Cook. *Immigration of the Irish Quakers into Pennsylvania 1682-1750*. Swarthmore, Pa., 1902.

———. *William Penn's Early Life in Brief 1644-1674*. Moylan, Pa., 1937.

Myers, William Starr. *The Story of New Jersey*. New York, 1945.

Ogilby, John. *Roads Out of London, Being Photographic Reprints Extracted from Ogilby's Britannia, 1675*. Edited by T. F. Ordish. London, 1911.

O'Hart, John. *Irish Landed Gentry When Cromwell Came to Ireland*. Dublin, 1887.

Ormonde, J. *The Life of James (Butler) Late Duke of Ormonde*. 1747.

Osgood, Herbert L. *The American Colonies in the Seventeenth Century.* New York, 1904.

Penington, Isaac. *Letters of Isaac Penington, Written to His Relatives and Friends, Now First Published from Manuscript Copies.* London, 1796.

Penn, Granville. *Memorials of the Professional Life and Times of Sir William Penn, Knt.* London, 1833.

Penn, William. *A Collection of the Works of William Penn. To Which is Prefixed A Journal of His Life* (attributed to Joseph Besse) *With Many Original Letters and Papers Not Before Published.* London, 1726. See Bibliography of William Penn's Writings.

———. *My Irish Journal 1669-1670*, Edited by Isabel Grubb. London, 1952.

Penney, Norman, Editor. *Extracts from State Papers Relating to Friends 1654 to 1672.* London, 1913.

———, Editor. *The Household Account Book of Sarah Fell of Swarthmoor Hall.* Cambridge, 1920.

Pepys, Samuel. *Diary and Correspondence of Samuel Pepys.* Life and Notes by Richard, Lord Braybrooke. Philadelphia, n.d., (First Edition was 1848).

Pound, Arthur. *The Penns of Pennsylvania and England.* New York, 1932.

Proffatt, John. *A Treatise on Trial by Jury.* San Francisco, 1880.

Proud, Robert. *The History of Pennsylvania in North America from the Original Institution and Settlement of that Province, under the First Proprietor and Governor William Penn, in 1681, Till after the Year 1742.* Philadelphia, 1797-98.

Rojinskii, Lillian. *Seventeenth Century Costume.* London, 1952.

Sanders, Lloyd. *The Holland House Circle.* London, 1908.

Scharf, J. Thomas, and Westcott, Thompson. *History of Philadelphia 1609-1884.* Philadelphia, 1884.

Sewel, William. *The History of the Rise, Increase and Progress of the Christian People Called Quakers.* New York, 1844.

Sharpless, Isaac. *Political Leaders of Provincial Pennsylvania.* New York, 1919.

Shepherd, William Robert. *History of Proprietary Government in Pennsylvania.* New York, 1896.

Smith, Samuel. *The History of the Colony of Nova-Caesaria, or New-Jersey.* Burlington, 1765.

Spilsbury, William Holden. *Lincoln's Inn, Its Ancient and Modern Buildings*. London, 1850.

Stephen, James Fitzjames. *A History of the Criminal Law of England*. London, 1883.

Stow, John. *A Survey of London*. Reprinted from the Text of 1603. Oxford, 1908.

Sydney, Algernon. *Discourses on Government*. New York, 1805.

Thornbury, Walter, and Walford, Edward. *Old and New London*. London, n.d.

Tregelles, J. A. *A History of Hoddesdon in the County of Hertfordshire*. Hertford, 1908.

Trevelyan, George Macaulay. *The English Revolution 1688-1689*. London, 1938.

———. *England Under the Stuarts*. New York, 1949.

———. *Illustrated English Social History*. London, 1942.

Varley, Frederick John. *The Siege of Oxford*. London, 1932.

Vincent, W. A. L. *The State and School Education 1640-60 in England and Wales*. London, 1950.

Vulliamy, C. E. *William Penn*. New York, 1934.

Walker, Edwin Robert. *The Lenni Lenape or Delaware Indians*. Somerville, New Jersey, 1928. (Pamphlet.)

Watson, Foster. *The English Grammar Schools to 1660*. Cambridge, 1908.

Watson, John F. *Annals of Philadelphia, Being a Collection of Memoirs, Anecdotes, and Incidents of the City and Its Inhabitants from the Days of the Pilgrim Founders*. Philadelphia, 1830.

Weslager, C. A. *A Brief Account of the Indians of Delaware*. Delaware, 1953. (Pamphlet.)

Whiting, John. *Persecution Exposed, in Some Memoirs Relating to the Sufferings of John Whiting, and Many Others of the People Called Quakers*. London, 1741.

Wight, Thomas and Rutty, John. *A History of the Rise and Progress of the People Called Quakers in Ireland from the Year 1653 to 1700*. London, 1811.

Wolfe, Don M. *Milton in the Puritan Revolution*. New York, 1941.

Wood, Anthony. *The History . . . of Oxford*. 1786.

Wragge, J. Philip. *The Debt of Robert Barclay to George Keith*. July, 1946. (A bound manuscript, property of Swarthmore College.)

Authors not indicated:

The Case of Edward Bushel, John Hammond, Charles Milson, and John Baily, citizens and free-men of London, stated, and humbly presented to the honourable House of Commons Assembled in Parliament. 1671. (A pamphlet, property of Lincoln's Inn.)

The Scheme for the Management of Chigwell School. (A pamphlet, property of the school.)

A *Report from the Committee to Enquire into the State of the Goals of this Kingdom relating to Newgate and the Sheriffs Marshal of Dublin.* 1729. (A pamphlet, property of National Library, Dublin.)

A *Genealogical Account of the Earls of Roscommon and Barons Dillon of Kilkenny West.* (Property of National Library, Dublin.)

Catalogus, Librorum Omnium in Bibliotheca Aedis Christi, etc. Circa 1665. (A rare hand-written volume, property of Christ Church Library, Oxford.)

Magazine Articles

Archaeologia

Bruce, John. "Observations Upon William Penn's Imprisonment in the Tower of London, A.D. 1668." Volume 35.

The Bulletin of Friends Historical Association

Vaux, George. "The Embarkation Voyage and Arrival of the Ship Welcome." Volume 21.

The Contemporary Review

Van der Mandere, H. Ch. G. J. "Hugo Grotius, Founder of Modern International Law 1625-1925." May, 1925.

English Historical Review

Watson, Foster. "The State and Education During the Commonwealth." January, 1900.

The Journal of the Friends' Historical Society

Mood, Fulmer. "William Penn and English Politics in 1680-1681." Volume 32.

Walton, Joseph S. "David Lloyd." Volume 3.

Author not given. "The Convincement of William Penn." Article includes complete text of Harvey Manuscript. Volume 32.

R. S. M. "Penn and His Printer." Volume 46.

The Nineteenth Century

Stewart, Charles Edward. "A Visit to London in the Year 1651." October, 1912.

The Pennsylvania Magazine of History and Biography

Cadbury, Henry J. "Early References to Pennsylvania in the London Press." Volume 75.

———. "Intercepted Correspondence of William Penn, 1670." Volume 70.

———. "William Penn's Journal: Kent and Sussex, 1672." Volume 68.

Clement, John. "William Penn and West New Jersey." Volume 5.

Eshleman, H. Frank. "The Struggle and Rise of Popular Power in Pennsylvania's First Two Decades." Volume 34.

Glenn, Thomas Allen. "The Blue Anchor Tavern." Volume 20.

Hough, Oliver. "Captain William Crispin, Proprietary's Commissioner for Settling the Colony in Pennsylvania." Volume 22.

Johnson, Joseph E. "A Quaker Imperialist's View of the British Colonies in America: 1732." Volume 60.

Lewis, Lawrence, Jr. "The Courts of Pennsylvania in the Seventeenth Century." Volume 5.

Pomfret, John E. "The Proprietors of the Province of West New Jersey, 1674-1702." Volume 75.

———. "The First Purchasers of Pennsylvania 1681-1700." Volume 80.

Sachse, Julius F. "Benjamin Furly." Volume 19.

Smith, Culver, H. "Why Pennsylvania Never Became a Royal Province." Volume 53.

Stone, Frederick D. "Penn's Treaty with the Indians." Volume 6.

Wainwright, Nicholas B. "Governor John Blackwell." Volume 74.

———. "The Mystery of Pennsylvania's Royal Charter." Volume 73.

Zimmerman, Albright G. "James Logan, Proprietary Agent." Volume 78.

Bibliography of William Penn's Writings

Dates are according to the Old Style calendar. Printer's date has been used wherever known. Where no printer's date was shown, or in a few cases where the piece was not published, the dateline is given instead. Spelling and punctuation of titles have been modernized.

Truth Exalted. In a Short, but Sure Testimony, Against All Those Religions, Faiths and Worships, That Have Been Formed and Followed in the Darkness of Apostasy, etc. Printed 1668.

The Guide Mistaken and Temporizing Rebuked. Printed 1668.

The Sandy Foundation Shaken, or Those So Generally Believed and Applauded Doctrines . . . Refuted. Printed 1668.

Innocency with Her Open Face. Presented by Way of Apology for the Book Entitled, The Sandy Foundation Shaken. Printed 1669.

A Relation and Description of the Nature and Fruits of the Two Kingdoms of Darkness and Light, etc. Copy in William Penn's Letter Book of 1667-1675, HSP. *Circa* 1669.

No Cross, No Crown: Or Several Sober Reflections Against Hat Honor, Titular Respects, You to a Single Person, etc. Printed 1669.

My Irish Journal 1669-1670. Published 1952, Edited by Isabel Grubb. See Foreword to this volume by Henry J. Cadbury for history of the manuscript.

A Letter of Love to the Young Convinced. Datelined February 19, 1669.

The People's Ancient and Just Liberties Asserted. See Notes to Chapter 8.

A Seasonable Caveat Against Popery. Printed 1670.

The Great Case of Liberty of Conscience, Once More Briefly Debated and Defended by the Authority of Reason, Scripture and Antiquity. Printed 1670.

Truth Rescued From Imposture, or A Brief Reply to a Mere Rhapsody of Lies, Folly and Slander. Datelined March 1671.

A Serious Apology for the Principles and Practices of the People Called Quakers, in Two Parts. Part I written by George Whitehead dated April 1, 1671; Part II by William Penn dated June 29, 1671. Printed 1671.

A Short Testimony of the Life, Death and Ministry of That Faithful Servant of the Lord, Josiah Coale. A Preface in *The Books and Divers Epistles, Josiah Coale*. Printed 1671.

My Journey on Truth's Account Through Kent, Sussex and the Skirt of Surrey Begun the 11th-7th Mo. 1672 and ended 4th-8th Mo. 1672. Copy in William Penn's Letter Book 1667-1675, HSP. Published with Dr. Henry J. Cadbury's notes in *Penn Mag*, Vol. 68.

The New Witnesses Proved Old Heretics, or Information to the Ignorant; in Which the Doctrines of John Reeve and Lodowick Muggleton . . . Are Proved to be Mostly Ancient Whimsies, Blasphemies, and Heresies, etc. Printed 1672.

The Spirit of Truth Vindicated, Against That of Error and Envy; Unseasonably Manifested in a Late and Malicious Libel, Entitled, The Spirit of the Quakers Tried. Printed 1672.

Plain-Dealing with a Traducing Anabaptist; or Three Letters Writ Upon Occasion of Some Slanderous Reflections, Given and Promoted Against William Penn by One John Morse. Printed 1672.

A Winding Sheet for Controversy Ended. Datelined February 16, 1672.

Quakerism a New Nickname for Old Christianity, Being an Answer to a Book, Entitled, Quakerism No Christianity, Subscribed by J. Faldo. Printed 1672.

The Invalidity of John Faldo's Vindication of His Book, Called, Quakerism No Christianity. Being a Rejoinder in Defense of the Answer, Entitled, Quakerism a New Nickname for Old Christianity. Printed 1673.

Wisdom Justified of Her Children, From the Ignorance and Calumny of H. Hallywell in His Book, Called, An Account of Familism, etc. Printed 1673.

The Spirit of Alexander the Coppersmith Justly Rebuked, or, An Answer to a Late Pamphlet, Entitled, The Spirit of the Hat, etc. Printed 1673.

Judas and the Jews, Combined Against Christ and His Followers, Being a Rejoinder to the Late Nameless Reply, Called, Tyranny and Hypocrisy Detected, Made Against a Book, Entitled, The Spirit of Alexander the Coppersmith, Rebuked, etc. *Which was an Answer to a Pamphlet, Called, The Spirit of the Hat.* Printed 1673.

Reason Against Railing, and Truth Against Fiction, Being an Answer to Those Two Late Pamphlets . . . by One Thomas Hicks, etc. Printed 1673.

A Just Rebuke to One and Twenty Learned and Reverend Divines (So Called), etc. Printed 1674.

The Christian Quaker and His Divine Testimony, etc. in two parts. Part I by William Penn and Part II by George Whitehead. Part I first printed 1673. Preface to complete tract datelined December 16, 1674.

Urim and Thummim, or The Apostalical Doctrines of Light and Perfection Maintained, Against the Opposite Plea of Samuel Grevill, etc. Printed 1674.

The Counterfeit Christian Detected and The Real Quaker Justified, etc. Printed 1674.

William Penn's Just Complaint Against, and Solemn Offer of a Public Meeting to, the Leading Baptists Assembled at Barbican, the 28th of the 6th Month, 1674. On the Behalf of Himself, George Whitehead and the Rest of His Friends. Datelined September 5, 1674.

Naked Truth Needs No Shift. Or, An Answer to a Libelous Sheet, Entitled, The Quakers Last Shift Found Out. Printed 1674.

Libels No Proofs. Datelined September 21, 1674.

Jeremy Ives's Sober Request, Proved in the Matter of It, to be False, Impertinent and Impudent. Datelined October 27, 1674.

An Answer to John Faldo's Printed Challenge. Printed 1674.

William Penn's Return to John Faldo's Reply, Called, A Curb for William Penn's Confidence, etc. *Writ in Defense of His Answer to John Faldo's Printed Challenge.* Datelined November 12, 1674.

Christian Liberty as It Was Soberly Desired in a Letter to Certain Foreign States, etc. . . . Printed 1675.

A Treatise of Oaths: Containing Several Weighty Reasons Why the People Called Quakers Refuse to Swear. Signed by both William Penn and Richard Richardson. Printed 1675.

England's Present Interest Discovered with Honor to the Prince, and Safety to the People, etc. Printed 1675.

Saul Smitten to the Ground: Being a Brief, but Faithful Narrative of the Dying Remorse of a Late Living Enemy . . . Matthew Hide, etc. Printed 1675.

The Continued Cry of the Oppressed for Justice, etc. Signed, "By the Author of England's Present Interest." Printed 1675.

The Skirmisher Defeated and Truth Defended, etc. Printed 1676.

To the Churches of Jesus Throughout the World. Printed 1677.

A Tender Visitation in the Love of God . . . to All the People in the High and Low Dutch Nations, etc. Written October 15, 1677. (In Penn's 1726 collected works.)

Tender Counsel and Advice, By Way of an Epistle to All Those Who Are Sensible of Their Day of Visitation, and Who Have Received the Call of the Lord, etc. Written October 15, 1677. Probably first printed 1695.

A Call to Christendom: In an Earnest Expostulation with Her, to Prepare for the Great and Notable Day of the Lord That Is at the Door. Written October 15, 1677. First printed 1694.

To All Those Professors of Christianity, That Are Externally Separated From the Visible Sects and Fellowships in the Christian World, etc. Written October 15, 1677. (In Penn's 1726 collected works.)

Journal of My Travels in Holland and Germany. Written 1677. Printed 1694, under the title: *An Account of W. Penn's Travels in Holland and Germany.*

To Friends Everywhere Concerning the Present Separatists and Their Spirit of Separation. Written September 16, 1677. (In Penn's 1726 collected works.)

A Brief Answer to a False and Foolish Libel, Called, The Quakers Opinions, etc. Printed 1678.

An Address to Protestants Upon the Present Conjecture. Printed 1678.

An Address to Protestants of All Persuasions, More Especially the Magistracy and Clergy, for the Promotion of Virtue and Charity. Printed 1679.

To the Children of Light in This Generation. Printed 1678.

England's Great Interest in the Choice of This New Parliament. Signed, "Philanglus." n.d. Probably printed 1679.

One Project for the Good of England: That Is, Our Civil Union Is Our Civil Safety. Signed, "Philanglus." n.d. Probably printed 1679.

The Testimony of William Penn Concerning Isaac Penington. Dated February 20, 1680/81. Printed 1681 in *The Works of the Long Mournful and Sorely Distressed Isaac Penington,* etc.

A Brief Account of the Province of Pennsylvania; Lately Granted by the King Under the Great Seal of England, to William Penn and His Heirs and Assigns. Printed 1681.

Some Account of the Province of Pennsylvania in America; Lately Granted Under the Great Seal of England to William Penn, etc.

Together with Privileges and Powers Necessary to the Well-Governing Thereof. Printed 1681.

A Brief Examination and State of Liberty Spiritual, Both with Respect to Persons in Their Private Capacity, and in Their Church Society and Communion. Printed 1681.

No Cross, No Crown. A Discourse Showing the Nature and Discipline of the Holy Cross of Christ, etc. Printed 1682.

An Epistle Containing a Salutation to All Faithful Friends; A Reproof to the Unfaithful; and a Visitation to the Enquiring, in a Solemn Farewell to Them in the Land of My Nativity. From The Downs, August 30, 1682. Printed 1682.

A Letter from William Penn, Proprietary and Governor of Pennsylvania in America, to the Committee of the Free Society of Traders of That Province, Residing in London . . . to Which Is Added an Account of the City of Philadelphia Newly Laid Out. From Philadelphia, August 16, 1683. Printed 1683.

Something Begun Toward a History of My Life from '84. Manuscript in Penn's hand, American Philosophical Society Library. Published in HSP *Memoirs*, Vol. 3, under the title, *Fragments of an Apology for Himself*.

True Interest of King and Kingdom. 1684. Manuscript described by Penn in his *Something Begun*, etc.

Fiction Found Out. To My Esteemed Friends, Called Quakers, On Occasion of Two Copies of Verses Printed and Subscribed W. P. Printed 1685.

A Further Account of the Province of Pennsylvania and Its Improvements. Datelined December 12, 1685.

A Persuasive to Moderation to Dissenting Christians, in Prudence and Conscience: Humbly Submitted to the King and His Great Council. Printed 1685.

Good Advice to the Church of England, Roman Catholic and Protestant Dissenter, etc. Penn's name not on first edition. "Beati Pacifici" appears on title page. Printed 1687.

Some Proposals for a Second Settlement in the Province of Pennsylvania. Printed 1690.

A Testimony to the Memory of Robert Barclay by his Faithful Friend William Penn. n.d. Printed in *Truth Triumphant Through Spiritual Warfare, Christian Labours, and Writings of That Able and Faithful Servant of Jesus Christ, Robert Barclay*, MDCXCII.

Just Measures in an Epistle of Peace and Love, to Such Professors of

Truth as Are Under Any Dissatisfaction About the Present Order Practiced in the Church of Christ. Printed 1692.

A Key Opening a Way to Every Common Understanding, How to Discern the Difference Betwixt the Religion Professed by the People Called Quakers and the Perversions, Misrepresentations and Calumnies of Their Several Adversaries. Printed 1692.

The New Athenians No Noble Bereans: Being an Answer to the Athenian Mercury of the 7th Instant, in Behalf of the People Called Quakers. Penn's name did not appear on the first edition. Printed 1692.

An Essay Towards the Present and Future Peace of Europe, by the Establishment of an European Diet, Parliament or Estates. Penn's name did not appear on the first edition. "Beati Pacifici" appears on the title page. Printed 1693.

Some Fruits of Solitude, in Reflections and Maxims Relating to the Conduct of Human Life. Penn's name did not appear on first edition. Printed 1693.

An Account of the Blessed End of Gulielma Maria Penn, and of Springett Penn, the Beloved Wife, and Eldest Son of William Penn. Printed 1696.

The Preface (to George Fox's *Journal*), *Being a Summary Account of the Divers Dispensations of God to Men, From the Beginning of the World, to That of Our Present Age, by the Ministry and Testimony of His Faithful Servant George Fox, as an Introduction to the Ensuing Journal.* The *Journal* was printed in 1694. The *Preface* was reprinted 1694 under the title, *A Brief Account of the Rise and Progress of the People Called Quakers,* etc.

A Reply to a Pretended Answer, by a Nameless Author, to William Penn's Key, etc. Printed 1695.

The Harmony of Divine and Heavenly Doctrines, etc. A collection of sermons by William Penn, George Whitehead and others, taken down in shorthand. Printed 1696.

Primitive Christianity Revived in the Faith and Practice of the People Called Quakers. Printed 1696

More Work for George Keith: Being George Keith's Vindication of the People Called Quakers with Himself, Against the Forgeries and Abuses of Thomas Hicks and William Kiffin, called Anabaptists, with the Rest of Their Confederate Brethren of the Barbican Meeting Held at London, 28th-6th Mo. 1674 Penn's name did not appear on this. Printed 1696.

Some Considerations Upon the Bill for the More Effectual Suppressing Blasphemy and Profaneness, Humbly Offered. Circa 1697. (In Penn's 1726 collected works.)

William Penn's Plan for a Union of the Colonies, February 8, 1697. Printed in HSP *Memoirs* Vol. 6 and in *Penn Mag.* Vol. 11.

Gospel Truths Held and Briefly Declared by the People Called Quakers, for Satisfaction of Moderate Enquirers. By William Penn, Thomas Story, Anthony Sharp and George Rooke. Datelined May 14, 1698.

The Quaker a Christian. By William Penn, John Everett and Thomas Story. Printed 1698.

A Defense of a Paper, Entitled, Gospel Truths, Against the Exceptions of the Bishop of Cork's Testimony. Printed 1698.

A Testimony to the Truth of God. Printed 1698.

An Epistle of Farewell to the People of God Called Quakers, Wherever Scattered or Gathered in England, Ireland, Scotland, Holland, Germany or in Any Other Parts of Europe. Printed 1699.

A Farewell Sermon, Preached by Mr. William Penn, on Sunday, Being the 6th Instant, at the Quakers Meeting, at Westminster. Printed 1699.

More Fruits of Solitude: Being the Second Part of Reflections and Maxims Relating to the Conduct of Human Life. Penn's name did not appear on the first edition. Printed 1702.

Preface to *Memorials of the English Affairs,* etc., by Sir Bulstrode Whitlocke. Printed 1709.

A Serious Expostulation with the Inhabitants of Pennsylvania in a Letter from the Proprietor and Governor. Printed 1710.

Fruits of a Father's Love: Being the Advice of William Penn to His Children Relating to Their Civil and Religious Conduct. Written Occasionally Many Years Ago, and Now Made Public for a General Good. By a Lover of His Memory. Printed 1726.

Christian Discipline, or Certain Good and Wholesome Orders, for the Well-Governing of My Family in a Right Christian Conversation, as Becometh the Children of Light and Truth of the Most High God. n.d. First published by Josiah Forster 1751. May be found in *Letters of Early Friends.*

A few short prefaces which Penn wrote for contemporary works have been omitted from the above list. A few pieces which have been attributed to him by one or more authorities have also been omitted since they do not bear Penn's name and their authorship remains in doubt.

Index